Journal of Semitic Studies Supplement 3

THE KNOWLEDGE OF LIFE

The Origins and Early History of the Mandaeans and Their Relation to the Sabians of the Qur'ān and to the Harranians

by

Şinasi Gündüz

Published by Oxford University Press
on behalf of the University of Manchester

Oxford University Press, Walton Street, Oxford OX2 6DP

Journal of Semitic Studies, Supplement 3

The Knowledge of Life

by

Şinasi Gündüz

A catalogue record for this book is available from the British Library

Library of Congress Cataloguing in Publication Data
(Data available)

ISSN 0022-4480
ISBN 0-19-922193-6

Subscription information for the *Journal of Semitic Studies* is available from

Journals Customer Services
Oxford University Press
Walton Street
Oxford OX2 6DP
UK

or

Journals Marketing Department
Oxford University Press
2001 Evans Road
Cary
North Carolina 27513
USA

Contents

Preface

This work is a revision of a dissertation submitted to the Department of Middle Eastern Studies of the Victoria University of Manchester. I would like to express my sincere thanks and appreciation to Dr J.F. Healey who taught and guided me at each step throughout my study, from the beginning to the very end. I am indebted to his careful interest and attention. It is a pleasure to state that without his help and guidance this work would not have been completed.

Among many other scholars to whom I am grateful I would particularly mention Prof. G. Rex Smith of Manchester University and Dr P.W. Coxon of the University of St. Andrews for their careful reading of the work as a dissertation, valuable suggestions and helpful criticism. I would also like to express my thanks to Dr E.C.D. Hunter of Cambridge University who kindly sent an unpublished paper to me and to Prof. P. Alexander of the Oxford Centre for Postgraduate Hebrew Studies who was kind enough to read the work.

I wish to thank the Editors of *JSS* for accepting this work into the Supplement Series. I also would like to thank the Spalding Trust who have supported the publication with a subsidy. I am particularly indebted to Prof. C.E. Bosworth for his help and advice in this connection.

I am grateful to Ondokuz Mayıs University of Samsun and Prof E. Sarıkçıoğlu, the Dean of the Faculty of Theology of the same University, for supporting me financially during my Ph.D. study. My thanks also go to the British Council in Ankara and particularly Mr D. Marler of the Council who supplied a grant to enable me to make a brief return visit to Manchester.

This volume is dedicated to my family, especially my wife, who have been generous enough to support and encourage me throughout my study.

Şinasi Gündüz
Manchester, October 1993

Abbreviations

AJSL	*The American Journal of Semitic Languages and Literature*
AM	*The Book of Zodiac* (tr. E.S. Drower, London 1949)
ARR	*Alma Rišaia Rba* (tr. E.S. Drower, *A Pair of Naṣoraean Commentaries*, Leiden 1963)
ARZ	*Alma Rišaia Zuṭa* (tr. E.S. Drower, *A Pair of Naṣoraean Commentaries*, Leiden 1963)
AS	*Anatolian Studies*
ATŠ	*The Thousand and Twelve Questions* (tr. E.S. Drower, Berlin 1960)
BASOR	*Bulletin of the American Schools of Oriental Research*
BSOAS	*Bulletin of the School of Oriental and African Studies*
BSOS	*Bulletin of the School of Oriental Studies*
BZNW	*Beihefte zur ZNW*
CAD	*Chicago Assyrian Dictionary*
CHI	*Cambridge History of Islam*
CP	*The Canonical Prayerbook of the Mandaeans* (tr. E.S. Drower, Leiden 1959)
DA	*Diwan Abatur* (tr. E.S. Drower, Vatican City 1950)
DC	Drower Collection of Mandaean Manuscripts in the Bodleian Library, Oxford
DMHZ	*Diwan Maṣbuta ḏ-Hibil Ziwa* (tr. E.S. Drower, Vatican City 1953)
DB	*A Dictionary of the Bible* (ed. J. Hasting)
EI	*Encyclopédie l'Islâm* (1913-34)
*EI**	*Encyclopaedia of Islam* (New Edition 1960-)
EJ	*Encyclopedia Judaica*
ER	*Encyclopedia of Religions* (ed. M. Eliade)
ERE	*Encyclopaedia of Religions and Ethics* (ed. J. Hastings)
GAS	*Geschichte des arabischen Schrifttums* (F. Sezgin, Leiden 1967-1984)
GL	*Ginza Left* (*Ginzā. Der Schatz oder das grosse Buch der Mandäer übersetzt und erklärt*, tr. M. Lidzbarski, Göttingen 1925)
GR	*Ginza Right* (*Ginzā. Der Schatz oder das grosse Buch der Mandäer übersetzt und erklärt*, tr. M. Lidzbarski, Göttingen 1925)
HCMM	*Handbook of Classical and Modern Mandaic* (R. Macuch, Berlin 1965)
HG	*The Haran Gawaita* (tr. E.S. Drower, Vatican City 1953)
HR	*History of Religions*

HUCA	*Hebrew Union College Annual*
JA	*Journal Asiatique*
Jb	*Das Johannesbuch der Mandäer* (tr. M. Lidzbarski, Giessen 1915)
JAOS	*Journal of the American Oriental Society*
JEOL	*Jaarbericht ex Oriente Lux*
JNES	*Journal of Near Eastern Studies*
JPOS	*Journal of the Palestine Oriental Society*
JRAS	*Journal of Royal Asiatic Society*
JSS	*Journal of Semitic Studies*
JThS	*Journal of Theological Studies*
LQR	*The London Quarterly Review*
MD	*A Mandaic Dictionary* (E.S. Drower, R. Macuch, Oxford 1963)
MII	*The Mandaeans of Iraq and Iran. Their Cults, Customs, Magic Legends and Folklore* (E.S. Drower, Oxford 1937)
MIT	*Mandaic Incantation Texts* (E.M. Yamauchi, New Haven 1967)
ML	*Mandäische Liturgien mitgeteilt, übersetzt und erklärt* (tr. M. Lidzbarski, Berlin 1920)
MW	*The Muslim World*
OCD	*The Oxford Classical Dictionary* (N.G.L. Hammond, H.H. Scullard, Oxford 1970)
Or	*Orientalia*
PBA	*Proceedings of the British Academy*
PRGS	*Proceedings of the Royal Geographical Society*
RLA	*Reallexicon der Assyriologie*
RQ	*Revue de Qumran*
SEL	*Studi Epigrafici e Linguistici*
SI	*Studia Islamica*
SPAW	*Sitzungsberichte der Preussischen Akademie der Wissenschaften*
ThLZ	*Theologische Literaturzeitung*
ThR	*Theologische Rundschau*
TU	*Texte und Untersuchungen*
WW	*Water into Wine* (E.S. Drower, London 1956)
ZDMG	*Zeitschrift der Deutschen Morgenländischen Gesellschaft*
ZfN	*Zeitschrift für Numismatik*
ZNW	*Zeitschrift für die Neutestamentliche Wissenschaft und die Kunde der Älteren Kirche*
ZRGG	*Zeitschrift für Religions- und Geistesgeschichte*

CHAPTER I

INTRODUCTION

The Mandaeans who live alongside the Tigris, Euphrates and Kārun rivers in Iraq and Iran are generally accepted as the last surviving representatives of the Gnostics. This small community, which consists of about 15,000 members,[1] is called by its neighbours *ṣubbā* or *ṣubbī*, though the Mandaeans do not call themselves by this name. They mostly live in small towns and villages in small communities in the marshy regions of south Mesopotamia. Also, because of better living standards some of them have moved to the big city centres of Baghdad and Basra where they generally earn their living as shopkeepers, and gold- and silversmiths. The number of faithful believers of the community is decreasing day by day because of the very slight connection of the younger generation with the religion.

1. The Mandaean community, its cult and rites

The Mandaeans call themselves either *mandaiia* (Mandaeans), "Gnostics", or *naṣuraiia* (Naṣoraeans), "observants".[2] The name "Mandaean" is used for the "laymen" while "Naṣoraean" is a name used for priests and those who have the secret knowledge of the mysteries of Mandaeism. In Mandaean literature this name is one of the earliest appellations of the Mandaeans.

The Mandaean community is divided into two groups: laymen and priests, but this division is not fundamental.[3] The priesthood has three divisions: (i)*riš ama* (or

[1]This is K. Rudolph's estimation in 1978. See Rudolph, K., *Mandaeism*, (Iconography of Religions, Section 21) Leiden (1978), p.1. Also see for recent information about the Mandaeans Franzmann, M., "Living Water. Mediating Element in Mandaean Myth and Ritual", *Numen*, 36, 1989, p.156; Sox, H.D., "The Last of the Gnostics", *King's Theological Review*, 6, 2,.1983, pp.43-44.

[2]See Drower, E.S. and R. Macuch, *A Mandaic Dictionary*, (hereafter *MD*) Oxford (1963), pp.247, 285.

[3]See Rudolph, K., *Mandaeism*, p.5.

rišaia), "the head of the people", (ii) *ganzibra*, "treasurer, head-priest, bishop", and (iii) *tarmida*, the ordinary priest. There are also lesser priestly functionaries, like the *šualia*, probationer priest, and *šganda*, deacon.

The Mandaean cult-hut is called *manda* (or *mandi*), *bitmanda* or *bimanda*, a small hut with an artificially constructed pool in front of it.[4]

The Mandaeans have an extensive literature which consists of many books, priestly commentaries and magical treatises.[5] The most extensive book is the *Ginza* (Treasure) which is also known as *Sidra Rba* (The Great Book). The *Ginza* contains two parts: The Right Ginza (*ginza iamina*) which is a large collection of mythological, theological, cosmological and moral treatises; and The Left Ginza (*ginza smala*) which is a small book of songs and hymns. *Drašia d̲-Iahia* (The Teachings of John) also known as *Drašia d̲-Malkia* (The Teachings of the Kings) and *Qolasta* (Praising or Collection) also known as *The Canonical Prayerbook* are also important Mandaean writings. The former includes mythological fragments and stories about the heavenly saviour Anuš and John the Baptist, called *iahia iuhana*, while the latter consists of hymns, daily prayers and songs. In addition there are important priestly documents such as *Alf Trisar Šuialia* (One Thousand and Twelve Questions), *Alma Rišaia Rba* (The Great First World), *Alma Rišaia Zuṭa* (The Lesser First World) and *Diwan Maṣbuta d̲-Hibil Ziwa* (Diwan of the Baptism of Hibil Ziwa). Moreover there are Diwans, like *Diwan Abatur* and the Diwan of the Great Revelation, called *Haran Gawaita*, and astrological books like *Sfar Malwašia* or *The Book of the Zodiac.*

Mandaean literature contains both old and new elements. It is therefore generally quite difficult to get a clear picture of the religious ideas from this literature.

The cult of the Mandaeans is stamped by a kind of Gnostic dualism:[6] the World of Light on the one side and the World of Darkness on the other. At the summit of the World of Light there is a supreme being called "Life", "Great Life", "Lord of Greatness", "Mighty Mana" or "King of Light". Around him there are countless Light beings called *uthria* (riches) and *malkia* (kings). It is believed that this World of sublime beings emanated from the supreme being in various stages known as the "Second", "Third" and "Fourth Life". Also the World of Darkness which emanates from the chaos or black waters is formed in the same way. There is a King of Darkness at the top of this world and all evil beings, including the seven planets and twelve

---

[4]See Drower, E.S., *The Mandaeans of Iraq and Iran. Their Cults, Customs, Magic, Legends, and Folklore*, (hereafter *MII*) Oxford (1937), pp.124ff; Rudolph, K., *Die Mandäer II. Der Kult*, Göttingen (1961), pp.306ff.

[5]For detailed information on Mandaean literature see Rudolph, K., "Die mandäische Literatur", in *Studia Mandaica*, ed. R. Macuch, Band I, Berlin, New York (1976), pp.147-70; Drower, E.S., "A Mandaean Bibliography", *JRAS*, 1953, pp.34-39.

[6]For the doctrine of Gnostic dualism in Mandaeism see below pp.214ff. Also for detailed information about the theology of Mandaean religion see Rudolph, K., *Theogonie, Kosmogonie und Anthropogonie in den mandäischen Schriften*, Göttingen (1965).

zodiac signs, are around him. There is a continuous hostility between the World of Light and the World of Darkness.

On the creation of man the Mandaeans believe that his body (*adam pagria*) was created by the demiurge Ptahil and his evil associates, i.e. the seven planets, but his soul (*adakas* or *adam kasia*) was given by the light beings. In the Mandaeans' doctrine every being has its partner (*dmuta*) in the heavenly worlds. Therefore the earthly Adam and Adamites are only the images of the heavenly Adam and Adamites. Consequently the salvation of the soul happens only when a soul leaves the earthly world and body and unites with the heavenly partner. The prototype of salvation is that of Adam. After the soul was put in the body of Adam, Manda ḏ-Hiia, the Light messenger, came to Adam and taught him the secret knowledge and the cultic rituals. Therefore in the belief of the Mandaeans, "knowledge" (*manda*) is not enough for reaching salvation. The cultic rituals are as important as (or more important than) knowledge for leaving the earthly world of darkness and bodies where the soul (*nišimta*) is prisoner, and ascending to the soul's native world of Light. Hence the rituals are necessary for every Mandaean.

Among the Mandaean rituals[7] baptism (*maṣbuta*) is the most important. Baptism can take place only in "flowing (living) water", i.e. in rivers or the Mandi pool. The flowing water of baptism is called "jordan" (*iardna*). The full baptism which must take place every Sunday involves immersion in water, signing of the forehead with water, drinking of water, crowning with the myrtle wreath, laying on of hands, the sacrament of bread and water and sealing. The ceremony always ends with the ritual handshake (*kušṭa*) between the priests and neophyte. Also *masiqta*, the ceremony for the ascent of the soul to the World of Light (or mass for souls), and *lofani* (communion) and *zidqa brika* (blessed alms), the funeral meals for the benefit of the soul, which consist of bread, water from the jordan and spices, are among the most important Mandaean rituals.

2. History of research and the problem of origins

The Mandaeans have been known by Westerners since as early as the 16th century. They were called "the Christians of St. John" by the Jesuit missionaries of Ormuz in the Persian Gulf in a report dated 1555.[8] The Christian missionaries

---

[7]For the description of various Mandaean rituals and discussion on this subject see below pp.217-20; *MII*, pp.100-24, 178-225; Drower, E.S., *Water into Wine. A Study of Ritual Idiom in the Middle East*, (hereafter *WW*) London (1956), pp.229-58; Rudolph, K., *Die Mandäer II. Der Kult*; Segelberg, E., *Maṣbūtā. Studies in the Ritual of the Mandaean Baptism*, Uppsala (1958). Also see the articles of E. Segelberg and J.J. Buckley to which we will give reference throughout the footnotes of the coming chapters.

[8]See Crehan, J.H., "The Mandaeans and Christian Infiltration", *JThS*, 19, 1968, pp.624-25.

presumably thought that these people must have belonged to a Christian sect of John the Baptist, since we know that the Mandaeans introduce themselves to any foreigner as the adherents of John the Baptist who has a positive role throughout the Mandaean literature.[9] The name "the Christians of St. John" (or "the Disciples of St. John the Baptist") was used for the Mandaeans by western scholars, particularly by New Testament scholars, for a long time.[10]

The first Mandaean manuscript was brought to Europe in 1652 by Ignatius à Jesu, a Carmelite missionary at Basra.[11]

At the beginning studies on the Mandaeans were mainly based on the information of missionaries and travellers. Only after the beginning of the publication of the Mandaean literature in the second half of the 18th century, especially by M. Norberg from 1781 onwards,[12] did scholars begin to carry out Mandaean research on the basis of Mandaean writings. Systematic studies on the theology, mythology, rituals and history of the Mandaeans, however, began almost a century later with W. Brandt's important study in 1889.[13]

From the earliest times scholars were interested in the problem of the origin of the Mandaeans. R. Simon in 1685 pointed out the relations between the Mandaeans and Manichaeans and regarded the present Mandaeans as a remnant of an ancient eastern Gnostic Chaldaean sect.[14] G. Peringer in 1691 supported Simon.[15]

In 1697 Barthélomy d'Herbelot pointed out the western origin of the Mandaeans and their connection with Jewish post-Christian sects.[16] In this he was followed by J.L. Mosheim in 1753.[17] In 1771 N. Barkey criticized d'Herbelot and supported Simon's theory, but suggested that Mandaeism was a Gnostic sect originating from the Ophites.[18] Later in the 18th century (1779) G. Conti, vicar of the Maronite patriarch, stated that the Nazaraeans of El Merkab near Lattakia were the disciples of St. John the Baptist and M. Norberg agreed with Conti in regarding this sect as a branch of the Mandaeans. Norberg too supported the western origin of the Mandaeans and stated that "Galilaeans" was the natural name for them. According to his theory the Mandaeans were originally connected with the Ebionite Nasaraeans.[19] In 1784 O.G. Tychsen

---

[9]See *MII*, pp.2-3. Also see below pp.68, 105f.
[10]See Pallis, S.A., *Essay on Mandaean Bibliography 1560-1930*, Amsterdam (1933), pp.17ff.
[11]See ibid, p.32.
[12]See ibid, pp.41, 52-53.
[13]Brandt, W., *Die mandäische Religion*, Leipzig (1889). For bibliography of the Mandaean studies see Widengren, G. (ed.), *Der Mandäismus*, Darmstadt (1982). Also for older studies see Houtum-Schindler, A., "Notes on the Sabaeans", *PRGS*, 13, 1891, pp.663-69; Kraeling, C.H., "A Mandaic Bibliography", *JAOS*, 46, 1926, pp.49-55; Pallis, S.A., op.cit.
[14]See Pallis, S.A., op.cit., pp.47ff.
[15]See ibid, pp.50-51.
[16]See ibid, p.49.
[17]Ibid, p.49.
[18]See ibid, p.50.
[19]See ibid, pp.11, 53.

criticized Norberg and entirely dismissed the idea that the Mandaeans from Galilee should have fled to El Merkab and thence, subsequently, a number of them to Chaldaea. He claimed that the Mandaeans were originally natives of Chaldaea and suggested a late origin for them in the 9th century A.D. He also claimed that perhaps a Nestorian monk, converted to Islam, was the founder of Mandaeism.[20]

C.W.F. Walch in 1782, following d'Herbelot, inclined to the theory of the western origin of the Mandaeans. He identified the Mandaeans with Hemerobaptists, who were mentioned by several Church Fathers and early Christian authors such as Epiphanius and Pseudo-Hieronymus. He also identified the Sabians of the Qur'ān with the Mandaeans, a view which was later supported by many scholars such as D. Chwolsohn and Lady Drower.[21]

In the 19th century scholars continued to discuss the problem of the origin of the Mandaeans and to support one of two main theories, i.e. either a western or an eastern origin. In 1828 A.J. Matter held the opinion of the western origin of the Mandaeans and stated that the origin of the Mandaeans must be sought in the Nasaraeans mentioned by Epiphanius.[22] This opinion later gained great support and was developed in this century particularly by E.S. Drower and R. Macuch.[23] Also E. Renan in the mid 19th century supported the idea of western origin for the Mandaeans and connected the Elchasaites with the Mandaean Gnosis.[24] D. Chwolsohn, in his monumental study on the Sabians, arrived at results similar to Renan's about the relationship between the Mandaeans and Elchasaites. Chwolsohn's theory, which is mainly based on the Arabic sources, consists of three points:

(i) Identification of the Mandaeans with the Elchasaites. He states that El'hasa'ih (Elchasai), coming from north-eastern Parthia, appeared at the close of the first century among the heathen Babylonians in South Mesopotamia and spread his Persian ideas among them. Then these Parsified Babylonians called themselves Mandaeans.

(ii) Mani was born of Mandaean parents and grew up among the Mandaeans, but later founded his own community.

(iii) The Sabians of the Qur'ān are the Mandaeans.[25]

---

[20]See ibid, pp.54-55.

[21]See ibid, p.54. Chwolsohn, D., *Die Ssabier und der Ssabismus*, St. Petersburg (1856), v.I, pp.21-22, 138; Drower, E.S., *The Secret Adam. A Study of Naṣoraean Gnosis*, Oxford (1960), p.ix.

[22]See Pallis, S.A., op.cit., p.59.

[23]See Drower, E.S., op.cit., pp.94ff; Macuch, R., "Anfänge der Mandäer", in *Die Araber in der Alten Welt*, eds. F. Altheim and R. Stiehl, v.II, Berlin (1965), pp.93ff.

[24]See Pallis, S.A., op.cit., p.60.

[25]See Chwolsohn, D., op.cit., v.I, pp.136ff.

Chwolsohn's opinion about the close relationship between the Mandaeans and Elchasaites was later supported by Lady Drower.[26] His view about Mani was also adopted by many scholars, such as Widengren and Rudolph,[27] until the discovery of the Cologne Mani Codex in 1970 which obviously demonstrated that Mani was brought up among the Elchasaites. However, his identification of the Sabians of the Qur'ān with the Mandaeans, which was earlier suggested by C.W.F. Walch, held ground longer than his other views and was defended by many scholars.

On the other hand some scholars rejected Chwolsohn's opinion. G. Flügel in 1896 raised objections to Chwolsohn's view of the relation between the Mandaeans and Manichaeans.[28] Also J. Pedersen in 1922 rejected his theory of identification of the Elchasaites with the Mandaeans and the Mandaeans with the Sabians of the Qur'ān.[29]

From 1881 onwards K. Kessler argued for an eastern homeland and origin for the Mandaeans which was earlier suggested by R. Simon in the 17th century. Kessler pointed to old Babylonian religion as the soil in which the Gnostic view of the world had grown up and emphasized the Babylonian elements in the Mandaean cult and mythology. Hence he suggested a Babylonian home for the Mandaeans.[30] Kessler's view of a Babylonian homeland for the Mandaeans was supported by scholars like W. Anz and H. Zimmern.[31] Also J.B. Segal recently held the opinion of an eastern origin of the Mandaeans.[32]

As we have earlier noted, systematic Mandaean researches began with W. Brandt. Brandt's theory on the origin and early history of the Mandaeans consists of two points:

(i) The oldest layer of the Mandaean tradition, which was the polytheistic material nourished from Semitic nature religion and Chaldaean philosophy, was pre-Christian. Other ideas and conceptions, like those of Gnostics, Jews and Persians, were adopted later. He also stated that the second stage of Mandaeism, the monotheistic period, extended from 300 to 600 A.D.

---

[26]See Drower, E.S., *The Secret Adam*, pp.92ff; idem, "Adam and the Elkasaites", *TU*, 79, (Studia Patristica, v.IV) 1961, pp.406-10.

[27]See Widengren, G., *Mani and Manichaeism*, tr. C. Kessler, London (1965), pp.25-26; Rudolph, K., *Die Mandäer I*, Göttingen (1960), p.239.

[28]See Pallis, S.A., op.cit., p.63.

[29]See Pedersen, J, "The Ṣābians", in *A Volume of Oriental Studies. Presented to Edward G. Browne*, eds. T.W. Arnold and R.A. Nicholson, Cambridge (1922), pp.383-91.

[30]See Pallis, S.A., op.cit., p.64. Also for Kessler's sdudies on the Mandaeans see ibid, pp.166f, 188ff.

[31]See ibid, p.64; Yamauchi, E.M., "The Present Status of Mandaean Studies", *JNES*, 25, 1966, p.91.

[32]Segal, J.B., Review of E.M. Yamauchi: *Gnostic Ethics and Mandaean Origins* (Cambridge, 1970), *BSOAS*, 36, 1973, p.134-35.

(ii) Secondly he pointed to the extensive eastern, particularly Babylonian, elements in Mandaean cult and ritual and argued for an eastern origin for the Mandaeans, not a western, Jewish or Christian, origin.[33]

On the problem of the identification of Qur'ānic Sabians with Mandaeans he remarked:

> "The passages in the Qur'ān and the name 'Ṣābians' would apply most approximately to the Mandaeans."[34]

Brandt has been criticized by scholars mainly because of his neglect of the Jewish, Gnostic and Christian elements in the Mandaean cult and rituals.[35]

At the beginning of this century the leading Mandaean scholar of his time, M. Lidzbarski, argued for a pre-Christian western origin of the Mandaeans. According to his theory it is impossible to locate the beginning of the Mandaeans in the Christian period. Lidzbarski stated that the Mandaeans were originally situated in Transjordan. Hence their original homeland was Syria-Palestine. He also stated that the Mandaeans had their spiritual home in heterodox circles of Judaism. He claimed that some of them probably saw the activities of John the Baptist, but he rejected the possibility that the Mandaeans could be traced back to John the Baptist. Moreover Lidzbarski located their migration to the East in the first Christian century. He remarked that this migration took place even before the destruction of the Jewish kingdom, i.e. before 70 A.D. According to his theory the Mandaeans came into contact with the Babylonian and Syrian cults in their new homeland and were influenced by the Babylonian planet cult and the Syrian cult of the mother-goddess. Further he stated that anti-Christian polemics entered the Mandaean tradition in the struggle against the Christian mission, while the hatred against the Jews had older roots.[36] As we will later see, Lidzbarski's theory was adopted by many scholars, such as C.H. Kraeling, R. Macuch and K. Rudolph.

In 1913 J.A. Montgomery, the publisher of some Mandaic incantation texts, stated on the beginning of Mandaeism:

> "The sect itself must have arisen in the age when Gnosticism was rife in the Orient and before the domination of Christianity."[37]

---

[33]See Brandt, W., *Die mandäische Religion*, pp.57-59, 178; idem, "Mandaeans", in *ERE*, v.8, pp.382ff. For a summary of Brandt's theory see Rudolph, K., "Problems of a History of the Development of the Mandaean Religion", (English translation by D.C. Duling, in consultation with J. Modschiedler) *HR*, 8, 1969, pp.211-12.

[34]Brandt, W., "Mandaeans", p.390.

[35]See Rudolph, K., op.cit., pp.212f.

[36]See Lidzbarski, M., *Ginzā. Der Schatz oder das grosse Buch der Mandäer übersetzt und erklärt*, (hereafter *GR* or *GL*) Göttingen (1925), pp.vi-xii; idem, "Alter und Heimat der mandäischen Religion", *ZNW*, 27, 1928, pp.321-27. Also see Rudolph, K., op.cit., pp.213ff.

[37]Montgomery, J.A., *Aramaic Incantation Texts from Nippur*, (University of Pennsylvania the Museum Publications of the Babylonian Section vol. III) Philadelphia (1913), p.39.

W. Bousset in 1917 supported the theory of western origin of the Mandaeans and remarked that the original home of the Mandaeans was near the Jordan. He also mentioned a migration of the Mandaeans to the lower Euphrates where they were influenced by strong elements of a Babylonian-Persian syncretism.[38] C.H. Kraeling too defended the theory of western origin and homeland of the Mandaeans. He pointed out the extensive Jewish elements in Mandaean tradition and repeated the theory of early migration of the Mandaeans to Mesopotamia.[39] He also says:

> "All that can therefore be said regarding the antiquity of the Mandaeans is that, as a sect, they are not without first century affinities."[40]

Kraeling located the beginning of the anti-Christian polemics in Mandaean tradition in the period antedating the arrival of the Jesuit mission in Mesopotamia in the sixteenth century A.D.[41]

On the other hand S.A. Pallis opposed both Lidzbarski and Brandt. He claimed that there was nothing of Judaism in Mandaean tradition, and that the effect of Babylonian and Persian religion on Mandaeism was quite subordinate and secondary.[42] Pallis rejected the idea that the Mandaeans always lived in Babylonia, but he was in difficulty about their original homeland. He says:

> "we must finally confess that we have no possible means of fixing more accurately the original dwelling-place of the Mandaeans; one thing, however, is certain, viz. that they did not always live in Southern Mesopotamia, but probably immigrated during the Sassanian age."[43]

R. Reitzenstein, from 1919 onwards, started a new discussion by suggesting that Christianity had emerged from Mandaeism.[44] He also suggested that Mandaeism represented the teaching of a pre-Christian Jewish sect, and that the earliest Mandaean doctrines and rituals had been originated by John the Baptist and his followers.

---

[38]See Bousset, W., "Die Religion der Mandäer", *ThR*, 20, 1917, pp.185-205.

[39]See Kraeling, C.H., "The Origin and Antiquity of the Mandaeans", *JAOS*, 49, 1929, pp.195-218; idem, "A Mandaean Bibliography", p.50.

[40]Idem, "The Origin and Antiquity of the Mandaeans", p.218.

[41]Ibid, p.198.

[42]See Pallis, S.A., *Mandaean Studies*, tr. E.H. Pallis, London and Copenhagen (1926), pp.115-16; idem, *Essay on Mandaean Bibliography 1560-1930*, p.65.

[43]Idem, *Mandaean Studies*, p.216.

[44]For summary of Reitzenstein's theory see Yamauchi, E.M., *Pre-Christian Gnosticism. A Survey of Proposed Evidences*, Tyndale Press (1973), p.24; Dodd, C.H., *The Interpretation of the Fourth Gospel*, Cambridge (1953, reprinted 1954), pp.121f, 127. Also for Reitzenstein's studies on the Mandaeans see Pallis, S.A., *Essay on Mandaean Bibliography 1560-1930*, pp.65, 196ff.

Reitzenstein's theory was followed by R. Bultmann and his students. Bultmann stated that the origin of the Mandaeans lay ultimately with a group of the adherents of John the Baptist. He also suggested that the Gospel of John represented a revised version of the myth current in the Baptist Mandaean tradition.[45] H.H. Schaeder proposed that the prologue of John's Gospel was a Mandaic hymn taken over from Baptist circles. Moreover the Bultmannian scholars H. Becker and E. Schweizer sought to reconstruct various ideas and concepts in John's Gospel from parallels found in Mandaean texts.[46]

This theory was generally criticized and rejected by New Testament scholars such as F.C. Burkitt and H. Lietzmann. W.F. Howard criticized the idea that Mandaean material was one of the sources for the Fourth Gospel.[47] E. Peterson claimed that Mandaeism was established in the 8th century A.D.[48] F.C. Burkitt examined Mandaeism in heretical Christian circles and claimed that the source of many ideas and conceptions in Mandaean tradition was the *Peshiṭta*, the Syriac version of the Bible. Therefore he argued for a late date for the beginning of Mandaeism,[49] and stated: "the Mandaeans may be regarded as heretical Christians".[50] H. Lietzmann suggested that the Mandaean baptismal rite was actually derived from the Nestorian rite and therefore argued for a Christian origin for the Mandaeans. He placed their origin in the 7th century A.D.[51] In 1940 V.S. Pedersen claimed that Mandaeism was not a Jewish but a Christian heretical sect. He stated that Mandaeism passed through a Jewish-Christian stage before it came into opposition with Christianity. He also claimed that anti-Jewish polemics in Mandaean tradition were derived from Christian anti-Jewish ideas.[52] Moreover C.H. Dodd, W.F. Albright and R.P. Casey criticized the theory represented by Reitzenstein and Bultmann and agreed with Burkitt.[53] These New Testament scholars have, however, in turn been criticized by many Mandaean scholars. For example, Lady Drower stated of Burkitt:

---

[45]See Yamauchi, E.M., *Pre-Christian Gnosticism*, p.29; Dodd, C.H., op.cit., p.122. Cf. Bultmann, R., *The Gospel of John: A Commentary*, tr. G.R. Beasley-Murray, eds. R.W.N. Hoare and J.K. Riches, Oxford (1971), p.8.

[46]See Yamauchi, E.M., "Jewish Gnosticism? The Prologue of John, Mandaean Parallels, and the Trimorphic Protennoia", in *Studies in Gnosticism and Hellenistic Religions Presented to Gilles Quispel on the Occasion of his 65th Birthday*, eds. R. Van den Broek and M.J. Vermaseren, Leiden (1981), p.470.

[47]See Howard, W.F., "The Fourth Gospel and Mandaean Gnosticism", *LQR*, 1927, pp.72-85.

[48]See Peterson, E., "Urchristentum und Mandäismus", *ZNW*, 27, 1928, pp.55ff.

[49]See Burkitt, F.C., *Church and Gnosis. A Study of Christian Thought and Speculation in the Second Century*, Cambridge (1932), pp.102-19; idem, "The Mandaeans", *JThS*, 29, 1928, pp.225-35.

[50]Idem, *Church and Gnosis*, p.106.

[51]See Lietzmann, H., "Ein Beitrag zur Mandäerfrage", *SPAW*, Phil.-Hist.Kl., 1930, pp.596-608.

[52]For Pedersen's theory see Rudolph, K., "Problems of a History of the Development of the Mandaean Religion", pp.215-16.

[53]See Dodd, C.H., op.cit., pp.121-30; Albright, W.F., *From the Stone Age to Christianity*, Baltimore (1946), pp.281-82; idem, "Recent Discoveries in Palestine and the Gospel of St. John", in *The Background of the New Testament and its Eschatology*, eds. W.D. Davies and D. Daube, Cambridge (1956), p.154; Casey, R.P., "Gnosis, Gnosticism and the New Testament", in *The Background of the New Testament and its Eschatology*, pp.54-55.

> "His acquaintance with Mandaean literature, however, was limited to Lidzbarski's translations."[54]

Also regarding the scholars who claimed a late dating for the beginning of Mandaeism, K. Rudolph stated:

> "While Nöldeke, Brandt and Lidzbarski — that is, those who were best informed about the material — were firmly convinced of a pre-Christian existence of this sect, other scholars, to be sure almost only those who once turned to the Mandaeans for a short time, prefer a late dating."[55]

Lady Drower, one of the leading Mandaean scholars of this century, first suggested an Iranian origin for the Mandaeans,[56] but later she gave up this view and adopted the theory of a western origin of the Mandaeans in heretical Jewish circles. Her opinion consists of three points: first she connected the beginning of Mandaeism with the pre-Christian Jewish dissidents, the Nasaraeans. She says:

> "early Naṣiruta, or *Ur-Mandäismus* to use the convenient German expression, was originally a sect which flourished in Judaea and Samaria then possibly in Parthian-Jewish settlements and in Transjordania, and ... was a hybrid strongly influenced by Magianism and Jewish gnosticism."[57]

Also regarding the migration of the Mandaeans she assumes that:

> "it might well follow that after the destruction of Jerusalem, when Jewish Christians for the most part settled in East Jordan, our Naṣoraeans, hating, and hated by, both Jew and Jewish-Christian, would naturally seek harbour in the friendlier atmosphere of Parthia and the Median hills."[58]

Secondly she suggested that there was a close relationship between the Elchasaites and Mandaeans.[59] Finally she claimed that there was a connection between the medieval pagans of Harran known as the Harranian Sabians and the Mandaeans.[60]

---

[54]Drower, E.S., "Mandaean Polemic", *BSOAS*, 25, 1962, p.443.
[55]Rudolph, K., "Problems of a History of the Development of the Mandaean Religion", p.211.
[56]See Drower, E.S., "The Mandaeans To-day", *The Hibbert Journal*, 37, 1938-39, p.435; *MII*, pp.xixff, 239.
[57]Drower, E.S., "Mandaean Polemic", p.448. Also see idem, *The Secret Adam*, pp.xiii-xv, 81ff.
[58]Idem, *The Secret Adam*, p.xi.
[59]See ibid, pp.92-98; idem, "Adam and the Elkasaites", pp.406-10.
[60]See below p.126.

In 1949 T. Säve-Söderbergh demonstrated that the Coptic Manichaean Psalms of Thomas were adaptations or almost translations of Mandaean hymns.[61] Also in an article published in 1967 he stated that the central part of Mandaeism is pre-Manichaean, but on the other hand criticized Rudolph's dating of the beginning of Mandaeism.[62]

E. Segelberg in 1958 stated that the essential western and Semitic origin of the Mandaean central ritual, baptism, must be accepted without any doubt.[63] Also in his later studies on various Mandaean rituals Segelberg pointed out the western origin of the Mandaean tradition and stated that the western background of Mandaeism could be traced back at least to the beginning of the Christian era.[64] R. McL. Wilson too held to a western origin of the Mandaeans.[65]

G. Widengren defended the theory of western origin. Widengren divided Mandaean history into three stages:

First was the Jewish West Semitic stage. Palestine was their original homeland. The Jewish elements as well as some Babylonian-Iranian elements were adopted by the Mandaeans during this period.

The second stage was the Mesopotamian. The Mandaeans adopted some Babylonian elements including their baptismal liturgies at this stage.

According to his theory the third and fundamental stage was the Iranian. The Mandaeans adopted many Iranian elements including plenty of cultic terms of Parthian origin and the teaching of redemption in the form of the "dogma of the redeemed Redeemer" in this period.[66]

R. Macuch, one of the leading Mandaean scholars, succeeded M. Lidzbarski and championed his thesis on the origin and early history of the Mandaeans.[67] He states of his study, "Anfänge der Mandäer":

---

61 Säve-Söderbergh, T., *Studies in the Coptic Manichaean Psalm-Book: Prosody and Mandaean Parallels*, Uppsala (1949).

62 See idem, "Gnostic and Canonical Gospel Traditions (with special reference to the Gospel of Thomas)", in *Le Origini dello Gnosticismo Colloquio di Messina 13-18 Aprile 1966*, ed. U. Bianchi, Leiden (1967), pp.552-62.

63 Segelberg, E., *Maṣbūtā*, p.182.

64 See idem, "The Pitha and Mambuha Prayers to the Question of the Liturgical Development among the Mandaeans", in *Gnosis Festschrift für Hans Jonas*, ed. B. Aland, Göttingen (1978), p.464; idem, "Trāṣa ḏ-tāga ḏ-Šišlām rabbā. Studies in the rite called the Coronation of Šišlām Rabbā", in *Studia Mandaica*, ed. R. Macuch, Band I, Berlin, New York (1976), p.183.

65 See Wilson, R. McL., *The Gnostic Problem. A Study of the Relations Between Hellenistic Judaism and the Gnostic Heresy*, London (1958), pp.66-67; idem, *Gnosis and the New Testament*, Oxford (1968), p.14.

66 See Widengren, G., "Die Mandäer", in *Handbuch der Orientalistik*, ed. B. Spuler, VIII, Pt.2, Leiden (1961), pp.83-101; idem, *Mani and Manichaeism*, pp.16-20; idem, "Heavenly Enthronement and Baptism. Studies in Mandaean Baptism", in *Religions in Antiquity*, ed. J. Neusner, Leiden (1968), pp.572-74.

67 See Macuch, R., "Alter und Heimat des Mandäismus nach neuerschlossenen Quellen", *ThLZ*, 82, 1957, pp.402-7; idem, "Zur Frühgeschichte der Mandäer", *ThLZ*, 90, 1965, pp.649-60; idem, "Anfänge der Mandäer", pp.76-191.

> "The essay of a historical picture of Mandaeism I have sketched there corresponds to the picture Lidzbarski had in mind, but its single traits are confirmed, reinforced and completed by new material unknown in Lidzbarski's days."[68]

Macuch sought the origin of the Mandaeans in pre-Christian heretical Jewish circles. He pointed to the pre-Christian Nasaraeans as the group among whom the Mandaeans originated. Also his theory contains an exodus of the Mandaeans first to Harran, then to Media under the protection of Artabanus III (c.12-38 A.D.) in the first Christian century, before 70 A.D.

Another leading Mandaean scholar K. Rudolph also defended the idea of pre-Christian western origin of the Mandaeans. He remarked that Mandaeism, originating in the region of Jordan, was a movement which splintered off official Judaism. On the other hand on the date of the migration of the Mandaeans he states:

> "A successive stage-by-stage migration from Transjordan is, of course, to be assumed in the first century and even earlier, but the invasion into the Parthian region that is, toward Ḥarran, ensued in my opinion only in the second century."[69]

In one of his later studies he says:

> "The emigration of the early Naṣoraean community from the Jordan valley in Palestine into eastern territories, brought about because of persecutions by 'orthodox' Jews, must have taken place at the latest during the second century A.D. ... Presumably the emigrants went first to Ḥarran, the ancient Carrhae, and the Median hills, and then entered the southern provinces of Mesopotamia (Mesene, Charakene)."[70]

In 1970 E.M. Yamauchi, criticizing Lidzbarski, Macuch, Drower and Rudolph, suggested a western proto-Mandaean component and an eastern proto-Mandaean component in connection with the problem of the origin of the Mandaeans. In his opinion western proto-Mandaeans, who were dwellers in Transjordan and worshippers

---

[68]Macuch, R., *Handbook of Classical and Modern Mandaic*, (hereafter *HCMM*) Berlin (1965), p.lxvii.

[69]Rudolph, K., "Problems of a History of the Development of the Mandaean Religion", p.224.

[70]Idem, *Mandaeism*, p.5. Also for Rudolph's discussion on the problem of the origin of the Mandaeans see idem, "Quellenprobleme zum ursprung und alter der Mandäer", in *Christianity, Judaism and Other Greco-Roman Cults. Studies for Morton Smith at Sixty*, ed. J. Neusner, Part 4, Leiden (1975), pp.112-42; idem, "Der Mandäismus in der neueren Gnosisforschung", in *Gnosis. Festschrift für Hans Jonas*, ed. B. Aland, Göttingen (1978), pp.268-74.

of the god of Hauran, were not Jews but hostile to the Jews. When the Jews attacked the areas east and southeast of the Sea of Galilee in 66 A.D. they migrated to the region of Antioch where they adopted Gnostic ideas. After that they moved eastward first to Harran, and then to Adiabene; finally they settled in southern Mesopotamia where they adopted Mesopotamian cult and magic. Therefore by the end of the 2nd century the new religion was born.[71] On the earliest date of Mandaeism he says:

> "a date in the 3rd cent. A.D. is most probable, and a date in the 2nd cent. A.D. is possible, but a pre-Christian date remains hypothetical and speculative."[72]

Yamauchi's thesis was criticized and rejected by many scholars, especially by Macuch and Rudolph.[73]

In an article published in 1975 G. Quispel suggested that the Mandaeans were dependant upon Jewish Christians. He claimed that the Mandaeans took their rituals and western elements from Elchasaites.[74] Quispel also connected the Mandaeans with the enigmatic Magharians. He states:

> "There cannot be any reasonable doubt that the Mandaeans have preserved the Jewish notions of the Magharians. ...at a certain moment Jewish Gnostics in Southern Babylonia, the heirs of the Magharians, thought it good to cover themselves with the name of the Nazoraeans. They also accepted the baptism and the ritual ablutions characteristic of the Elkesaites. ... It was only then that Mandaeanism, as a religion at the same time ritual and gnostic, came into being."[75]

On the other hand there is no agreement between scholars about the history of the Magharians, who believed in the existence of a high God and an angelic creator of the world. For example Quispel claimed that the Magharians existed in the pre-Christian era in Palestine, while N. Golb suggested that they flourished in Egypt during the first

---

[71] See Yamauchi, E.M., *Gnostic Ethics and Mandaean Origins*, (Harvard Theological Studies XXIV) Cambridge (1970), pp.86ff.
[72] Ibid, p.71.
[73] See Macuch, R., "Gnostische Ethik und die Anfänge der Mandäer", in *Christentum am Roten Meer*, v.II, eds. F. Altheim and R. Stiehl, Berlin, New York (1973), pp.254-73; Rudolph, K., Review of E.M. Yamauchi: *Gnostic Ethics and Mandaean Origins* (Cambridge, 1970), *ThLZ*, 97, 1972, pp.733-37. Also see J.S. Segal's Review in *BSOAS*, 36, 1973, pp.134-35.
[74] Quispel, G., "Jewish Gnosis and Mandaean Gnosticism. Some Reflections on the Writing *Bronté*", in *Les Textes de Nag Hammadi*, ed. J.-É. Ménard, (Nag Hammadi Studies, eds. M. Krause, J.M. Robinson, F. Wisse, VII) Leiden (1975), pp.115f.
[75] Ibid, pp.121-22.

few centuries of the present era.[76] On the other hand the earliest source for this sect, Qirqisani, comes from the 10th century A.D.[77]

Finally J.C. Greenfield recently supported the theory of western Jewish origin of the Mandaeans[78] and D. Cohn-Sherbok in his articles gave further evidences for the heretical Jewish connections of the Mandaean tradition.[79]

As we have seen various ideas on the origin and early history of the Mandaeans have been discussed by scholars. In this study we therefore face the following problems:

(i)First we have the problem of the origin and early history of the Mandaeans. Is Mandaeism an eastern or western tradition? Where is the original homeland of the Mandaeans? Also, depending upon these questions, what is the true picture of the early history of the Mandaeans?

(ii) The second problem we face is whether there is a connection between the Sabians of the Qur'ān and the Mandaeans. Who are the Sabians of the Qur'ān?

(iii) Finally we face the problem of whether there is a connection between the pagans of Harran, known as the Sabians of Harran in medieval times, and the Mandaeans.

We will first discuss the Sabian problem in Islamic sources, and particularly examine the identification of the Sabians of the Qur'ān, which has been discussed from the earliest Islamic times. We will discuss whether there is a connection between the Sabians of the Qur'ān and modern Mandaeans. We will also examine the source of speculation on the Sabians especially in later Muslim sources.

Secondly we will examine the problem of the origin and early history of the Mandaeans. After discussing the date of the Mandaean writings and Mandaeans' own version of their origin and history we will examine various internal and external evidences on this subject.

Finally we will examine whether there is a relationship between the Harranians and Mandaeans. We will first give a description of the Harranian religion and, then, make a comparison between the Mandaean and Harranian traditions.

---

[76]See ibid, p.120; Yamauchi, E.M., *Pre-Christian Gnosticism*, pp.158-59.

[77]See Yamauchi, E.M., *Pre-Christian Gnosticism*, p.158.

[78]See Greenfield, J.C., "A Mandaic 'Targum' of Psalm 114", in *Studies in Aggadah, Targum and Jewish Liturgy in Memory of Joseph Heinemann*, eds. J.J. Petuchowski and E. Fleischer, Jerusalem (1981), pp.23-31; idem, "A Mandaic Miscellany", *JAOS*, 104, 1984, pp.81-84.

[79]See Cohn-Sherbok, D., "The Alphabet in Mandaean and Jewish Gnosticism", *Religion*, 11, 1981, pp.227-34; idem, "The Mandaeans and Heterodox Judaism", *HUCA*, 54, 1983, pp.147-51.

CHAPTER II

THE SABIANS ACCORDING TO ISLAMIC SOURCES

The Muslim scholars were interested in the Sabians from the earliest time, since they are mentioned by the Qur'ān, though only a few times. We can classify these scholars under two categories:

A. The aim of most Muslim scholars is either to explain the term *ṣābi'ūn* (or *ṣābi'īn*) in the Qur'ān or to make clear their situation in Islamic law. All of the Muslim scholars before the second half of the ninth century A.D. and almost all of the commentators on the Qur'ān, traditionists and Islamic jurists after this date belong to this group. Their statements are generally brief and often only a few sentences.

B. Some Muslim scholars examine the Sabians as a special subject. All are later in date, i.e. after the 9th century A.D. For example, al-Mas'ūdī, who is generally accepted as one of the earliest references on this subject, lived in the 10th century A.D.

Studies on this subject are not many. In modern Muslim scholarship a few writers, such as 'Abd al-Razzāq al-Ḥasanī,[1] Rushdī 'Alyān,[2] and Nājiyah Ghāfil Marrānī,[3] have been interested in the subject, but they simply summarized the opinions of medieval Muslim scholars and gave some basic information about the Mandaeans.

On the other hand the studies of western scholars are also few. Chwolsohn's monumental two-volume study on this subject[4] is still one of the most important sources, though it was written almost one and half centuries ago. Chwolsohn, in this study, generally used the Arabic sources which he had seen. However, some of the important sources on this subject, such as al-Bīrūnī, are absent from Chwolsohn's study. He was also not sufficiently familiar with the Mandaeans and their literature because of the lack of studies on them at that time.

---

[1]al-Ḥasanī, 'Abd al-Razzāq, *al-ṣābi'ah qadīman wa ḥadīthan*, Cairo (1350/1931); idem, *al-ṣābi'ūn fī ḥāḍirihim wa māḍihim*, Saida (1374/1955); idem, *ṣābi'ah al-baṭā'ikh wa ṣābi'ah ḥarrān*, n.p. (1968).
[2]'Alyān, Rushdī, *al-ṣābi'ūn ḥarrāniyyīn wa mandā'iyyīn*, Baghdad (1976).
[3]Marrānī, N.G., *mafāhīm ṣābi'iyyah mandā'iyyah tārikh.dīn.lughah*, 2nd edition, Baghdad (1981).
[4]Chwolsohn, D., op.cit.

After Chwolsohn, so far as we know, only a few studies on the Sabian problem in Islamic sources have been carried out by western scholars.[5]

In this chapter we divide the medieval Muslim scholars into two groups, early Muslim scholars before the death of the Abbasid caliph al-Maʾmūn (832-33) and later Muslim scholars after al-Maʾmūn, because, as we will see later, there is a remarkable difference between those who lived before this date and those who lived after it.

1. The problem of the Sabians in the Islamic sources

The main point of discussion in all of the classical Islamic sources on this subject is the identification and localization of the Sabians. There is a noticeable difference between the comments made by early and later Muslim scholars.

On the one hand early Muslim scholars describe as Sabians a group of people who live in Iraq and have a monotheistic kind of belief-system, though there is not complete agreement between them. Later Muslim scholars, on the other, mostly refer to the people of Harran as the Sabians, though they also mention another group of people who lived in Iraq and disagreed with the beliefs and rituals of the Sabians of Harran. Moreover some of them claim that the people of Harran are not real Sabians. Apart from the Harranians and the group in Iraq, the later Muslim scholars also use the term Sabians for all pagans from China to Greece.

Who, then, are the Sabians of the Qurʾān? Where did they live? What is the source of the speculation on this subject? What is the relation between the Sabians of the Qurʾān and the Harranians?

The same problems arise over the situation of the Sabians in Islamic law. Although the Sabians are mentioned among the people of the book, i.e. with the Christians and the Jews, in the Qurʾān, some medieval Muslim jurists did not accept them as such. Some, such as al-Jaṣṣāṣ (d. 370/981), even claimed that they had no right to pay poll-tax in order to live in an Islamic country.

---

[5] See Pedersen, J., op.cit., pp.383-91; Segal, J.B., "The Sabian Mysteries: The Planet Cult of Ancient Harran" in *Vanished Civilizations: Forgotten Peoples of the Ancient World*, ed. E. Bacon, London (1963), pp.201-20; Dodge, B., "The Ṣabians of Ḥarrān" in *American University of Beirut Festival Book (Festschrift)*, eds. F. Sarruf and S. Tamim, Beirut (1967), pp.59-85; Hjärpe, J., *Analyse critique des traditions Arabes sur les Sabéens Harraniens*, Uppsala (1972); Buck, C., "The Identity of the Ṣābiʾūn: An Historical Quest", *MW*, 74, 1984, pp.172-86; Tubach, J., *Im Schatten des Sonnengottes*, Wiesbaden (1986), pp.143ff; Tardieu, M., "Ṣābiens Coraniques et 'Ṣābiens' de Ḥarrān", *JA*, 274, 1986, pp.1-44.

2. The Sabians in the Qurʾān

The earliest source which mentions the Sabians is the Qurʾān (7th century A.D.).[6] The Sabians appear in three verses of the Qurʾān:[7]

> "Those who believe, and the Jews, and the Christians, and the Sabians, whoever believes in God and the last day and does good, they shall have their reward from their Lord, and there is no fear for them, nor shall they grieve." (2:62)
>
> "Those who believe and the Jews and the Sabeans [Sabians] and the Christians — whoever believes in God and the last day and does good — they shall have no fear, nor shall they grieve." (5:69)
>
> "Those who believe and those who are the Jews and the Sabeans [Sabians] and the Christians and the Magians and those who set up gods (with God) — God will decide between them on the day of resurrection; for God is a witness over all things." (22:17)

The Qurʾān does not give any information about the Sabians apart from mentioning them among the People of the Book (*ʾahl al-kitāb*) with the Jews and the Christians.

First of all we must examine how the term "Sabians" and its derivative forms were used in the Arabic-speaking community at the time of the Qurʾān. Two groups of usage are noticeable:

A. *ṣābiʾūn* is the plural of *ṣābiʾ*, a *fāʿil* form (pl. *fāʿilūn*). There are two verbal roots associated with this term:

i. *ṣabaʾa* (imp. *yaṣbaʾu*) means "to change, to come out, to convert, to return". According to medieval scholars the Arabs used this verb for the stars when they came out at night and one would say "so-and-so came suddenly upon us at such-and-such a place". They would also use it for a camel when it returned.[8] Moreover they would use it for anyone who left his religion. For instance, when somebody became a Muslim at

---

[6] Here the Qurʾān translations are from M.M. Ali, *Translation of the Holy Quran*, Lahore (1934). The numbers in parenthesis show the numbers of chapters and verses.

[7] In addition some commentators state that *ṣawāmiʿ* (plural of *ṣawmaʿah* which means "monastery") which is mentioned in the Qurʾān 22:40 refers to the holy buildings of the Sabians (ʾIbn Qutaybah, ʾAbū Muḥammad ʿAbd ʾAllāh ʾibn Muslim, *taʾwīl mushkil al-qurʾān*, 2nd edition, Cairo (1393/1973), p.210), but there is no clear evidence which supports this view.

[8] al-Ṭabarī, ʾAbū Jaʿfar Muḥammad ʾibn Jarīr, *jāmiʿ al-bayān an taʾwīl āy al-qurʾān*, 3rd edition, Cairo (1388/1968), v.I, pp.318-19; al-Zamakhsharī, ʾAbū al-Qāsim Jārullah Maḥmūd ʾibn ʿUmar, *ʾasās al-balāghah*, Beirut (1965), p.345.

the time of the prophet they would say *ṣaba'a fulānun*, "so-and-so changed his religion".[9] For example the people of Bani Jazimah said *ṣaba'nā ṣaba'nā*, "we have changed our religion, converted", when Khālid 'ibn al-Walīd called them to become Muslim.[10]

ii. *ṣabā* (imp. *yaṣbū*) means "to incline, to turn over". The Arabs would use this verb for a man when he left his religion and inclined to another.[11]

It is clear that these two verbal roots are connected. The only difference between them is that the *hamzah* in the former appears as long *ā* in the latter.

B. The pagan Arabs used the term *ṣābi'* for the prophet Muhammad himself in his Meccan period.[12] The reason for this usage, according to some Islamic sources, was simply because of its meaning as "one who changed his religion". Therefore they called the prophet *ṣābi'*.[13]

On the other hand some Muslim scholars who lived in the early Islamic period remark that there is a specific connection between the term *ṣābi'*, used for the prophet, and his teaching. ʿAbd al-Raḥmān 'ibn Zayd (d.182/798)[14] states:

> "The polytheists used to say of the prophet and his companions: 'These are the Sabians', comparing them to them, because the Sabians, who live in Jazīrat al-Mawṣil, would say 'there is no god but God'."[15]

Also 'Ibn Jurayj (d.150/767)[16] and ʿAtā 'ibn 'Abī Rabāh (d.114/732)[17] pointed out the relationship between the Sabians who lived in Sawād and the saying of the Meccan polytheists about the prophet, "he has become a Sabian."[18]

According to this point of view the Arab pagans connected the teaching of the prophet with the beliefs of the Sabians who lived in Iraq. The most striking characteristic of his teaching was the Unity of God: "There is no god but Allah". The

---

[9]al-Ṭabarī, op.cit., v.I, p.318; 'Ibn Ḥanbal, 'Aḥmad, *musnad*, Beirut (n.d.), v.2, p.452; al-Bukhārī, 'Abū ʿAbd 'Allāh Muḥammad 'ibn 'Ismāʿīl, *al-jāmiʿ al-ṣaḥīḥ*, Istanbul (1981), v.4, p.242; al-Zamakhsharī, *al-fā'iq fī gharīb al-ḥadīth*, Cairo (1945-1971), v.2, p.10.

[10]al-Bukhārī, op.cit., v.8, p.118; al-Nasā'ī, 'Abū ʿAbd al-Raḥmān 'ibn Shuʿayb, *sunan* Cairo (1383/1964), v.8, p.208.

[11]'Abū Layth al-Samarqandī, Naṣr 'ibn Muḥammad 'ibn 'Ibrāhīm, *tafsīr*, Süleymaniye Library, Fatih Bölümü Nu: 227, Istanbul, v.I, p.19-B; 'Ibn 'Athīr, 'Abū al-Saʿādat Mubārak 'ibn Muḥammad, *al-nihāyah fī gharīb al-ḥadīth wa al-'āthār*, Beirut (n.d.), v.3, p.11; Fakhruddīn al-Rāḍī, Muḥammad 'ibn ʿUmar al-Khattāb, *mafātīḥ al-ghayb*, Istanbul (1307 A.H.), v.I, p.548.

[12]al-Bukhārī, op.cit., v.I, p.89; 'Ibn Ḥanbal, op.cit., v.5, pp.174-75; Muslim 'ibn Ḥajjāj, 'Imām 'Abī al-Ḥusayn al-Qurashī, *ṣaḥīḥ*, n.p. (1955), v.4, pp.1920-21.

[13]See 'Ibn 'Athīr, op.cit., v.3, p.3.

[14]ʿAbd al-Raḥmān 'ibn Zayd 'ibn 'Aslam al-ʿAdawī al-Madanī is one of the important sources of al-Ṭabarī who gives the name shortly "'Ibn Zayd". See Sezgin, F., *Geschichte des arabischen Schrifttums*, (hereafter *GAS*) Leiden (1967-1984), v.I, p.38.

[15]al-Ṭabarī, op.cit., v.I, p.319; 'Ibn Kathīr, 'Abū al-Fidā 'Ismaʿil al-Qurashī, *tafsīr al-qur'ān al-ʿazim*, 3rd edition, Cairo (1376/1956), v.I, p.104.

[16]See Chwolsohn, D., op.cit., v.I, p.187.

[17]'Abū Muḥammad ʿAtā 'ibn 'Abī Rabah 'Aslam al-Qurashī was born in 27/647. See *GAS*, v.I, p.31.

[18] al-Ṭabarī, op.cit., v.I, p.319.

polytheist Arabs knew the people known as "Sabians" who had a kind of monotheistic belief-system. They therefore thought there was a connection between his teaching and the Sabians', and called the prophet *ṣābiʾ*. An account at the time of the prophet seems to support this:

> "Rabīʿah ʾibn ʿUbbād said: 'I saw the prophet when I was a pagan. He was saying to people, "if you want to save yourselves, accept there is no god but Allah". At this moment I noticed a man behind him, saying: "He is a *ṣābiʿ*." When I asked somebody who he was he told me he was ʾAbū Lahab, his uncle."'[19]

In connection with the etymology of *ṣābiʾūn*, Arab lexicographers explain the word *ṣābiʾ* or *ṣābī* as derived from verbs meaning "arise, apostatize" or "incline, turn away from the (true) religion".[20] *ṣābiʾūn*, therefore, means "those who take on a new religion other than their own" like a Muslim apostate from his religion.[21]

Most western scholars do not accept this derivation. They agree that the word is of non-Arabic origin, but differ about its etymology.

E. Pocock, in 1649, suggested that *ṣābiʾ* was to be derived from the Hebrew word *ṣâbā* "army, troops", a view which was recently supported by M. Tardieu.[22]

R. Bell is inclined to think that the word is just a play on the name of the Sabaeans of South Arabia, though he himself notes the difficulties of this theory because of confusion of "*s*" sounds which are quite distinct in Arabic.[23] H. Grimme looked to South Arabia for the origin of the word, which he would relate to Ethiopic *ṣbḥ*, whose secondary meaning is "tributum pendere" (weigh tribute), and which he would interpret as "Almosen spendend" (dispensing alms).[24]

On the other hand a number of western scholars, such as J. Wellhausen, D. Chwolsohn and E.S. Drower, suggested that this term was connected with the Syriac

---

[19] ʾIbn Ḥanbal, op.cit., v.3, p.492; v.4, p.341. Also see Waardenburg, J., "World Religions as Seen in the Light of Islam", in *Islam: Past Influence and Present Challenge*, eds. A.T. Welch and P. Cachia, Edinburgh (1979), p.248.

[20] See above pp.17f. Also see ʾIbn Manẓūr, ʾAbū Faḍl Jamāl al-Dīn Muḥammad, *lisān al-ʿarab*, Beirut (c. 1975), v.I, p.108; Segal, J.B., "Pagan Syriac Monuments in the Vilayet of Urfa", *AS*, 3, 1953, p.110; Wansbrough, J., *The Sectarian Milieu. Content and Composition of Islamic Salvation History*, Oxford (1978), pp.101f.

[21] See al-Ṭabarī, op.cit., v.I, p.318; al-Qurṭubī, ʾAbū ʿAbd ʾAllāh Muḥammad ʾibn ʾAḥmad, *al-jāmiʿ al-ʾaḥkām al-qurʾān*, Cairo (1387/1967), v.I, p.434; al-Zamakhsharī, *ʾasās al-balāghah*, p.345; Fakhruddīn al-Rāḍī, op.cit., v.I, p.548; al-Naysābūrī, Nizām al-Dīn al-Ḥasan ʾibn Muḥammad ʾibn Ḥusayn al-Qummī, *gharāʾib al-qurʾān wa raghāʾib al-furqān*, Cairo (1381/1962), v.I, p.333.

[22] See Tardieu, M., "Ṣabiens Coraniques et'Ṣabiens' de Ḥarrān", p.41. Also see Chwolsohn, D., op.cit., v.I, p.31. Tardieu suggested that the term *ṣābiʾūn* in the Qurʾān was the Arabic equivalent of a Greek name meaning "celestial armies". See Tardieu, M., op.cit., p.42.

[23] Bell, R., *The Origin of Islam in its Christian Environment*, London (1926, new edition 1968), p.60.

[24] Jeffery, A., *The Foreign Vocabulary of the Qurʾan*, Baroda (1938), p.191.

verb *ṣbʿ* which means "to dip, moisten, dye, baptize".[25] J.B. Segal, rejecting this derivation, stated that the development of Syriac *ṣabiʿ* > *ṣabiʾ* into Arabic *ṣābiʾ*, postulated by this theory, was difficult and he simply derived it from a geographical term "Ṣôbā", applied at this period to the city of "Niṣibis".[26] Segal's explanation of the origin of the term is not free from serious objections.[27]

In fact the Arabs might not have taken the term directly from Syriac, but from the Mandaic verb *ṣbʾ*.[28] The *ʿayn* of Syriac words mostly disappears in Mandaic and sometimes turns to *alaf*.[29] We find *ṣbʾ* means "to baptize, immerse, dip in" in Mandaic, a changed form of Syriac *ṣbʿ*.[30] This derivation, supported by many scholars, such as C.C. Torrey and A. Jeffery,[31] seems the best.

The question whom this term of the Qurʾān refers to is at least as important a subject of argument as its etymology. We will examine the opinions of the medieval Muslim scholars later.[32] We have various theories on this problem proposed by western scholars.

We saw, earlier, the suggestion made by R. Bell that the Sabians were the Sabaeans of South Arabia.[33]

J. Pedersen who begins from the statement that the terms *ḥanīf* and *ṣābiʾūn* in the Qurʾān are synonymous and refer to the same thing, claims that the Qurʾān uses this term (*ṣābiʾūn*) for a number of Gnostic and Hellenistic sects, including the Harranians, scattered over the whole of North Arabia. He states:

---

[25]See Chwolsohn, D., op.cit., v.I, pp.110-11; *MII*, p.16; Drower, E.S., *The Secret Adam*, p.ix; Jeffery, A., op.cit., p.191; Yamauchi, E.M., "The Present Status of Mandaean Studies", p.89.

[26]See Segal, J.B., "Pagan Syriac Monuments in the Vilayet of Urfa", p.110; idem, "The Sabian Mysteries: The Planet Cult of Ancient Ḥarran", pp.212, 214.

[27]Some Syriac writers named the city of Niṣibis (modern Nusaybin) as "Ṣôbā": cf. Addai, the Apostle, *The Teaching of Addai*, tr. G. Howard, Chico (1981), p.36. The name "Niṣibis" (ancient form Naṣībina) has been used for Nusaybin since the 10th century B.C. The only name, used for this city in Neo-Assyrian texts is "Naṣībina", cf. Parpola, S., *Neo-Assyrian Toponyms*, Kevelaer (1970), pp.258-59. Yāqūt al-Rūmī mentions another Niṣibis (*naṣībin al-rūm*), a city between Āmid and Ḥarran on the bank of Euphrates. See Yāqūt al-Hamawī al-Rūmī, Shihāb al-Dīn ʾAbī ʿAbd ʾAllāh, *muʿjam al-buldān*, Beirut (1376/1957), v.5, p.289. But there is no place known as "Sôbā" in classical times, including the early times of Islam, around Ḥarran and Niṣibis. The medieval geographers only describe a village near Jerusalem under the name "Sôbā" (cf. ibid, v.3, p.432). All of these points support scholars, such as R.P. Smith and E. Honigmann, who state that these Syriac writers used this name, Sôbā of the Bible, for Niṣibis by mistake. Moreover we cannot find such a usage in any other source; cf. Smith, R.P., *Thesaurus Syriacus*, Oxford (1879-1901), Tom.2, p.3373; *EI*, v.III, pp.917-20; Fiey, J.-M., *Nisibe*, Louvain (1977), pp.18, 104.

[28]See Chwolsohn, D., op.cit., v.I, p.111.

[29]Cf. *HCMM*, pp.90ff; Nöldeke, Th., *Mandäische Grammatik*, Halle (1875), pp.69-70.

[30]*MD*, pp.388-89.

[31]See Torrey, C.C., *The Jewish Foundation of Islam*, New York (1933), p.3; Jeffery, A., op.cit., p.192. Therefore the term acquires the sense of "the Baptists", cf. Huart, Cl., "Notice sur les Mandéens", in *Études Linguistiques. Deuxième Partie. Textes Mandaïtes*, J. de Morgan, Paris (1904), p.ix.

[32]See below pp.29ff.

[33]See above p.19.

> "Before the time of Muhammad the word (Ṣabiūn) must have had a meaning that connects it closely with his doctrines otherwise he would not be able to use it in this way... They (the Ḥanīfs) too are the people who believe in God, neither Jews, nor Christians; the nearest model for the believers, as Abraham himself was Ḥanīf... A so strongly emphasized religious community could not fail to be mentioned in the three places where Ṣabiūn are mentioned... Therefore the word is synonymous with the designation Ḥanīf. The words Ḥanīf and Ṣabian stand thus in the some relation as 'Hellenistic' and 'Gnostic' in our usage."[34]

Pedersen's view was supported by J.B. Segal,[35] and recently by J. Hjärpe with a small variation.[36]

This point of view is questionable. First of all we must examine the term *ḥanīf* which occurs a number of times in the Qur'ān. In connection with the etymology of the word, many scholars, such as Th. Nöldeke and M. Watt, have been inclined to connect it with Syriac *ḥnp'*, "heathen".[37] But some, such as A. Sprenger, C.C. Torrey and C.S. Lyall, insisted that it was connected with Hebrew *ḥānef*, "heretic, profane".[38] The other possibilities on the origin of *ḥanīf* are that it is a loan from Ethiopic, and that it is connected with some South Arabian cult as claimed by H. Grimme.[39] Finally, according to the suggestion which was made by medieval Muslim philologists (except al-Masʿūdī),[40] and supported by some western scholars, such as R. Bell, *ḥanīf* is, simply, a proper Arabic form, derived from the Arabic verb *ḥanafa* which means "declined" or "turned away from". *ḥanīf* would then mean "one who turns aside or secedes from his community in the matter of religion".[41]

In the usage of the Qur'ān, Ḥanīf acquires the sense of pure monotheism.[42] The term is used especially for Abraham, who was not a Jew, nor a Christian, nor one of the polytheists, but a Ḥanīf, a Muslim.[43] The Qur'ān divides religions into two sections: Islam which is the true and pure monotheistic religion of God on the one side,

---

[34]Pedersen, J., op.cit., pp.386-90.

[35]See Segal, J.B., op.cit., pp.214-15; idem, *Edessa 'The Blessed City'*, Oxford (1970), p.60 n.1.

[36]Hjärpe, too, accepts the suggestion that *ṣābi'ūn* and *ḥanīf* have the same meaning and the same content, which is "Gnosticism". As a different point he states that *ṣābi'ūn* is a term of opprobrium indicating a Gnostic sect; but *ḥanīf* refers to the good Gnostics. cf. Hjärpe, J., op.cit., pp.23-24.

[37]For the etymology of the word, see Jeffery, A., op.cit., pp.112-15; Margoliouth, D.S., "On the Origin and Import of the Names Muslim and Ḥanif", *JRAS*, 1903, pp.467-93; *EI**, v.III, pp.165-66; *EI*, v.III, pp.258-60.

[38]Torrey, C.C., op.cit., p.51; Lyall, C.S., "The Words Ḥanīf and Muslim", *JRAS*, 1903, p.781.

[39]See Jeffery, A., op.cit., p.115.

[40]al-Masʿūdī remarks that it is a foreign word, borrowed from Syriac, cf. al-Masʿūdī, 'Abū al-Ḥasan ʿAli 'ibn Ḥusayn, *kitāb al-tanbīh wa al-'ishrāf*, ed. M.J. de Goeje, Leiden (1967), p.91.

[41]Cf. Bell, R., op.cit., p.58.

[42]See idem, *Introduction to the Qur'an*, Edinburgh (1958), p.12; idem, "Who were the Ḥanīfs?", *MW*, 20, 1930, p.124.

[43]See *Qur'ān*, 3:67; 6:161; 16:120, 121, 123.

and the others, including Judaism, Christianity and all kinds of paganism, on the other side. All prophets, mentioned in the Qur'ān, like Adam, Abraham, Moses, Jesus and Muhammad are representatives of Islam.[44] Therefore all of them carry the name "Muslim". Since "Muslim" is the name, used for these prophets as well as for their followers, the term *ḥanīf*, used for the prophet Abraham, Muhammad and all Muslims, is synonymous with the term "Muslim". There are a number of verses in the Qur'ān which support this.[45]

On the other hand the term *ṣābi'ūn* in the Qur'ān obviously refers to the people who are not Muslims, but among the People of the Book (*'ahl al-kitāb*), like the Christians. In that case how can we think there is a connection between the terms *ḥanīf* and *ṣābi'ūn*?

More recently M. Tardieu, who bases his theory on E. Pocock's etymology of the term *ṣābi'* and on the characteristics of the Harranian pagans known as "the Sabians from Harran" from the 10th century A.D., suggested that the Sabians of the Qur'ān were nothing else but Gnostics.[46]

Finally concerning this subject, the most popular theory, suggested by C.W.F. Walch (18th century) and D. Chwolsohn (19th century) and supported by many scholars of this century, such as C.H. Kraeling, Lady Drower and C. Buck, is that the term *ṣābi'ūn* refers to the Mandaeans of South Iraq.[47] We will discuss this theory in coming sections.

3. The Sabians according to early Muslim scholars before 832-33 A.D. (the date of death of the Abbasid caliph al-Ma'mūn)

Western scholars interested in the Sabians, with a few exceptions such as D. Chwolsohn and D.S. Margoliouth, did not pay attention to these early Muslim scholars,[48] though they are vitally important if we are to recognize who the Sabians of

[44]See *Qur'ān*, 2:127, 128, 133; 3:19, 84, 85.

[45]See *Qur'ān*, 3:67; 10:105; 16:123; 22:31; 30:30.

[46]See Tardieu, M., op.cit., pp.40ff.

[47]See above pp.5-6. Also see Drower, E.S., *The Secret Adam*, p.ix; Krealing, C.H., "The Origin and Antiquity of the Mandaeans", p.203; Brandt, W., "Mandaeans", p.390; Browne, E.G., *A Literary History of Persia*, Cambridge (1964), v.I, pp.301f; Hitti, P.K., *History of Syria*, London (1951), p.485; idem, *History of the Arabs*, London (1937), p.233; Rudolph, K., "Problems of a History of the Development of the Mandaean Religion", p.218; idem, *Gnosis: The Nature and History of an Ancient Religion*, translation ed. R. McL. Wilson (trs. R.McL. Wilson, P.W. Coxon and K.H. Kuhn), Edinburgh (1983), p.343; Gätje, H., *The Qur'ān and its Exegesis*, tr. A.T. Welch, London (1976), p.265; Buck, C., op.cit., pp.172ff.

[48]Cf. Chwolsohn, D., op.cit., v.I, pp.183ff; Margoliouth, D.S., "Ḥarranians", in *ERE*, v.6, p.519. E.S. Drower's suggestion, which is that from the earliest time they were dependent upon hearsay, and their reports can only be accepted as such (*MII*, p.xvi), is difficult to accept because we find the statements of some of them, like 'Abū Yūsuf (d. 182/ c.797) and al-Shāfi'ī (d. 204/819), in their own books. In connection with the others, we do not have the books which were written by them, because

the Qur'ān are and analyze the speculations on the Sabians which take place in later Islamic sources. We can explain this importance in two points:

a. First of all these authors lived in the early times of Islam, mostly in the first two centuries A.H. (c. 7th-8th century A.D.). Therefore they are closer to the Qur'ān in which the Sabian people were mentioned for the first time, and to the first generation of Islam than the others. Their views give us a clear idea of how the people at the time of the Prophet knew the Sabians.

b. Secondly they have had a big effect upon the later Islamic scientific movements like Tafsīr, Ḥadīth and Fiqh. All of them are amongst the most important sources of later Muslim scholars such as 'Ibn Hishām (d. 218/833), al-Balādurī (d. 279/892), al-Ṭabarī (d. 310/923) and al-Mas'ūdī (d. 346/954).

A. The identification of the Sabians

Although their statements on the Sabians are generally just a few sentences, they give us important clues on who the Sabians are. The main aim of these scholars was to explain to whom this term of the Qur'ān referred.

'Abd 'Allāh 'ibn al-'Abbās, who lived in the middle of 7th century A.D.,[49] states that the religion of the Sabians is a sect of Christianity. He also remarks that the animals which they slaughtered cannot be eaten and their women cannot be married — they are banned to the Muslims.[50]

In the opinion of Ziyād 'ibn 'Abīhī (d. 53/672),[51] who was the governor of Iraq at the time of the first Umayyad caliph Mu'āwiyah, the Sabians believe in the prophets and pray five times daily.[52] According to the information given by Ḥasan al-Baṣrī (d. 110/728) Ziyād had met them and wanted to exempt them from the poll-tax (*jizyah*), but when he was informed that they worshipped the angels (*malā'ikah*) he changed his decision.[53]

---

they did not write any book about this subject. But, on the other hand, it is possible to find their opinions in a number of later sources, and to compare them to each other.

[49]One of the companions of the Prophet, he was born 3 years before the Hijrah (619 A.D.) and died in 687 A.D. See *GAS*, v.I, pp.25ff; *EI**, v.I, pp.40ff.

[50]See al-Qurṭubī, op.cit., v.I, p.434; 'Abū al-Faraj, 'Abd al-Raḥmān 'ibn al-Jawzī al-Qurashī al-Baghdādī, *zād al-masīr fī 'ilm al-tafsīr*, Beirut (1384/1964), v.I, p.92. Also 'Ibn al-'Abbās states that their beliefs are between Judaism and Christianity. See 'Ibn Ḥayyān, 'Athīr al-Dīn 'Abī'Abd 'Allāh al-'Andalūsī, *al-tafsīr al-kabīr al-muthammā bi al-bahr al-muḥīt*, Riyad (n.d.), v.I, p.239.

[51]Ziyād 'ibn 'Abīhī (or Ziyād 'ibn 'Abī Sufyān) was half-brother of Mu'āwiyah. See *GAS*, v.I, pp.261-62; *EI*, v.IV, p.1302.

[52]'Ibn Kathīr, op.cit., v.I, p.104.

[53]al-Ṭabarī, op.cit., v.I, p.319; 'Ibn Ḥayyān, op.cit., v.I, p.239.

Mujāhid 'ibn Jarīr (d. 104/722), the famous commentator,[54] remarks that the Sabians have no distinctive religion. He states that their religion is between Judaism and Magianism.[55]

Ḥasan al-Baṣrī (d. 110/728)[56] states that the Sabians look like the Magians and worship the angels (*malā'ikah*).[57] He also remarks that they read *zabūr*[58] and pray in the direction of *qiblah* .[59] Moreover al-Ṭabarī relates that Ḥasan claimed the religion of the Sabians was between Judaism and Magianism.[60] 'Ibn 'Abī Nujayh (d. 132/749)[61] and Suddī (d. 128/745)[62] too accept the latter opinion.[63]

Wahb 'ibn Munabbih (d. 110-14/728-32), who was originally from Iran,[64] points out that they believe "there is no god but God", but they do not have a certain canonical law.[65]

In the opinion of ʿAṭā' 'ibn 'Abī Rabāh (d. 114/732),[66] the famous commentator, the Sabians are a tribe who live in "Sawād",[67] and who are not identical with Magians, Jews and Christians. 'Ibn Jurayj, who lived in the 8th century A.D.,[68] too accepts his opinion and points out that the polytheists said of the Prophet: "He is a Sabian".[69]

Qatādah 'ibn Diʿāmah (d. 118/736)[70] states that the Sabians worship the angels (*malā'ikah*), read *zabūr* and pray the five ritual prayers.[71] Moreover he points out that they pray to the Sun.[72]

---

[54] 'Abū al-Ḥajjāj Mujāhid 'ibn Jarīr al-Makkī was born in 21/642. See 'Ibn Qutaybah, 'Abū Muḥammad ʿAbd 'Allah, *al-maʿārif*, Cairo (1934), p.196.

[55] Mujāhid, 'Abū al-Ḥajjāj 'Ibn Jabr al-Makkī, *tafsīr mujāhid*, ed. ʿAbd al-Raḥmān Ṭāhir 'ibn Muḥammad al-Surātī, Duha (1396/1976), p.77; al-Ṭabarī, op.cit., v.I, p.319; al-Qurṭubī, op.cit., v.I, p.434. On the other hand there are various statements which are related from Mujāhid: the religion of the Sabians is between Magianism, Judaism and Christianity; they are neither Jews nor Christians. See 'Ibn Kathīr, op.cit., v.I, p.104. Cf. al-Ṭabarī, op.cit., v.I, p.319.

[56] He was born in 21/642. See *GAS*, v.I, p.30.

[57] See 'Ibn Kathīr, op.cit., v.I, p.104; 'Abū al-Faraj al-Baghdādī, op.cit., v.I, p.92.

[58] *zabūr* is the Book of Psalms, revealed to David. See *Qur'ān*, 4:163; 17:55; 21:105.

[59] al-Qurṭubī, op.cit., v.I, p.434; 'Ibn Ḥayyān, op.cit., v.I, p.239.

[60] al-Ṭabarī, op.cit., v.I, p.319.

[61] See 'Ibn Qutaybah, op.cit., p.206.

[62] 'Abū Muḥammad 'Ismāʿil 'ibn ʿAbd al-Raḥmān al-Suddī. See *GAS*, v.I, pp.32f.

[63] 'Ibn Kathīr, op.cit., v.I, p.104; 'Ibn Ḥayyān, op.cit., v.I, p.239.

[64] See 'Ibn Qutaybah, op.cit., p.202.

[65] 'Ibn Kathīr, op.cit., v.I, p.104.

[66] 'Abū Muḥammad ʿAṭā 'ibn 'Abī Rabah 'Aslam al-Qurashī was born in 27/647. See *GAS*, v.I, p.31; 'Ibn Qutaybah, op.cit., p.202.

[67] The region of Iraq conquered by the Muslims at the time of the second caliph ʿUmar. See Yāqūt al-Ḥamawī al-Rūmī, op.cit., v.3, p.272. Also see Map I (below p.53).

[68] ʿAbd al-Mālik 'ibn ʿAbd al-ʿAzīz 'ibn Jurayj. See Chwolsohn, D., op.cit., v.I, p.187; 'Ibn Qutaybah, op.cit., p.214.

[69] al-Ṭabarī, op.cit., v.I, p.319.

[70] 'Abū al-Khaṭṭāb Qatādah 'ibn Diʿāmah al-Sadūsī, who was born in 60/679, spent his life in Basra and Wasit and died in Wasit. See 'Ibn Qutaybah, op.cit., p.203; *GAS*, v.I, p.31.

[71] al-Ṭabarī, op.cit., v.I, p.320; al-Qurṭubī, op.cit., v.I, p.434; 'Ibn Kathīr, op.cit., v.I, p.104.

[72] al-Naysābūrī, op.cit., v.I, p.333.

ʾAbū al-Zanād (d. 130/747), who was from Iraq,[73] remarks that they are a tribe who live in "Kūtha" in Iraq.[74] He also states that they believe in prophets, fast 30 days in a year and pray 5 times daily towards Yaman.[75]

In the opinion of ʾAbū Ḥanīfah (d. 150/767), who is the founder and the greatest *ʾimām* of the Ḥanafite school of Islamic Law,[76] the Sabians are a tribe who read *zabūr*, and whose religion is between Judaism and Christianity.[77] ʾAwzāʿī (d. 157/773), the main representative of the ancient Syrian school of religious law,[78] and Mālik ʾibn ʾAnas (d. 179/795), the jurist and the traditionist,[79] agree with ʾAbū Ḥanīfah, but they think that the Sabians have no scriptures.[80]

According to the statement of Khalīl ʾibn ʾAḥmad, who died at Basra in 170/786-87,[81] the Sabians believe that they belong to the religion of the prophet Noah; they read *zabūr* and worship the angels (*malāʾikah*). Also he remarks that their religion looks like Christianity.[82]

ʿAbd al-Raḥmān ʾibn Zayd (d. 182/798) states that their religion is a religion in itself. He points out that they live in the area around Mosul (*jazīrat al-mawṣil*)[83] and believe in only one God, but they have no cult, no scripture and no prophet; it is their belief that "there is no god but God". He also remarks that they do not believe in the Messenger of God (the Prophet Muhammad). Moreover he states that the polytheists used to say of the Prophet and his companions: "these are the Sabians", comparing them to them.[84]

Finally ʾAḥmad ʾibn Ḥanbal (d. 241/855), the *ʾimām* of Baghdad,[85] states that the religion of the Sabians is a sect of Christianity or Judaism.[86]

Briefly, about the Sabians these early Muslim scholars remark on:

a) The location in which they live:

1. Around Mosul (ʿAbd al-Raḥmān ʾibn Zayd).
2. Sawād (ʿAtā ʾibn ʾAbī Rabāh and ʾIbn Jurayj).

---

[73]ʿAbd ʾAllāh ʾibn Zakwān ʾAbī al-Zanād. See ʾIbn Qutaybah, op.cit., p.204.

[74]Kūtha is a city in Babylonia in Iraq. See Yāqūt al-Hamawī al-Rūmī, op.cit., v.4, p.487. Also see Map I (below p.53).

[75]ʾIbn Kathīr, op.cit., v.I, p.104.

[76]ʾAbū Ḥanīfah Nuʿmān ʾibn Thābit who was born in 80/699 spent his life in Baṣrah and Kufah. See ʾIbn Qutaybah, op.cit., pp.216-17.

[77]See ʾAbū Layth al-Samarqandī, op.cit., v.I, p.19-B.

[78]ʿAbd al-Raḥman ʾibn ʿAmr al-ʾAwzāʿī. See ʾIbn Qutaybah, op.cit., p.217; *EI**, v.I, pp.772-73.

[79]The founder of the school of the Mālikis. See *EI*, v.III, pp.218-22.

[80]See Jaṣṣāṣ, ʾAḥmad ʾibn ʿAlī, *ʾaḥkām al-qurʾān*, Cairo (1347 A.H.), v.3, p.113.

[81]See Chwolsohn, D., op.cit., v.I, p.188.

[82]al-Qurṭubī, op.cit., v.I, p.434; ʾIbn Kathīr, op.cit., v.I, p.104; ʾIbn Ḥayyān, op.cit., v.I, p.239.

[83]Mosul is a city on the bank of Tigris in North Iraq. Yāqūt al-Hamawī al-Rūmī, op.cit., v.5, pp.223ff. See Map I (below p.53).

[84]See al-Ṭabarī, op.cit., v.I, p.319; ʾIbn Kathīr, op.cit., v.I, p.104; ʾAbū al-Faraj, op.cit., v.I, p.92; ʾIbn Ḥayyān, op.cit., v.I, p.239.

[85]Founder of one of the four major Sunni Schools, the Ḥanbalī. See *EI**, v.I, pp.272-73.

[86]See ʾIbn Qudāmah, Muwaffaq al-Dīn ʾAbī Muḥammad ʿAbd ʾAllāh ʾibn ʾAḥmad, *al-mughnī*, Beirut (1392/1972), v.10, p.568.

3. Kūtha (ʾAbū al-Zanād).

b) The definition of their religion:

1.It is a religion between Judaism and Magianism (Mujāhid, Ḥasan al-Baṣrī, ʾIbn ʾAbī Nujayh and Suddī).

2. It is a religion between Judaism and Christianity (Qatādah, ʾAbū Ḥanīfah, ʾAwzaʿī, Mālik ʾibn ʾAnas and ʾAḥmad ʾibn Ḥanbal).

3. It is a sect of the Christianity (ʾIbn ʿAbbās and Khalīl).

4. It is a separate religion (ʿAtā and ʿAbd al-Raḥmān ʾibn Zayd).

c) Their beliefs and characteristic rites:

1. They believe in only one God (Wahb ʾibn Munabbih and ʿAbd al-Raḥmān ʾibn Zayd).

2. They suppose they are the followers of the religion of the prophet Noah (Khalīl).

3. They worship the angels (*malāʾikah*) and read *zabūr* (Qatādah, Khalīl, Ḥasan al-Baṣrī, ʾIbn ʾAbi Nujayh and Suddī).[87]

4. They pray to the Sun (Qatādah).

5. They believe in the prophets (ʾAbū al-Zanād and Ziyād ʾibn ʾAbīhī).

6. They do not have any cult, scripture and prophet (ʿAbd al-Raḥmān ʾibn Zayd).

7. They pray 5 ritual prayers daily (ʾAbū al-Zanād, Ziyād ʾibn ʾAbīhī and Qatādah).

8. They pray in the direction of the south (Ḥasan al-Baṣrī and ʾAbū al-Zanād).

9. They fast 30 days in a year (ʾAbū al-Zanād).

It is an important feature of these statements about the Sabians that these early scholars, who generally lived in Iraq, accept the religion of the Sabians as a religion between Magianism, Judaism and Christianity, though they apparently have some different opinions. In another words the religion of the Sabians in their explanation is either a sect which is related to one of these three religions, i.e. Magianism, Judaism or Christianity, or a separate religion which carries various elements of these three religions.

Secondly, according to the statements of some of them, the Sabians, whom they localize in Iraq, have a monotheistic belief system, though, on the other hand, they worship the *malāʾikah* and even (in one report) pray to the Sun.

There are important similarities between the characteristics of the Sabians according to these early scholars and the features of the religion of the Mandaeans. First

[87] ʾAbū Yūsuf (d. 182/798), the head-judge of the Abbasid caliph Hārūn al-Rashīd, the father of al-Maʾmūn, and Muḥammad ʾibn Ḥasan (d.189/804), both lived in Iraq (see ʾIbn Qutaybah, op.cit., pp.218f), too remark that the Sabians worship the angels. See ʾAbū Layth al-Samarqandī, op.cit., v.I, p.19-B. In addition, ʾAbū al-ʾĀliyah (d. 90/708), Daḥḥaq ʾibn Mazāhim (d. 102/720) and Rabiʿ ʾibn ʾAnas al-Baṣrī (d. 139/756) (see ʾIbn Qutaybah, op.cit., pp.200, 201, 205) state that they read *zabūr*. cf al-Bukhārī, op.cit., v.I, p.90; al-Qurṭubī, op.cit., v.I, p.434; ʾIbn Kathīr, op.cit., v.I, p.104; ʾIbn Ḥayyān, op.cit., v.I, p.239.

of all, like the Sabians of the early Muslim scholars the Mandaean tradition carries a number of Jewish, Iranian and Christian elements which we will discuss later.[88]

Another notable point is the statement of the early Muslim scholars that the Sabians worship the *malā'ikah*, "angels". *mlaka* in Mandaic means "angel" and "devil". This term is used for both good and bad spirits.[89] Good spirits are preferably indicated as *malkia*, "kings", semi-divinities who carry out the will of the Great Life. All are subordinate to the Creator, whose first manifestation they were.[90] The highest Malka is *malka d̲-nhura*, "King of Light". No one is like him and no one has tried to dispute his power. Malka d̲-Nhura is one of the names given to the Supreme Being in Mandaean religion.[91] It is possible that the Muslims, who lived alongside the Mandaeans (known to them as the Sabians) from the 7th century A.D., noted the term "Malka" (particularly "Malka d̲-Nhura") in the Mandaean tradition, since it is quite often used by the Mandaeans, and that they confused this term with *malak* (pl. *malā'ikah*), "angel", in Arabic. Consequently they supposed that the Sabians worshipped the angels.

The statement that they read *zabūr* is notable as well. Zabūr is the Psalms of David, as we have seen before. An important part of the Mandaean literature is in hymn style, e.g. a number of parts of the *Ginza* and *Qolasta*.[92]

Another important point is that Noah is indicated in the Mandaean writings as one of the great ancestors and leaders of the Mandaean people.[93]

Even the statement about praying to the Sun is partly supported by the Mandaean literature. Although in the Mandaean tradition the seven planets are regarded as evil beings and planet-worshipping is therefore certainly rejected, the Sun, *šamiš* is sometimes regarded as a power for good rather than evil.[94]

The statements of the early Muslim scholars about the Sabians praying five times daily are also notable. In the *Ginza* the Mandaeans are invited to pray five times daily to the Lord of all the worlds.[95]

---

[88]See Chapter IV.
[89]See *MD*, pp.243-44.
[90]See *MII*, p.94.
[91]See ibid, p.38. Cf. *GR*, pp.5ff.
[92]See *GR* and *GL*; *The Canonical Prayerbook of the Mandaeans*, (hereafter *CP*) tr. E.S. Drower, Leiden (1959).
[93]See below pp.88-9.
[94]See *MII*, pp.75-76: "It is the day of Habšaba (the First of the Week). This is our symbol (type): it is that which is called good fortune. We taught them all about it (*enjoining*) love of that day. Šamiš (Sun), Bringer of good fortune, assigned the first type to himself: and it is his symbol": Drower, E.S., *The Thousand and Twelve Questions*, (hereafter *ATS*) Berlin (1960), p.253.

But, on the other hand, Šamiš, one of the seven evil planets, is sometimes associated with "Adonai", "Qadoš" and "El-El". See *GR*, p.25.

[95]See below pp.225-6.

Finally the places where these early Muslim scholars locate the Sabians are almost the same areas where the Mandaeans live.[96]

B. The situation of the Sabians in Islamic law

The Muslim scholars who lived before the Abbasid caliph al-Ma'mūn agree with each other that the Sabians are among the non-Muslim groups who can live in the Muslim community by paying a poll-tax (*jizyah*). According to Islamic law the poll-tax can be taken not only from the People of the Book (*'ahl al-kitāb*), like the Jews and Christians, but from any non-Muslims who live in the Islamic state except the Muslim apostates and the Arab pagans.[97]

As a matter of fact when the lands of Iraq (Sawād), including Mosul and Kūtha, were conquered by the Muslims at the time of the second caliph ʿUmar, all non-Muslim peoples including the Magians and the Sabians who lived in this area were inserted into the poll-tax system.[98] Moreover the account of the relations between Ziyād 'ibn 'Abīhī, the Governor of Iraq, and the Sabians, we have remarked earlier,[99] definitely indicates that they paid the poll-tax.

But these early scholars differ about whether the Sabians are one of the Peoples of the Book. They are divided into two groups:

a. In the opinions of 'Abū al-'Āliyah (d. 90/708), Suddī (d. 128/745) and 'Abū Ḥanīfah (d. 150/767),[100] the Sabians are People of the Book because they read

---

[96]D.S. Margoliouth, in connection with Jazīrat al-Mawṣil, maintains that it would not suit the Mandaeans. See Margoliouth, D.S., "Harranians", p.519. We disagree with him, because we know that the Mandaeans live scattered over a wide area. Therefore al-Bīrūnī, who lived in the 11th century, emphasized that "they live very much scattered and nowhere in places that belonged exclusively to them alone". al-Bīrūnī, 'Abū al-Rayhān Muḥammad 'ibn 'Aḥmad, *The Chronology of Ancient Nations*, ed. and tr. E. Sachau, London (1879), pp.188, 314. Also according to Bar Konai's account the Mandaean community in Mesene was founded by the group who migrated from Adiabene, a district to the north of Mosul. See below p.124.

[97]See 'Abū Yūsuf, Yaʿqub 'ibn 'Ibrāhīm, *kitāb al-kharāj*, 5th edition, Cairo (1396 A.H.), p.139; al-Shāfiʿī, 'Abū ʿAbd 'Allāh Muḥammad 'Idrīs, *al-'umm*, Cairo (1381/1961), v.4, pp.174-75.

[98]See al-Shāfiʿī, op.cit., v.4, pp.179-81.

[99]See above p.23.

[100]'Ibn Butlān (d. 1052-63 A.D.) claims that 'Abū Ḥanīfah forbade marriage with the Sabians and the eating of meat slaughtered by them, while his two companions ('Abū Yūsuf and Muḥammad) allowed them. See Schacht, J. and M. Meyerhof, *The Medico-Philosophical Controversy Between 'Ibn Butlān of Baghdad and 'Ibn Ridwān of Cairo*, Cairo (1937), pp.101-2. In our opinion, it is difficult to accept this claim because 'Abū Layth al-Samarqandī (d.373/983), who lived about one century before 'Ibn Butlān, stated that 'Abū Ḥanīfah thought that the Sabians were among the People of the Book, and that therefore the meat slaughtered by them might be eaten and their women married. He also pointed out that two close companions of 'Abū Ḥanīfah, 'Abū Yūsuf and Muḥammad, disagreed with him. See 'Abū Layth al-Samarqandī, op.cit., v.I, p.19-B.

zabūr.[101] Therefore meat slaughtered by them may be eaten and their women married.[102]

b. According to the views of Mujāhid (d. 104/722), 'Abū Yūsuf (d. 182/798) and Muḥammad 'ibn Ḥasan (d. 189/804) they are not among the People of the Book because they worship the angels. Therefore their situation and that of the Magians are the same in the Islamic law, i.e. meat slaughtered by them may not be eaten and their women may not be married.[103]

The main obvious difference between the two groups is on the definition of the People of the Book or *'ahl al-kitāb*. In the opinion of Muslim scholars who accept the Sabians as one of the Peoples of the Book, the term *'ahl al-kitāb* includes every non-Muslim community which has a Holy Book which the Qur'ān mentions, like the Christians and Jews.[104] Therefore the Sabians are one of them because they too have a Holy Book, *zabūr*, which the Qur'ān mentions. Consequently there is no objection to eating their meat and to marrying their women.

But the group who compare the Sabians with the Magians define the *'ahl al-kitāb* as the non-Muslim people whose religion has a monotheistic character like that of Christians. They especially pointed out that the Sabians worshipped the angels, and presumably thought that was similar to the worshipping of fire in Magianism. Consequently, in their opinion, they are not among the People of the Book, like the Magians, and the status of their meat and women in Islamic law is the same as that of the Magians.

4. The Sabians according to later Muslim scholars after the caliph al-Ma'mūn

Although al-Mas'ūdī (d. 346/957) was the first scholar who made a systematic study on the Sabians[105] there were some scholars before him, such as 'Aḥmad 'ibn al-Ṭayyib (d. 286/899) and 'Abū Bakr 'ibn Zakariyyā al-Rāzī (d. 320/932), who were interested in the Sabians. We unfortunately do not have their books on the Sabians, such as the book of 'Aḥmad 'ibn al-Ṭayyib, *kitāb risālatih fī waṣf madhāhib al-*

[101] 'Umar 'ibn al-Khaṭṭāb (d. 22/642), the second caliph, and 'Abd 'Allāh 'ibn 'Abbās (d. 68/687) too state that they are one of the People of the Book. 'Umar 'ibn al-Khaṭṭāb also remarks that their meat may be eaten. See al-Baghawī, 'Abū Muḥammad al-Ḥusayn 'ibn Mas'ūd, *ma'ālim al-tanzīl* with *tafsīr 'ibn kathīr*, Cairo (1343 A.H.), v.I, pp.188-89.

[102] See al-Bukhārī, op.cit., v.I, p.90; al-Ṭabarī, op.cit., v.I, p.320; 'Abū Layth al-Samarqandī, op.cit., v.I, p.19-B; al-Qurṭubī, op.cit., v.I, p.434; 'Ibn Kathīr, op.cit., v.I, p.104. al-Shāfi'ī (150-204/767-819) too states that meat slaughtered by them may be eaten and their women married. See al-Shāfi'ī, op.cit., v.5, p.7.

[103] See 'Abū Layth al-Samarqandī, op.cit., v.I, p.19-B; al-Ṭabarī, op.cit., v.I, p.319; Jaṣṣāṣ, op.cit., v.2, pp.401-2.

[104] The Qur'ān clearly mentions the Christians and Jews as the People of the Book. See *Qur'ān*, 3:65-67.

[105] See below pp.31f.

ṣābi'īn, "Book of Description of the Religious Views of the Sabians",[106] but we learn what they say from other sources such as al-Mas'ūdī, al-Maqdisī (d. 342/950) and 'Ibn al-Nadīm (d. 377/987).

Chronologically the first Muslim scholar after al-Ma'mūn who comments on the Sabians is 'Aḥmad 'ibn al-Ṭayyib.[107] The quotations from him which are found in the books of al-Maqdisī and 'Ibn al-Nadīm[108] are probably based on his book *kitāb risālatih fī waṣf madhāhib al-ṣābi'īn*, but, on the other hand, the term "Sabians" never occurs in either of the quotations. 'Ibn al-Ṭayyib only uses the name "Harranians" in his statements found in the book of al-Maqdisī. al-Maqdisī himself also does not use the term Sabians, but only remarks at the beginning of the quotations: "This is about the Harranians."[109]

According to the statement which is found in 'Ibn al-Nadīm's book, 'Ibn al-Ṭayyib narrates the opinions of his master, the philosopher al-Kindī.[110]

'Ibn al-Ṭayyib gives plenty of information about the Harranians. He describes their theology, i.e. of the planetary deities, the Creator and the order of the World, their rites such as prayers, fasts and sacrifices to the planets, festival days and various regulations.[111] He also narrates that al-Kindī, his teacher, said that he had examined a book which was considered authoritative by these people, namely some treatises of Hermes about the Unity (of God) which Hermes had written for his son.[112]

We know very little about 'Ibn 'Ishūn al-Ḥarrānī al-Qāḍī who died just after 300 A.H. (912 A.D.), the second person who is interested in the Harranians. He, according to al-Mas'ūdī's statement, describes the belief system, rites, temples, idols and various rites of the Harranians in a long poem (*qaṣīdah*).[113]

Also at the beginning of the 10th century A.D., 'Abū 'Ishāq al-Farasī al-'Iṣṭakhrī (c. d. 303-307/915-919), the geographer, mentions Harran as a city of the Sabians and states that there are seventeen holy places there. Also he remarks that there is a great hill related to the prophet Abraham on which the Sabians pray.[114]

---

[106]See Rosenthal, F., *Ahmad B. aṭ-Ṭayyib as-Sarahsī*, New Haven (1943), p.40; al-Qifṭī, Jamāl al-Dīn 'Abī Ḥasan 'Alī 'ibn Yūsuf, *tārikh al-ḥukamā*, ed. J. Lippert, Leipzig (1903), p.78.

[107]'Abū al-'Abbās 'Aḥmad 'ibn Muḥammad 'ibn Marwān al-Ṭayyib al-Sarakhsī was probably born 218-22/833-37, just after al-Ma'mūn. See Rosenthal, F., op.cit., pp.16, 25.

[108]See al-Maqdisī, al-Muṭahhar 'ibn Ṭāhir, *kitāb al-bad'i wa al-tārīkh*, Paris (1899-1919), v.4, pp.22-24; 'Ibn al-Nadīm, Muḥammad 'ibn 'Ishāq, *kitāb al-fihrist*, ed. G. Flügel, Leipzig (1872), pp.318-19 [for English translation see Dodge, B., *The Fihrist of al-Nadim*, (hereafter Dodge) New York-London, (1970), v.II, pp.746-49]; Rosenthal, F., op.cit., pp.41-51.

[109]al-Maqdisī, op.cit., v.4, p.22.

[110]'Ibn al-Nadīm, op.cit., p.318. 'Abū Yūsuf Ya'qub 'ibn 'Ishāq al-Kindī, the philosopher of the Arabs, approximately lived between 185-252 A.H. (801-866 A.D.). See *EI**, v.5, pp.122ff.

[111]For the beliefs and rituals of the Harranians see Chapter VI.

[112]'Ibn al-Nadīm, op.cit., p.319.

[113]al-Mas'ūdī, 'Abū al-Ḥasan 'Ali 'ibn Ḥusayn, *murūj al-dhahab wa ma'ādin al-jawhar*, text and translation into French by C.B. de Meynard, Paris (1861-1877), v.4, p.63.

[114]al-'Iṣṭakhrī, 'Abū 'Ishāq al-Farasī, *kitāb al-'aqālīm*, ed. J.H. Moeller, Gotha (1839), p.42.

ʾAbu Jaʿfar Muḥammad ʾibn Jarīr al-Ṭabarī (224-310/838-922) who is one of the earliest sources of commentary on the Qurʾān and the history of Islam, in his commentary on the Qurʾān, examines the etymology of *ṣābiʾūn* and points out that it is the plural of *ṣābī* which means someone who takes on a new religion other than his own, like a Muslim apostate from his religion.[115] On the other hand, in his history, he derives *ṣābiʾūn* from a personal name: he claims *ṣābī* is another name of Lamech, the father of the prophet Noah, and the Sabians took their name from Lamech.[116]

al-Ṭabarī also uses the name "Sabians" for idolaters in general. He states, for instance, that Būdasab (Buddha) in his early period called the people to the religion of the Sabians[117] and that Bishtasb and his father Luhrasb, the ruler of the Persians after Kaykhusraw, embraced the religion of the Sabians until Sāmi and Zoroaster came to Bishtasb with their tenets.[118]

The famous physician and chemist ʾAbu Bakr Muḥammad ʾibn Zakariyyā al-Rāḍī (d. 311/923),[119] according to the information given by al-Masʿūdī, discusses the Sabians in his book *al-manṣūrī*.[120] He divides them into two groups: the Sabians from Harran and the *kīmāriyyūn*. In his opinion the latter is a different Sabian sect and opposed to the former.[121] al-Masʿūdī also states that al-Rāḍī said a lot about the religion of the Sabians, but he does not give any detail.

The first systematic study on the Sabians which we have belongs to ʾAbū al-Ḥasan ʿAlī ʾibn Ḥusayn al-Masʿūdī (d. 346/957). First of all he uses the term *ṣābiʾūn* for the members of the various ancient and contemporary sects scattered in a wide area from China to Egypt and from Syria to Greece. In his opinion the Shemniyyah (Tesminah, Ind. Chramana) of China, the ancient Egyptians, the Harranians and the ancient Greeks, are all Sabians.[122] Also the Copts before the Christian era and ancient Roman emperors before Constantine's conversion were of the Sabian religion.[123] Consequently, on the whole, he associates the Sabians with idol and star-worshippers. He thinks of the Sabians as pagans in general.

On the other hand his special interest is in the people of Harran, the Sabians of Harran. Because of his particular knowledge of these people he gives plenty of information about their rites, belief-system, temples, prophets and philosophy.[124] al-

---

115al-Ṭabarī, op.cit., v.I, pp.318-19.

116Idem, *tarīkh al-rusūl wa al-mulūk*, ed. M.J. de Goeje, Leiden (1964), v.I, p.178.

117Ibid, v.I, p.176.

118Ibid, v.2, p.683.

119See Kaḥḥālah, ʿUmar Riḍā, *muʿjam al-muʾallifīn tarājīm muṣannifiyyi al-kutub al-ʿarabiyyah*, Damascus (1379/1960), v.10, p.67; *GAS*, v.III, pp.274ff.

120"Liber Almansoris". See *EI*, v.3, pp.1213f; *GAS*, v.III, p.281; Chwolsohn, D., op.cit., v.II, p.643.

121al-Masʿūdī, op.cit., v.4, p.68.

122Idem, *al-tanbīh wa al-ʾishrāf*, p.161.

123Ibid, p.19.

124See idem, *murūj al-dhahab wa maʿādin al-jawhar*, v.4, pp.61-71.

Masʿūdī also states that he made a visit to Harran in 332 A.H. (c. 943 A.D.) and saw the last temple of the Harranians, named *mughallītiyā* (or *maghlītiyā*) in Bāb al-Rikʿa and some words of Plato written in Syriac on the gate of Harran, and spoke to a number of learned men of the Harranians, including Mālik ʾibn ʿUqbūn, about their religion.[125]

Moreover he relates the opinions of some persons who lived before him about the beliefs and rites of the Harranians. These are Ḥāris ʾibn Sunbāt, ʾIbn ʿIshūn al-Qāḏī and ʾAbū Bakr ʾibn Zakariyyā al-Rāḏī, the philosopher. He also checks the information given by al-Rāḏī and remarks:

> "I have spoken to Mālik ʾibn ʿUqbūn and other learned men of the Harranians about the accounts of al-Rāḏī. While they confirmed certain points, they denied others such as the account of sacrifice."[126]

About the *kīmāriyyūn* al-Masʿūdī accepts al-Rāḏī's opinion that they oppose the beliefs of the Harranians and are the other sect of the Sabians. He also points out that they live in the marshes and the places overgrown with reeds between Basra and Wasit in Iraq.[127] On the other hand he states in his other book, *al-tanbīh wa al-ʾishrāf*, that the people who live in the marshes between Basra and Wasit are *kaldāniyyūn*, "Chaldaeans", who are the remnants of the Babylonians and remarks that their direction in prayer is to the north.[128] The *kīmāriyyūn* and *kaldāniyyūn* who are mentioned by al-Masʿūdī in his two books probably refer to the same people who live in the marshes between Wasit and Basra in Iraq.

There is an obvious relationship between the *kīmāriyyūn* (or *kaldāniyyūn*) of al-Masʿūdī and the modern Mandaeans, because the characteristics of the *kīmāriyyūn* are very similar to those of the Mandaeans who have lived in the same area at least since the time of the Muslim conquest and have a different belief-system and rites from the Harranians. The Mandaeans too turn towards the north for prayer.[129]

The first Muslim scholar who brought forward a new point of view on the identification of the Harranians (known as the Sabians of Harran) is Ḥamzah al-ʾIṣfahānī (d. 350/961). In his point of view the Chaldaeans lived in the north-west. He states:

---

[125]Ibid, v.4, pp.62-64, 68.
[126]Ibid, v.4, p.68.
[127]Ibid, v.2, p.112.
[128]Idem, *al-tanbīh wa al-ʾishrāf*, p.161.
[129]See below p.226.

> "Today (10th century A.D.) their descendants live in the city of Harran and Rūḥā (modern Urfa). They gave up this name (Chaldaeans) from the time of the caliph al-Ma'mūn and adopted the name *ṣābi'ūn*."[130]

According to this statement the Harranians began to use the name Sabians after al-Ma'mūn. Before him they were known as the Chaldaeans like their ancestors who lived in the same area.

Before moving to the opinions of other scholars about the Sabians we would like to see whether there are other scholars who support Ḥamzah al-'Iṣfahānī's view that the Harranians adopted the name "Sabians" after caliph al-Ma'mūn.

'Abū ʿAbd 'Allāh Muḥammad 'ibn Mūsā al-Khawārizmī (d. 370-71/980-81)[131] who lived in the same period as Ḥamzah al-'Iṣfahānī, supports this view. He names the Harranians as *kaldāniyyūn* and states:

> "Their members live in Harran and Iraq. They adopted the name *ṣābi'ūn* at the time of the caliph al-Ma'mūn."[132]

He also remarks in connection with the real Sabians that they are a group of Christians.[133]

This view was later supported also by an account found in *al-fihrist* of 'Ibn al-Nadīm. 'Abū Yūsuf 'Absha'a (or 'Īsha'a) al-Qaṭīʿī, the narrator of this account, probably lived at the same time as al-'Iṣfahānī.[134] 'Ibn al-Nadīm quotes this account from a book of 'Abū Yūsuf 'Absha'a al-Qaṭīʿī which is about the thoughts of the Harranians. Unfortunately we do not have this book.

'Ibn al-Nadīm states:[135]

> "'Abū Yūsuf Īsha' al-Qaṭīyʿī, the Christian, said in his book on an investigation of the school of thought of the Ḥarnānīyūn,[136] who are known in our time as the Ṣābians (al-Ṣābah), that at the end of his life (days) al-Ma'mūn journeyed through the regions of Muḍar, heading towards the Byzantine country for a raid. The people met him and prayed

---

[130] Ḥamzah al-'Iṣfahānī, *tārīkh sinī mulūk al-ʿarḍ wa al-'anbiyā*, ed. Jawad al-Irani al-Tabrizi, Berlin (1340 A.H.), p.7.

[131] See al-Qifṭī, op.cit., p.286; Chwolsohn, D., op.cit., v.I, p.286.

[132] al-Khawārizmī, 'Abū ʿAbd 'Allāh Muḥammad, *mafātīḥ al-ʿulūm*, ed. Van Vloten, Leiden (1968), p.36.

[133] Ibid, p.36.

[134] 'Abū Yūsuf 'Absha'a presumably lived just before 'Ibn al-Nadīm (d. 385/995) who quotes from his book, because in his story about the Harranians he mentions Sinān 'ibn al-Thābit who died in 942 A.D. See al-Qifṭī, op.cit., pp.190f.

[135] Here we will follow B. Dodge's translation, but we will make some comments about the text in the footnotes.

[136] *ḥarnāniyyūn* is another spelling of the term *ḥarrāniyyūn*, "Harranians".

for him. Among them there was a group of the Ḥarnānīyūn, whose mode of dress was the wearing of short gowns and who had long hair with side bands (ringlets), like the long hair of Qurrah,[137] the grandfather of Sinān 'ibn Thābit. Al-Ma'mūn found fault with their dress, saying to them, 'which of the subject peoples are you?' They said: 'We are the Ḥarnāniyah.' He said: 'Are you Christians?' They replied: 'No'. Then he said: 'Are you Jews?' 'No,' they said. He inquired: 'Are you Magians?' They answered: 'No.' So he said to them, 'Have you a book or a prophet?' When they stammered in replying he said to them: 'Then you are unbelievers, the slaves of idols, Aṣḥāb al-Ra's,[138] who lived during the days of my father al-Rashīd! As far as you are concerned, it is legitimate to shed your blood, as there is no contract established for you as subjects.'

Then they said, 'we will pay the poll tax.'[139] He replied to them, 'The poll tax is accepted only from persons who are members of those non-Islamic sects which Allāh, may His name be exalted and magnified, mentioned in His book, and who have a book of their own, assuring them of good relations with the Muslims. As you do not belong to one or other of these groups, now choose one of two alternatives: Either embrace the religion of Islām, or else one of those religions which Allāh mentioned in His Book. Otherwise I will slay you to the last man. I am going to grant you a delay until I return from journey of mine. Then, unless you have entered into Islām or one of the religions among the faiths mentioned by Allāh in His Book, I will order your slaughter and the extermination of your evil doing.'

Al-Ma'mūn moved on, heading for the territory of the Byzantines. Then they changed their style of dress, cut their hair, and left off wearing short gowns. Many of them became Christians and wore girdles, while others accepted Islām, and a small number remained in their original state. Being troubled in mind, they used stratagems until one of the people of Ḥarrān who was a shaykh appealed to them, saying, 'I have found a means by which you can be delivered and saved from death.' So they brought him a large sum from their treasury, which they had maintained from the days of al-Rashīd until this time, making it ready for emergencies... Then he [the shaykh] said to them, 'When al-Ma'mūn

---

[137]Thābit 'ibn Qurrah 'ibn Marwān al-Ḥarrānī (221-88/835-900). See al-Qifṭī, op.cit., pp.115ff.

[138]*'aṣḥāb al-ra's*, "Adherents of the Head", were a group who worshipped the planetary deities. See 'Ibn Nadīm, op.cit., p.321.

[139]It is more correct to translate this sentence as "we pay the poll-tax" or "we are paying the poll-tax", because in the Arabic original the tense of this sentence is present, not future (نحن نؤدى الجزية).

> returns from his journey, say to him, 'We are Ṣābians (Ṣāb'ūn),' for this is the name of a religion which Allāh, may His name be exalted, mentioned in the Qur'ān. Profess it and you will be saved by it.'"[140]

According to this account the Harranian pagans accepted this recommendation and, consequently, from this time (833 A.D.) on they were called the Sabians of Harran. 'Abū Yūsuf 'Absha'a states that before this time there had not been a group in Harran and its vicinity called Sabians.[141]

'Abū Yūsuf 'Absha'a also states that al-Ma'mūn died on this journey, and that when the Harranians heard this news many of them who became Christians returned to their old religion; however, those who became Muslims could not recant because they feared they might be killed.[142]

Finally al-Bīrūnī who lived in the first half of the 11th century A.D. also supports this. He emphasizes the Harranians adopted this name in the Abbasid period, but does not mention the caliph al-Ma'mūn. He states:

> "This sect (al-Ḥarrāniyyūn) is much more known by the name of Ṣābians than the others (who live in Wasit and its vicinity), although they themselves did not adopt this name before 228 A.H. under Abbasid rule, solely for the purpose of being reckoned among those from whom the duties of Dhimma are accepted, and towards whom the laws of Dhimma are observed. Before that time they were called heathens, idolaters and Ḥarrānians."[143]

According to these sources the pagans of Harran adopted the name "Sabians" after al-Ma'mūn's visit to Harran in order to secure their status. Before this event they were known as "heathens", "idolaters", "Chaldaeans" or simply "Harranians". We also understand from the account of 'Abū Yūsuf 'Absha'a that al-Ma'mūn did not accept them as a non-Muslim group who could live in the Muslim country according to the law of Dhimma, because he remarked that this status was only valid for those non-Muslims who were mentioned in the Qur'ān or who had a holy book.

Western scholars divide into two groups about this account of the Harranians. Some of them, such as D. Chwolsohn and E.G. Browne, believe that it is true and deduce that the Harranians are pseudo-Sabians.[144] On the other hand, others, such as

---

140 Ibn al-Nadīm, op.cit., p.320 (Dodge, v.II, pp.751-52).
141 Ibid, p.320.
142 Ibid, pp.320-21.
143 al-Bīrūnī, op.cit., p.315.
144 See Chwolsohn, D., op.cit., v.I, pp.139ff; Browne, E.G., op.cit., v.I, pp.301f.

Lady Drower, J.B. Segal and J. Pedersen, are suspicious of this account. Lady Drower, who claims the identity of the Harranians with the Mandaeans,[145] criticizes it and the views of Chwolsohn and claims that the brilliant Harranian scholars of the medieval period, such as Thābit 'ibn Qurrah, may have been not pseudo-Sabians but genuine members of Mandaeism.[146]

Also J. Pedersen[147] and J.B. Segal criticize the account in *al-fihrist*. The latter says that we must hesitate to accept the account of 'Abū Yūsuf al-Qaṭīʿī, since he was a Christian, and there was a long history of bitter strife between the pagans of Harran and the Christians.[148]

Segal also states:

> "This story is in fact improbable. Barely twenty years earlier the Governor of Ḥarrān permitted the pagans to perform their ritual in public — to the dismay and disgust of their Christian neighbours, who alleged, somewhat uncharitably, that the Governor had been bribed."[149]

In our opinion there is nothing to oppose the account of 'Abū Yūsuf 'Abshaʿa found in *al-fihrist* and supported by some Muslim scholars, like al-Khawārizmī and Ḥamzah al-'Iṣfahānī. The problem was, in fact, about al-Ma'mūn's policy towards the subject people. As is stated in this account, the caliph al-Ma'mūn did not approve of them paying the poll-tax after he spoke to the Harranians because in his opinion the poll-tax was to be accepted only from those whom the Qur'ān mentioned or who had a sacred book. But the Harranians did not fit this condition, and al-Ma'mūn forced them to do so in order to continue as a subject people.

We see from this account that the Harranians said to al-Ma'mūn that they were subject to the poll-tax. As a matter of fact according to the earliest sources the Harranians were included among the subject people (*'ahl al-dhimma*), like the Christians of Rūḥā, their neighbours, just after ʿIyād 'ibn Ghanam conquered the city at the time of the second caliph ʿUmar 'ibn al-Khaṭṭāb,[150] which caliph al-Ma'mūn quite probably knew. On the other hand it is well known that during al-Ma'mūn's reign there was no toleration of views on various subjects which were against the opinion of the central government.[151] In that period there was presumably intolerance about the poll

---

[145]See below p126.

[146]See Drower, E.S., *The Secret Adam*, p.111.

[147]See Pedersen, J., op.cit., pp.390-91.

[148]See Segal, J.B., "The Sabian Mysteries: The Planet Cult of Ancient Harran", p.212.

[149]Idem, *Edessa and Harran*, London (1963), pp.21-22.

[150]See al-Balādhurī, 'Imām 'Abī al-Ḥasan, *futūḥ al-buldān*, Beirut (1398/1978), pp.178-79; 'Abū Yūsuf, op.cit., p.43; al-Ṭabarī, op.cit., v.2, p.197; al-Yaʿqūbī, 'Aḥmad 'ibn 'Abī Yaqub 'ibn Jaʿfar, *tarīkhu yaʿqūbī*, Beirut (1960), v.2, p.150.

[151]For al-Ma'mūn's reign see *EI**, v.VI, pp.331-39.

tax by contrast with earlier times, when there was great elasticity. al-Ma'mūn's statements about the subject people which are found in the account of 'Abū Yūsuf 'Absha'a obviously support this.

Another important point in favour of the account in *al-fihrist* is that there is no evidence that the Harranians carried the name "Sabians" before the death of al-Ma'mūn. As a matter of fact the Harranians were called "Heathens", "Idolaters", "Chaldaeans" or simply "Harranians" by their neighbours before this time.[152] Moreover, when he talks about Harran, 'Abū Yūsuf, the head-judge of the caliph Ḥārūn al-Rashīd, states that the people of this city are Nabataeans and refugees from Greece (*rūm*).[153]

The question when this people began to use *ṣābī* as an epithet attached to personal names is another important point. The first Harranian called *al-ṣābī* is Thābit 'ibn Qurrah 'ibn Marwān al-Ḥarrānī al-Ṣābī (221-88/835-900) who became a famous physician and philosopher at the time of Abbasid caliph al-Mu'tadi' Billāh. He was born a few years later than al-Ma'mūn and approximately 40 years later became a well-known person in the capital of the Caliph.[154] After him a number of persons called *al-ṣābī* who were famous in philosophy and science appeared. For example 'Ibrāhīm 'ibn Hilāl al-Ḥarrānī al-Ṣābī (320-84/932-94), Thābit 'ibn Sinān 'ibn Thābit al-Ḥarrānī al-Ṣābī (d. 365/975) and Hilāl 'ibn al-Muḥassin al-Ṣābī (d. 448/1056).[155] All of them were originally from Harran. It is clear that the Harranians began to use *ṣābī* as an epithet after al-Ma'mūn.

All of these points support the medieval sources, such as Ḥamzah al-'Iṣfahānī, al-Khawārizmī and *al-fihrist*, which indicate that the Harranians adopted the name "Sabians" after al-Ma'mūn in order to continue their status as a subject people.

Having seen that Ḥamzah al-'Iṣfahānī was probably correct when he stated that the Harranians adopted the name *ṣābi'ūn* after al-Ma'mūn,[156] we can continue examining the statements of the medieval Muslim sources about the identification and characteristics of the Sabians.

'Abū Bakr 'Aḥmad 'ibn 'Alī al-Jaṣṣāṣ (d. 370/981), another commentator on the Qur'ān, states that there are two groups of people known as Sabians in his time. He remarks:

---

[152]See al-Balādhurī, op.cit., pp.178-79; al-Bīrūnī, op.cit., p.315.

[153]Cf. 'Abū Yūsuf, op.cit., p.43. Here the term "Nabataeans" probably refers to the Syriac-speaking people. See al-Mas'ūdī, *al-tanbīh wa al-'ishrāf*, p.31. Also as an important point 'Abū Yūsuf, when he talks about the Harranians, never uses the term "Sabians".

[154]See al-Qifṭī, op.cit., pp.115-22; al-Ziriklī, Khayr al-Dīn, *al-'a'lām*, 3rd edition, Beirut (1389/1969), v.2, pp.81ff.

[155]See Yāqut al-Hamawī al-Rūmī, *mu'jam al-'udabā' (or) ṭabaqāt al-'udabā'*, 3rd edition, Cairo (1924), v.2, p.397; al-Ziriklī, op.cit., v.I, p.73; al-Qifṭī, op.cit., pp.111-15. Also see Marquet, Y., "Sabéens et iḫwān al-ṣafā'", *SI*, 24, 1966, pp.35-80; 25, 1966, pp.77-109.

[156]See above p.32f.

> "The belief of these two groups who live in al-Baṭā'iḥ around Wasit and in Harran is, in fact, the same, which is the worship of the seven planets and belief that they are deities. Therefore they are idolaters. But they [he probably means the Sabians from al-Baṭā'iḥ] could not practice this openly after the Iranians conquered Iraq, because the Iranians did not permit them... The only difference between the Sabians from Harran and the Sabians from al-Baṭā'iḥ concerns their rites."[157]

al-Jaṣṣāṣ also states that they are certainly not People of the Book (*'ahl al-kitāb*). He therefore believes that it is not permitted to them to pay the poll tax, because of the worship the stars. There are only two ways for them, he remarks: either to become Muslim or to be killed.[158]

Moreover al-Jaṣṣāṣ uses the term Sabians for pagans in general. For example he calls the ancient people of Syria and Iraq, and the Greeks before Constantine "Sabians".[159]

'Abū Layth al-Samarqandī (d. 373/983), another commentator on the Qur'ān, supports al-Ṭabarī on the etymology of the term *ṣābi'ūn*. He too derives *ṣābi'* from the Arabic verbal root *ṣaba'a-yaṣba'u* and *ṣabā-yaṣbū* and claims it means "someone who changed his religion". He also states that the Sabians are people who worship the angels.[160]

The second important reference on the Sabians after al-Mas'ūdī is Muḥammad 'ibn 'Ishāq 'ibn al-Nadīm (d. 385/995) who wrote his book in 377 A.H. (c. 987 A.D.). We have earlier seen the account of 'Abū Yūsuf 'Absha'a about the adoptation of the name Sabians by the Harranians which is quoted in 'Ibn al-Nadīm's book. Here we will examine 'Ibn al-Nadīm's own view about the Sabians.

First of all 'Ibn al-Nadīm, like al-Mas'ūdī, uses the term Sabians for the idolaters and star-worshippers in general. For example, he remarks about the baptizing sect which he calls *ṣābat al-baṭā'iḥ* that they belong to the community of the Sabians known as al-Ḥarrāniyyūn, although it is said that they are different from them, both in general and in particular beliefs.[161]

'Ibn al-Nadīm divides the Sabians into two groups:

i. He examines the Harranians under the title "The Chaldaean Harranians known as the Sabians".[162] About the theology, rites, festival days, temples, idols and prophets of the Harranians he makes some quotations from 'Aḥmad 'ibn al-Ṭayyib al-

---

[157] al-Jaṣṣāṣ, op.cit., v.2, pp.401-2.
[158] Ibid, v.2, p.402.
[159] Ibid, v.2, p.401.
[160] See 'Abū Layth al-Samarqandī, op.cit., v.I, p.19-B.
[161] See 'Ibn al-Nadīm, op.cit., p.341. Also cf. Chwolsohn, D., op.cit., v.II, pp.543-44.
[162] See 'Ibn al-Nadīm, p.318.

Sarakhsī,[163] ʾAbū Yūsuf ʾAbshaʿa al-Qaṭīʿī[164] and ʾAbū Saʿīd Wahb ʾibn ʾIbrāhīm.[165] Moreover he quotes some information from the books of the Harranians through secondary sources.[166] We will later examine all this information about the Harranians.[167]

ii. Secondly he mentions another group whom he calls *ṣābat al-baṭāʾiḥ*, "the Sabians of the Marshs". Calling them *al-mughtasilah*, "the Baptists", he says:

> "These people are very numerous in the regions of al-Baṭāʾiḥ; they are [called] the Ṣābat al-Baṭāʾiḥ. They observe ablution as a rite and wash everything which they eat. ... Until this our own day, some of them venerate the stars."[168]

Also, in another place, he points out that they live around Dastumīsān[169] and states:

> "There is still a remnant of them in those regions and watered districts, even in this our own time."[170]

Finally his theory on the origin of this baptizing sect is noteworthy. Firstly he refers to a person named as al-Ḥasīḥ (Elchasai) as the founder of the sect.[171] He states that they assert that the two eternal beings are male and female and that the herbs are from the likeness of the male, whereas the parasite plants are from the likeness of the female, the trees being veins (roots).[172] Secondly he remarks that there is a connection between al-Mughtasilah and Manichaeism. He claims Futtaq, Mani's father, was in contact with al-Mughtasilah, when his wife was pregnant with Mani. He also claims that they (al-Mughtasila) belonged to the cult which Futtaq was ordered to join. This included the requirements: "do not eat meat, do not drink wine and do not marry a human being".[173] But, in another place he emphasizes, "they agreed with the Manichaeans at the beginning, but, later, their sect became separate".[174]

---

163 See ibid, pp.318-19.
164 See ibid, pp.320-21.
165 See ibid, pp.321-25.
166 See ibid, pp.326-27.
167 See Chapter VI.
168 ʾIbn al-Nadīm, op.cit., p.340 (Dodge, v.II, p.811).
169 Dastumīsān was a place between Wasit and Baṣrah in Iraq. See Yāqūt al-Hamawī al-Rūmī, *muʿjam al-buldān*, v.2, p.574. Also Bar Konai stated that Mesene was a centre for the Mandaean community in his time. See below p.124.
170 ʾIbn al-Nadīm, op.cit., p.328 (Dodge, v.II, p.774).
171 Ibid, p.340.
172 See ibid, p.340.
173 See ibid, p.328.
174 Ibid, p.340.

It is clear that 'Ibn al-Nadīm did not know this baptizing sect well enough. But all the information which he gives on this people, who lived in the marshs between Basra and Wasit in his time (10th century A.D.), is closely connected with the Mandaeans, as many scholars have stated before.[175] The Mandaeans have lived in the same area at least since the Muslim conquest. Also their central rite is baptism and they wash everything, except salt and oil, which they prepare as a ritual meal, three times before eating, and consecrate in "the Name of Life".[176] Although the Mandaeans do not adore the heavenly bodies they believe that stars and planets contain animating principles, spirits subservient and obedient to Malka ḏ-Nhura (the King of Light), and that the lives of men are governed by their influences.[177] These characteristics of the Mandaeans are almost the same as the features of al-Mughtasilah of 'Ibn al-Nadīm.[178]

Another Muslim scholar who is interested in the Sabians is ʿAbd al-Qāhir al-Baghdādī (d. 429/1037). He divides them into two groups: the Sabians from Harran and the Sabians from Wasit (or *wāsitiyyah*).[179] He also divides the Sabians from Harran into two sections: the first group claims that the Universe is eternal,[180] while the second group denies it. The latter are divided into two as well: one is a group from Greece who claim the Maker of this Universe is "ever-living, speaking, seeing and organizing the world". The other says: "we do not say the Maker has such qualities, but we say He is far from every deficiency".[181]

As is clearly seen, the only subject of argument between the Harranians is about the qualities of the Holy Being. They have various philosophical sects which have

---

[175]See Chwolsohn, D., op.cit., v.I, pp.109ff; Drower, E.S., *The Secret Adam*, pp.ix, xiii.
[176]See *MII*, pp.100ff, 191-92.
[177]See ibid, p.xviii.
[178]J. Pedersen points out the statement in *al-fihrist* "do not eat meat, do not marry and do not drink wine" as characteristics of al-Mughtasila and remarks that all of these are opposite to what the Mandaeans believe. Hence he claims that the Mandaeans and al-Mughtasila are two separate baptizing sects. See Pedersen, J., op.cit., pp.384-85. We agree with Pedersen that the Mandaeans evidently oppose the restrictions against marriage, eating meat and drinking since marriage and procreation of children are very important for every Mandaean, and the Mandaeans eat meat and drink a specially prepared drink in their ritual ceremonies. On the other hand we disagree with him in his view that al-Mughtasila and the Mandaeans are two separate sects. We have two kinds of information about al-Mughtasila in *al-fihrist*: first, 'Ibn al-Nadīm describes the people known as *al-mughtasila* or *ṣābat al-baṭā'iḥ* who lived in his time (10th century A.D.). He gives some information about their characteristics and place where they lived. Secondly, he gives his own opinion about the origin of this sect: he mentions Elchasai as the founder of community. We see the same situation in Bar Konai's account on the Mandaeans. On the one hand Bar Konai describes the characteristics of the Mandaeans who lived in his time, but on the other hand he gives his own view about the origin and founder of Mandaeism (see below p.124). As we have already mentioned the characteristics of al-Mughtasila in *al-fihrist* completely fit to that of the Mandaeans. On the other hand we do not agree with 'Ibn al-Nadīm's view about the origin of the Mandaeans, because, as we will examine later, there are quite important differences between the two traditions. See below p.116f.
[179]See al-Baghdādī, 'Abū Manṣūr ʿAbd al-Qāhir 'ibn Ṭāhir, *al-farq bayn al-firāq*, Cairo (1328/1910), p.263.
[180]Ibid, p.348.
[181]Idem, *'uṣūl al-dīn*, Istanbul (1346/1928), pp.324-25.

different theories on this subject. We will later see a similar separation of the Harranians in al-Shahrastānī's book (12th century A.D.).[182]

ʿAbd al-Qāhir al-Baghdādī also gives plenty of information about the beliefs, rites (such as daily prayers and fasts), prophets and various rules of the Harranians. Almost all his explanations are the same as those which were given by ʾAḥmad ʾibn al-Ṭayyib and al-Masʿūdī, though he does not mention them as sources.[183]

The second group of the Sabians in ʿAbd al-Qāhir al-Baghdādī's book live in Wasit in Iraq. They, also known as *wāsitiyyah*, disagree with the Harranians on a number of subjects. For example, they eat pork and turn towards the north in their prayer. They also claim that they are followers of the religion of Shīth (Seth), Adam's son, and that his Holy Book is in their hands.[184]

All of these characteristics of *wāsitiyyah*, except the eating of pork, are similar to those of the Mandaeans.[185]

ʿAbd al-Qāhir al-Baghdādī also remarks a relationship between the Harranians and al-Bāṭiniyyah,[186] one of heretical Islamic sects. He claims that al-Bāṭiniyyah adopted some of its characteristics, like the principle of secrecy, from the Harranians. He also points out that the founder of this sect, Ḥamdān Qirmiṭ, was originally a Sabian from Harran.[187] Moreover he narrates the view of al-Yazīdiyyah,[188] another heretical sect, on the Sabians. According to this the people known as the Sabians who live in Wasit and Harran are not real Sabians. The real Sabians of the Qurʾān are the followers of an Iranian prophet whom God will send in future.[189]

Finally he narrates the various views on the situation of the Sabians in Islamic law. His own opinion is that they are one of the subject peoples.[190]

Probably the most important medieval Muslim scholar in this subject is ʾAbū al-Rayhān Muḥammad ʾibn ʾAḥmad al-Bīrūnī (362-440/972-1048) who lived almost at the same period as ʿAbd al-Qāhir al-Baghdādī. His theories on the identification and origin of the Sabians are noteworthy.

al-Bīrūnī too examines the people known as Sabians in his time under two sections:

182See below pp.45ff.

183See al-Baghdādī, *al-farq bayn al-firāq*, p.279; idem, *ʾuṣūl al-dīn*, p.325. cf. ʾIbn al-Nadīm, op.cit., pp.318f; al-Masʿūdī, *murūj al-dhahab wa maʿādin al-jawhar*, v.4, pp.61-71.

184al-Baghdādī, *ʾuṣūl al-dīn*, p.325.

185E.S. Drower states that camel, horse, pig, rabbit, hare and cat are forbidden to the Mandaeans. See *MII*, p.47. On the other hand according to the Mandaean literature, incense, dipped in pig's blood, is used as an exorcism against demons. See Drower, E.S., *The Book of the Zodiac*, (hereafter *AM*) Oriental Translation Fund, vol.36, London (1949), p.84. For the acceptance of north as direction of prayer by the Mandaeans see below p.226. Also for Seth in Mandaean tradition see below pp.223f.

186Another name of the sect of the Ismāʿīlis in medieval times. Cf. *EI**, v.I, pp.1098ff.

187al-Baghdādī, *al-farq bayn al-firāq*, p.278.

188One of the sects of the Khārijītes. See *EI*, v.2, p.960.

189See al-Baghdādī, op.cit., p.263; idem, *ʾuṣūl al-dīn*, p.325.

190Idem, *al-farq bayn al-firāq*, p.348; idem, *ʾuṣūl al-dīn*, p.324.

i. The first group are the Harranians who live in Harran. He claims that their name, *al-ḥarrāniyyah*, is derived from their place.[191] As we mentioned before, in his opinion, although the Harranians are much more known by the name of Sabians than the others, they are not real Sabians. The Harranians, he states, are called in the books "Heathens" and "Idolaters". They are, in fact, the remains of the followers of the ancient religion of the West, cut off from it since the Ionian Greeks (i.e. the ancient Greeks) adopted Christianity. al-Bīrūnī also points out that the Harranians did not adopt this name before 228 A.H. under Abbasid rule, solely for the purpose of being reckoned among those from whom the duties of Dhimma are accepted.[192]

He also examines their theology and gives some descriptions of their deities and monuments symbolizing the planetary beings. He states:

> "All, however, we know of them is that they profess monotheism and describe God as exempt from anything that is bad... The rule of the Universe they attribute to the celestial globe and its bodies, which they consider as living, speaking, hearing and seeing beings."[193]

He also points out the moon cult in Harran and the offerings to the stars, their images and temples. He says:

> "The city of Harran was attributed to the moon, it being built in the shape of the moon."[194]

Finally he mentions their rites such as daily prayer and fasting, regulations for eating and sacrifices. He also narrates the opinions of the scholars before him on the rites and beliefs of the Harranians. These are ʾIbn Sankīlā (Syncellus), ʿAbd al-Masīḥ ʾibn ʾIsḥāq al-Kindī who claims the Harranians are notorious for their sacrificing human beings, and Muḥammad ʾibn ʿAbd al-ʿAzīz al-Ḥāshimī.[195]

ii. The second group of the Sabians, he states, are those who are mostly settled at Wasit, in Sawād al-Irāq, in the district of Jaʿfar, al-Jāmida and Nahr al-Sila. They live very much scattered and nowhere in places that belong exclusively to them alone. He also points out that they differ from the Harranians, opposing their doctrines and not agreeing with them except in a few matters.[196]

---

[191] al-Bīrūnī, op.cit., p.186.
[192] See ibid, pp.188, 314-15.
[193] Ibid, p.187.
[194] Ibid, pp.187-88.
[195] See ibid, pp.186-87, 315-18.
[196] Ibid, pp.188, 314.

al-Bīrūnī states that these are real Sabians. On the origin of this group he states they are the remnant of the captive Jews in Babylonia, whom, Nebuchadnezzar had transferred from Jerusalem to that country. They found it inconvenient to return to Syria; therefore they preferred to stay in Babylonia. Their religion wanted a certain solid foundation, in consequence of which they listened to the doctrines of the Magians and inclined towards some of them. So their religion became a mixture of Magian and Jewish elements like that of the so-called Samaritans who were transferred from Babylonia to Syria.[197] He also states in connection with their beliefs and rites that they pretend to be the descendants of Anosh, the son of Seth, and in praying they turn towards the north.[198]

The second group, whom al-Bīrūnī calls the real Sabians, are closely connected with the Mandaeans, since all of their characteristics and the place where they lived fit to the Mandaeans.[199]

Finally he also uses the term Sabians for idolaters in general, like the other medieval Muslim scholars of that period. For example, he states that Budasaf (Buddha) who came forward in India after the first year of Tahmurath, introduced Persian writing and called people to the religion of the Sabians.[200]

ʾAbū Muḥammad ʾibn ʾAḥmad ʾibn Ḥazm al-Qurṭubī (384-456/ 994-1063) brought forward a new point of view on the Sabians. First of all he, like the other Muslim scholars in his time, starts from the point that the Sabians are idol and star-worshippers in general. He states:

> "The Sabians are those who believe in the seven planets and twelve zodiac signs to whom they sacrifice and make idols."[201]

In his opinion, therefore, the Indians and Harranians who worship the planets and make idols symbolizing them are among the Sabians. Again he remarks that the Christians too are among the Sabians in certain points, like the belief in the Trinity.[202]

Secondly he connects the people of the prophet Abraham to the Sabians. He states:

> "The religion of the Sabians was the oldest from the historical aspect and the most common religion until they [the members of this religion]

197Ibid, p.314.
198Ibid, p.188.
199See Drower, E.S., *The Haran Gawaita and the Baptism of Hibil-Ziwa*, Studi e Testi 176, Vatican City (1953), p.viii.
200See al-Bīrūnī, op.cit., p.186. Also see ibid, pp.188-89.
201ʾIbn Ḥazm, ʾAbū Muḥammad ʿAlī ʾibn ʾAḥmad al-ʾAndalusī, *kitāb al-faṣl fī al-milal wa al-ʾahwāʾi wa al-niḥāl*, Cairo (1317 A.H.), v.I, p.34.
202Ibid, v.I, p.35.

> fabricated some new [bad] things and therefore changed their binding law (*sharīʿah*) with these things which we mentioned [i.e. worshipping the planets, making idols etc.]. Consequently God sent the prophet Abraham with the religion of Islam and Ḥanīf, which God also revealed to the prophet Muhammad and, now, we are followers of it, in order to correct what they changed. Also God drew attention to, as the Qurʾān mentions, these things which they fabricated, like worshipping the planets and idols... They were called 'Ḥunafāʾ' at that time (of Abraham) and after him. Today [11th century A.D.] some of them live in Harran, but they are really few."[203]

ʾIbn Ḥazm obviously claims that the Sabian religion in very early times was a monotheistic religion. But its adherents later changed the features of this religion and fabricated a lot of polytheistic beliefs and rites such as worshipping the planets and making idols. Then God sent his prophet, Abraham, in order to correct this and to establish monotheism again.

This theory, in general points, is in accordance with the Qurʾān, though, of course, the Qurʾān does not mention the religion of the Sabians as a religion before Abraham. Nor does it mention that this religion had a monotheistic character in early times. The Qurʾān only mentions them among the People of the Book as we saw before.[204] But, on the other hand, according to the Qurʾān, every community from Adam to the prophet Muhammad, adhered to the true religion, i.e. Islam, before the people changed the religion with polytheism. Consequently God sent to them the prophets with the true religion, Islam, in order to establish monotheism again.[205]

ʾIbn Ḥazm probably supposed some of the Sabians at the time of Abraham accepted his teaching and therefore became Ḥanīfs. According to his statement there were still some people in Harran who claimed that they were the adherents of the religion of the prophet Abraham.

Finally he gives some information about the rites such as daily prayer and fasting, prophets and various rules of the Harranians.[206]

ʾAbū al-Qāsim Saʿīd ʾibn Saʿīd al-ʾAndalusī (d. 463/1070) too accepts the Sabians are idolaters and pagans in general. He states:

> "These seven groups of people, i.e. the Chaldaeans, the Greeks, the Persians, the Egyptians, the Turks, the Indians and the Chinese, all of

---

[203]Ibid, v.I, p.35; v.4, p.7. For Ḥanīf see above pp.20-22.
[204]See above p.17.
[205]See *Qurʾān*, 7: 59-93; 21: 51-93.
[206]ʾIbn Ḥazm, op.cit., v.I, pp.34-35, 98.

them, are Sabians. They worship idols which are the representatives of the Holy Beings and seven planets."[207]

In another place he also remarks that there was a group of the Sabians at the time of the Abbasid dynasty.[208]

He divides the Chaldaeans into the groups: "Suryanians" and "Babylonians". He also subdivides them as *al-'āthūriyyūn*, *al-kūthā'iyyūn* and *al-'ārāmiyyūn*.[209] In this division "al-Kūthā'iyyūn", the people of Kūtha, a city in Iraq, are presumably the Sabians mentioned in 'Abū Zanād's account, because he (d. 130/747) states that the Sabians live in Kūtha in Iraq.[210]

Another important source on the Sabians among the medieval Muslim scholars is 'Abū al-Fatḥ Muḥammad 'ibn ʿAbd al-Karīm al-Shahrastānī (479-548/1086-1153). Firstly he examines in his famous book on comparative religions and Islamic sects the etymology of the term *ṣābi'ūn*. He too accepts the opinions of earlier commentators, like al-Ṭabarī and 'Abū Layth al-Samarqandī, on this subject, saying:

"In the literary language *ṣaba'a* means 'left the true way of the prophets'. They who left the true way are named *ṣābi'ah*."[211]

Then he, like the other medieval Muslim scholars in this period, remarks that the Sabians are the pagans and idolaters. The ancient Egyptians, Greeks and Indians were Sabians.[212] He also distinguishes the Sabians into two groups from the historical point of view: the ancient or the first Sabians and the Harranians.[213]

In the early chapters of his book, al-Shahrastānī mentions the ancient Sabians among those who have laws and binding judgements (*sharīʿah*) without a revealed book and those who deny the prophecies.[214] Although there is no certain statement he generally uses the name "the first Sabians" for the Sabians at the time of Abraham. In relation to them, he states that at the time of Abraham there were two different religious groups: the Sabians and Ḥunafā. The Sabians were those who said that they needed some mediators in order to understand God and his orders, judgements and way.[215]

207'Ibn Saʿīd al-'Andalusī, 'Abū al-Qāsim Saʿīd 'ibn 'Aḥmad, *kitāb al-taʿrīf bi ṭabaqāt al-'umam*, Cairo (n.d.), pp.5, 12.

208Ibid, p.39.

209Ibid, p.4.

210See above p.25.

211al-Shahrastānī, 'Abū al-Fatḥ Muḥammad 'ibn ʿAbd al-Karīm, *kitāb al-milal wa al-niḥāl*, ed. W. Cureton, London (1842), p.203.

212Ibid, pp.180, 230, 444.

213Ibid, pp.24, 202, 248.

214Ibid, pp.24-25. But in later chapter he states that the ancient Sabians accept only Hermes and Adīmūn who are the prophets 'Idrīs and Shīth (Seth), but do not accept the others. See ibid, p.202.

215Ibid, pp.180-81.

He also subdivides these ancient Sabians into two sects: *ʾaṣḥāb al-hayākil* and *ʾaṣḥāb al-ʾashkhāṣ*. The former are the star-worshippers and the latter are the idol-worshippers, who called the idols deities corresponding to the Heavenly Beings.[216] al-Shahrastānī tells how the worship of idols developed in the Sabian community:

> "According to Sabian belief these mediators of God must be spiritual beings, not physical, like us... Then they began to worship at the temples which were built for these spiritual beings, i.e. the seven planets, because they did not find a way to reach the spiritual beings directly... After that they directed (their worship) to physical things (idols) which neither could see, nor hear, nor be useful to human beings."[217]

Hereafter he mentions the prophet Abraham and his relation with the Sabians. He states:

> "The prophet Abraham grew up among two sects of the Sabians. First he was with *ʾaṣḥāb al-ʾashkhāṣ* (the idol-worshippers)... Secondly he inclined to *ʾaṣḥāb al-hayākil* (the star-worshippers)... But finally he chose the religion of Ḥunafā and announced that the religion of the Sabians was untrue and the religion of Ḥunafā was true."[218]

As has been seen, his statements about the life of the prophet Abraham are based on the Qurʾān.[219]

al-Shahrastānī also states that Hanifianism (Ḥunafā) is the contrary of the Sabian religion.[220] The section depicting the dispute between Sabians and Ḥunafā illustrates not only the differences between the two groups but also their common orientation to inspiration and revelation outside the realm of reason.[221]

al-Shahrastānī describes the philosophic doctrine of the Sabians, which he sets forth partly in the form of an imaginary debate between Sabians and adherents of Abraham (i.e. of the true religion). The philosophic system which he ascribes to the Sabians (i.e. to pagans in general) is, in the main, a Greek system based on Plato and

---

[216]Ibid, pp.244, 246.
[217]Ibid, pp.180-81.
[218]Ibid, pp.246-48.
[219]Cf. *Qurʾān* 6: 74-80.
[220]al-Shahrastānī, op.cit., p.203.
[221]See ibid, pp.203ff. Also see Lawrence, B.B., *Shahrastani on the Indian Religions*, Paris (1976), p.68.

Aristotle, i.e. a form of Neoplatonism which the Arabic philosophers had learned from the Greeks.[222]

Finally al-Shahrastānī remarks that the Harranians whom he calls *ḥarbāniyyah* are the adherents of the Sabian religion.[223] He gives plenty of information on their theology, prophets, rites and traditions.[224]

Maḥmūd ʾibn ʿUmar al-Zamakhsharī (d. 538/1143), in his commentary on the Qurʾān and the other books, derives the term *ṣābiʾūn* from *ṣabaʾa-yaṣbaʾu* in Arabic. He therefore states that it means "those who changed religion".[225] In his opinion the Sabians who worship the angels are an offshoot from Christianity. They were called Sabians because of being separated.[226]

Jamāl al-Dīn ʾAbū al-Faraj ʾibn al-Jawzī (d. 597/ c.1200) accepts the usual etymology of the term. He too derives it from *ṣabaʾa* in Arabic and summarizes the statements of the Muslim scholars before him on the identity of the Sabians.[227]

Muḥammad ʾibn ʿUmar al-Khattāb Fakhruddīn al-Rāḍī (544-606/1149-1209), another commentator on the Qurʾān, mostly repeats the opinion of ʾIbn Ḥazm and al-Shahrastānī, though he does not mention them explicitly. He states that the term *ṣābiʾūn* was derived from the Arabic verbal root *ṣabā-yaṣbū* and it is possible to pronounce it as *ṣābūn* or *ṣābiyūn*.[228] In his opinion the Sabians worship the stars and planets which they claim are the creator and organizer of the Universe.[229]

In connection with the development of the worship of idols in the Sabian community he claims that they used to worship the stars, when they appeared in the night. Then they made idols symbolizing the stars in order to pray to them at all times, and began to worship them. As a result idol-worshipping became common everywhere.[230] Moreover he states that the people were the adherents of the Sabian religion when Abraham was sent as a prophet. He adds that Abraham struggled against them, as the Qurʾān mentions.[231]

ʾAbū al-Saʿādāt al-Mubārak ʾibn Muḥammad ʾibn ʾAthīr (d. 606/1209) too derives the term *ṣābiʾūn* from *ṣabā-yaṣbū* in Arabic.[232]

---

222 See Chwolsohn, D., op.cit., v.I, pp.167, 684; Scott, W. and A.S. Ferguson, *Hermetica*, Oxford (1936), v.IV, p.258.
223 al-Shahrastānī, op.cit., p.248.
224 See ibid, pp.204, 224, 240-41, 248-51.
225 See al-Zamakhsharī, *al-kashshāf ʿan ḥaqāʾiq al-tanzīl wa ʿuyūn al-ʾaqāwīl fī wujūh al-taʾwīl*, Cairo (1966-1968), v.I, p.285; idem, *ʾaṣāṣ al-balāghah*, p.345.
226 Idem, *al-kashshāf ʿan ḥaqāʾiq al-tanzīl wa ʿuyūn al-ʾaqāwīl fī wujūh al-taʾwīl*, v.I, pp.285, 631-32.
227 ʾIbn al-Jawzī, Jamāl al-Dīn ʾAbī al-Faraj ʿAbd al-Raḥmān, *talbīs ʾiblīs*, Beirut (1368 A.H.), p.74.
228 Fakhruddīn al-Rāḍī, op.cit., v.I, p.548.
229 See ibid, v.I, p.549; idem, *ʾiʿtiqād firaq al-muslimīn wa al-mushrikīn*, Cairo (1978), p.143.
230 Ibid, p.143.
231 Ibid, p.143.
232 ʾIbn ʾAthīr, op.cit., v.3, pp.3, 11.

'Ibn 'Athīr (d. 631/1233), historian and the writer of *al-kamil wa al-tarīkh*, points out that the Sabians are idolaters. He claims that the ancient Greeks were Sabians.[233]

The famous jurist Muwaffaq al-Dīn 'Abū Muḥammad ʿAbd 'Allāh 'ibn Qudāmah (541-620/1146-1223) states that the Sabians are idol and star-worshippers in general. In his opinion they especially pray to the seven planets.[234]

'Abū ʿAbd 'Allāh Muḥammad 'ibn 'Aḥmad al-Qurṭubī (d. 681/1282) remarks that *ṣābi'ūn* means "those who inclined to another (religion) rather than their own". He also states that the Sabians are the people who were the adherents of the religions with a revealed book, but they left their religion and began to believe in the power of the stars.[235]

'Ismāʿīl 'ibn ʿAlī 'Abū al-Fidā (d. 710/1310), the historian, uses the term Sabians for pagans in general. For instance he claims the ancient Egyptians and the Greeks before Christianity were Sabians.[236]

On the other hand he uses the term Sabians in a particular sense for the people of Harran. In his opinion they took their religion from 'Idrīs (Hermes) and Shīth ('Adīmūn), and they have a holy book named "The Pages of Shīth" (*ṣuḥufu shīth*). He also states that they are respectful to the pyramids in Egypt.[237] Moreover he gives some information about their rites and festival days.[238] Finally he points out the Sabians' claim that they are descendants of Ṣābī, son of Shīth.[239]

Shams al-Dīn Muḥammad al-Dimashqī (654-727/1256-1326), the geographer, like the other Muslim scholars in this period, uses the term Sabians for idolaters in general and claims that the ancient people of Iraq (Chaldaeans), Greeks, Indians, Persians, Copts before Christianity and Arabs before Islam were Sabians.[240]

On the other hand al-Dimashqī uses the term in a particular sense for the people of Harran. He describes the temples of the Harranians[241] and gives plenty of information about their theology and monuments. His statements are almost the same as 'Aḥmad 'ibn al-Ṭayyib's and al-Masʿūdī's.[242] On the theology of the Harranians he states that they believe in a holy Creator whom nobody can understand. Therefore

233See 'Abū al-Fidā 'Ismāʿīl 'ibn ʿAlī, *al-mukhtaṣar fī 'akhbār al-bashar*, ed. H. Fleischer, Vogel (1831), p.106.
234'Ibn Qudāmah, op.cit., v.10, pp.568-69.
235al-Qurṭubī, op.cit., v.I, p.435.
236'Abū al-Fidā, op.cit., pp.98, 110.
237Ibid, p.148.
238Ibid, p.148.
239Ibid, p.14.
240al-Dimashqī, Shams al-Dīn 'Abī ʿAbd 'Allāh Muḥammad, *nukhbat al-dahr fī ajā'ib al-barr wa al-bahr*, ed. M.A.F. Mehren, St. Petersbourg (1866), pp.45-46.
241See below pp.147ff.
242al-Dimashqī, op.cit., pp.39-43.

mediators who are the saints and angels are necessary to reach the creator. These saints govern the stars and each of them has an idol.[243]

In his opinion the term *ṣābiʾūn* comes from Ṣāb, the name of the son of Hermes. He remarks that the Sabians claim that one of the pyramids is the tomb of Ṣāb; therefore they make pilgrimage and sacrifice there every year.[244]

Finally he, like al-Shahrastānī, divides the Sabians into two sects: the star-worshippers and the idol-worshippers,[245] but in fact there is no difference between them except some philosophical tenets on the character of the spiritual beings.

Taqiaddīn ʾAḥmad ʾibn ʿAlī al-Maqrīzī (d. 845/1441) too claims that the Sabians are star-worshippers. They worship the idols which they made to represent the stars.[246] al-Maqrīzī too divides the Sabians into two sects: the Sabians from Babylon (*bābiliyyūn*) and the Sabians from Harran (*ḥarrāniyyūn*).[247] On the other hand he is particularly interested in the Harranians. Therefore he gives some information about their monuments, holy days etc.[248]

Nizāmuddīn Ḥasan ʾibn Muḥammad al-Naysābūrī (d. 728/1327) derives the term *ṣābiʾūn* from *ṣabaʾa-yaṣbaʾu* in Arabic and states that the Sabians are those who are seperated from all religions.[249] In his opinion the Chaldaeans (*kaldāniyyūn*) at the time of Abraham, whose most characteristic feature was planet-worship, were Sabians.[250]

ʾAbū al-Fidā ʾIsmaʿīl ʾibn Kathīr (d. 774/1372), famous historian and commentator on the Qurʾān, states that the Sabians are those who left their religion.[251] He also remarks that at the time of the prophet Abraham star-worshipping was very common in Harran and Damascus and there were many idols symbolizing the planets.[252]

ʾIbn Khaldūn (d. 808/1405) too states that the Sabians are the people who worship the stars and the monuments symbolizing them.[253]

Finally Muḥammad ʾibn Muḥammad al-ʾAʿmādī ʾAbū al-Suʿūd (d. 951/1544) derives the term *ṣābiʾūn* from the Arabic *ṣabaʾa-yaṣbaʾu*[254] and states that the

---

243 Ibid, p.47.
244 Ibid, p.34.
245 Ibid, p.44.
246 al-Maqrīzī, Taqiaddīn ʾAḥmad ʾibn ʿAlī ʿAbd al-Qādir ʾibn Muḥammad, *al-mawāʿiz wa al-ʾiʿtibār fī dhikr al-khiṭāt wa al-ʾāthār*, ed. M.G. Wiet, Cairo (1911-1924), v.3, p.258.
247 Ibid, v.3, p.100.
248 Ibid, v.3, pp.28, 100-101.
249 al-Naysābūrī, op.cit., v.I, p.233; v.6, p.132.
250 Ibid, v.I, p.333.
251 ʾIbn Kathīr, op.cit., v.I, p.104.
252 See idem, *al-bidāyah wa al-nihāyah*, Cairo (1932), v.I, pp.150-51.
253 See ʾIbn Khaldūn, *The Muqaddimah: An Introduction to History*, tr. F. Rosenthal, New York (1958), v.2, pp.258, 264.
254 ʾAbū al-Suʿūd, Muḥammad ʾibn Muḥammad al-ʾAʿmādī, *ʾirshād ʿaql al-salīm ʾilā mahāyā al-qurʾān al-karīm*, Cairo (n.d.), v.I, p.108.

Sabians have no special religion. He says: "Some time ago, they were the adherents of certain religions, but they left them and, therefore, were called the Sabians".[255]

It is difficult to classify these later Muslim scholars in clear categories, because their statements contain a lot of speculations. But we can, briefly, summarize their opinions in these points:

a. Almost all of them derive the term *ṣābiʾūn* either from *ṣabaʾa* (imperf. *yaṣbaʾu*) which means "changed his religion" or from *ṣabā* (imperf. *yaṣbū*) which means "inclined" in Arabic. Hence they state that *ṣābiʾūn* means "those who changed their religion" or "who left their religion and inclined to another". Generally the commentators on the Qurʾān and the historians hold this opinion.

b. In connection with the identification of the Sabians almost all of these scholars use the term Sabian for pagans who worship the planets and idols which are the representatives of them.

i) Some of them use it for all star- and idol-worshippers scattered in a wide area from China to Greece and from the central Asia to Egypt.

ii) Some, like ʾAbū al-Suʿūd, use the term for the people who are separate from all known religions. In other words they have no clear religion.

iii) Some scholars related this term especially to the community of Abraham. Abraham tried to correct these people, whose most important characteristic was the worship of the stars and their idols.

c. All of these scholars are particularly interested in the Harranians and they use the term Sabian in a particular sense for the pagans of Harran. They extensively describe their theology, rites, monuments, festivals, customs and various rules. According to their statements, the most important characteristic features of the Harranians are belief in the seven planets as creator and governors of the Universe and the worship of the idols symbolizing them.[256]

d. On the other hand some of these scholars mention another particular group of people under the name Sabians. They give them different names, but their descriptions are similar to each other and quite probably refer to the same community. The names given are *al-mughtasilah*, *kīmāriyyūn* (or *kanyāriyyūn*), *al-wāsitiyyah*, *ṣābat al-baṭāʾiḥ*, *bābiliyyūn* and *al-kūthāʾiyyūn*. These people opposed the beliefs and rites of the Harranians. Important features are that they wash everything they eat as a ritual meal, baptize themselves, turn to the north in prayer and show great respect for Anosh and Seth (Shīth).

e. Finally some of these later Muslim scholars, such as Ḥamzah al-ʾIṣfahānī, al-Khawārizmī and al-Bīrūnī, state that the Harranians are not the real Sabians, but are

---

[255]Ibid, v.I, p.109.
[256]For the striking characteristics of the Harranians see below pp.192ff.

Chaldaeans, adherents of ancient paganism. In their opinion they adopted the name Sabians as a trick under the Abbasid dynasty, specifically at the time of the caliph al-Ma'mūn, in order to continue their status as a subject people.

5. Conclusion

The Sabians whom the Qur'ān mentions as People of the Book, i.e. with the Jews and Christians, were described in a way appropriate to the statements of the Qur'ān by early Muslim scholars before 832-33 A.D., the date of death of the Abbasid caliph al-Ma'mūn. These early scholars stated that the Sabians had a monotheistic belief-system which carried a lot of features of Judaism, Christianity and, also, Magianism, and they located them in the region of Iraq, especially around Mosul and Kūtha.[257]

From the last quarter of the 9th century the people of Harran appeared under the name of Sabians of Harran, though, in the earlier sources, they were called only Harranians or Nabataeans (non-Arab Syriac-speaking people of North Arabia). For example, 'Abū Yūsuf (d.182/798), the head-judge of the Abbasid caliph al-Rashīd, al-Ma'mūn's father, states that the people of Harran are Nabataeans and refugees from Greece.[258] Most of the medieval Muslim scholars after al-Ma'mūn described the people of Harran who worshipped the seven planets and the idols representing the stars as Sabians. At the same time they also mentioned another Sabian sect known under various names such as al-Mughtasilah, al-Wāsitiyyah, Kīmāriyyūn and al-Kūthā'iyyūn, whose location was Iraq, particularly Wasit, Basra and al-Baṭā'iḥ, the marshy regions of southern Babylonia.[259]

Apart from these particular senses of the word, the term Sabians acquired a new sense in the usage of the later Muslim scholars in that they used the term in general for all idol and star-worshippers, ancient or not, from China to Greece and from central Asia to Arabia and Egypt.

Concerning the Harranians, the account of events between caliph al-Ma'mūn and the people of Harran in approximately 832 A.D., mentioned by 'Abū Yūsuf 'Absha'a, Ḥamzah al-'Iṣfahānī and al-Khawārizmī, explains their connection with the name *ṣābi'ūn*. According to this account they adopted this name after that date, as a way of getting the toleration of al-Ma'mūn and his successors. Before this date they were known only as Chaldaeans or simply Harranians. All the evidence which we have discussed supports this view. The pagans of Harran, whose most characteristic features

---

[257]See Map I (below p.53).
[258]See Chapter II n.153.
[259]See Map II (below p.54).

were belief in the planets as the creators and governors of the Universe and the worship of them and their idols, cannot be the Sabians of the Qur'ān, whom the Qur'ān definitely mentions among the People of the Book, i.e. with the Christians and Jews.

Obviously the most important reason why later Muslim scholars were particularly interested in the Harranian Sabians and put the Sabians of southern Iraq into the background was the glorious success of the Harranian scholars in Baghdad, the capital of the Muslim Empire, in science and philosophy. As a matter of fact, from the last quarter of the 9th century, many Harranian pagan scholars, like Thābit 'ibn Qurrah (d. 288/900) and 'Ibrāhīm 'ibn Hilāl (d. 384/994), were accepted into the palace of the caliphs and some of them, for instance Thābit 'ibn Qurrah, refused to become Muslim and strongly defended paganism.

On the other hand there are two main reasons why the term acquired a new sense as "pagans and idolaters" in general in the statements of later Muslim scholars.

i. In connection with the etymology of the term they derived it from the Arabic verbal roots *ṣaba'a* (imperf. *yaṣba'u*) which meant "changed, turned over" and *ṣabā* (imperf. *yaṣbū*) which meant "inclined". Therefore, since they took *ṣābi'ūn* to mean "those who changed their religion for another or turned from the religion of the prophets to false religion", they called all non-Muslims except Jews and Christians Sabians.

ii. The other reason for the usage of the term for pagans in general is the Harranians. The later Muslim scholars called all idol and star-worshippers Sabians, comparing them to the Harranians who worshipped the planets and idols, because the Harranians particularly became famous under this name.

On the other hand the statements of early Muslim scholars and later Muslim scholars on the Sabians who live in Iraq quite probably refer to the Sabians of the Qur'ān. There is a notable similarity between the characteristics of these people stated by early and later Muslim scholars, and those of the Mandaeans of today whom their neighbours still call *ṣubbā* or *ṣābi'ūn*. The Mandaeans have lived in the same area since at least the Muslim conquest. Consequently the Sabians of the medieval Muslim scholars whom they also called by various other names, like al-Mughtasilah and al-Wāsitiyyah, were presumably the progenitors of the Mandaeans.

Map 1
The Location of the Sabians According to Early Muslim Scholars

Map 2
The Location of the Sabians According to Later Muslim Scholars

CHAPTER III

THE MANDAEAN SOURCES

1. Date of the Mandaean writings

The Mandaean literature consists of many parts which belong to different historical periods. Even in one manuscript we can see the sections which reflect different periods. Consequently the Mandaean writings sometimes contain contradictory elements. Some parts of this literature can be clearly dated, from the colophons and historical events recorded in the manuscripts. Much of it can be dated less clearly and with some difficulty.

For dating the Mandaean writings, we will examine in this section (i) the colophons and the historical events and persons which appear in the manuscripts, and (ii) some external evidences which reflect the possible date of some parts of this literature.

The extant Mandaic manuscripts are generally dated quite late, mostly from the 18th or 19th century A.D. However, it seems that many of the texts were originally collected just after the Muslim invasion into the area where the Mandaeans lived. Some statements in the literary texts support this. For example, concerning the Muslim conquest we read in *Haran Gawaita*:

> "...and then the Son of Slaughter, the Arab, set up as king, went forth and took a people to himself and performed circumcision. ... And Anuš (-ʿUthra?) instructed the Son-of-Slaughter, as he had instructed Anuš-son-of Danqa, about this Book (compiled) by his fathers, upon which all kings of the Naṣoraeans stood firm... in order that they (the Moslems) should not harm the Naṣoraeans who lived in the era of his government."[1]

---

[1] *Haran Gawaita* (hereafter *HG*), in *The Haran Gawaita and the Baptism of Hibil-Ziwa*, tr. E.S. Drower, Studi e Testi 176, Vatican City (1953), pp.15-16.

Here the Book on which Anuš instructed the Muslims probably refers to the literary texts, such as the *Ginza* and *Qolasta*.[2]

Among the main Mandaean writings the *Ginza* was, as the leading Mandaean scholars suggested,[3] presumably collected in the second half of the seventh century A.D., although its liturgical fragments are amongst the oldest texts of the Mandaean literature. In the eighteenth book of the *Ginza Right* there is a list of Parthian and Sassanian kings which ends with "Kasrau son of Hurmiz" and this prophecy:

> "after the Persian kings there will be Arabian kings. They will reign seventy-one years."[4]

Mesopotamia was conquered by the Muslims in 639 A.D.[5] Consequently this fragment of the *Ginza* must have been written during the first Islamic century. In addition the *Ginza* gives references to Muhammad and to the Islamic period.[6]

Also *The Book of John* (*Drašia d̠-Iahia*) was probably redacted after the Muslim conquest, probably in the eighth century A.D.[7] It mentions Muhammad[8] and gives the name of John the Baptist as *iahia iuhana*.[9] A number of scholars agree that the form of the name *iahia* (Ar. يحيى, *yaḥyā*) is an Arabic influence in Mandaean literature,[10] which also shows that the collection was made during the Islamic period.

In contrast to the *Ginza* and *The Book of John*, *Qolasta* was presumably edited in pre-Islamic times, although according to its colophons the present manuscript was re-copied by Rabbi Adam Yuhana son of Sam son of Bihram son of Sa'dan who lived in the first half of the thirteenth century A.H. (in the 19th century).[11] Also in the colophons of *Qolasta*, which give long lists of the copyists, three important early copyists appear: Ramuia son of ʿQaimat, Ašganda son of Yasmin and Zazai d̠-Gawazta

stacy

[2]Ibid, p.16 n.2. Also see ibid, p.15 n.10.

[3]See *MII*, p.20; *HCMM*, pp.lxvi-lxvii; Rudolph, K., "Der Mandäismus in der neueren Gnosisforschung", p.272; idem, *Gnosis*, p.346.

[4]*GR*, p.414 (English translation from *MII*, p.20).

[5]See al-Balādhurī, op.cit., p.179.

[6]"Then comes Ahmaṭ, son of the demon Bizbaṭ, and makes a cry, which is no (true) cry, brings about widespread wickedness in the world, and leads the family (*kanna*) of souls astray into error": *GR*, p.30 (English translation from Rudolph, K., "Mandean Sources" (hereafter Rudolph, "Man.Sour."), in *Gnosis. A Selection of Gnostic Texts*, ed. W. Foerster, English translation edited by R.McL. Wilson (trs. R.McL. Wilson, P.W. Coxon and K.H. Kuhn), v.II, Part 2, Oxford (1974), p.300). Also see *GR*, pp.54, 300.

[7]See Rudolph, K., "Der Mandäismus in der neueren Gnosisforschung", p.272.

[8]"Muhammad the Arab", Lidzbarski, M., *Das Johannesbuch der Mandäer*, (hereafter *Jb*) Giessen (1915), p.88.

[9]See ibid, pp.70ff. The same name also appears in the *Ginza* as "*iahia* son of *zakaria*". See *MD*, p.185.

[10]See Drower, E.S., *The Secret Adam*, p.101; Mead, G.R.S., *The Gnostic John the Baptizer. Selections from the Mandaean John-Book*, London (1924), p.31; Yamauchi, E.M., *Gnostic Ethics and Mandaean Origins*, p.5. Also cf. *Jb*, pp.73ff; Pallis, S.A., *Mandaean Studies*, p.117.

[11]See *CP*, pp.69, 148, 169; *Alma Rišaia Rba* (hereafter *ARR*), in *A Pair of Naṣoraean Commentaries (Two Priestly Documents). The Great 'First World' and the Lesser 'First World'*, ed. and tr. E.S. Drower, Leiden (1963), p.51.

son of Hawa.[12] The first copyist, *ramuia br ʿqaimat*, who is also the editor of *The Thousand and Twelve Questions*, lived in Ṭib in the early Islamic period.[13] We read in one of the colophons of *Qolasta*:

> "And Ramuai son of ʿQaimat said 'I wrote this Diwan in the town of Ṭib in the years when Anuš son of Danqa departed with the heads of people (ethnarchs), in the years when the Arabs advanced'."[14]

Consequently Ramuai copied this book in about 639 A.D. According to another statement which occurs in *Qolasta*, Ramuai collected the Mandaean writings, including *Qolasta*, in the scroll named "the Great Wellspring". From this scroll the Mandaean priests later copied the texts, and distributed them among the people.[15]

The second copyist, *ašganda br iasmin*, presumably lived in Ṭib in the sixth century A.D., just before the beginning of the Islamic period.[16] A passage in *Haran Gawaita* refers to Ašganda and states:

> "About eighty-six years before the Son-of-Slaughter, the Arab, Adonai sent Šurbiš-Ruha who is his spouse, to the city of Ṭib, called locally the City of Ašganda because of all that was done (*during*) his rule in Baghdad. (For) Ašganda (*dwelt?*) in Ṭib; it was his native place; and it was called 'the city of Šganda' (*also*) because in it there were Naṣoraeans and *rišamia* (ethnarchs)."[17]

The third copyist, *zazai d̲-gauazta br haua*, who, according to the colophons, is the earliest liturgist, lived in the second half of the third century. In one of the colophons of *Qolasta* Ramuai, who wrote about 639 A.D., says:

> "From the day on which it fell from (*was written by*) Zazai-d̲-Gawazta son of Hawa till now, the years in which I wrote it, is (*a space of*) 368 years in the ages."[18]

---

[12] See *CP*, pp.32, 71, 150, 171. Also see Macuch, R., "Anfänge der Mandäer", pp.158ff; Rudolph, K., "Quellenprobleme zum ursprung und alter der Mandäer", pp.125f.

[13] See *ATŠ*, p.289. According to Yāqut al-Rūmī, who wrote about 626 A.H., Ṭīb, a small town between Wasit and Khuzistan, was in his time inhabited by the Nabataeans who spoke Nabataean, and claimed to be descendants of Seth, son of Adam, and were the Sabians. See Yāqut al-Hamawī al-Rūmī, *muʿjam al-buldān*, v.6, p.76. Lady Drower remarks that this information fits very neatly the Mandaeans who are today called *ṣubbā*. See *CP*, p.32, n.2; *ATŠ*, p.4.

[14] *CP*, p.71.

[15] See ibid, p.12.

[16] See Rudolph, K., "Quellenprobleme zum ursprung und alter der Mandäer", p.125; idem, "Der Mandäismus in der neueren Gnosisforschung", p.271; Macuch, R., "Anfänge der Mandäer", pp.163ff.

[17] *HG*, p.12.

[18] *CP*, p.71.

According to this statement Zazai d-Gawazta wrote his copy c. 272 A.D. This date cannot be accepted as an exact date of composition of *Qolasta*, but it is certain that the texts traced back to Zazai must have been redacted before the Islamic times, because, apart from this statement, they do not contain anything about the Islamic period.[19]

Zazai d-Gawazta is also mentioned as the earliest copyist in the priestly documents, *The Thousand and Twelve Questions*, *Alma Rišaia Zuṭa*, and *Diwan Maṣbuta d-Hibil-Ziwa*.[20] The manuscript of *The Thousand and Twelve Questions* is dated 1088 A.H. (c.1684 A.D.).[21] The latest copyist, mentioned in the colophons, is Zakia-Zihrun son of Rabbi Ram son of Rabbi Yahia-Yuhana.[22] The colophon at the end of "Book I, Part I" mentions Zazai d-Gawazta as the earliest copyist of this text.[23] Since this priestly document contains polemical references to the Magians and Christians, but is silent about the Muslims, it might have been redacted before the Islamic period.[24]

The date of the manuscript of *Alma Rišaia Zuṭa*, of which the earliest copyist, according to its colophon, is again Zazai d-Gawazta, is 972 A.H. (1564 A.D.).[25] Adam-Zihrun son of Rabbi Bihram-Šitlan appears as the latest copyist.[26]

Zazai also appears as the earliest copyist of another literary text, *Diwan Maṣbuta d-Hibil Ziwa*. The manuscript, of which the latest copyist is Yahia-Bihram son of Adam-Yuhana, is dated from 1247 A.H. (1831 A.D.).[27]

Moreover Zazai, with the other two important copyists we have mentioned, is mentioned in the famous prayer "Abahatan Qadmaiia".[28]

---

[19]This conclusion is shared with Macuch. See Macuch, R., "The Origins of the Mandaeans and Their Script", *JSS*, 16, 1971, p.185.

[20]Cf. *ATŠ*, p.159; *Alma Rišaia Zuṭa* (hereafter *ARZ*), in *A Pair of Naṣoraean Commentaries (Two Priestly Documents). The Great 'First World' and the Lesser 'First World'*, ed. and tr. E.S. Drower, Leiden (1963), p.90; *Diwan Maṣbuta ḏ-Hibil Ziwa* (hereafter *DMHZ*), in *The Haran Gawaita and the Baptism of Hibil-Ziwa*, ed. and tr. E.S. Drower, Studi e Testi 176, Vatican City (1953), p.84. Another priestly commentary, *Alma Rišaia Rba*, of which the latest copyist is Rabbi Adam-Yuhana son of Sam son of Bihram who wrote in 1224 A.H., and who is also the latest copyist of the manuscript of *Qolasta*, mentions Anuš son of Naṭar as the earliest copyist of this commentary: "And Ramuai copied it from Ašganda son of Yasmin and Ašganda copied it from the Diwan of Anuš son of Naṭar. And Anuš-Uthra copied it from the Diwan of Hibil-Ziwa": *ARR*, p.52.

Here Anuš son of Naṭar is possibly identical with Zazai d-Gawazta son of Hawa because (i) Naṭar is the father of Zazai (his mother is Hawa) (see *CP*, p.150), (ii) Ašganda generally copies from Zazai, and (iii) in the liturgical texts, copied from Zazai, no person (copiest) is mentioned before Zazai, but a heavenly being like the First Life or Manda ḏ-Hiia (see *CP*, pp.71, 150, 171; *DMHZ*, p.84). In this text it is also mentioned that Anuš son of Naṭar copied it from a heavenly being, Hibil-Ziwa.

[21]*ATŠ*, pp.160, 230, 261.

[22]Ibid, pp.158, 194, 230, 261.

[23]Ibid, p.159.

[24]See ibid, p.162.

[25]*ARZ*, pp.89-90.

[26]Ibid, pp.89-90.

[27]*DMHZ*, pp.84ff.

[28]See *CP*, p.154.

In these writings, traced back to Zazai, Zazai is mentioned as the copyist who copied from a heavenly being, sometimes from the First Life, and sometimes from Manda d̲-Hiia. In other words no copyist is mentioned before him except the heavenly beings. A most important characteristic of the texts traced back to Zazai is that no sign of Islamic times is seen.[29]

Other Mandaean writings are quite late in date. The manuscript of *Haran Gawaita*, which gives a number of references to the Islamic period, is dated from 1088 A.H. (1677 A.D.). The copyist of this manuscript is Zakia-Zihrun son of Rabbi Ram son of Rabbi Yahia-Yuhana, who mentions only one copyist before him and remarks: "And he had no copy but this".[30]

There are three manuscripts of *Sfar* (or *Asfar*) *Malwašia*, another Mandaean book, dated from 1212, 1247 and 1350 A.H.[31] The lists of the names of the copyists differ in the three manuscripts, but they coincide in the very earliest copyists.[32] The earliest copyists are Adam Bulfaraj, Ram Baktiar and Anuš Muailia son of Anuš Bihdad̲.[33] *Sfar Malwašia* too gives some references to the Islamic period. For example, there is a charm concerned with the Qur'ān and the sura *yāsīn* (sura 36).[34]

Another Mandaean book is *Diwan Abatur*, which was first brought to the West by a Carmelite father in the 17th century.[35] *Diwan Abatur* too gives some references to the Islamic times. For example it refers to the persecution of the Mandaean community from time to time during that period.[36]

The Coronation of the Great Šišlam was copied by Zihrun son of Yahia-Yuhana in 1289 A.H. (1872 A.D.), who mentions only one copyist before him without giving his name, and states: "He had no copies."[37]

The Phylacteries, translated and published by Lady Drower, are dated from 1249 and 1273 A.H.[38]

As we have seen, the earliest manuscript is dated from the late 16th century A.D. The others are generally from the 18th or 19th centuries A.D. On the other hand some priestly liturgical texts, like *Qolasta*, are said to be edited first by Zazai d̲-Gawazta

---

[29]Also see *HCMM*, pp.lxvi-lxvii.
[30]*HG*, p.22. Also see Rudolph, K., "Problems of a History of the Development of the Mandaean Religion", p.223.
[31]See *AM*, p.1.
[32]Ibid, p.157.
[33]Ibid, p.156.
[34]See ibid, p.83.
[35]See *Diwan Abatur or Progress Through the Purgatories* (hereafter *DA*), ed. and tr. E.S. Drower, Studi e Testi 151, Vatican City (1950), p.v.
[36]"Some of them enforce circumcision upon them; and some of them set up mosques and crosses, doing that to the souls of the Naṣoraeans which sullies their garments..": ibid, p.17.
[37]Drower, E.S., *The Coronation of the Great Šišlam. Being a Description of the Rite of the Coronation of a Mandaean Priest According to the Ancient Canon*, Leiden (1962), p.36.
[38]See Drower, E.S., "A Phylactery for Rue. An Invocation of the Personified Herb", *Or*, 15, 1946, p.324; idem, "A Mandaean Phylactery", *Iraq*, 5, 1938, p.45.

in the second half of the third century A.D. Although we cannot accept this date as the exact date of the editing of this literature it is certain that these liturgical texts which, by contrast with the others, do not bear any Islamic elements, were redacted at least a few centuries before the Islamic period. The external evidences, too, as we will see, support this conclusion.

Besides the literary texts we have a number of Mandaic magical bowl texts and lead amulets which were published by scholars such as H. Pognon, M. Lidzbarski, J.A. Montgomery, W.S. McCullough, C.H. Gordon and R. Macuch.[39] As far as we know more than 50 bowl texts and 8 lead rolls have been published.

The magical bowl texts were generally dated by scholars to the pre-Islamic period, about 600 A.D., because of their similarities with other Aramaic bowls from this date.[40] These texts, except the one which was published by E.M. Yamauchi, which was dated to the 7th century A.D. by Yamauchi because of the occurrence of the Arabic word *ʿiz*, "powerful", in the text,[41] do not bear any Islamic influence, but, on the other hand, Semitic, ancient Mesopotamian and Iranian influences (names and ideas) can be seen.

The first Mandaic lead amulet, published by Lidzbarski in 1909,[42] was dated by him to 400 A.D. because of orthographic considerations.[43] This date was generally accepted by scholars as the earliest date of the Mandaean writings,[44] but Lidzbarski in his last article, written, according to Macuch, on his death-bed and published only after his death, stated that the year 400 was too late rather than too early a dating, and, as Macuch points out, he was prepared to change his assessment of the chronology of the amulet.[45]

---

[39]The information about Mandaic magical bowl texts and lead amulets, published until 1967, is found in E.M. Yamauchi's *Mandaic Incantation Texts* (hereafter *MIT*), American Oriental Series, vol. 49, New Haven 1967. Also see Sokoloff, M., "Notes on Some Mandaic Magical Texts", *Or*, 40, 1971, pp.448-58. See, for later publications, McCullough, W.S., *Jewish and Mandaean Incantation Bowls in the Royal Ontario Museum*, (Near and Middle East Series 5) Toronto (1967); Yamauchi, E.M., "A Mandaic Magic Bowl from the Yale Babylonian Collection", *Berytus*, 17, 1967-68, pp.49-63; Macuch, R., "Altmandäische Bleirollen", in *Die Araber in der Alten Welt*, eds. F. Altheim and R. Stiehl, Berlin, v.IV (1967), pp.91-203, 626-31; v.V/1 (1968), pp.34-72, 454-69; Caquot, A., "Un phylactère Mandéen en plomb", *Semitica*, 22, 1972, pp.67-87; Naveh, J., "Another Mandaic Lead roll", *Israel Oriental Studies*, 5, 1975, pp.47-53; Greenfield, J.C. and J. Naveh, "A Mandaic Lead Amulet with Four Incantations", *Eretz-Israel*, 18, 1985, pp.97-107.

Three more Mandaic incantation bowls from Nippur were recently unearthed during an excavation at Nippur under the directorship of McGuire Gibson in January-March 1989. See Hunter, E.C.D., "Incantation bowls from the 18th Nippur season", Paper read at the 4th Annual Conference of the British Association of Near Eastern Archaeology 9-11th November, 1990, Birmingham University.

[40]See Montgomery, J.A., op.cit., p.38; McCullough, W.S., op.cit., pp.xi-xii; Yamauchi, E.M., *Gnostic Ethics and Mandaean Origins*, p.6; *MIT*, p.2.

[41]See Yamauchi, E.M., "A Mandaic Magic Bowl from the Yale Babylonian Collection", p.51.

[42]Lidzbarski, M., "Ein mandäische Amulett", in *Florilegium dédié à M. Vogué*, Paris (1909), pp.349-73. Also see *MIT*, No. 22.

[43]See Yamauchi, E.M., "The Present Status of Mandaean Studies", p.94.

[44]On the other hand W.F. Albright, who suggested that Mandaeism arose in southern Iraq in the 5th century A.D., criticized Lidzbarki's dating, and claimed that a date a century or more later was probable. See Albright, W.F., *From the Stone Age to Christianity*, p.338 n.38.

[45]See Lidzbarski, M., "Alter und Heimat in den mandäischen Religion", p.325; Macuch, R., "Anfänge der Mandäer", p.139.

Macuch dated one of the Mandaic lead amulets, published by himself, to the first half of the third century A.D. because of palaeographical considerations. Another basis of his dating is the occurrence of an angel named Estaqlos both in the section of *The Canonical Prayerbook* assigned to this early date and in this lead amulet.[46] Later he stated that this scroll, as well as the amulet published previously by Lidzbarski, belonged to the third or fourth centuries at the latest.[47] Macuch's dating was criticized by J. Naveh and K. Rudolph. The former suggested that such an early date could not be based on paleographical evidence,[48] while Rudolph pointed out that this dating was not yet provable.[49] Macuch also dated the second and third rolls to the end of the pre-Islamic period, and the fourth roll to the Islamic period.[50]

The language of the pre-Islamic magical texts is, as Pognon and Montgomery stated,[51] identical with that of the liturgical texts of *Qolasta* and the *Ginza*. Mandaean scholars are in agreement that the oldest texts of the Mandaean literature are to be found in the liturgical documents, like *Qolasta* and the *Ginza Left*.[52] As we will later see, T. Säve-Söderbergh, in his comparative study of the Coptic Manichaean *Psalms of Thomas*, showed that the *Psalms of Thomas* were adaptations of early Mandaic hymns in the *Ginza Left*.[53] Manichaeism was established in the first half of the third century A.D., and Thomas was one of Mani's first disciples.[54] Therefore these Mandaean liturgical texts must have been redacted before the third century A.D.[55] If, consequently, we consider Lidzbarski and Macuch's dating of the lead amulets to the third or fourth centuries A.D. in the light of this Manichaean evidence, it is obvious that this dating for these magical texts is quite reasonable. We must also bear in mind the statement of the colophon in *Qolasta* that some parts of the Mandaean literature were redacted in the third century A.D.

As we have seen the earliest Mandaean texts, the lead amulets, come from the third or fourth centuries A.D. On the other hand the Mandaean manuscripts are quite late in date, the earliest dated to the 16th century A.D., but it is certain from the internal and external evidence, such as the colophons of the manuscripts and the Manichaean

---

46 See Macuch, R., "Altmandäische Bleirollen", *Die Araber in der Alten Welt*, v.IV, pp.96-97, 189.

47 Idem, "The Origins of the Mandaeans and Their Script", p.185. G. Widengren too remarks that the Mandaean invocatory texts are attributable on palaeographical grounds to 400 A.D. See Widengren, G., *Mani and Manichaeism*, p.16.

48 Naveh, J., "The Origin of the Mandaic Script", *BASOR*, 198, 1970, p.33. For Macuch's answer to this, see Macuch, R., "The Origins of the Mandaeans and Their Script", pp.177ff.

49 Rudolph, K., "Problems of a History of the Development of the Mandaean Religion", p.225.

50 See Macuch, R., "Altmandäische Bleirollen", in *Die Araber in der Alten Welt*, v.IV, pp.93ff.

51 See Montgomery, J.A., op.cit., p.39.

52 See *HCMM*, p.lxv; Rudolph, K., *Gnosis*, p.346.

53 See below pp.122-23.

54 See Säve-Söderbergh, T., op.cit., pp.155-56.

55 See below p.123.

Psalms of Thomas, that some liturgical hymns and prayers had already been edited in the third century A.D.

2. The origin and history of the Mandaeans according to their own tradition

The most important written tradition of the Mandaean version of their origin and history is found in *Haran Gawaita*. Some references to their history are also found in other Mandaean texts such as the *Ginza*, *The Book of John* and *The Canonical Prayerbook*. Besides these written sources we have the oral traditions of the Mandaeans about their origin and history, which are mainly collected by Lady Drower at the end of her study, *The Mandaeans of Iraq and Iran*.[56]

We will use the written and oral traditions together in order to construct a history of the Mandaeans according to their own version.

The *Haran Gawaita* version of their history is very confused, legendary and contradictory.[57] There is a break at the beginning of the manuscript. After a prologue by the copyist the text begins:

> "...and Haran Gawaita receiveth him and that city in which there were Naṣoraeans, because there was no road for the Jewish rulers. Over them was King Ardban. And sixty thousand Naṣoraeans abandoned the Sign of the Seven and entered the Median hills, a place where we were free from domination by all other races. And they built cult-huts (*bimandaia*) and abode in the Call of the Life and in the strength of the high King of Light until they came to their end."[58]

From where did sixty thousand Naṣoraeans migrate, and when did it happen? To answer these questions we have to follow their tradition about their history from the beginning.

---

[56]See *MII*, pp.251-399.

[57]Macuch attributes at the most 5 per cent historical value to *Haran Gawaita*. See Macuch, R., "Anfänge der Mandäer", p.117. Despite this he uses this source very widely in his theory about the early history of the Mandaeans. See idem, "Alter and Heimat des Mandäismus nach neuerschlossenen Quellen", pp.401ff; idem, "Anfänge der Mandäer", pp.110ff. Also Lady Drower, K. Rudolph and E.M. Yamauchi used the information of this book to reconstruct the migration (or exodus) of the Mandaeans from west to east, though the last two scholars criticized Macuch because he based far-reaching results upon this text. See Drower, E.S., *The Secret Adam*, pp.xiii-xiv; *MII*, pp.5f.; Rudolph, K., "Quellenprobleme zum ursprung und alter der Mandäer", pp.119ff.; idem, "Der Mandäismus in der neueren Gnosisforschung", pp.269f.; idem, "Problems of a History of the Development of the Mandaean Religion", pp.221, 223; Yamauchi, E.M., *Gnostic Ethics and Mandaean Origins*, pp.68ff.

[58]*HG*, p.3.

The Mandaeans believe that their religion was established by the World of Light at the time of Adam and Eve. They consequently understand their religion as a kind of proto-religion. They believe that the body of the first man Adam (*adam pagra*) was created by the demiurge Ptahil and his companions, 7 planets and 12 zodiac signs, but the soul of Adam (*adam kasia* or *adakas*) was provided by Manda ḏ-Hiia, one of the important Light spirits.[59] According to their belief Adam was baptised, taught and given hymns and ritual books by the powers of Light.[60] They believe that from that time their religion spread out into the world.

According to the Mandaeans there have been three catastrophes of mankind from the time of Adam until now. At the end of each, mankind was destroyed with the exception of one couple.[61]

The Mandaeans believe that Shem (*šum*), the son of Noah from his true wife, and his wife Anhar are their progenitors after the third catastrophe. On the other hand the progenitors of other people are, in their belief, Ham, Yam and Japhet, who are the children of Noah from Ruha.[62]

---

[59]See *GR*, pp.107ff.

[60]"We will give Adam a wife
and make a companion (*ṣautā*) for him.
A companion (*ṣautā*) will we make for him,
and we will make his family numerous.
Hymns and ritual books will we recite,
and the Life shall erect the building": *GR*, p.115 (Rudolph, "Man.Sour.", p.194).
"When I (Manda dHaiyê) installed Adam
I appointed three uthras over him.
I set myself at the head
of the uthras whom I set over Adam and Eve.
I stood before them and taught them
wonderful hymns (*drašê*).
I instructed them in the ritual books (*sidrê*)
so that they might perform the masiqtas (after the manner) of the uthras.
I taught them prayers
so that they might be confirmed through the prayers of the Life": *GR*, p.119 (Rudolph, "Man.Sour.", p.197). Also see *CP*, pp.29f.

[61]"Then the world is carried off by sword and by pestilence, and it is appointed for souls that at that departure they depart from the body, and the souls rise up without sin or guilt to the light. Then Ram, the man, and Rud, the woman, remain behind. ... From Adam, the man, to Ram and Rud there are thirty generations, and they all ascend in *one* ascent (or: by *one* masiqta) to the light... Then the world is carried off by flames of fire and Šurbai, the man, and Šarhabêl, the woman, remain behind... Then the world is made (anew) and (once more) expanded. From Ram and Rud to Šurbai and Šarhabêl there are twenty-five generations. Then after Šurbai and Šarhabêl the world is carried off by the flood, and Noah of the ark and Šem, Noah's son, (*Šum bar Nu*) remained behind. ... From the generation of Šurbai and Šarhabêl to the generation of Noah there are fifteen generations. From Noah, the man, the world will (again) expand": *GR*, pp.27-28 (Rudolph, "Man.Sour.", pp.297-98). Also see *GR*, pp.408ff.

For the oral tradition of the Mandaeans about these catastrophes see *MII*, pp.258ff. The Mandaeans believe that at the end of the world there will be another destruction of mankind by air or wind. See *GR*, p.28; *MII*, p.93.

[62]"Ruha came forth and saw Noh and assumed the appearance of his wife. She greeted him saying 'I am Anhuraita, your wife!' and he took her and she became pregnant and brought forth three sons, Ham, Yam, and Yafet. These were the fathers of the human race, Ham becoming father of the blacks, the *ʿabīd* or slaves; Yam of the white nations, Abraham and Jews; and Yafet of the gypsies (*Kauliyah*). But Sam and his wife Anhar are the progenitors of the Mandai": *MII*, p.261.

The Mandaeans believe that after the flood, according to one legend 6,000 years later,[63] Ruha and her seven sons, the seven planets, built Jerusalem where they gave power to the Jews and Moses, the prophet of Ruha.[64]

Oral Mandaean tradition makes a connection between the ancient Egyptians and their early history. According to this tradition the ancient Egyptians were co-religionists of the Mandaeans.[65] According to Mandaean legends Moses, who was against Mandaeism,[66] quarrelled with the Mandaeans in Egypt. Then Ardban Malka of the Mandaeans had a vision and commanded the people to be taken out of Egypt. The story follows:

> "He [Ardban] rose and took the Mandai and they went out of Egypt and came to the sea which became shut off, leaving a road with mountains of sea on either side. Thus they went from Egypt. But Firukh Melka, brother of Ardwan Melka, remained in Egypt and fought with the Jews there and was surrounded and discomfited by them and fled. Seeing the road through the sea still remaining, he went with his people upon it, but when they were in the midst of the sea, the mountains of water closed upon them and they were all drowned."[67]

Here we have a Mandaean version of the Exodus story of the Bible. The modern Mandaeans prepare a ritual meal every year in memory of their ancestors who perished in the sea.[68]

Then, the story continues, King Ardban and sixty thousand Mandaeans travel until they reach the *ṭura ḏ-madai*, the Median hills. They settled down there. Moses, when he reached the Median hills, could not go further and turned back to Jerusalem.[69]

Here we reach the beginning of the *Haran Gawaita* story, which mentions sixty thousand Naṣoraeans who abandoned the Sign of the Seven and entered the Median hills, under King Ardban.[70] It also mentions *haran gauaita*, "inner Haran", and calls it:

---

[63]See ibid, p.261.
[64]See *GR*, pp.340-41; *MII*, p.261.
"They built Jerusalem,
in which the Jews came into being (or: were).
.....
They conjured them with exorcisms,
and handed over Jerusalem to the Jews": *GR*, p.341 (Rudolph, "Man.Sour.", p.304).
[65]See *MII*, p.10.
[66]Also see below p.89.
[67]*MII*, p.261.
[68]*MII*, p.10. Lady Drower remarks that this story must come through some Israelitish source. See ibid.
[69]Ibid, p.261.
[70]*HG*, p.3.

"...that city in which there were Naṣoraeans, because there was no road for the Jewish rulers. Over them was King Ardban."[71]

Scholars have often discussed the problem of identification of the terms *haran gauaita* and *ardban*, the King. First of all the text itself identifies Haran Gawaita with the Median mountains:

"Anuš-ʿUthra went to the 'Ṭura ḏ-Madai' (Median mountains), called *Haran Gawaita.*"[72]

Also in the *Ginza* there is a reference to "cedars from Haran",[73] which Lidzbarski identified with the Amanos mountains.[74] Moreover Jabal Haran, "Haran mountain", is mentioned in one of the legends of the modern Mandaeans, collected by Lady Drower, but this time it is spelled as Harrān because the narrator tells the story in Arabic.[75]

Lady Drower first inclined to identify Haran Gawaita with the Ḥaurān, one of the important terms in Mandaean literature which occurs both in the earliest magical texts and in the literary texts.[76] Later she favored identification with Harran in northwestern Mesopotamia. She also suggested that there is a connection between the Mandaeans and the Sabians of Harran, the Harranians.[77] R. Macuch accepted the identification with Harran and cited the Sabians of Harran from the Islamic period, without identifying the Mandaeans with the latter.[78] E.M. Yamauchi, too, accepts the identification with the city of Harran.[79] On the other hand K. Rudolph remarks that Haran Gawaita was in Iranian territory between Harran and Nisibis or Media.[80] Finally J.B. Segal, who does not accept the migration of the Mandaeans from west to east at all, criticizes the other scholars, particularly Yamauchi, who suggested that the Mandaeans first migrated to Harran. Segal states:

---

[71]Ibid, p.3.
[72]Ibid, p.10.
[73]*GR*, p.409.
[74]See ibid, p.409 n.2.
[75]See *MII*, p.258; *HG*, p.vii.
[76]Lady Drower says: "Is this the city Ḥarran or the Ḥaurān? Probably the latter": *HG*, p.3 n.2. For Haurān see *GR*, p.302; *GL*, p.593; *Jb*, p.232. Also see below pp.112-13.
[77]See Drower, E.S., *The Secret Adam*, pp.xiii-xiv, 111ff. For the discussion of the relationship between the Mandaeans and the Harranians see Chapter VII.
[78]See Macuch, R., "Anfänge der Mandäer", pp.113ff.
[79]See Yamauchi, E.M., *Gnostic Ethics and Mandaean Origins*, pp.69 n.340, 87.
[80]Rudolph, K., "Mandean Sources", p.140.

> "It is highly improbable... that a sect devoted to baptism in running water could have been so imprudent as to make even a short sojourn at Harran; that place is notoriously ill-supplied with water."[81]

In fact, it is really difficult to accept the identification of Haran Gawaita with the city of Harran. In addition to Segal's point, the text itself, as we have already mentioned, identifies it with the Median mountains where, the text states, there was no road for the Jewish rulers. By contrast the city of Harran is not a mountainous place, though there are a few small hills around the area. The identification with Harran, therefore, contradicts the text. It must therefore be a mountainous area in Media, presumably in northern Mesopotamia.[82]

Another problem is the identification of King Ardban. The name King Ardban is once mentioned in the *Ginza* where it refers to Artabanus V.[83] There were five Parthian kings named Artabanus: Artabanus I (c.211-191 B.C.), Artabanus II (c.128-123 B.C.), Artabanus III (c.12-38 A.D.), Artabanus IV (c.80-81 A.D.), and Artabanus V (c.213-224 A.D.).[84] R. Macuch and Lady Drower favor identifying King Ardban in *Haran Gawaita* with Artabanus III.[85] Macuch noted that this had been anticipated by N.C. Debevoise in 1938, when he wrote: "Perhaps it was Artabanus III who brought the Mandaeans to the country of the Two Rivers".[86] Macuch also gives other reasons for this identification. He remarks that the exodus of the Mandaeans was before the destruction of Jerusalem which happened in 70 A.D. Moreover he points to the account of Pliny that an Arabian people called *Mardani* (other variations are *Mandani* and *Vandani*), whom Macuch associates with the Mandaeans, migrated into the Parthian kingdom under Artabanus III.[87] On the other hand K. Rudolph, who remarks that Macuch's identification is not impossible, suggests that Artabanus V is intended.[88] Finally E. Bammel states that the exodus of the Mandaeans took place during the short reign of Artabanus IV, and King Ardban in the text consequently refers to him.[89]

As far as *Haran Gawaita* is concerned we face legendary and confused stories about the history of the Mandaeans, as we have earlier remarked. Like the term *haran*

---

[81] Segal, J.B., Review of E.M. Yamauchi: *Gnostic Ethics and Mandaean Origins*, p.135.
[82] Also see below p.124.
[83] See *GR*, p.411; *MD*, p.36.
[84] See Macuch, R., "Anfänge der Mandäer", p.121.
[85] See Macuch, R., op.cit., pp.121ff; Drower, E.S., *The Secret Adam*, p.xi.
[86] See Macuch, R., "Alter und Heimat des Mandäismus nach neuerschlossenen Quellen", p.406. Cf. Debevoise, N.C., *A Political History of Parthia*, Chicago (1938), p.157.
[87] See Macuch, R., "Anfänge der Mandäer", pp.127-33; *HCMM*, p.lxvii.
[88] See Rudolph, K., "Der Mandäismus in der neueren Gnosisforschung", p.269; idem, "Quellenprobleme zum ursprung und alter der Mandäer", pp.120f. On the other hand Rudolph once remarked that the identification of this Ardban (Artabanus) was difficult, and stated the migration of the Mandaean community into Iranian territory took place during the later Parthian period, the first or second century A.D. See Rudolph, K., "Mandean Sources", p.140.
[89] See Bammel, E., "Zur Frühgeschichte der Mandäer", *Or*, 32, 1963, p.225 n.2.

gauaita which, as we have discussed, presumably refers to the Median mountains, the name King Ardban became legendary. What we understand from the Mandaean sources, both *Haran Gawaita* and the other written and oral sources, is that when they were persecuted by the ruling Jews, the Mandaeans migrated towards the Median mountains under the protection of the Parthian rulers. As we will later see, Mandaean tradition speaks of the Parthians in a quite positive way because under Parthian rule they were living in freedom, so that, according to *Haran Gawaita*, they built 400 cult-huts in Babylonia.[90] The Mandaeans consequently hold the Parthians in great respect. The name Artabanus of a number of Parthian kings was very well-known. Therefore it is possible that the Mandaean writers did not mean any particular Parthian king known as Artabanus, but the Parthian rulers in general. In other words King Ardban in the Mandaean tradition may refer to the Parthian dynasty in general.

On the other hand if we are obliged to identify King Ardban of the Mandaean tradition with one of the kings of the Parthians of that name we prefer to identify him with Artabanus III for a number of reasons. First of all, as we will later see,[91] there are a number of evidences such as the adaptation of some Mandaean texts by the Manichaean writers in the third century A.D. and the *Kartīr* inscription from the third century A.D. that the Mandaeans were already in Mesopotamia during the second and third centuries A.D. This probably rules out Artabanus V. Also, according to the Mandaean sources, the exodus of the Mandaeans took place before the destruction of Jerusalem, hence before 70 A.D. Therefore King Ardban cannot be identified with Artabanus IV or Artabanus V, since they were later than 70 A.D. On the other hand Artabanus I and Artabanus II were quite early. King Ardban, mentioned in the Mandaean tradition, must consequently be Artabanus III (c.12-38 A.D.).

As we have seen, the Mandaeans produced a new story from the Exodus and Red Sea crossing stories of the Bible. Here we must point out that according to oral Mandaean tradition the exodus of their ancestors under the leadership of King Ardban took place before Yahya Yuhana (John the Baptist).[92] Also in *Haran Gawaita* the story of King Ardban is mentioned before the story of Yahya.

In *Haran Gawaita*, after the statements concerning King Ardban and sixty thousand Naṣoraeans, a story of Christ and the Christians is found. Mary is mentioned as "a daughter of Moses", and Christ (*mšiha*) is called "the prophet (*nbiha*) of the Jews".[93]

---

[90]See *HG*, p.10.
[91]See below pp.120ff.
[92]See *MII*, pp.261ff.
[93]See *HG*, p.3; *GR*, p.28.
"And he took to himself a people and was called by the name of the False Messiah. ... And he and his brother dwell on Mount Sinai, and he joineth all races to him, and perverteth and joineth to himself a people, and they are called Christians": *HG*. p.4. Also see *GR*, pp.50ff.

According to Mandaean tradition John the Baptist (*iahia*) too was born at that time (as in Christian tradition). His father Zakharia (*zakria*) and mother Elizabeth (*ʿnišbai*) were very old when his mother became pregnant with him.[94] They believe that the seed of John was sown in the womb of his mother when she drank water.[95]

John is called "the prophet of Kušṭa, the apostle... who dwelt at the city of Jerusalem".[96] After the birth John is taken by the powers of Light to Parwan, the mythological white mountains. He is fed miraculously, and taught by Anuš Uthra until his 22nd year.[97] *Haran Gawaita* also points out a possible Mandaean community in the Median mountains at that time, who are far from the powers of Ruha:

> "...all belonged to her and to her seven sons except (*those from*?) the Median hills."[98]

Then John returns to Jerusalem and begins his teaching. He continues until his 42nd year. Also Jesus comes to John and is baptized by him. After being baptized he becomes wise through John's wisdom, but then he proceeds to pervert the word of John and changes the baptism of Jordan.[99]

According to *Haran Gawaita* sixty years after John, Ruha and her powers, the Jews, became arrogant, and a persecution of the Naṣoraeans (Mandaeans) took place in Jerusalem. Many of them were killed by the Jews.[100] Also the *Ginza* tells of the persecution of a community of the Mandaeans, more precisely of 365 disciples, in Jerusalem by the Jews.

> "From Yaqif and Bni-Amin
> 365 disciples (*tarmidê*) went forth.
> 365 disciples went forth
> in the city of Jerusalem.
> The Jews flew into a rage
> and murdered my disciples, who pronounced the name of the Life."[101]

---

[94]See *GR*, p.51; *Jb*, pp.75ff; *MII*, p.262.

[95]"They have taken the child out of the basin of Jordan and laid him in the womb of Enišbai": *Jb*, p.82 (Translation from G.R.S. Mead, op.cit., p.40).
"And in the great Jordan a pure seed was formed... and came and was sown in the womb of ʿNišbai, so that from it a child might come into being, a prophet of the great Father of Glory, praised be His name! in order to destroy the building of Ruha and Adonai": *HG*, p.5. Also see *MII*, p.262.

[96]*HG*, p.5.

[97]See ibid, pp.6-7.

[98]Ibid, p.7. Another possibility is that those who were in the Median mountains might be the Parthians, since the Mandaean writers held the Parthians, who protected the Mandaeans and allowed them to settle in Parthia, in great respect.

[99]See *GR*, p.51. Also *The Book of John* gives a long dialogue between John and Jesus. See *Jb*, pp.103ff.

[100]See *HG*, p.8.

[101]*GR*, p.341 (Rudolph, "Man.Sour.", p.305).

According to *Haran Gawaita* after the persecution of the Mandaeans Ruha scatters the Jews. Then comes another version of the story of the Red Sea crossing:

> "Then Ruha scattered the Jews... who is called 'of the House of the Seven', and then Adonai sent a staff... And he spoke over it and struck Suf-Zaba and the waters that abide in Suf-Zaba were divided like the two mountains of a gorge and there was a road. And Ruha brought these (*Jews?*) over Suf-Zaba. And she built for them, and pressed out for them clay brick that is sacred, and constructed a building and they set up for it column after column of falsehood, and raised up each (*fallen?*) column..."[102]

We have seen that oral and written Mandaean sources speak of the persecution of their ancestors in Jerusalem. We have also remarked that there is an oral Mandaean tradition that their ancestors were persecuted by the Jews in Egypt. In our opinion both persecution stories refer to the same event, the persecution of the Mandaeans in Jerusalem, because there are a number of parallels, such as that Moses is the head of the powers of Ruha in both stories. We have mentioned that the Mandaeans produced a new story from the Exodus and Red Sea crossing stories of the Bible. It is obvious that the Mandaeans knew the story of struggle between the Jews and Egyptians. Because of their hatred against the official Jews the Mandaeans made a connection between their ancestors and the ancient Egyptians who were also against the Jews and Moses. They thus produced another version of the story of the persecution and exodus of their ancestors.

According to the Mandaean tradition, after the persecution of the Mandaeans, Hibil Ziwa comes and destroys Jerusalem and the Jews.[103] According to *Haran Gawaita* Hibil Ziwa then goes to Baghdad, kills all the priests of the Jews, and takes the government from them, which they have had for 800 years.[104]

102*HG*, p.8.

103"I destroyed the city of Jerusalem,
in which the blood of my disciples was poured out.
I slew the Jews,
who had persecuted the Family of Life": *GR*, p.343 (Rudolph, "Man.Sour.", pp.306-7). Also see ibid, pp.341-42.

HG says: "...and Hibil-Ziwa came and burnt and destroyed Jerusalem and made it like heaps of ruins": *HG*, p.9. Lady Drower notes that the destruction referred to here must be that by Titus (70 A.D.). She also states that it is unlikely to be Hadrian's massacre and conquest of the Jews in 135 A.D. after Bar-Kokhba's rebellion. See *HG*, p.9 n.3.

104"And he went to Baghdad and killed (*there*) all the *cohens* and took away government from them and pounded (*to*) dust every city in which there were Jews. Moreover for the eight hundred years that their government was in Baghdad...": *HG*, p.9.

After this event, according to *Haran Gawaita*, the Mandaeans migrated from the Median mountains, known as *haran gauaita*, into Babylonia. A Mandaean community was set up there under the rule of Bhire son of Šitil, a descendant of king Artabanus.[105]

According to the Mandaean sources their ancestors lived in Babylonia in peace and freedom for 280 years. After this period a confusion ensued amongst them so that there was a great disagreement in the community which presumably divided into two sections.[106] Another schism amongst the Mandaeans about 86 years before Islam is also mentioned in *Haran Gawaita*.[107] They state that because of this schism and confusion amongst the Mandaeans non-Mandaean beliefs became many, and sovereignty and freedom were taken from the Mandaeans.

According to *Haran Gawaita*, during the Sassanian dynasty the religious freedom of the Mandaeans was limited, so that more than half of their cult-huts were destroyed.[108] This is supported by the *Karfīr* inscription.[109]

Although we cannot find polemics against the Muslims as much as against Jews and Christians in Mandaean literature, the Mandaeans do not talk about the Muslims and the Islamic period positively. In their literature the prophet Muhammad is identified with the demon Bizbaṭ and usually called "the Son of Slaughter, the Arab".[110] They state, however, that when the Muslims invaded the area where they lived they were treated as *ʾahl al-kitāb*, "people of the book", and therefore no tribulation happened against them.[111] On the other hand the Muslim invasion must have caused some problems as well. Some of them must have migrated north-east just before or during the invasion because they state that after the invasion only sixty banners remained in Babylonia:

[105] "Anuš-Uthra went to the 'Ṭura ḏ Madai' (Median mountains), called *Haran Gawaita*, and brought Bhira son of Šitil, a descendant of Artabanus king of the Naṣoraeans and set him up in Baghdad (*Babylon*) and installed him in sovereign power (*as its sovereign*). And in his company there were sixty Naṣoraeans, and the Naṣoraeans in Baghdad (*Babylonia*) multiplied and became many. Some of the tribe of Bhira son of Šitil, Naṣoraeans, came with him until there were four hundred *mašknia* in Baghdad": *HG*, p.10.

[106] See ibid, pp.11-12.

[107] "About eighty-six years before the Son-of-Slaughter, the Arab, Adonai sent Šurbiš-Ruha who is his spouse, to the city of Ṭib, called locally the city of Ašganda... So schism ensued amongst the Naṣoraeans and candidates for priesthood as result of those writings which he had written": *HG*, pp.12-13.

[108] "Thus, before the appearance of the Son-of-Slaughter, the Arab, the Christian, Idumaean, Jewish, Hurdabaean and Dilbilaean peoples became many. The peoples were divided and languages became numerous; even the languages of Naṣoraeans multiplied. This; and then sovereignty was taken from the descendants of King Artabanus, and (*they were driven*) from Baghdad; the Hardbaeans (*Sasanians*) taking over the kingdom. (*Nevertheless*) there remained one hundred and seventy banners and *bimandia* in Baghdad. And so a Hardabaean (*Sasanian*) dynasty ruled for three hundred and sixty years..": ibid, pp.14-15.

[109] See below pp.120ff.

[110] See *GR*, pp.30, 54; *Jb*, p.88; *HG*, pp.12-16.

[111] See *HG*, pp.15f.

> "...after this had happened and these events had taken place, sixty banners (*still*) remained and pertained to me in Baghdad."[112]

Perhaps for this reason they called Muhammad "the Son of Slaughter".

From the statements in the colophons and some religious writings we understand that from time to time persecution of the Mandaeans caused by local governors took place.[113]

Finally the Mandaean version of their history ends with a prophecy. They claim that the period of Muslim domination will continue 4,000 years. After this period the false Messiah, the son of Miriam (Mary), will succeed him, and his reign will last 6,000 years. During this period all kinds of evil will increase. At last people's senses will return to them. They will stop doing evil, and the Mandaeans will increase again. Then, 50,000 years will pass in calm before the end of the world. Finally a destruction of the world by one cry or utterance will happen.[114]

Although the Mandaean written and oral traditions about the history of the sect are, as we have earlier remarked, full of legends, contradictory statements and confusion, they hint at the following important clues:

a. The Mandaeans tell of a western homeland. This homeland is the area of Jerusalem where Yahya Yuhana (John the Baptist) appears as a great disciple or prophet of the Mandaean religion. Here we must state that the Mandaeans never mention John as the founder of their religion, since their religion is a proto-religion, beginning with Adam and Eve.[115]

b. They speak of a persecution of their ancestors in Jerusalem by the Jews. After the persecution, Jerusalem and the Jews are destroyed by the powers of Light.

c. They state that after the persecution their ancestors who were under the leadership of King Ardban migrated to the Median mountains, called "Haran Gawaita". This migration certainly happened during the Parthian period, presumably in the first century A.D.

d. Then under Parthian protection they migrated from the Median mountains to the south, Babylonia. During the Parthian period Mandaeism lived its golden age so that up to 400 cult-huts were built.

---

[112] Ibid, p.15.

[113] "In that period and epoch — from the rule of the Arab Son-of-Slaughter unto the end of the worlds — persecution and tribulation will increase for Naṣoraeans; purity will decrease and pollutions, adultery, theft and fraud will increase. ... Hibil Ziwa taught concerning this age — that is, the age of the Arab Law... (*During*) this Arab age every evil creature multiplieth like evil weeds that grow apace, and peoples, nations and languages disperse and become measureless and numberless": ibid, pp.18-19.

For persecution of the Mandaeans by the local governors see the colophon of *DMHZ* (particularly p.90).

[114] See *HG*, pp.19ff; *GR*, p.28.

[115] See below p.106.

e. During the Sassanian period there was persecution against the Mandaeans.
f. Finally they speak of confusion and schism amongst their ancestors about a century before Islam.

In the coming chapters we will examine various internal and external evidences about the origin and history of the Mandaeans, and discuss the points mentioned above.

Map 3
Possible Migration Route of the Mandaeans

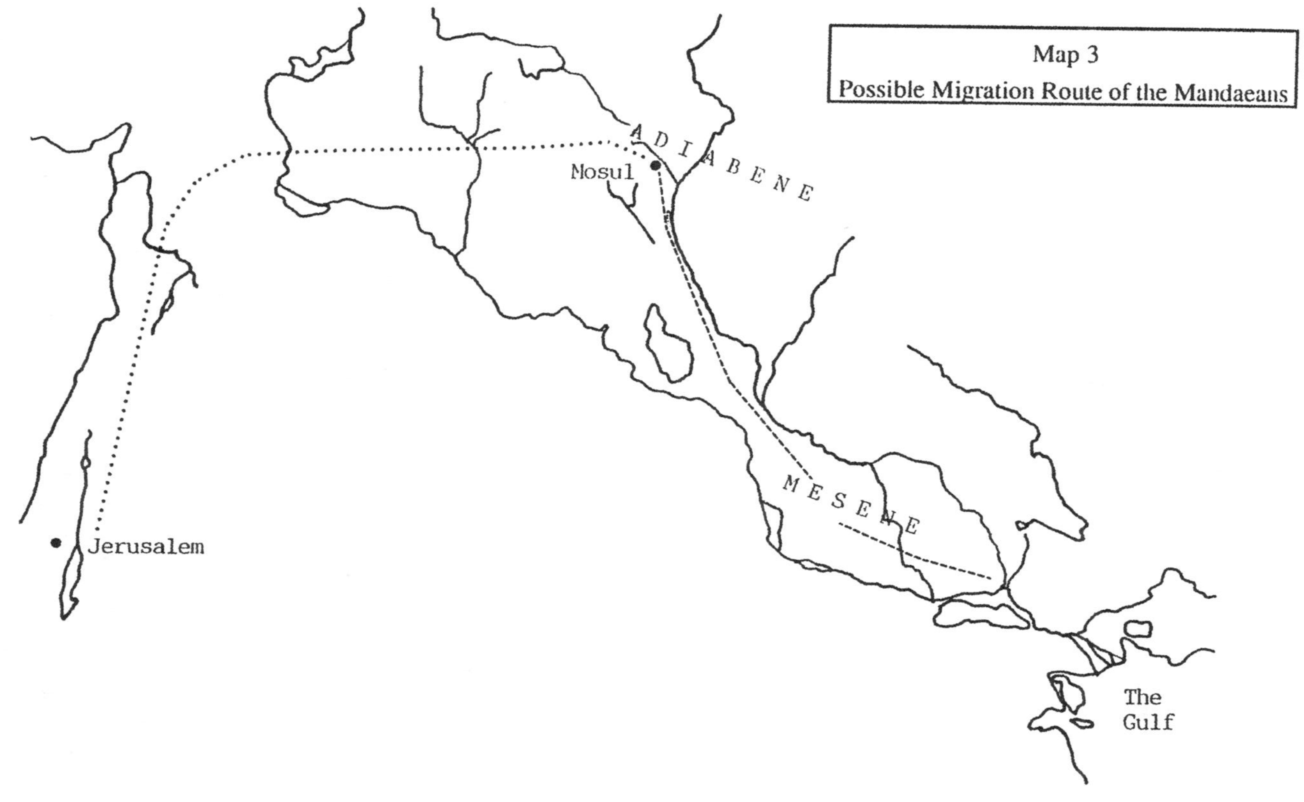

.... First Stage: From Palestine to the Median Mountains
------------- Second Stage: From Media to Southern Mesopotamia

CHAPTER IV

VARIOUS FOREIGN ELEMENTS IN MANDAEISM AND THE WESTERN CONNECTIONS OF THE MANDAEANS

Mandaean religion bears a number of foreign elements. We can classify them in two groups on the basis of their importance: (i) Jewish, ancient Mesopotamian, Iranian and Christian elements; (ii) Egyptian, Minoan, ancient Greek and Islamic influence. The second group is not so important because the elements which were regarded as connected with these traditions by some scholars can, as we will show, be assigned to the first group.[1] Therefore in this section we will examine the elements in Mandaean religion connected with the first group. We will examine them in two categories: ancient Mesopotamian and Iranian elements and western elements.

1. Ancient Mesopotamian and Iranian elements

Some western scholars, especially those who argued for an eastern homeland for the Mandaeans, such as Brandt and Kessler,[2] have pointed out a number of ancient Mesopotamian and Iranian elements in Mandaean religion. Some of these points were later criticized by Mandaean scholars, when Mandaean studies settled down after the

---

[1]The main Egyptian influence is seen in the name of the Mandaean demiurge Ptahil. Almost all Mandaean scholars, such as Lidzbarski and Drower, state that Ptahil is a combination of Ptah, the Egyptian demiurge, and El, the Semitic deity. See *Jb*, pp.xxviif; *MII*, p.95 n.5; Drower, E.S., *The Secret Adam*, p.xv; Rudolph, K., *Die Mandäer*, I, p.81 n.4; *MIT*, p.63. On the other hand C.H. Kraeling suggests that Ptahil is derived from the word *ptḥ*, "to open", and argues that in the Mandaean cosmology the word "to open" is used in the sense of "create". He also suggests that Ptahil therefore refers to the Supreme Deity in his creative power. See Kraeling, C.H., "The Mandaic God Ptahil", *JAOS*, 53, 1953, p.164; idem, "The Origin and Antiquity of the Mandaeans", pp.206-7. But bearing in mind the striking resemblence between the name Ptah and Ptahil, and the similar characteristics of these two demiurges, the theory of Lidzbarski and other scholars who follow him seems to be correct. We must also remember the Mandaean tradition that they once had fellow religionists in Egypt. See above p.64.

Some scholars, such as Yamauchi, pointed out the similarity between the name of Mandaean Šišlam, who is the guardian spirit of Mšunia Kušta, the Mandaean ideal world, and the Minoan deity Yašašlam. See Gordon, C.H., "Towards a Grammar of Minoan", *Or*, 32, 1963, p.293; *MIT*, pp.65-66.

[2]See above pp.6-7.

publication of so many Mandaean texts and studies of their rituals and cults. The Mandaeans have lived in Mesopotamia for a long time, where they have naturally been in contact with their neighbours who held ancient Mesopotamian and Iranian beliefs and rituals, and they may have adopted some of these foreign elements later. We will examine first ancient Mesopotamian elements in Mandaeism.

A. Ancient Mesopotamian elements

The ancient Mesopotamian influence upon Mandaeism may be considered in three categories: (1) Magic and astrology, (2) loanwords, and (3) some religious motifs and rituals.

(1) The most important influence upon Mandaean magic and astrology is that of the Babylonians.[3] Both the earliest Mandaean magical bowl texts and lead amulets such as Lidzbarski's lead amulet from the third or fourth century A.D., and the astrological and magical literary texts from a later date, like *Sfar Malwašia*, bear magical formulas, ideas and lists of names which are quite similar to those of the Babylonians. For example we have a dialogue formula in the lead amulet published by Lidzbarski in 1909. In this amulet it is stated that the magician Yokabar appeals to Manda ḏ-Hiia to help Per Nukraya, son of Abandukt, against misfortune and the evil destroyers, the planets. Then the Life, the great Deity, calls to Hibil. Hibil tells the Life and Yawar about the troubles. After that the Life wants Yawar to help Nukraya and to chase the evil planets. Hibil himself, who, it seems, goes in the personality of Yawar, chases the planets away.[4] There is a resemblance between this story and the well-known theme of Marduk and Ea which recurs in the Sumerian and Akkadian incantations. In this motif Marduk goes to his father Ea to report a calamity that has happened and to ask for Ea's advice.[5] There is, consequently, a noticeable parallelism between the roles of Marduk and Manda ḏ-Hiia or Hibil in these dialogue formulas.

The planetary deities of ancient Mesopotamia also appear in the Mandaean magical texts. In the Mandaean literature they are generally described as evil beings or children of Ruha, the evil spirit, but in the magical texts sometimes they are invoked positively, although they are frequently described as demons. For example in Lidzbarski's amulet they are described as the "evil destroyers", and Šamiš (compare Mesopotamian Šamaš) is called the "Blind one who is over the spheres and Lame one who is over the chariots".[6] In the magical bowl texts Nergal is called "Nergal of the

---

[3]See Drower, E.S., *The Secret Adam*, p.x; Pallis, S.A., *Mandaean Studies*, pp.19ff; Yamauchi, E.M., "The Present Status of Mandaean Studies", p.94; *MIT*, p.62.
[4]Cf. *MIT*, Text 22: 14-100.
[5]See ibid, pp.42f; Baumgartner, W., "Zur Mandäerfrage", *HUCA*, 23, 1950-51, pp.64-65. Also see Rudolph, K., *Die Mandäer*, I, p.196.
[6]Cf. *MIT*, Text 22: 10, 21-23, 123-135.

wasp", while Ishtar is called "the queen" who has three-hundred and sixty tribes and amulet spirits. It is also said that there are eighty Ištars and sixty male temple spirits amongst the demons.[7] On the other hand the seven planets and twelve zodiac signs are sometimes invoked as friendly deities to strengthen the protective spell.[8] In a Mandaic bowl from Khuabir, Ishtar is invoked by saying: "You will come with this wine and perfume and myrtle".[9]

Moreover the list of the cursers, which includes father and mother, brother and sister, etc., is based on a Mesopotamian prototype. The comprehensive list of the baleful spirits is similar. Many of the spirits are directly derived from Mesopotamian originals. The most important spirits are the liliths. The Šedim are no longer protective genii, but have been demoted to the status of devils.[10]

In the Mandaic magical texts we also find the symbolism of the right and left sides as Light and Darkness, which is one of the characteristics of Mandaean thought.[11] Symbolism of the right and left sides is also seen in Babylonian magic.[12] The Mandaeans might have adopted this from the Babylonian tradition.

Finally the modern Mandaean priests meet together at New Year and carefully read the pages of *Sfar Malwašia*, which is their main astrological and magical book, in order to guess future events. In so doing they obviously carry on the Babylonian traditions of ceremonies to "fix the fates" of the coming year which took place in the New Year Festival.[13]

(2) It has also been observed that in the Mandaic dialect more than 80 words are Akkadian loanwords, some of them ultimately derived from Sumerian.[14] The names of the seven planets, who, as we have earlier noted, are regarded as the powers of darkness in the Mandaean tradition, are the same as those of the ancient Babylonian planetary deties. These names, which occur both in the literary texts, like the *Ginza* and

---

[7]See ibid, pp.165, 167, 169, 229, 277.

[8]"...Šamiš (the Sun) in his brilliance has
strengthened it. Bel (Jupiter), Nergal (Mars),
and Kewan (Saturn) have strengthened it. The
Moon in its brightness has strengthened it.
Dlibat (Venus), and Daniš have strengthened
it. Nebo (Mercury), his priest and worshipper, have strengthened it. The seven
Planets have strengthened it.
Their twelve angels
have strengthened it": *MIT*, p.253.

[9]Cf. ibid, pp.205-6.

[10]See *MIT*, p.63; Yamauchi, E.M., "The Present Status of Mandaean Studies", p.94.

[11]"...(sealed) bound is Duktana Prauk (daughter of Bzurgantai) from the right hand to the left hand, from the left hand to the right hand, from the hair which is on the head and unto the toe nails which is on the foot..": McCullough, W.S., op.cit., p.14.

[12]See ibid, p.21.

[13]See *AM*, p.1.

[14]For these loanwords see Baumgartner, W., op.cit., pp.57ff; Widengren, G., "Heavenly Enthronement and Baptism. Studies in Mandaean Baptism", pp.573-74; Rudolph, K., *Die* Mandäer, I, p.28.

The Book of John, and also in the magical lead amulets and bowl texts,[15] are: *sin* (Akk. *sīn*), "the Moon",[16] *šamiš* (Akk. *šamšu*), "the Sun",[17] *kiuan* (Akk. *kaimānu*), "Saturn",[18] *bil* (Akk. *bēlu*), "Jupiter",[19] *nbu* or *ʿnbu* (Akk. *nabū*), "Mercury", which is identified with Christ in the Mandaean literature,[20] *nirig* or *nʿrig* (Akk. *nirgallū*), "Mars", which is sometimes identified with Muhammad and regarded as a symbol of the Arabs,[21] and *ʿstira* or *ʿstra* (Akk. *ištar*), "Venus", which is also named *libat* or *dlibat*.[22]

(3) The Babylonian influence is also seen in religious language and some cultic institutions. There is a similarity between the Mandaean and ancient Mesopotamian religious language in the blessing formula. In the Mandaean liturgical texts we find a special blessing formula which shows a few variations but of which a standard version runs as follows:

> "Healing, victory, soundness, speech and a hearing, joy of heart and forgiving of sins for me..."[23]

Similar formulas occur in Akkadian texts which are often used in prayers, such as: "speaking and hearing (and favour)..." and "Health and joy of heart".[24]

There might be a connection between the *ʿngirta* ceremony of the Mandaeans and a legal act in ancient Mesopotamia, as J.C. Greenfield noted.[25] In Mandaean funeral ceremonies a letter, called *ʿngirta*, which is actually a sealed bottle of oil, is sometimes left with the garment worn by the corpse.[26] In the description of this letter, given in *CP*, the following steps are involved: writing, sealing, tying with a cord, and sealing the letter again with the nail.[27] This is also seen in a legal act in Mesopotamia from Old Babylonian times to the Seleucid period.[28]

---

[15]See *GR*, pp.28, 46, 176; *Jb*, p.217; *MIT*, pp.165, 167, 191, 243, 253, 277; Macuch, R., "Altmandäische Bleirollen", in *Die Araber in der Alten Welt*, v.IV, pp.129, 135, 137. Also see Pallis, S.A., *Mandaean Studies*, pp.33ff.

[16]*MD*, p.327.

[17]Ibid, p.443.

[18]Ibid, p.212.

[19]Ibid, p.60.

[20]Ibid, p.287.

[21]Ibid, p.299.

[22]Ibid, pp.234-35, 355.

[23]*CP*, p.1. Also see for variations, ibid, pp.5, 64, 72.

[24]See Widengren, G., "Heavenly Enthronement and Baptism. Studies in Mandaean Baptism", pp.576-77. Widengren has also seen a resemblance between the usage of the liturgical language of ritual directions in the Mandaean liturgical texts and that in the ancient Mesopotamian *bīt rimki* ritual texts. See ibid, pp.575-76.

[25]See Greenfield, J.C., "A Mandaic Miscellany", p.82.

[26]See *MII*, pp.169ff.

[27]See *CP*, p.61.

[28]See Greenfield, J.C., op.cit., p.82.

Moreover the use of myrtle which symbolizes life and immortality in the Mandaean rituals is also seen in the Babylonian ceremonies, but it is difficult to suggest that the Mandaeans inherited it from the Babylonians because myrtle is widely used in the Persian and presumably Syrian cults as well.[29]

From the beginning of the century some scholars, such as H. Zimmern, G. Widengren and recently E.M. Yamauchi, pointed out some similarities between Mandaean baptism and the Mesopotamian water-purification ceremonies and argued for a Mesopotamian origin of Mandaean baptism.[30] For example, Widengren has noted the similarities between the actions of the water purifications of Tammūz and those of Mandaean baptism.[31] Also E.M. Yamauchi points out the similarities between the Mandaean baptismal ceremonies and Mesopotamian magical lustrations. Thus the water is, according to both traditions, a vivifying force which washes away sins and protects against demons. Yamauchi also remarks that according to the Mesopotamian Šurpu texts divine river water flows from the pure Euphrates, and he points out the resemblance of this to the Mandaean tradition which mentions *praš-ziua*, "the Light Euphrates", which is regarded as a celestial river flowing from the mountains.[32]

We disagree with those scholars who argued because of these similarities for a Mesopotamian origin of Mandaean baptism. In fact these points of resemblance, like the acceptance of the power of water against demons and sins, were common among the various peoples of the area, such as the Greeks, the Iranians and the Hebrews.[33] With regard to the term *praš ziua* in the Mandaean tradition we know that this is a late name, adopted by the Mandaeans for their baptismal water, as some Mandaean scholars remark.[34] On the other hand it is certain that in the Mandaean literature the most ancient term used for the baptismal water is *iardna*, which refers to the famous river in Palestine.[35]

Although there are some points of similarity between the Mandaean baptism and ancient Mesopotamian water purifications, we cannot talk about direct influence from ancient Mesopotamia upon Mandaean baptism, since these points of resemblence were common among the various cultures. On the other hand, as we will see later,[36] there is a close parallelism between the central acts and technical terms of the Mandaean

---

[29]See Rudolph, K., *Die Mandäer*, II, p.47; *MII*, p.121; Widengren, G., "Heavenly Enthronement and Baptism. Studies in Mandaean Baptism", p.572. Segelberg, E., "Trāṣa ḏ-tāga ḏ-Šišlām rabbā", p.223.

[30]See Zimmern, H., "Das vermutliche babylonische Vorbild des Pethā and Mambūhā der Mandäer", in *Orientalische Studien Theodor Nöldeke zum siebzigsten Geburtsag gewidmet*, ed. C. Bezold, Giessen (1906), Bd.2, pp.959-67; Widengren, G., op.cit., pp.552ff; Yamauchi, E.M., *Gnostic Ethics and Mandaean Origins*, pp.84-85.

[31]See Widengren, G., op.cit., p.579.

[32]See Yamauchi, E.M., op.cit., pp.84-85.

[33]See Pallis, S.A., *Mandaean Studies*, p.46; Rudolph, K., "Problems of a History of the Development of the Mandaean Religion", p.217.

[34]See Segelberg, E., *Maṣbūtā*, p.38.

[35]See below pp.111f.

[36]See below pp.114ff.

baptism and that of the various western baptismal cults, and the western background of the Mandaean rite is quite certain.

The ancient Mesopotamian influence upon Mandaeism is, as we have seen, mainly in magic and astrology. The most striking characteristic is that the planetary deities of ancient Mesopotamia are regarded as demons, the power of darkness and the children of Ruha, though a few times they are mentioned as benevolent beings, and invoked in magical texts. This means that although the Mandaeans preserved the names of the planetary deities of ancient Mesopotamia, they rejected the old gods and the old official cult of Mesopotamia.

B. Iranian elements

We will examine the Iranian influence upon Mandaeism in five categories: (1) cultic institutions, (2) loanwords, (3) the mass of the dead and ritual meals, (4) some gnostic concepts, and (5) cosmology.[37]

(1) One of the important Iranian influences upon Mandaean tradition is the use of fire. Fire-cult is one of the characteristic features of the Iranian tradition. It appears on the coins of the pre-Christian Frataraka dynasty of Fars, about 200 B.C., on which king (priest), fire-altar and banner are represented.[38] Mandaean tradition has different opinions about the use of fire in the ritual actions. On the one hand the power of fire is denied and the fire-worshippers are reviled in the Mandaean literature, both in the bowl texts and in the liturgical writings,[39] but on the other hand fire is one of the objects used in the ritual ceremonies of the modern Mandaeans. The small fire-brazier upon which sacramental bread is baked and incense constantly cast is very important to all Mandaean rites. Without it no rite can be performed. It is kindled by the priest, fed with ritually immersed and ritually pure fuel, tended by the celebrant or ašganda, and without this fire no baptism is valid.

---

[37]H. Field in his anthropological study on the Mandaeans stated that they were connected racially with western Iran. Field, H., *The Anthropology of Iraq, I, 2: The Lower Euphrates-Tigris Region*, Anth. Ser. Field Museum of Natural History, vol. 30, Publ. 631, Chicago (1949), p.310.

[38]See Drower, E.S., "Mandaean Polemic", p. 444; idem, *The Secret Adam*, p.61.

[39]In the bowl text, published by W.S. McCullough, the bowl-writer regards fire as an evil element: "...bound and tied are the wings of the chariots of fire in which they dwell": McCullough, W.S., op.cit., p.14. Also see ibid, p.21.

Also in the prayers of baptism the power of fire is denied and its worshippers are reviled:

"'If I go with you to the Jordan
Who will be your witness?'
'Lo, there burns a fire.
It will bear witness for us'.
'That is not what I seek,
.....
Fire, is vanity and cometh to naught
And its worshippers come to naught and are vanity'": *CP*, p.17.

Besides the fire some other cult objects of the Mandaeans are connected to the Iranian tradition. One is the *drabša*, "banner", used in many rituals. The term is of Persian origin.[40] The banner is, as we have mentioned, represented on the coins of the pre-Christian dynasty of Fars.[41]

Another cult object, the ring, which is used by the priests, is an ancient symbol, known from both Iranian and Semitic spheres.[42] It is consequently difficult to connect it only to the Iranian tradition.

There is also a connection between the Mandaean calendar which consists of twelve months of thirty days each, with five intercalary days called Panja, and ancient Persian practise.[43]

The points of resemblance are also seen between the festivals of the Mandaeans and those of the Iranians. The Mandaeans use the Persian "Nauruz Rba" which is the name given to the solemn festival in *Alf Trisar Šuialia*.[44] There are some resemblances between the Mandaean Panja festival, celebrated in the five intercalary days of the year, and the Panja or Fanja festival of the Iranian tradition which precedes the New Year.[45]

(2) Mandaean texts contain a number of terms and proper nouns of Iranian derivation. It has been stated that there are about 125 Iranian loanwords in Mandaic.[46] In the Mandaean magical bowl texts and the lead amulets many Persian names are found. The *daevin* come in as degenerate demons in these texts.[47] Also in the liturgical texts many names of Iranian origin appear. For example, Bihram, which is originally an Iranian *yazata* or angel, is a name which often occurs in the baptismal liturgies and in which the Mandaeans are baptized.[48] Moreover many of the names of the ritual objects of the Mandaeans are Iranian loanwords. For example, the names of the parts of the ritual dress and of ritual objects such as the *burzinga*, the turban, *taga*, the crown, *himiana*, the girdle, *šaruala*, the trousers, *margna*, the staff, *gauaza*, the staff, *drabša*, the banner, and *aštargan*, the bridegroom's staff, are Iranian.[49]

---

[40]Lady Drower states that the Persian origin of the word may offer some clue as to the time when it was adopted as a symbol used in the cult. See Drower, E.S., *The Secret Adam*, p.61.

[41]The term Fars (or Pars) occurs in one of the banner hymns of the Mandaeans. See *CP*, p.233.

[42]See Rudolph, K., *Die Mandäer*, II, p.57; Segelberg, E., "Trāṣa ḏ-tāga ḏ-Šišlām rabbā", p.231.

[43]See Taqizadeh, S.H., "An Ancient Persian Practice Preserved by a Non-Iranian People: The Mandaean Calendar", *BSOS*, 9, 1938, pp.603-19.

[44]See *MII*, p.85; Taqizadeh, S.H., op.cit., pp.607-8.

[45]See *MII*, pp.88-89, 98 n.18, 99 n.20.

[46]See Yamauchi, E.M., *Gnostic Ethics and Mandaean Origins*, p.72 n.354. Also see Pallis, S.A., *Mandaean Studies*, pp.104ff; Rudolph, K., *Die Mandäer*, I, pp.128f; *HCMM*, p.lxii; Segelberg, E., *Maṣbūtā*, pp.178ff.

[47]See *MIT*, pp.63-64.

[48]See *MD*, pp.59-60; Drower, E.S., *The Secret Adam*, p.65.

[49]See Widengren, G., "Heavenly Enthronement and Baptism. Studies in Mandaean Baptism", pp.554-56. Also see idem, *Mani and Manichaeism*, pp.17-19. Widengren states that all these loanwords could be of Parthian origin. However, some of these words may have been adopted by the Mandaeans already in the West, since some of them also appear in western sources. For example, for *šaruala* see Dan 3:21.

(3) There are some resemblances between the beliefs and rituals of the Mandaeans about the dead and those of the Iranian tradition. Many actions of the funeral ceremonies of Mandaeans, such as washing the dead and putting the body in a white sheet, are closely connected to those of the Parsis.[50] The Mandaean doctrine of "the soul's heavenly journey"[51] and the purgatories (*maṭarata*), through which every soul must pass, is also found in the Iranian tradition.[52]

There is also a close relationship between the Mandaean and Parsi ritual meals, as has been pointed out by Lady Drower in her detailed comparative study of the ritual meals of the Parsis and Mandaeans.[53]

(4) Some of the gnostic concepts of Mandaeism may have been derived from Iranian tradition. One of them is the dualism of Light and Darkness or good and bad, which is one of the striking characteristics of Mandaean religion.[54] Also in Iranian tradition the constrast between the worlds of Ahura-Mazda and Ahriman is the most important characteristic.[55]

Another concept which is seen to be connected to Iranian tradition is *dmuta*, the principle of "ideal counterpart". According to Mandaeism each individual on earth has his counterpart or likeness in *mšunia kušṭa*, the Mandaean ideal world.[56] As Lady Drower remarked there is a striking similarity between this concept and the *frawashi* doctrine of the Zoroastrians. According to the Zoroastrians "on the death of a person, his soul (*urwân* or *rawân*) meets with justice according to his merits or demerits. If he has deserved well, he goes to heaven, if not, to hell. His Fravashi, which guided him through life as a guiding spirit, parts from his soul and goes to its abode or place among all the Fravashis."[57] The Fravashi is pure and perfect. Therefore it is the soul (*urwân*) that meets with the good and evil consequences of its actions.[58] Also in the Mandaean tradition, at the time of death the soul leaves the body and proceeds to the world of light, through the purgatories and the scales of Abatur. When the soul has completed its

---

[50]See *MII*, pp.201-202 n.12.

[51]Also the close parallelism between the Mandaean sources and Fourth Gospel on the theme of "Descend and Ascent of the Soul" has been argued by the scholars. See Meeks, W.A., *The Prophet-King. Moses Traditions and the Johannine Christology*, Leiden (1967), p.297.

[52]See Widengren, G., *Mani and Manichaeism*, p.18; Pallis, S.A., *Mandaean Studies*, p.92. Also see Rudolph, K., *Die Mandäer*, I, p.123; idem, "Problems of a History of the Development of the Mandaean Religion", pp.230-31. Widengren states that the Mandaean concepts of the dead and of funerals, i.e. the tarrying of the demons around the corpse, the return to the "treasure-house" of the souls, the viaticum of good deeds, the meeting with the image of the soul, the delivery of robe and crown, sitting on the throne prepared in heaven, and reception by the godhead, are derived from the Iranian tradition. See Widengren, G., op.cit., pp.18-19.

[53]See *MII*, pp.225-39. Also see ibid, pp.204-24.

[54]For this concept in Mandaean religion see below pp.214ff.

[55]See Pallis, S.A., op.cit., p.50; Drower, E.S., *The Secret Adam*, p.x. Also see Rudolph, K., *Die Mandäer*, I, pp.118f.

[56]See *MII*, pp.54-55; *ATŠ*, pp.189-90.

[57]*MII*, p.55 (quoted from J.J. Modi, *The Religious Ceremonies and Customs of the Parsees*, Bombay (1922), p.423).

[58]*MII*, p.55.

purification it reaches the world of Light and joins its counterpart. The resemblance of the two doctrines to each other is obvious.[59]

(5) The similarities between the Mandaean and Iranian traditions about the world-ages and the periodic destruction of the world are notable. According to the Mandaeans the world-age is divided into four epochs. At the end of each mankind is destroyed with the exception of one couple; first by sword and plague, second by fire, third by flood, and finally there will be a destruction by air at the end of the fourth epoch.[60] According to the Persian doctrine also, the world-age is divided into four periods which will take 12,000 years. Each period lasts 3,000 years. There will be a destruction by fire at the end of the last millennium of the last period.[61] Obviously there are many differences as well as similarities between the two traditions about the world periods. For example, according to the Persian doctrine man does not appear in the first two periods. In the Persian doctrine it is also stated that the destruction by fire will occur at the end of the last period. A tradition about the destruction of mankind by flood and later by fire, sulphur and asphalt is also found in the *Apocalypse of Adam* from Nag-Hammadi.[62]

Some other similarities between Mandaean and Iranian traditions have been pointed out. For example, the Mandaean genie of the upper air, Ayar Ziwa, which occurs both in the bowl and literary texts, has been compared with the Parsi Ram-Khvastra, the angel of rarefied air, and with the Iranian Vayu (Ether).[63] Lady Drower also points out the resemblance between the Mandaean *dukrana*, a sacramental commemorating of a person or persons by reciting their name, and the Parsi *yâd* ceremony.[64]

We have seen that the Iranian influence upon Mandaeism is generally found in rituals, like the funeral ceremonies and ritual meals. A number of names of ritual objects are of Iranian origin. Moreover there is an obvious similarity between the Iranian and Mandaean tradition in the principles of ideal counterpart and of dualism. However, the Mandaeans may have received at least some of these Iranian elements such as the *dmuta* principle and dualism between the Light and Darkness already in the west,

---

[59]Also see Rudolph, K., *Die Mandäer*, I, p.127; Drower, E.S., *The Secret Adam*, p.40. Lady Drower also points out the similarity between the Mandaean ideal world, *mšunia kušṭa* and the Parsi world of prototypes and Plato's ideal world. See Drower, E.S., op.cit., p.41.

[60]See Chapter III n.61.

[61]For a summary of Iranian doctrine see, Pallis, S.A., op.cit., pp.60-61.

[62]See MacRae, G.W., "The Apocalypse of Adam", in *Nag Hammadi Codices, V, 2-5 and VI with Papyrus Berolinensis 8502, 1 and 4*, ed. D.M. Parrott (Nag Hammadi Studies, eds., M. Krause, J.M. Robinson and F. Wisse, XI) Leiden (1979), pp.163ff, 173ff.

[63]See *MD*, p.14; *MII*, p.58 n.13; *MIT*, p.64.

[64]See *MII*, p.223 n.7.

before their migration to the east, since it is well known that the Iranian tradition, like the Mithra cult, was influential in the west before the Christian period.[65]

2. Western elements

The western tradition is the most important influential factor in Mandaeism. The western elements are mainly divided into two groups: Jewish elements and Christian elements. We may add reference to the Nabataeans, since the relationship between the script of the Nabataeans (and Palmyrenes) and that of the Mandaeans has been pointed out by scholars such as Lidzbarski and Macuch.[66] Also *nbaṭ*, eponym of the Nabataeans, is a Light spirit of the Mandaeans.[67]

A. Jewish elements and influence

Studies of Mandaeism have demonstrated that the Mandaean literature from the very early magical texts to the late literary texts bears a number of Jewish elements and influences. Strong anti-Jewish polemics are also found, especially in the literary texts. In this section we will first discuss the anti-Jewish polemics in the Mandaean tradition, and, then, examine some essential Jewish elements.

a. Anti-Jewish polemics

In the magical bowl texts and the lead amulets, the earliest of which reaches back to the third or fourth century A.D., no evidence of strong hostility towards Judaism such as that which appears in the later texts is found. Instead, the names of Jewish angels are as important for the removal of curses as are the Uthras. The name of Adonai, the head of the temple spirits and the leader of all the great chariots of darkness, is sometimes used in a positive way to remove curses.[68] On the other hand throughout the rest of Mandaean literature we see strong anti-Jewish feelings. The Jews are called "the powers of darkness" and "an evil nation":

---

[65]See Rudolph, K., "Problems of a History of the Development of the Mandaean Religion", p.218; Drower, E.S., *The Secret Adam*, p.45.

[66]See below pp.118-19.

[67]See *MD*, p.287; Rudolph, K., *Die Mandäer*, I, p.61; idem, *Theogonie, Kosmogonie und Anthropogonie in den mandäischen Schriften*, pp.71f; Kraeling, C.H., "The Origin and Antiquity of the Mandaeans", p.211.

[68]See *MIT*, pp.155, 295. Also see Morony, M.G., *Iraq After the Muslim Conquest*, New Jersey (1984), pp.413f.

"The Jews, an evil nation, accursed and blasphemous ..."[69]

The Jews are believed to be the source of confusion and disagreement:

"Do not mix with the Jews, who do not agree on a *single* utterance. All peoples and gates proceed from the Jewish people."[70]

Also the Jews are reviled because of their rituals and customs, like circumcision.[71] On the other hand the main reason for the Mandaeans' hate against the Jews is the belief that the Jews have persecuted their ancestors in Jerusalem.[72]

Strong anti-Jewish feelings are also seen in the hymns of Miriai.[73]

The polemical usage of certain words and verbal roots in Mandaean literature is also noticeable. The root *qdš* originally meant "be holy" or "sacred"; in the Mandaean literature the words derived from this root are never used to describe Mandaean beings, personages, ceremonies or objects. They are used for the Jews and Christians to express obloquy.[74] For example the sun which is identified with Adonai is called

---

[69]*CP*, p.251.
"They built Jerusalem,
in which the Jews came into being (or: were).
They gave the works of darkness to them,
and the seven pronounced a blessing over them": *GR*, p.341 (Rudolph, "Man.Sour.", p.304).

[70]Ibid, p.25 (Rudolph, "Man.Sour.", p.296).

[71]"He, Adonai, chose a people for himself and called together a community (*kništa*) for himself. The place Jerusalem was built, the city of the Jews, who circumcise themselves with the sword and sprinkle their faces with their blood and (in this way) worship Adonai. Husbands abandon their wives, go forth and lie with one another. The womenfolk lie in the bosoms of their husbands during their menstrual periods. They strayed from the first doctrine (*šuta*) and produced a 'book' (*ktaba*) for themselves": *GR*, p.25 (Rudolph, "Man.Sour.", p.296).

[72]See above p.68.

[73]Miriai, who is the daughter of the king of Babylon, the ruler of Jerusalem, is an important figure in the Mandaean literature. According to the Mandaean tradition she leaves Judaism and becomes a Mandaean. The Jews force her to leave Mandaeism, but she does not change her beliefs and leaves Jerusalem:
"I am Miriai, daughter of the king of Babylon,
daughter of the mighty ruler of Jerusalem.
The Jews gave birth to me,
the men, the priests reared me": *Jb*, p.126 (Rudolph, "Man.Sour.", p.311).
"She hath hated Jewry and loved Naṣirutha;
She hath conceived hate for the synagogue-door
And love for the door of the *maškna*.
.....
Miriai scattereth the dust with her foot
And sayeth "Dust on the mouth of the Jews!
Ashes on the mouths of all the cohens (priests)!
And dung beneath the horses' hooves
Be upon the Elders who are in Jerusalem!
That which I have come to love I cannot hate.
That which I (now) hate, I cannot love": *CP*, p.130. Also see *GR*, p.341; *Jb*, pp.123ff; *CP*, pp.129f; Rudolph, K., *Die Mandäer*, I, pp.95ff; Buckley, J.J., "The Mandaean Appropriation of Jesus' Mother Miriai", *Novum Testamentum*, 35, 1993, pp.181-96.

[74]*MD*, p.405; Drower, E.S., "Mandaean Polemic", p.439.

qaduš.[75] Also Christian saints and nuns are called *qadišia* and *qadišiata*, "holy men and women".[76]

Another polemical word is *iahuṭaiia*. *iahudata*, Judaism, is changed to *iahuṭaiia* associating it with the root *iahṭa*, "abortion", and the root *hṭa*, "to sin".[77] Thus we have the sentence in the *Ginza*: *iahuṭaiia iahṭia unipṣia*, "the Jews — abortions and excrement".[78]

Moreover in the Mandaean literature the Jewish god Adonai (my lord) is seen as a false and evil god or demon and identified with the sun. Therefore the Jews are believed to be the worshippers of the sun.[79]

Moses is described as "a prophet of Ruha" and "a false prophet".[80] He is also mentioned as the Jewish ruler who persecuted the Mandaeans and followed them to Ṭura d̲-Madai.[81]

b. Jewish features

In spite of the strong anti-Jewish polemics Mandaean tradition bears a number of essential Jewish elements. Some scholars, such as Brandt and Pallis, minimize the Jewish elements in Mandaeism. Brandt does not entertain a Jewish origin of the Mandaean sect. In his opinion there are only a few Jewish elements.[82] Pallis went further and believed that there was no single point in Mandaeism taken from Judaism though he is thereby in difficulty in trying to explain Biblical names in the Mandaean literature.[83]

Jewish elements in Mandaeism can be examined in 5 categories: Old Testament figures and allusions; legal terminology; parallels to the ethics of Judaism; ritual ceremonies; and similarities between the Mandaeans and the heretical sects of Judaism.

---

[75]See *GR*, pp.25, 43.
[76]See Drower, E.S., op.cit., p.439.
[77]See *MD*, p.184; *HCMM*, p.429 n.71; Segelberg, E., "Old and New Testament Figures in Mandaean Version", in *Syncretism*, ed. S.S. Hartman, (Scripta Instituti Donneriani Aboensis III) Stockholm and Uppsala (1969), p.236.
[78]*GR*, p.232; *MD*, p.184.
[79]See *MD*, p.7; Rudolph, K., *Die Mandäer*, I, pp.81-82; idem, *Mandaeism*, p.4. "...Šamiš whose name is Qadoš, whose name is Adōnai, whose name is Ēl-Ēl": *GR*, p.43. Also see ibid, p.25.
[80]See ibid, pp.43, 46; *HG*, p.8. Also Abraham is described as "the prophet of Ruha". See *GR*, pp.43, 46.
[81]See above p.64.
[82]For a summary of Brandt's theory see Rudolph, K., "Problems of a History of the Development of the Mandaean Religion", pp.211-12.
[83]Pallis states: "While all the names mentioned in this section ... showed absolutely no connection between Mandaeism and Judaism, in the case of the names *hibil*, *šitil* and *'Anuš* or ʿEnuš we are on more difficult ground": Pallis, S.A., *Mandaean Studies*, p.126. Also see ibid, pp.115-16.

1) Old Testament figures and allusions

In the Mandaean literature, both in the magical bowl texts and lead amulets and in the literary texts, we find a number of Old Testament characters. According to the Mandaean tradition Adam, who is the primal man of the Old Testament, created by God from the earth into which he breathed the spirit of life, is the first man, called *adam gabra qadmaia*, "Adam the first man".[84]

In the priestly documents of the Mandaeans two figures of Adam appear: one is the spiritual Adam, *adam kasia*, the Mystic or Secret Adam who is the primordial first man, *adam qadmaia*, and the other is *adam pagria*, the physical man. Adam Kasia precedes the human Adam by many myriads of years, for the Universe as a whole precedes the microcosm.[85] In these documents also a comparison of the created universe with the limbs and organs of the human body is made.[86] Here, the body, *ʿṣṭun* or *ʿṣṭuna*, is that of Adam Qadmaia.[87] Therefore the primal Adam, Adam Qadmaia, is depicted as the macrocosmos. In other words he is the cosmos in human shape. In his formation the letters of the alphabet play an instrumental role.[88]

There is a parallelism between this aspect of the Mandaean tradition and the Jewish sources. The reference to a cosmic Adam is found also in the Rabbinic literature.[89]

There is also a relationship between the Mandaean Adam Qadmaia and Adam Qadmon of Kabbalism: Adam Qadmon is the archetypal man in the Kabbalah.[90]

According to the Mandaean creation story of the earthly man the body of the first man, *adam pagria*, is created by the demiurge, Ptahil, associated with the evil planets, but, on the other hand, his soul, *adam kasia* or *adakas*, is derived from the world of Light.[91] Here, we have a kind of gnostic dualism: on the one hand there is a holy being, the world of Light (or the king of Light), who gives the soul, the living essence, to the earthly Adam; on the other there is a demiurge and his evil helpers, the planets, who carry out the action of creation. There is also a parallelism between the Mandaeans and heretical Judaism in this motif. In the Jewish sources the rabbis sometimes polemicized against the notion that the Name of God was associated with

---

[84]See *MD*, p.7

[85]See Drower, E.S., *The Secret Adam*, pp.21-22. Cf. *ATŠ*, p.173.

[86]See *ATŠ*, pp.161ff.

[87]See Drower, E.S., *The Secret Adam*, p.21.

[88]See *ATŠ*, pp.181ff. For the parallelism between the Mandaean tradition and heretical Jewish traditions about the role of alphabet in the creation see below pp.100f.

[89]D. Cohn-Sherbok states: "In Sanh. 38f. for example, R. Meir implies that Adam represents all creation by saying that the dust to make him was taken from every place on earth. R. Judah states in the name of Rab that Adam had cosmic dimensions at first": Cohn-Sherbok, D., "The Mandaeans and Heterodox Judaism", p.149 n.16. Also see Schonfield, H.J., *The Authentic New Testament*, London (1956), p.309 n.59.

[90]See Scholem, G., *Major Trends in Jewish Mysticism*, London (1955), p.265.

[91]See *GR*, pp.107ff.

another object or person.[92] Also the earliest parts of the theological and liturgical literature of the Samaritans contain some polemics against a teaching to the effect that God had an "associate" or "second" in the creation and government of the universe.[93] In Rabbinic literature there are several references to the belief of the Jewish heretics called *minim* that there was a helper to God in creation. For example in the *Tosefta* (Sanhedrin 8: 7) we read:

> "A. Man was created last [in the order of creation].
> B. And why was man created last?
> C. So that the *minim* should not be able to say 'There was a partner with him in his work [of creation].'"[94]

As in the Old Testament, in the Mandaean tradition Adam is given a wife, *haua*,[95] Eve of the Scriptures. There are confused traditions about the origin of Hawwa. She appears in both positive and negative aspects. According to Mandaean literature she was given to Adam as a wife by the powers of Light.[96] Also in the *Ginza* and the liturgical texts Hawwa is given a high place.[97] Ptahil created Adam after his own image and Hawwa after Adam's image.[98] This tradition corresponds to the tradition of the Old Testament that Adam is said to be created in the image and likeness of the Creator,[99] and that Eve was formed from a rib of the first man.[100] On the other

---

[92]See Fossum, J.E., *The Name of God and the Angel of the Lord,* (Wissenschaftliche Untersuchungen zum Neuen Testament 36) Tübingen (1985), p.264.

[93]See ibid, p.264.

[94]Neusner, J., *The Tosefta*, New York (1981), p.224. Also see Cohn-Sherbok, D., op.cit., p.149. Cohn-Sherbok states that according to the Rabbinic literature the *minim* believed that this helper was Adam, a divine heavenly being. See Cohn-Sherbok, D., op.cit., pp.148-49. He also remarks that in Genesis Rabba the rabbis warn that it is a mistake to believe that Adam is a divine creature: ibid, p.149.

Moreover Rudolph states that the inability of the demiurge and his powers to make Adam stand up is also found in western gnosis. See Rudolph, K., "Mandean Sources", p.187 n.3. Also see idem "Ein Grundtyp gnostische Urmensch-Adam-Spekulation", *ZRGG*, 9, 1957, pp.1-20.

[95]See *MD*, p.117.

[96]"and we gave him a wife.
We gave Hawwa (Eve) to him as a wife,
(just) as she had been planted in her place": *GR*, p.115 (Rudolph, "Man.Sour.", p.195).

[97]"I made Eve equal with Anana-dNhura (cloud of Light).
mistress of the whole world.
When I (Manda dHaiyê) installed Adam
I appointed three uthras over him.
I set myself at the head
of the uthras whom I set over Adam and Eve": ibid, pp.118-19 (Rudolph, "Man.Sour.", p.197). Also see *CP*, pp.67, 151.

Also *The Apocalypse of Adam* from Nag Hammadi states that Adam receives a vision of three man. See MacRae, G.W., op.cit., p.159. Also see Böhlig, A., *Mysterion und Wahrheit*, Leiden (1968), p.149.

[98]Cf. *GR*, p.242.

[99]Cf. Gen 1: 26-27.

[100]Cf. Gen 2: 21ff.

hand, in another chapter of the *Ginza* it is stated that Hawwa was created in the image of Ruha, an evil figure in the Mandaean tradition.[101]

The names of three important uthras, Hibil, Šitil and Anuš, which appear both in the magical bowl texts and lead amulets and in the literary texts,[102] are based on the names of the Biblical characters, Abel, Seth and Enosh.[103] These three important figures appear in two forms in the Mandaean literature: i) They are the first generations after the earthly Adam and Eve. Hibil is called *hibil br adam*, Hibil the son of Adam, or Adam's son from Eve, though his virgin birth from Eve is described in the *Ginza*.[104] Šitil is the son of Hibil, and Anuš is the son of Šitil.[105] Therefore they relate to each other as grandfather, father and son. ii) They are also three heavenly beings, the three saviours called "uthras". The three reside in the Light-world before the earthly world is created. During this time Hibil, accompanied by his two invisible brothers, descends to the underworld in order to find out which of the creatures down there plan to wage war against the Light-world. After the creation of the earthly world the three uthras act as guardians of the three earthly epochs.[106]

As we have seen these Old Testament figures are transformed in the Mandaean tradition. Being regarded as belonging to the first links in the human genealogy in the Old Testament Hibil, Šitil and Anuš have become heavenly beings and Saviours in Mandaeism.

The Old Testament figures Noah, *nu*, and his sons, Shem, Ham and Japhet,[107] who are known as *šum*, *iam* and *iapit*, also appear in Mandaean literature. According to Mandaean tradition Noah is the person who is commanded to build an ark before the destruction of mankind by flood.[108] This is the story which appears in Genesis.[109] The name of his wife, which is not preserved in Genesis, is *nuraita*. This name is also used

---

[101]In the *Ginza* Ptahil says to Ruha and her angels: "I will form my image as man and your image as woman. We shall call the man Adam and the woman Hawwa": *GR*, p.266 (English translation from Buckley, J.J., "A Rehabilitation of Spirit Ruha in Mandaean Religion", *HR*, 22, 1982, p.67).

Also according to the *Ginza* at the death of Adam, Ruha tempts Hawwa into mourning for him. This behaviour is strongly repudiated in the Mandaean religion. See *GL*, p.438; *MII*, pp.180-81. Also see Rudolph, K., *Theogonie, Kosmogonie und Anthropogonie in den mandäischen Schriften*, pp.281f; Segelberg, E., "Old and New Testament Figures in Mandaean Version", p.230.

[102]See *MIT*, p.64; *CP*, p.108; Rudolph, K., *Die Mandäer*, I, p.81.

[103]Moreover Lady Drower has seen a connection between the Biblical Cain and the Mandaean Qin, the queen of the Darkness. She states that Qin is possibly derived from the root *qyn*, "to fabricate, work in iron", hence it refers to the Cain of the Bible. See Drower, E.S., *The Secret Adam*, p.57.

[104]"A young lad lay with Eve, whilst Adam lived with her as an unmarried man. And Eve said: 'Where does the young lad come from, who was not sown with a man's seed? The womb (of a woman) swelled not and had no fullness. His words are pleasant and his voice clear": *GR*, p.243 (Rudolph, "Man.Sour.", p.199).

[105]"Hibil begot a son, whose name was Šitil, and Šitil begot a son, whose name was Anoš": ibid, p.243 (Rudolph, "Man.Sour.", p.199).

[106]See Buckley, J.J., "The Mandaean Šitil as an Example of 'The Image Above and Below'", *Numen*, 26, 1979, pp.185f.

[107]See Gen 5:32.

[108]See *GR*, pp.28, 263; *MII*, pp.93, 258-61; Rudolph, K., *Die Mandäer*, I, p.83 n.1.

[109]Cf. Gen, 6: 9ff.

for the wives of Shem and Denanukht.[110] Among the sons of Noah Shem has a growing importance in the Mandaean tradition, whereas Ham and Japhet do not play an important role.[111]

Mandaean literature also contains reference to the Old Testament figures Abraham, Moses, David and Solomon, known as *abram* or *abraham*, *miša*, *daud* and *šlimun*.[112] Abraham does not appear in the pre-Islamic bowl texts and lead amulets as far as we know. On the other hand he is mentioned a few times in the literary texts.[113] In the *Ginza* he is called "the prophet of Ruha".[114] Moses appears once in the pre-Islamic bowl texts, where he is mentioned positively and called "Moses of the myriads",[115] but in the literary texts he never appears in a positive role, and is called "the prophet of Ruha".[116] Therefore there is an obvious difference between the early and late tradition of the Mandaeans about Moses. The same difference is also valid for other important Jewish figures, like Adonai, which we will discuss later.[117]

For David and Solomon we do not find such a polemical tradition. Both are mentioned in the bowl texts. The "seal (or seal-ring) of Solomon" is used to remove curses and to protect people against evil spirits in these magical texts.[118] David is only mentioned as the father of Solomon (in both pre-Islamic bowl texts and literary texts).[119] Also in the Ginza Solomon appears as a king whom demons and devils serve,[120] an idea which does not stem from the Old Testament. Solomon's power over the demons was known as a tradition by the first century A.D.[121]

Satan, another Old Testament figure, known as *saṭana* in Mandaean literature, appears both in the magical bowl and literary texts.[122] According to the Mandaean

---

[110]See *MD*, p.294; *CP*, p.152. Also see Rudolph, K., op.cit., I, p.83 n.1; Stroumsa, G.A.G., *Another Seed: Studies in Gnostic Mythology*, Leiden (1984), pp.54ff.
[111]See above p.63.
[112]See *MD*, pp.5, 198, 270, 468; Rudolph, K., op.cit., I, p.83.
[113]See *GR*, pp.43, 46, 410; *Jb*, p.81.
[114]*GR*, p.43.
[115]"Amen Moses of the myriads: I myself am Moses": McCullough, W.S., op.cit., p.32. Also see ibid, p.40.
[116]See *GR*, pp.43, 46; *MD*, p.270.
[117]See below pp.93f.
[118]"... Bound and sealed are the liliths, male and female, with the seal-ring of King Solomon, the son of David..": *MIT*, p.233. Also see ibid, p.261.
[119]Cf. *GR*, p.28; *MIT*, p.233.
[120]Cf. *GR*, p.28.
[121]See Josephus, *Antiquities*, VIII [*The Works of Flavius Josephus*, Whiston's translation, Revised by A.R. Shilleto, London (1889), v.II, pp.79f].
[122]See *MD*, p.311; *MIT*, p.265; McCullough, W.S., op.cit., pp.32, 42. Also Simiael, a demon of blindness, mentioned in the Mandaean literature (*GR*, p.200; *CP*, p.248) is identified with Samael, a name for Satan, which appears in Jewish literature. G. Scholem states that Simiael in the Mandaean literature is simply a variant of Samael, which is the major name of Satan in Judaism from the Amoraic period onward, and which first appears in the account of the fall of angels in the Ethiopic Book of Enoch 6, which includes the name, although not in the most important place, in the list of the leaders of the angels who rebelled against God. See Scholem, G., *Kabbalah*, New York (1974), pp.385ff. G. Quispel also pointed out the similarity between the description of Yaltabaoth in the *Apocryphon of John* and that of the King of Darkness in the Mandaean literature. See Quispel, G., "Jewish Gnosis and Mandaean Gnosticism. Some Reflections on the Writing *Brontē*", pp.117-18. In

tradition Satans are a subclass of evil spirits. However, some scholars point out the Iranian influence in the development of the concept of Satan in Jewish tradition.[123]

Some of the Jewish angels also appear in Mandaean literature. In the magical texts these angels, whose names are used for the removal of curses, are as important as the Uthras.

Gabriel, *gabr'il*, occurs both in the bowl texts and in the literary texts.[124] He is given the title *šliha*, "apostle", and identified with Ptahil, the Mandaean demiurge, and sometimes with Hibil.[125] In the *Ginza*, Gabriel is mentioned as a secret name which was given to Ptahil Uthra by Bhaq Ziwa, another name of Abatur, the Third Life.[126] In the magical texts his name is used against curses. Rudolph suggested that the figure of Gabriel was derived from Islam.[127] It is difficult to accept this view because the angel Gabriel in Islam is the bringer of revelation to the Prophet; he is not a demiurgic figure.[128] The Mandaeans probably adopted it from Jewish circles. The title *šliha*, "apostle", which is given to Gabriel in the Mandaean texts, is closely connected with the Jewish sources where *šlyḥ* was used to designate a person having the power of attorney of another, and the angels could be seen as God's "apostles".[129]

As we have mentioned, Gabriel, according to Mandaean literature, is a secret name of the demiurge. There might be a connection between this and the doctrine of the "Hidden Names" in the Jewish tradition.[130]

---

the *Apocryphon of John* Yaltabaoth, one of whose names is Saklas, "fool", is described as a lion-faced serpent whose eyes were like lightning fires which flash. See Wisse, F., "The Apocryphon of John", in *The Nag Hammadi Library in English*, General ed. J.M. Robinson, 3rd edition, Leiden (1988), p.110.

"Now the archon who is weak has three names. The first name is Yaltabaoth, the second is Saklas, and the third is Samael. And he is impious in his arrogance which is in him. For he said, 'I am God and there is no other God beside me', for he is arrogant of his strength, the place from which he had come": Wisse, F., op.cit., p.111. Also see Giversen, S. *Apocryphon Johannis*, (Acta Theologica Danica, v.V) Copenhagen (1963), pp.65, 67.

The *Ginza* gives a similar description of the King of Darkness: "That King of Darkness assumed all the forms of earthly creatures: the head of the lion, the body of the dragon, the wings of the eagle, the back of the tortoise, the hands and feet of a monster. ... But he is stupid, muddled, his ideas are confused, and he knows neither the First nor the Last... He became arrogant and exalted himself and said: 'Is there anyone who is greater than I?'": *GR*, pp.278-79 (Rudolph, "Man.Sour.", pp.160-61).

For Samael also see Stroumsa, G.A.G., op.cit., p.44 n.34. On the other hand Lidzbarski identified Simiael in Mandaean literature with Ishmael who is also mentioned in the Mandaean texts and described as the ancestor of the Arabs. See *GR*, p.200 n.1. Also see *CP*, p.248 n.4; *MD*, p.327.

[123]See *ER*, v.13, pp.81-84.

[124]See *MD*, p.73; *MIT*, p.295; McCullough, W.S., op.cit., p.32. For the appearance of Gabriel in the Old Testament see Dan 8:16; 9:21.

[125]See *GR*, pp.14, 15, 89, 98.

[126]See ibid, p.98.

[127]See Rudolph, K., *Theogonie, Kosmogonie und Anthropogonie in den mandäischen Schriften*, pp.199f.

[128]See Qur'ān, 2:97, 98.

[129]See Fossum, J.E., op.cit., pp.261-64.

[130]See ibid, p.261.

Michael and Yhadiel appear in the magical bowl texts where their names are used against the curse.[131] Michael is known as a Jewish angel in a special sense, a kind of Patron saint and celestial champion of Israel.[132]

A figure called Yophin-Yophaphin (*iupin iupapin*) often appears in the Mandaean literature, especially in both parts of the *Ginza* (*GR* and *GL*) and in the liturgical texts.[133] The name frequently occurs in a praying formula where it occupies the place of the Fourth Life.[134] Since this formula occurs several times in Mandaean literature, Lidzbarski holds it to be very old.[135] Yophin-Yophaphin is to be derived from the Jewish angel names Yophiel and Yophiphyah.[136] Yophiel is said to be one of the secret names of Metatron.[137] The earliest appearance of Metatron in Jewish literature is in the Palestinian Midrash on Deuteronomy, which dates from about 150-225 A.D.[138] The name Metatron also appears in one of the pre-Islamic Mandaean bowl texts.[139] In this text the name occurs with other Jewish names, El, Yh and Qadosh.

Raphael, *rupi*(a)*ʿi*(*i*)*l*, is also mentioned in Mandäean literature.[140] Although Raphael does not appear in the Bible he is one of the four archangels of Jewish tradition and he appears in the apocryphal *Book of Tobit* and in the *Talmud*.[141]

Some scholars, such as Pallis, claimed that the Mandaeans adopted these Old Testament figures either from Christianity or from Islamic sources.[142] They state that the Old Testament knowledge of the Mandaeans is secondhand and does not exactly fit the Old Testament.[143] Although the Mandaean tradition contains some Christian elements which we will later discuss[144] there are reasons to believe that the Mandaeans adopted these Old Testament figures from heretical Jewish circles. Most of them, figures such as Adam and the Adamites, Satan, Moses, and the angels, Gabriel, Michael and Raphiel, appear in the pre-Islamic magical bowl texts and the lead amulets, the earliest of which goes back to the third or fourth century A.D.[145] In these magical

---

131"In the name of the angels Gabriel, Michael... in the name of the angel Yhadiel": McCullough, W.S., op.cit., p.32.

132See Dan 10:13, 21; 12:1. Also see McCullough, W.S., op.cit., p.38; Fohrer, G., *History of Israelite Religion*, tr. D.A. Green, London (1972), p.374. Yhadiel appears as a personal name in the Hebrew Bible (1 Chron 5:24).

133See *MD*, p.191.

134"I adore, laud and praise the Mighty, Strange (other-worldly) Life, and the Second Life and the Third Life; and Yufin-Yufafin": *CP*, p.7. Also cf. ibid, pp.84, 155; *GR*, p.191.

135See *GR*, p.191 n.1.

136See *Jb*, p.xxvii.

137See Fossum, J.E., op.cit., p.262 n.23.

138See McCullough, W.S., op.cit., p.35. For Metatron also see *EJ*, v.11, pp.1443ff.

139"... in the name of Metatron": ibid, p.32.

140See *MD*, p.431. Also he appears in one of the lead amulets as *rupʿil*: "In the name of the angel Rūfiēl": Macuch, R., "Altmandäische Bleirollen", in *Die Araber in der Alten Welt*, IV, p.133.

141See *EJ*, v.13, p.1549.

142See Pallis, S.A., *Mandaean Studies*, pp.116ff, 127ff.

143See Yamauchi, E.M., *Gnostic Ethics and Mandaean Origins*, p.54.

144See below pp.101ff.

145For the bowl texts and lead amulets see above pp.60-61.

texts neither Christian elements nor polemics against Christianity appear. Neither Christ nor John the Baptist appears. On the other hand in the literary texts which, except for certain liturgical texts, are dated from the post-Islamic period, we see polemics against Christianity and some Christian elements.[146] Therefore it is clear that the Mandaeans had these elements before they came into contact with the Christians. With regard to the point that these figures in the Mandaean tradition are secondhand and do not fit the Old Testament, we may remark that we have here a heretical version of these figures, not an orthdox one. It is quite wrong to look for an exact Old Testament account of these figures in Mandaean literature, which is full of hatred and polemics against orthodox Judaism. The reason why these figures do not exactly fit the Old Testament is that the Mandaeans gave them new characteristics and roles according to their own tradition.

Besides these Old Testament figures Mandaean literature contains some passages adopted from or influenced by the Old Testament. The resemblance between a passage in *The Canonical Prayerbook*[147] and Psalm 22:1[148] is notable. Another passage in *The Canonical Prayerbook* is almost a translation of Psalm 114, to which is added Psalm 29:5, 9.[149] A slightly different version of the same passage is also found in the *Ginza*.[150] This is a free imitation in Mandaic rather than a quotation or paraphrase. Scholars held different opinions on how the Mandaeans adapted this text. Some, such as F.C. Burkitt and H. Lietzmann, attempted to prove that the text was borrowed from the Syriac *Peshiṭta*,[151] but they were in difficulty over some points in

---

[146]See below pp.103f.

[147]"Spirit (*ruha*) lifted up her voice,
She cried aloud and said, 'My Father, my Father
Why didst Thou create me? My God, my God,
My Allah, why hast you set me afar off
And cut me off and left me in the depths of the earth.": *CP*, p.74.

[148]"My God, my God, why have you left me?
[Why are you] far from saving me.
[From] the words of my roaring?": *Ps* 22:1.

[149]"At Thy radiance the riders were afraid,
At Thy light gates and kingdoms were troubled.
On seeing Thee the Jordan turned about,
The waves of the sea rolled back
And the islands of the sea were thrown into confusion.
Chariots were overthrown and they fell on their faces.
Cedars of Lebanon were rent, mountains shook and leaped like stags.
They opened and gave praise.
Does in the desert shed their young untimely;
The heights arise and speak in (Thy) honour.
The earth trembled and was shaken.
Jordan! whom didst thou behold that thou didst turn back?
Waves of the sea! wherefore did ye roll back?
Isles of the sea! why were ye thrown into confusion?
Chariots! wherefore did ye overturn and fall on your faces?
Cedars of Lebanon! why were ye rent?
Mountains! wherefore were ye shaken and why did ye leap like stags?
(Why) did ye open and give praise?": *CP*, p.73 (For a slightly different translation see Greenfield, J.C., "A Mandaic 'Targum' of Psalm 114", pp.24-25). Cf. Ps 29:5-9; 114: 3-7.

[150]See *GR*, pp.178-79.

[151]See Burkitt, F.C., "Note on Ginza Rabba 174", *JThS*, 29, 1928, pp.235-37; Lietzmann, H., op.cit., pp.604-5.

the text.[152] Others, such as Baumstark, Widengren and very recently Greenfield, preferred to explain the text from an origin in Jewish circles.[153] Bearing in mind the strong Jewish connection of the Mandaeans, it is more reasonable to suggest that the Mandaeans adapted these verses in Jewish circles.

In another case a passage in the *Ginza* has been compared to Isaiah 5:12.[154]

There is also a resemblance between the statement of the Old Testament about sevenfold daily prayers (Ps 119:164) and the passage in *The Canonical Prayerbook* in which the Mandaeans are called to sevenfold daily-prayer.[155]

Further, a formula of ending, *amin sala* or *amin amin sala*, is frequently used in the Mandaean magical texts, both in the bowl and literary texts.[156] Both of the words, *amin*, Amen, and *sala*, Selah, are familiar in the Hebrew Scriptures.

We also see the polemical usage of a number of words about Judaism in the Mandaean writings. One is *adunai*, "my Lord", which refers to the God of the Jews.[157] In the literary texts Adonai is described as a false God and identified with the sun, one of the evil planets.[158] On the other hand in the magical bowl texts his name is sometimes mentioned in order to remove curses.[159] In *Haran Gawaita* an interesting statement about Adonai is found. After the narration of the story that sixty thousand Naṣoraeans under the leadership of King Ardban migrated into the Median mountains the text states:

152For a critique of this theory see Greenfield, J.C., op.cit., pp.27ff.

153See Baumstark, A., "Der Mandäerpsalm Ginza R V 2- Qolasta 75", *Br.Christ.*, 35, 1938, pp.157ff; Widengren, G., "Die Mandäer", p.90; Greenfield, J.C., op.cit., pp.28ff. Greenfield states that this is an additional indication of the western, i.e. ultimately Jewish, origin of the Mandaeans. For the connection of this text to Ps 144 and Ps 29 also see Brandt, W., *Die Mandäische Religion*, pp.134-37; *Jb*, pp.xxif; Pallis, S.A., op.cit., p.133; Rudolph, K., *Die Mandäer*, I, p.107.

154See Yamauchi, E.M., *Gnostic Ethics and Mandaean Origins*, pp.54-55. Cf. *GR*, p.180.

155"Every Naṣoraean who reciteth these secret sayings will seek and find, will speak and be heard seven times daily. And seven sins will be forgiven him in the great Place of Light and Eternal Abode": *CP*, p.39.Also see Segelberg, E., "The Pitha and Mambuha Prayers to the Question of the Liturgical Development among the Mandaeans", p.467.

156See *MD*, pp.22, 312; McCullough, W.S., op.cit., p.32; *MIT*, pp.167, 283; Macuch, R., "Altmandäische Bleirollen", in *Die Araber in der Alten Welt*, IV, p.133. Also see *MII*, p.27; Yamauchi, E.S., *Gnostic Ethics and Mandaean Origins*, p.55.

157"He, Adonai, chose a people for himself and called together a community (*kništa*) for himself": *GR*, p.25 (Rudolph, "Man.Sour.", p.296).

"Adonai calls Moses from Mount Sinai and acknowledged Moses and gave him a people for himself": ibid, p.43 (Rudolph, "Man.Sour.", p.296 n.1).

In the Mandaean literature Adonai is also sometimes given the name *ṣbabut*, "hosts". See *MD*, p.389. In one of the Mandaic manuscript (*DC* 44) he is called: "*adunai ṣbabut*, the great god of Israel". See *MD*, p.389. Also see *MD*, p.7; Rudolph, K., *Die Mandäer*, I, p.82 n.1.

The term Adonai frequently occurs in the Scriptures. On the usage of the term in Jewish literature G. Fohrer says: "there was increasingly reluctance to use the name 'Yahweh', out of fear of desecrating it. Within the Holy Scriptures outside the Pentateuch the word *'ădônāy*, 'Lord', was frequently used in addition to or instead of the divine name": Fohrer, G., op.cit., p.373.

158See *GR*, pp.25, 43; *Jb*, 192.

159"And they are removed from her by the power of Adonai Yorba, the head of all the temple-spirits and the leader of all the great chariots of darkness": *MIT*, p.155. Also see ibid, pp.159, 165, 167, 195, 295; Macuch, R., "Altmandäische Bleirollen", in *Die Araber in der Alten Welt*, IV, p.137.

> "And they built cult-huts (*bimandia*) and abode in the Call of the Life and in the strength of the high King of Light until they came to their end. And they loved the Lord, that is, Adonai, until in the House of Israel there was created something which was not placed in the womb of Mary, a daughter of Moses."[160]

This statement clearly indicates that the Mandaeans recognized Adonai as a God until the coming of Christ, and supports the theory of the Jewish origin of the Mandaeans.

Other names used for the God of the Jews in Mandaean literature are *iurba*, *ʿil* and *qaduš*, which appear both in the bowl and literary texts. Yurba[161] is a name of sun-spirit, identified with Adonai, in literary texts. The term Yahu, *iahu*, also occurs in the Mandaean texts.[162] It is freely and repeatedly used as a word of power in exorcisms and magic. El or El El[163] and Qadosh[164] are also designations of the Jewish God. Although these names are identified with the sun in the literary texts, they, like Adonai, are used positively in the bowl texts.[165]

Mandaean literature also contains a number of Jewish loanwords. For example *maškna*, another name for the Mandaean cult-hut or sacred building, *mandi*, is related to the Hebrew *miškan*. Also *škinta*, the heavenly prototype of the *maškna*,[166] is related to the well known Hebrew word *šᵉkīnā*.[167]

We also find a number of place-names related to the Jewish tradition, such as *karimla* or *ṭur karimla*, Mount Carmel,[168] *libnan*, Lebanon,[169] *ʿurašlam*, Jerusalem,[170] and Bethlehem.[171] Of course names such as *iardna*, Jordan, and *hauran* (or *haurarar*), Ḥaurān, which we will discuss later,[172] are more than a memory for the Mandaeans, as Lady Drower remarks.[173]

---

[160]*HG*, p.3.
[161]See *MD*, p.191; *MIT*, pp.155, 159, 195, 249.
[162]See *MD*, p.184; *Jb*, pp.xxiiff. Also it has been suggested that *iušamin*, a mediator between good and evil (see *MD*, p.191), in the Mandaean literature is a transformation of Hebrew *yahwe shamin*. See *Jb*, pp.xxiif. *iušamin* is an ancient figure in the Mandaean tradition since besides the literary texts it appears in the earliest magical lead amulet. See *MIT*, p.253.
[163]See *MD*, p.348; McCullough, W.S., op.cit., p.32; *MIT*, p.291.
[164]See *MD*, p.399; McCullough, W.S., op.cit., p.32.
[165]"...the great El": *MIT*, p.291. "... in the name of El, Yh, ...Qadosh": McCullough, W.S. op.cit., p.32. "In the name of the angel Qadushan".
[166]See Rudolph, K., *Die Mandäer*, II, p.21.
[167]See Segelberg, E., "Trāṣa ḏ-tāga ḏ-Šišlām rabbā", pp.182-83; *MD*, 255. Segelberg also states that the term *maškna* and *škinta* indicate the western origin of the Mandaeans. Segelberg, E., op.cit., p.183. Further, it has been suggested that there is a similarity between the early non-institutionalized Jewish usage of the term *rabbī* and the Mandaean *rba*, a title for the Mandaean priests. See ibid, p.175.
[168]*MD*, p.201.
[169]Ibid, p.235.
[170]Ibid, p.346.
[171]See *GR*, p.338.
[172]See below pp.111ff.
[173]Drower, E.S., "Mandaean Polemic", p.441.

2) Legal terminology

In Mandaean literature we find narratives behind which Jewish legal terminology and practices lie. In one of the pre-Islamic Mandaean bowl texts the terminology of the Jewish divorce formula is used to drive off the lilith:

> "This have I written against you, Haldas the lilith, and thus
> have I banished you from the house and the body of Hormiz the son of Mahlapta, and from his wife Ahata
> the daughter of Dade, and from his sons and daughters, as the demons write a bill of divorce for their wives
> in truth, and may not return again and may not..... Behold! Take your bill of divorce and receive your oath, Haldas.
> O Haldas the lilith, flee, depart, escape, and remove yourself from the house, the dwelling, the mansion
> and building, from the bed and pillow of Hormiz the son of Mahlapta, and from his wife Ahata..."[174]

This basic formula is also found in some of the Aramaic incantation bowls, published by Montgomery and Gordon.[175] The legal term, *giṭa*, "divorce, bill of divorce", used in this text, occurs in the bill of divorce from Wadi Murabbaʿat (A.D.111).[176] The same divorce formula of *geṭ* is also found in the *Mishnah* (Giṭṭin 9:3).[177]

This practice of divorce also appears in *Jb*, in the narrative of the challenge of Aba Saba Zakharia, John's father, to Elizar, the high priest.[178] In this story Aba Saba Zakharia tells Elizar that Elizar's mother was a wanton, and that his father did not have the amount of 100 Staters (*ma satira zuzia*) which was needed to write her a bill of divorce; he therefore left her and did not ask for her again. The resemblance between the phrase *ʿngirta ḏ-šbuqia*, the bill of divorce, in this text and the *ʾggeret šibbuqīn*, known from the traditional formulation in *Mishnah Giṭṭin* 9:3, is notable.[179]

---

174 *MIT*, p.231.
175 See ibid, p.47.
176 See Benoit, P., J.T. Milik and R. de Vaux, *Les Grottes de Murabbaʿât*, Oxford (1961), pp.104-5.
177 "The essential formula in the bill of divorce is, 'Lo, thou art free to marry any man', R. Judah says: 'Let this be from me thy writ of divorce and letter of dismissal and deed of liberation, that thou mayest marry whatsoever man thou wilt'. The essential formula in a writ of emancipation is, 'Lo, thou art a freedwoman: lo, thou belongest to thyself'": Danby, H, *The Mishnah*, Oxford (1933), p.319.
178 *Jb*, p.79.
179 See ibid, p.79 n.5; Greenfield, J.C., "A Mandaic Miscellany", p.84. Greenfield also remarks that the sum of 100 Staters must reflect the sum of 100 or 200 *zūzīn* that was the normal amount written into the *ketubba*, depending on the bride's previous marital status. See ibid, p.84.

These two accounts may indicate that the Jewish legal formula of *geṭ* was known by the Mandaeans from early times, since it also occurs in the pre-Islamic bowl texts.

We find another detail of the Jewish law of divorce in the Mandaean literature. According to *Jb*, when Enišbai, John's mother, was told of the arrival of Yahia-Yuhana in Jerusalem, she ran out of her house without a proper cover (*kusia*). On seeing this, Aba Saba Zakharia writes her a bill of divorce, *ʿngirta ḏ-šbuqia.*[180] According to this story Enišbai was not fully wrapped up and in all likelihood had her hair uncovered, and this was enough reason for Aba Saba Zakharia for divorce. We find this ground for divorce in the Jewish law. According to *Mishnah Ketubbot* 7:6 "going out bareheaded" and "spinning in the market place" are among the grounds for divorce.[181]

3) Parallels to the ethics of Judaism

We also find points of similarity between Mandaean tradition and Judaism in ethics. For example, one of the important duties of every Mandaean is the giving of alms (*zidqa*),[182] which is also seen in Judaism.[183] According to the Mandaeans marriage and procreation are among the important duties of the members of the community:

> "Take a wife and found a family, so that the world may multiply through you."[184]

This high regard for marriage and for procreation is also seen in Judaism.[185]

We can add more points of resemblance to the ethics of Judaism. For example the Mandaeans have a similar restriction about the eating of animals:

> "Do not eat the blood of animals, not one dead, not one pregnant, not one casting its young (?), not one standing (?), and not one which a wild animal attacked. But slaughter with iron and rinse, wash, purify, cook, and eat it."[186]

---

180 Cf. *Jb*, p.117.

181 See Greenfield, J.C., op.cit., p.85. Cf. Danby, H., op.cit., p.255.

182 "If you see a prisoner who is believing and true, (then) pay the (necessary) ransom and release him. ... Give alms (*zidqa*) to the poor and be a guide (*parwanga*) to the blind": *GR*, p.17 (Rudolph, "Man.Sour.", p.291).

183 See Rudolph, K., *Die Mandäer*, I, p.85.

184 *GR*, p.16 (Rudolph, "Man.Sour.", p.292).

185 See Rudolph, K., *Die Mandäer*, I, p.85. Rudolph considers this as a clear proof of the Jewish background of the Mandaeans.

186 *GR*, p.20 (Rudolph, "Man.Sour.", p.292). Cf. Gen 9:4; Lev 17:14.

There is an obvious similarity between the ethics of the Mandaean religion and of Judaism on these points. On the other hand it is also possible to find the same characteristics in other traditions of the area, such as Christianity and Islam. For example the resemblance of the statements about the giving of alms in the *Ginza* to the passages of the New Testament and the Qur'ān is noticeable.[187] High regard for marriage and procreation is also seen in other cultures, such as Mesopotamian, Iranian and Muslim.[188] Again the restriction against eating the blood of animals and the flesh of the animals which are not positively slaughtered is also seen in the Harranian and Islamic regulations.[189]

If we therefore consider these parallels to Jewish ethics without considering also other Jewish elements in Mandaean religion and the evidences which reflect the western Jewish background of the Mandaeans, we would not treat them as peculiarly Jewish, because they occur so widely in various traditions of the Middle East. On the other hand when we bear in mind the other strong Jewish connections of the Mandaeans, we can see that it is probable that the Mandaeans have taken these regulations from Jewish circles.

4) Ritual ceremonies

Some Mandaean rituals reflect a Jewish background, in that they contain many points of resemblance to the Jewish rituals. We see many parallels between the ordination ritual of the Mandaeans, the *tarmida* initiation, and that which appears in the Jewish sources.[190] Although we find some Christian influence in the Mandaean ordination ritual, such as absolution and foot-washing, many central acts, such as enthronement, imposition of hands and kissing, are most easily derived from late Jewish or Rabbinic sources, as Segelberg demonstrates.[191] There is also an obvious

---

[187]In the *Ginza* we read: "...when you give alms, my chosen, do not give ostentatiously. If you give alms ostentatiously, do not do it a second time. If you give with your right hand, (then) do not tell it to your left. If you give with your left hand, (then) do not tell it to your right. Whoever gives alms ostentatiously, will find them blotted out and not reckoned to him": *GR*, p.17 (Rudolph, "Man.Sour.", p.291).

Identical statements to this are found in Mt 6:3 and *Qur'ān* 2:261-74. Also the giving of alms is, as Yamauchi remarked, one of the pillars of Islam. See Yamauchi, E.M., *Gnostic Ethics and Mandaean Origins*, p.56.

[188]See Yamauchi, E.M., *Gnostic Ethics and Mandaean Origins*, p.56.

[189]See *Qur'ān*, 5:3. For the Harranian regulations see below pp.184f.

[190]Rudolph suggested that the Mandaean ordination ritual, was derived from Persian sources, although he was aware of certain parallels also with Jewish ordination ritual. See Rudolph, K., *Die Mandäer*, II, pp.304ff. For description of the Mandaean ordination ritual see *MII*, pp.146-68; Segelberg, E., "The Ordination of the Mandaean *tarmida* and its Relation to Jewish and Early Christian Ordination Rites", in *Studia Patristica*, ed. F.L. Cross, v.x, Part 1, Berlin (1970), pp.419ff; idem, "Trāṣa ḏ-tāga ḏ-Šišlām rabbā", pp.184ff; Buckley, J.J., "The Making of a Mandaean Priest: The Tarmida Initiation", *Numen*, 32, 1985, pp.194-217.

[191]For a comparison between central acts of the Mandaean ordination ritual and those of the late Jewish or Rabbinic and Christian sources see Segelberg, E., "Trāṣa ḏ-tāga ḏ-Šišlām rabba", pp.201ff.

terminological affinity between Mandaean and Jewish sources in ordination ritual, like the similar usage of a number of words such as *talmīda* (Man. *tarmida*), *kwrsy*ʾ and the root *yšb* (Man. *itb*).[192]

The central Mandaean ritual, baptism in running water, is also closely connected to western, particularly Jewish, traditions. For example the fundamental features of the Mandaean baptismal rites, such as repeated baptisms, and the baptist terminology and baptist figurative discourse of Mandaeism, are also found in the baptismal and lustration rites of heretical Judaism. We will discuss the relationship between Mandaean baptism and the western baptismal cults (such as those of Qumran) in another section.[193]

5) Similarities to heterodox Judaism

Many points of similarity between Mandaeism and Jewish heterodox Judaism are notable. Besides the similarities between the baptism of the Mandaeans and that of the Qumran community we find some other resemblances between the two communities such as the use of white vestments which is found in both traditions.[194] Also well known Mandaean concepts such as *bhire zidqa*, "chosen righteous" or "proven righteous", one of the earliest self-designations of the Mandaeans, *mara ḏ-rabuta*, "Lord of Greatness", *raba*, "great", and *raza*, "mystery" or "secret", recur in the Qumran literature.[195]

It is difficult to accept Braun's theory, which attempts, on the basis of those similarities we have mentioned, to trace the Mandaeans to the Essenes, because as well as similarities there are many differences between the two traditions.[196] On the other hand the similar concepts and a number of parallel points between them indicate that both traditions had a common western background, though some of the similarities such as the use of white garments are common to many communities. White clothing also appears among the Babylonian priests.[197]

Also see idem, "The Ordination of the Mandaean *tarmida* and its Relation to Jewish and Early Christian Ordination Rites".

[192]See idem, "Trāṣa ḏ-tāga ḏ-Šišlām rabba", pp.202, 205-7. Also see idem, "The Ordination of the Mandaean *tarmida* and its Relation to Jewish and Early Christian Ordination Rites", p.422.

[193]See below pp.114ff.

[194]See Braun, F., "Le Mandéisme et la secte essénienne de Qumrân", *L'Ancien Testament et l'Orient: Études Présentées aux VI Journées Bibliques de Louvain 1954*, Louvain (1957), pp.193ff.

[195]See Rudolph, K., "Problems of a History of the Development of the Mandaean Religion", p.231; idem, "War der Verfasser der Oden Salomos ein 'Qumran-Christ'?" Ein Beitrag zur Diskussion um die Anfänge der Gnosis", *RQ*, 16, 1964, pp.532-39. Also see Quispel, G., "Jewish Gnosis and Mandaean Gnosticism. Some Reflections on the Writing *Bronté*", pp.107-8; *MD*, pp.53, 251, 417, 420. Rudolph also notes that there is a similar tradition in the Samaritan tradition. See Rudolph, K., "Problems of a History of the Development of the Mandaean Religion", p.231 n.106.

[196]For differences between the Mandaeans and Essenes see Yamauchi, E.M., op.cit., pp.57ff.

[197]See Yamauchi, E.M., op.cit., p.57.

There are also some parallels between Mandaeism and Samaritanism. Many terms and concepts are found in both Samaritan and Mandaean sources. One of these is "the Life", which is used as a name of God in both traditions.[198] Almost all the Mandaean texts, liturgies, magical texts and others, begin with the formula: "In the name of the Great Life".[199] Since the formula appears in even the earliest magical lead amulets and almost all of the liturgical texts it must be quite ancient. On the other hand, the title "the Life" in Samaritanism can also be transferred to the Law.[200]

Moreover such expressions as "the Word of Life" and "the Treasure of Life" occur in both Samaritan and Mandaean literature.[201]

There is also a connection between the usage of the term *qušṭa* in Samaritanism and *kušṭa* in Mandaeism. In Samaritan tradition *qušṭa* is a name of God.[202] In Mandaean tradition we find three kinds of usage of the term *kušṭa*: (i) in the literature it is used as a term which means "truth", "good-faith", "faithfulness", etc.; (ii) it is used for the ritual hand-clasp during the sacraments such as baptism and marriage; (iii) it is often personified as a celestial being.[203]

Another point of resemblance between the Mandaean and Samaritan tradition is seen in the usage of the term *šliha*, "apostle". In Mandaeism the title "Apostle" is used as a designation of the Saviour who is sent to earth. In the *Ginza* the Saviour speaks:

> "I am the Apostle of Light whom the Great One has sent into this world. I am the true Apostle with whom there is no lie."[204]

"Apostle" occurs as a pregnant title of Moses, the Saviour, in Samaritanism.[205] In Mandaeism, correspondingly, "prophet" is a synonym of "apostle", since the Jewish

---

[198]See Widengren, G., *The Ascension of the Apostle and the Heavenly Book (King and Saviour III)*, (UUA, 7) Uppsala-Leipzig (1950), p.57; Fossum, J.E., op.cit., p. 157.

[199]See *MD*, p.143.

[200]See Fossum, J.E., op.cit., p.157.

[201]See Widengren, G., op.cit., p.57. Rudolph also remarks that in the Mandaean literature the word *qaiim*, "constant, stable", is used in connection with "the Life", and he points out the parallel usage of *qʿim* in Samaritanism. See Rudolph, K., *Die Mandäer*, I, pp.173-74 n.4; *MD*, p.400. Also see Fossum, J.E., op.cit., p.157.

[202]See Fossum, J.E., op.cit., p.156. Fossum states that there can be no doubt that the Samaritan and the Mandaean terms are related.

[203]For the usage of *kušṭa* in Mandaean literature see Sundberg, W., *Kushṭa. A Monograph on a Principal Word in Mandaean Texts, I. The Descending Knowledge*, Lund (1953), pp.15-41; *MD*, pp.209-11.

[204]*GR*, p.58 (Translation from Fossum, J.E., op.cit., p.156). As we have mentioned earlier the title "Apostle" is also used for the demiurge Gabriel in the Mandaean literature. See above p.90. Widengren compares the term "the true Apostle" in the Mandaean literature with "the true Prophet" in Samaritanism. See Widengren, G., op.cit., pp.56f.

[205]For "Apostle" as a title of Moses in Samaritan literature see Fossum, J.E., op.cit., pp.145ff.

prophets are said to "call themselves prophets and say: 'We are apostles'" in the *Ginza*.[206]

The name of the Mandaean cult-hut, *maškna*,[207] is derived from *mškn*, the desert sanctuary, in the Samaritan tradition.[208] It was erected on Mt.Gerizim but hidden by God when Eli disrupted the cult at Shechem and moved to Shiloh, the place of worship before Jerusalem.[209]

As we have seen, many Samaritan terms and ideas are appear in Mandaean tradition.[210] Concerning the question of how these terms and ideas entered into Mandaean tradition we can say that the Mandaeans (or proto-Mandaeans) may have adopted them already in the West before their migration to the East.

We have earlier mentioned some parallels between the Mandaeans and the Jewish heretics of the tannaitic and amoraic periods, the so-called *minim* in the Rabbinic literature.[211] A parallelism is also seen between the Mandaean doctrine of the role of the alphabet in creation and that found in the *Sefer Yeṣirah*,[212] a Book of Creation composed between the third and sixth centuries.[213] According to the *Sefer Yeṣirah* the elements of the world are sought in the ten elementary and primordial numbers and the twenty-two letters of the Hebrew alphabet.[214] These letters are of three types: mothers, doubles and singles. According to some versions of the *Sefer Yeṣirah* each letter corresponds to particular parts and organs of the body.[215] A similar

---

[206]See *GR*, p.44. Fossum further points out the occurrence of the term "the Apostle of the Truth" in the Mandaean literature and remarks that this is the title of Moses in *Memar Marqa*. See Fossum, J.E., op.cit., p.156. Also see *GR*, p.56.

[207]In the Mandaean literature the term *maškna* usually designates the Mandaean cult-hut, but it, however, sometimes is used for the pagan temples. See *MD*, p.255. Other names, used for the Mandaean cult-hut in the Mandaean sources, are *mandi* and *škinta*. The term *manda* or *mandi*, which is used as another name of the Mandaean cult-hut, is accepted as a late name. See *MD*, p.247; Fossum, J.E., op.cit., p.158.

[208]See *Jb*, pp.xxf; Adam, A., *Die Psalmen des Thomas und das Perlenlied als Zeugnisse vorchristlicher Gnosis*, (*BZNW*, 24) Berlin (1959), p.79; Fossum, J.E., op.cit., p.158. Fossum states that this was one piece of evidence in particular which showed that the Mandaeans had appropriated Samaritan tradition.

[209]Fossum, J.E., op.cit., p.158.

[210]Besides these similarities mentioned above Rudolph points out other terms and ideas occurring in both Mandaeism and Samaritanism such as the concepts "the Tree of Life" and "Living Water". See Rudolph, K., "Randerscheinungen des Judentums und das Problem der Entstehung des Gnostizismus", *KAIROS*, 9, 1967, p.116 (*Gnosis und Gnostizismus*, ed. K. Rudolph, Darmstadt (1975), p.789). Also see Fossum, J.E., op.cit., p.157 n.233.

[211]See above p.87. For *minim* see Scholem, G., *Kabbalah*, p.12; Cohn-Sherbok, D., "The Mandaeans and Heteredox Judaism", pp.148-49.

[212]See Drower, E.S., *The Secret Adam*, pp.17ff; Cohn-Sherbok, D., "The Alphabet in Mandaean and Jewish Gnosticism", pp.227-32.

[213]See Scholem, G., *Major Trends in Jewish Mysticism*, p.76.

[214]"God has formed, weighed, transmuted, composed, and created with these twenty-two letters every living being, and every soul yet uncreated": *Sefer Yeṣirah*, 2.2 (cited in Cohn-Sherbok, D., op.cit., p.230).

[215]See Cohn-Sherbok, D., op.cit., pp.230-31.

doctrine of the role of alphabet in creation and its relation with the various parts and organs of the body of man is found in Mandaean literature.[216]

B. Christian elements and influence

The relationship between Mandaeism and Christianity has often been discussed by both Mandaean and New Testament scholars. Two important problems have been at the centre of discussion: whether Mandaeism was a pre-Christian tradition or post-Christian and, closely connected to this, the relationship between the Fourth Gospel and Mandaean doctrine.

From the beginning of this century a number of scholars, such as Lidzbarski, Reitzenstein, Bultmann and Schweizer, argued for a pre-Christian existence of the Mandaeans (or proto-Mandaeans) in Palestine.[217] Some of them, such as Reitzenstein and Bultmann, argued for Mandaean influences in Christianity, especially in the Fourth Gospel. The leading Mandaean scholars of the second half of the century, Drower, Macuch and Rudolph, also agreed with the pre-Christian existence of the Mandaeans and some Mandaean gnostic influence upon Christianity.[218] On the other hand some New Testament scholars, such as Burkitt, Petermann, Lietzmann and Casey, opposed the idea of pre-Christian existence of Mandaeism and argued for the Christian origin of the Mandaeans.[219]

In fact, one of the important bases of the arguments of these scholars was concerned with the nature and origin of Gnosticism. From early times the Church Fathers considered Gnosticism as a movement within Christian circles, or a Christian heresy. They regarded Simon Magus as the father of all heresy.[220] Consequently, the existence of a pre-Christian Gnosticism was certainly rejected, and traditionally Gnostic movements have been treated by Christian New Testament scholars as Christian heresies.[221] On the other hand from the beginning of the century many modern scholars turned to other sources, such as Hellenic, Babylonian, Egyptian and Iranian, for the

---

216See *ATŠ*, pp.181ff; *ARR*, p.9. Also see Drower, E.S., *The Secret Adam*, pp.17-20; Cohn-Sherbok, D., op.cit., pp.227-30. Cohn-Sherbok states that: "These striking similarities suggest that the concept of the creative power of the alphabet stems from a common source, and there is no doubt that such a belief was deeply rooted in early rabbinic Judaism": ibid, p.232.

Lady Drower, however, remarks that the origin of this doctrine may be sought in schools of thought influenced by Pythagoras. She also says: "In all gnostic writings the 'Word' (Logos) is full of creative power, for the act of pronunciation was the act of creation": Drower, E.S., op.cit., p.17.

217See above pp.8ff.

218See above pp.10ff.

219See above p.9.

220See Jonas, H., *The Gnostic Religion*, Beacon Hill (1958), pp.32, 103.

221See Yamauchi, E.M., "Jewish Gnosticism? The Prologue of John, Mandaean Parallels, and the Trimorphic Protennoia", p.497.

origins of Gnosticism, and argued for the pre-Christian existence of Gnostic movements.[222]

Scholars such as Bultmann, who accepted the existence of a pre-Christian Gnosticism, considered Mandaean texts in particular as an example of the earliest Gnostic literature. Also scholars such as Rudolph and Jonas compared the Mandaean gnostic tradition to that which appears in the various sources, such as *The Odes of Solomon*, *The Apocalypse of Adam* and *The Hymn of the Pearl*.[223]

Scholars who accepted Mandaeism as a pre-Christian gnostic tradition compared some of the characteristics of the Mandaeans to those of Christianity, especially in the Fourth Gospel. They suggested that the Gospel of John contained a number of Mandaean elements, such as the figure of a revealer, and gnostic language and imagery.[224] The redeemer figure in Christianity has also been examined by some scholars in the context of pre-Christian gnosticism and Mandaeism. Bultmann stated that one of the purest extant forms of the early oriental Gnostic Redeemer myth is preserved in the Mandaean literature.[225] Rudolph remarked:

> "I am hence of the well-grounded conviction that the gnostic redeemer myth is of pre-Christian origin. ... In my opinion Paul and the anonymous author of the Gospel of John presuppose a gnostic-type doctrine of the redeemer; they use its terminology, but also oppose it. For them the mythological redeemer or revealer has been transcended by the historical redeemer Jesus Christ."[226]

In a review of the E.M. Yamauchi's *Gnostic Ethics and Mandaean Origins* Macuch stated:

---

[222]Of Simon Magus H. Jonas remarked: "He was a contemporary of the apostles and a Samaritan, and Samaria was notoriously unruly in matters of religion and regarded with suspicion by the orthodox... Simon was not a dissident Christian, and if the Church Fathers cast him in the role of the arch-heretic, they implicitly admitted that Gnosticism was not an inner-Christian phenomenon": Jonas, H., op.cit., p.103.

A number of scholars, such as J. Daniélou, E. Haenchen, W. Schmithals and H.-M. Schenke, have accepted that Simon was a Gnostic before he made contact with Christianity. Also Daniélou has remarked that the Simonian gnosis was an example of the pre-Christian Jewish Gnosticism. See Daniélou, J., *The Theology of Jewish Christianity*, tr. and ed. J.A. Baker, (The Development of Christian Doctrine before the Council of Nicaea, v.1) London (1964), p.73; Yamauchi, E.M., *Pre-Christian Gnosticism*, p.61. Also Lady Drower has compared the Simonian gnosticism to Mandaeism and remarked some parallel points between the two traditions. See Drower, E.S., *The Secret Adam*, pp.89f.

[223]See Jonas, H., op.cit., pp.113, 116ff; Rudolph, K., "War der Verfasser der Oden Salomos ein 'Qumran-Christ'?", pp.523-55; idem, "Stand und Aufgaben in der Erforschung des Gnostizism", in *Tagung für allgemeine Religionsgeschichte*, ed. Th. Lohmann, 1963 (Sonderheft der Wissenschaftlichen Zeitschrift der Friedrich-Schiller-Universität Jena. 13, 1964), pp.89-102 (*Gnosis und Gnostizismus*, ed. K. Rudolph, Darmstadt (1975), pp.510-53).

[224]See Bultmann, R., op.cit., p.8; Schweizer, E., *Ego Eimi*, Göttingen (1965), p.37.

[225]See Yamauchi, E.M., *Pre-Christian Gnosticism*, p.29.

[226]Cited in Robinson, J.M. and H. Koester, *Trajectories Through Early Christianity*, Philadelphia (1971), p.263. Cf. Rudolph, K., "Stand und Aufgaben in der Erforschung des Gnostizism", pp.93f.

"Das Johannesevangelium ist mit 'mandäischen' Elementen so saturiert, daß sie nur von einem Blinden nicht gesehen werden."[227]

In this limited study we will not enter the problem of the relationship between the Fourth Gospel and Mandaean doctrine which needs further research.

a. Anti-Christian polemics

Before discussing the Christian elements and influences in Mandaeism we will examine the anti-Christian feelings in the Mandaean tradition. In fact, polemics against Christianity are not so strong as the polemics against Judaism. Neither polemics against Christianity nor figures and ideas from Christianity appear in the pre-Islamic magical bowl texts and lead amulets, in which, on the contrary, a number of Jewish figures and ideas are found, as we have earlier noted.[228] Neither Jesus nor John the Baptist appears in these early texts. Also in the earlier Mandaean books and in priestly commentaries there is little polemic against Christianity. Most of the polemic is directed against the Jews.[229] This fact suggests that the Christian influence in Mandaeism is later than the Jewish.

Yamauchi once stated that the strongest criticism that the Mandaeans had of the Christians was that against the celibacy of monks and nuns.[230] In fact, when we examine the Mandaean texts we see that the most important anti-Christian feeling is about Jesus Christ. The chief accusation against Jesus in the earlier books is the falsity of his messiahship.[231] Jesus, *ʿišu*, is always described as a "false (or pseudo-) messiah", "a liar" and "the prophet of the Jews", and identified with the evil planet Mercury, *nbu*. Therefore the Mandaeans are commanded not to listen to or believe in him:

"Beware, my friends of Jesu, the pseudo-Messiah,

227Macuch, R., "Gnostische Ethik und die Anfänge der Mandäer", p.267.

228See above p.83.

229Drower, E.S., "Mandaean Polemic", p.441.

230See Yamauchi, E.M., *Gnostic Ethics and Mandaean Origins*, p.41. Also see *GR*, pp.67, 226. On the other hand Lady Drower remarks that it is only late Mandaean polemic which tilts against Christian monasticism and attitudes towards sex. See Drower, E.S., op.cit., p.443.

231See Drower, E.S., op.cit., p.443. Also Lady Drower points out the polemical usage of the verbal root *mšh* in the Mandaean literature. She states that the Mandaeans do not use this verbal root to mean 'to anoint', because the word *mšiha* (anointed one, Messiah) is derived from it. In the baptismal liturgy the verb used to describe this rite is *mša*, not *mšh*. She also remarks that when referring to the Christian baptism the Mandaeans use the term *amd*, not *ṣba* because *ṣba* is used for the Mandaean baptism. See Drower, E.S., op.cit., p.440; idem, "Adam and the Elkasaites", p.410.

And of those who misconstrue appearances."[232]

In the *Ginza* Jesus is called "Christ the Roman":

"After John the world will continue in lies and Christ the Roman will split the peoples; the twelve seducers roam the world."[233]

In *The Book of John* he is also called "Christ-Paulis".[234] Christ is further accused of falsifying the message of John after being baptized by John in the Jordan and becoming wise through John's wisdom:

"Jesus Christ comes (*ʿšu mšiha*), moves about in humility, is baptized with the baptism of John, and becomes wise through John's wisdom. He then proceeds to pervert the word of John and change the baptism of Jordan, altering the words of kušṭa, and summoning wickedness and falsehood into the world."[235]

Finally the Mandaeans consider the Holy Spirit, *ruha d̠-qudša*, as the mother of Jesus and an evil female demon, identified with Dlibat or the planet Venus.[236]

The New Testament scholar Burkitt claimed that the attitude of the Mandaeans against Jesus is based on the beliefs of heretical Christian sects. He states that we ought not to be too much influenced by the attitude of the Mandaeans against Christ.[237]

It is difficult to accept this view. In fact, as we have earlier discussed, the Mandaeans oppose the idea of the messiahship of Jesus completely and this is the most important anti-Christian characteristic of the Mandaean tradition. It is impossible to find one single positive pronouncement about Jesus in the whole Mandaean literature. On the other hand in the Christian-gnostic texts, such as the *Evangelium Veritatis* and

---

[232]*CP*, p.119. "And Christ (*mšiha*), the prophet (*nbiha*) of the Jews, appeared. He summoned the planets with a cry, he brought them over to his side; each one fights for him. Seven dēvs, the seducers, seduce all the children of Adam. ... The dēvs of Nbu-Christ (*mšiha*) make an insidious attack upon mankind... they seize the body and torment spirit and souls": *GR*, pp.28-29 (Rudolph, "Man.Sour.", p.298).

"His name is Immanuel (*Amunēl*) and he called himself 'Jesus the Saviour' (*išu mahiana*). ... He appears to you and says to you: 'Come, stand beside me and you shall not be burned.' Do not believe him, for he practises sorcery and treachery. ... He says: 'I am God (*alaha*), and the son of God, I have been sent here by my father.' And he says (further) to you: 'I am the first messenger (*šliha*), I am Hibil-Ziwa, I have come from the heights.' Give him no recognition, for he is not Hibil-Ziwa": ibid, p.29 (Rudolph, "Man.Sour.", p.298-99). Also see *GR*, p.50.

[233]Ibid, p.51 (Rudolph, "Man.Sour.", p.308).

[234]See *Jb*, p.108.

[235]*GR*, p.51 (Rudolph, "Man.Sour.", p.308).

[236]See *GR*, p.52; *MD*, pp.428-29.

[237]See Burkitt, F., *Church and Gnosis*, pp.108ff.

Evangelium Philippi, Jesus is accepted as the mediator or one of the mediators, or prophets. Even in Manichaeism Jesus is accepted among the revealers.[238]

On the problem of when the anti-Christian and anti-Jesus feelings entered into the Mandaean tradition we can say that the Mandaeans lived in close contact with Syrian Christianity for a long time and that during that time they probably accepted some Christian traditions, but as soon as the Christian mission became more conscious, more active and perhaps more orthodox, Mandaean consciousness about Christian tradition changed, and anti-Christian and anti-Jesus pronouncements appeared.[239]

b. Possible Christian influences

Besides these polemics against Christianity Mandaean tradition contains some Christian elements and influences. The most important is the acceptance of Sunday, *habšaba*, the first day of the week, as a holy day, instead of Saturday.[240]

> "I did not forget baptism
> or my pure sign
> I did not forget Sunday,
> and the dawn of the day damned me not."[241]

The stories of John the Baptist, particularly the confrontation between John and Christ may have been adopted by the Mandaeans in heretical Christian circles. At the beginning of the century some scholars, such as Reitzenstein,[242] based their theories about the origin of the Mandaeans and the relationship between Mandaeism and the other traditions, especially Christianity, on the idea that John the Baptist was a central figure in the Mandaean tradition, but, today, it is completely accepted by Mandaean scholars that John the Baptist is not a central figure in Mandaeism.[243]

---

[238]See Segelberg, E., "Old and New Testament Figures in Mandaean Version", p.238.

[239]See ibid, p.239.

[240]See Rudolph, K., *Gnosis*, p.360; Segelberg, E., op.cit., p.238; idem, "The Mandaean Week and the Problem of Jewish Christianity and Mandaean Relationship", in *Judéo-christianisme: recherches historiques et théologiques offerts en hommage au Cardinal Jean Daniélou*, eds. B. Gerhardsson et al., Paris (1972), pp.280ff. On the other hand Lady Drower once suggested that the Mandaeans probably inherited their tradition from the Iranians, since the special honour for Sunday was also seen in the Mithra cult. See *MII*, p.96 n.7.

[241]*Jb*, p.83 (Rudolph, "Man.Sour.", pp.309-10). Sunday is often personified as a celestial being in the Mandaean literature. See *MD*, p.115.

[242]See above p.8.

[243]See Drower, E.S., *The Secret Adam*, p.101; Segelberg, E., "Old and New Testament Figures in Mandaean Version", p.236; Rudolph, K., *Gnosis*, p.363; idem, *Mandaeism*, p.4. On John stories in the Mandaean literature C.H. Kraeling states: "...the Mandaic stories concerning John merely repeat the facts of Gospel narrative, clothing them in a garment of legendary expatiation such as one finds in the Syriac Life of John the Baptist recently published by Mingana": Kraeling, C.H., op.cit., p.213.

John, *iahia iuhana*, does not appear in the pre-Islamic bowl texts. Also he hardly appears in the priestly documents such as *The Canonical Prayerbook* and *Alf Trisar Šuialia*. On the other hand the figure of John and the confrontation between John and Christ mainly appear in *The Book of John* and *Haran Gawaita*, both of which are accepted as post-Islamic. As we have earlier mentioned, the Arabic form of the name of John, *iahia* (Ar. يحيى), in the Mandaean literature also suggests that John may have been inserted into the Mandaean tradition at a late date.[244]

Another point of influence from Christianity is found in the *Ginza* in connection with the description of Anuš Uthra, one of the three celestial beings (the others being Hibil and Šitil):

> "On the contrary, Enoš (or: Anoš)-Uthra comes and proceeds to Jerusalem, clothed as with a garment in water-clouds. ...He emerges and comes during the years of Pilate, king of the world. Enoš-Uthra comes into the world with the power of the sublime King of Light. He heals the sick and opens (the eyes of) the blind, makes the lepers clean, raises the crippled and the lame so that they can move, he makes the deaf and dumb to speak and gives life to the dead (cf. Matt. 11:5). He gains believers among the Jews and shows them that there is death and life, darkness and light, error and truth (*šrara*). He leads the Jews forth in the name of the sublime King of Light. 360 prophets (*nbihê*) go forth from the place Jerusalem."[245]

These statements in the *Ginza* come after the polemical statements against Jesus whom the Mandaeans are commanded not to recognize. From this definition of Anuš Uthra some New Testament scholars such as Burkitt and Dodd, who claimed a Christian origin of the Mandaeans, suggested that Anuš Uthra was the true Jesus in the Mandaean tradition, adopted from Marcionite and Manichaean teaching about Jesus.[246] In other words, they claimed that the Mandaeans rejected the Jesus of the developed post-Nicene Church, whom they called "Jesus Christ", "pseudo-messiah", "lying messiah" and "the son of the Holy Spirit", but accepted Anuš Uthra as a true Jesus. In fact this highly hypothetical theory is closely associated with the idea of the Christian origin of the Mandaeans. As we have discussed earlier, the Christian influence upon Mandaeism is later than the Jewish one. In the magical bowl texts and lead amulets neither polemics against Jesus and Christianity nor Christian influence appears. As we

---

[244]See above p.56.

[245]*GR*, pp.29-30 (Rudolph, "Man.Sour.", p.299). Also see *Jb*, p.243.

[246]See Burkitt, F.C., *Church and Gnosis*, pp.110ff; idem, "The Mandaeans", pp.229ff; Dodd, C.H., op.cit., pp.125-26.

have earlier remarked the main polemic against Jesus is about his doctrine, his messiahship. The Mandaeans never identify Anuš Uthra with Jesus; and they are not simply Christian heretics, but, as Yamauchi pointed out, anti-Christians.[247]

On the other hand the similarity between the description of Anuš Uthra in this text quoted above and the statements of the miracles of Jesus in the New Testament is striking.[248] In Mandaean literature both Anuš Uthra and John the Baptist are described with almost the same characteristics:

> "Then Yahia-Yuhana took the jordan and the medicine Water (*of Life*)... and he cleansed lepers, opened (*the eyes of*) the blind and lifted the broken (*maimed*) to walk on their feet...by the strength of the lofty King of Light."[249]

This story is probably a polemic against Christianity in which the miracles of Jesus are attributed to Anuš and sometimes to John the Baptist.[250] Obviously this story of miracles was adopted in Christian circles and given a Mandaean shape during the time when the Mandaeans adopted the legends about John from heretical Christianity.

Some resemblances between the ritual ceremonies of the Mandaeans and those of the Christians are also notable. We have earlier mentioned that some actions in the Mandaean ordination ceremonies, such as absolution and the washing of the feet, may be an influence from Christian tradition.[251] As we will later examine,[252] there are also some similarities between the central acts of the Mandaean baptism and those of the ancient western Christian baptismal rite preserved by Hippolytus.

Some scholars have also seen a connection between the figure of *miriai* in the Mandaean literature and the figures of the Virgin Mary and Mary Magdalene of the Christian tradition.[253] It is difficult to accept the identification of Miriai with Mary, the mother of Jesus, who is called *miriam* or *mariam* in the Mandaean literature.[254] Miriai is a Jewish princess, converted to Mandaeism.[255] In *The Book of John* she is

---

[247] Yamauchi, E.M., "The Present Status of Mandaean Studies", p.89.
[248] Cf. Mt 11:4-5.
[249] *HG*, p.7.
[250] See Drower, E.S., *The Secret Adam*, pp.39-40; *HG*, p.5 n.7.
[251] See above p.97.
[252] See above pp.115-16.
[253] Of the Mandaean tradition W.F. Albright says: "the figure of Miryai, the Virgin Mary, has, for example, been assimilated to the Babylonian Sabitu-Sambethe": Albright, W.F., *From the Stone Age to Christianity*, p.338. On the other hand Burkitt identifies Mandaean Miriai with Mary Magdalene of the New Testament and claims that she has no doubt come into the Mandaean mythology through the Marcionite Gospel, Burkitt, F.C., *Church and Gnosis*, pp.119, 122. Cf. Mt 27:56; Mk 16:1; Lk 8:2, 24:10. However, Buckley, in a recent article, identified Miriai with Jesus' mother Mary, Buckley, J.J., "The Mandaean Appropriation of Jesus' Mother Miriai", p.182.
[254] See *MD*, pp.254, 270;Drower, E.S., "Mandaean Polemic", p.443.
[255] See Chapter IV n.73.

mentioned with the mother of John, weeping with her.[256] On the other hand it is possible that the Mandaeans adopted the figure of Mary Magdalene in the Christian tradition and gave it a Mandaean shape, as they did in the case of John.

As we have seen Mandaeism contains a number of elements from various traditions. Among them Jewish influence and elements are obviously the most important, since we find many Jewish concepts and ideas both in the magical bowl texts and lead amulets and in the literary texts. We have also a number of similarities between Mandaeism and various heretical sects of Judaism such as Samaritanism and the Essenes. On the one hand we see strong polemics against official Judaism and against the beliefs and rituals of the Jews, but, on the other, we sometimes find different, more positive, traditions about some important Jewish figures such as Adonai and Moses. Even in *Haran Gawaita* the Naṣoraeans (Mandaeans) are once mentioned as the worshippers of Adonai. If we take all of these points together with (i) the famous Mandaean tradition about their early history, that their ancestors lived in Palestine until they were persecuted by the (official) Jews and migrated into the East, and (ii) the other evidences which, as we will see later,[257] point to a western homeland for the Mandaeans, we clearly see that the Jewish elements in Mandaeism do not simply refer to an ordinary Jewish influence upon Mandaeism but demonstrate the origin of the Mandaeans in Jewish circles.

We also find Iranian and ancient Mesopotamian elements in Mandaean religion. Some of these elements may have been adopted by the Mandaeans already in the West. After their migration from the West, first to the mountainous lands of Media and then to south Babylonia, the Mandaeans lived for a long time in an area open to Iranian and ancient Mesopotamian influence, where they adopted some Iranian and Babylonian elements.

Finally we see some Christian influences in Mandaean doctrine, presumably taken from Syrian Christianity after the migration to the East. The Christian elements do not appear in the early texts. Presumably when the Christian mission became more active and orthodox in an area where the Mandaeans lived the Mandaean attitude to Christianity changed and strong polemics against Christian concepts and ideas were produced.

256"When Yahyā thus spake, the two women weep. Mirjai and Enishbai weep, and for both tears flow": *Jb*, p.85 (Translation from Mead, G.R.S., op.cit., p.44).
257See below pp.109ff.

3. Some characteristics of the Mandaean tradition which reflect the western connection of the Mandaeans

We have seen that the Mandaean written and oral tradition points to Palestine as the original homeland of the Mandaeans, where their ancestors were persecuted and forced to migrate to the Median mountains. We have also seen that a number of Jewish elements in Mandaean literature support their tradition about their western origin. In this section we will examine some particular characteristics of the Mandaeans, such as various technical terms (like *naṣurai* and *iardna*) and baptism, which suggest a western origin of the Mandaeans.

A. Important technical terms

Mandaean literature contains some essential technical terms which refer to the western background and origin of the Mandaeans.[258] These terms are quite important in the study of Mandaeism since they belong to its earliest phase.

a. Naṣoraeans

In the Mandaean literature the term *naṣuraiia*, "Naṣoraeans", which comes from the verbal root *nṣr* (=Heb., Ar. *naẓara*, Akk. *naṣāru*), "to observe, to keep, to guard, to mutter incantations",[259] appears in two kinds of usage. Firstly, it is one of the earliest self-designations of the Mandaeans.[260] We generally see this term referring to the Mandaeans in the texts concerning their history, like *Haran Gawaita*. Secondly the term is used for a certain group of the Mandaeans, those who possess secret knowledge and rites. At the same time the Mandaean laity are called *mandaiia*, "Mandaeans", which is of more recent date.[261] In the texts, not only historical persons such as John the Baptist but also heavenly beings such as Hibil, Šitil and Anuš, who symbolize the faith of the Mandaeans, are called "the Naṣoraeans".[262]

---

[258]See *Jb*, pp.xviff; *GR*, pp.viff; Macuch, R., "Anfänge der Mandäer", pp.82ff.
[259]See *MD*, p.306; Drower, E.S., "The Mandaeans To-day", p.438; idem *The Secret Adam*, p.xiv; Segelberg, E., "Trāṣa ḏ-tāga ḏ-Šišlām rabbā", p.178.
[260]See Rudolph, K., *Gnosis*, p.343. Also the term *naṣaruta*, "Naṣoraeism", is used for the doctrine of the Mandaeans:
"Your weapon is Naṣoreism (*naṣaruta*),
the true words which have come to you from the Place of Light": *GL*, p.508 (Rudolph, "Man.Sour.", p.223).
[261]See Rudolph, K., *Gnosis*, p.343; Drower, E.S., *The Secret Adam*, p.ix. Lady Drower once remarked that the word Naṣurai indicated a person skilled in exorcism of evil spirits, interpretation of omens, in healing arts and knowledge of white magic. See Drower, E.S., "The Mandaeans of To-day", p.438.
[262]"They are our brothers Hibil, Šitil, and Anoš, the Nāṣōraeans, the perfect, the elect righteous (*bhirê zidqa*), who did not forget rewards and alms (*zidqa*)": *GL*, p.424 (Rudolph, "Man.Sour.", p.300). Also see Drower, E.S., op.cit., p.438.

On the origin of the term *naṣuraiia* C.H. Dodd pointed out the Arabic term *al-naṣārā*, which, in the Qur'ān, regularly refers to the Christians.[263] Dodd claimed that the Mandaeans adopted the name, *al-naṣārā*, by which the Christians were known to the Muslim conquerors in order to secure status under Muslim rule.[264] Dodd's explanation is, of course, connected with his theory of the Christian origin of the Mandaeans. In fact the name *naṣuraiia* is much earlier than the Qur'ān and the usage of the term in the Mandaean literature clearly shows that the Mandaic term is older than Arabic *al-naṣārā*.[265] We must also bear in mind that the Qur'ān distinguishes the Christians *(al-naṣārā)* and the Sabians *(al-ṣābi'ūn)*, who, as we have discussed earlier,[266] are the Mandaeans.

On the other hand Epiphanius, a Christian Church Father from the fourth century A.D., speaks of the existence of a pre-Christian Jewish sect, Nasaraeans (Nasaraioi), who lived in Gilead, Bashan and the Transjordan, and he distinguishes the Nasaraeans from the Christian or Judeo-Christian sect of Nazoraeans (Nazōraioi).[267] Of the first Christians he says:

> "They did not call themselves Nasaraeans either; the Nasaraean sect was before Christ, and did not know Christ."[268]

According to the account of Epiphanius the characteristics of the pre-Christian Nasaraeans are that: (1) they rejected the sacrificial system, notions of fate and astrology, (2) abstained from the eating of meat, (3) observed the Sabbath and (4) practiced circumcision.[269]

Some scholars, such as Lady Drower and Macuch, have seen a connection between the term Naṣoraeans, one of the early self-designations of the Mandaeans, and

---

Besides the Mandaean sources Iranian and Manichaean sources too mention the Naṣoraeans, probably referring to the Mandaeans. In the *Kartīr* inscription from Naqsh-i Rustam (from about 275 A.D.) the Naṣoraeans are mentioned among those who perished. Also in the Manichaean *Kephalaia* there are some arguments with the Naṣoraeans. See below pp.120ff.

263 See Dodd, C.H., op.cit., p.124 n.2. Some scholars also pointed out the Akkadian phrase *nāṣir piristi*, "guardian of mysteries". See Zimmern, H., "Nazoräer", *ZDMG*, 74, 1920, p.433; Yamauchi, E.M., *Gnostic Ethics and Mandaean Origins*, p.60.

264 Dodd, C.H., op.cit., p.124 n.2.

265 See *MD*, p.285.

266 See Chapter II.

267 See Williams, F., *The Panarion of Epiphanius of Salamis. Book I (Sects 1-46)*, (Nag Hammadi Studies, XXXV, vol. ed. J.M. Robinson) Leiden (1987), pp.42ff, 116. Also see Drower, E.S., *The Secret Adam*, pp.xiv, 94ff; Macuch, R., "Anfänge der Mandäer", pp.98-99; Black, M., *The Scrolls and Christian Origins: Studies in the Jewish Background of the New Testament*, London (1961), pp.68ff.

Of the usage of the name Nasaraeans for some pre-Christian Jews Lady Drower says: "The name could have been applied to any strictly law-observing Jewish sect, for the root נצר means 'to keep, observe, guard' and could have been used as a laudatory term for more than one group of Jewish dissidents, particularly if they had secret teachings": Drower, E.S., op.cit., p.xiv.

268 Williams, F., op.cit., p.116.

269 See ibid, pp.42f.

pre-Christian Nasaraeans in Epiphanius' account.[270] Macuch states that the movement of separation from official Judaism in the pre-Christian period described by Epiphanius developed in two forms. One group migrated to the East where they were influenced by Babylonian, Iranian and Syrian Christian traditions: these are the later Mandaeans. The other group stayed in Palestine and later was absorbed into Jewish-Christianity.[271]

Since Epiphanius describes this movement as a heresy before the Christian period we can certainly accept Nasaraeanism as a Jewish heretical movement from pre-Christian times and it is our view that the Naṣoraeans in Mandaean tradition can be traced back to the pre-Christian separatist group described by Epiphanius. There are many reasons for this. A number of central points in Mandaeism refer to a Jewish background. On the one hand Mandaean tradition is, as we have seen earlier,[272] full of statements of struggle against ruling Jews in Palestine. We find strong polemics against official Judaism, both in the magical bowls and lead amulets and in the literary texts. On the other hand we have also seen that Mandaean tradition contains many central elements from Jewish tradition, which is the most powerful influence upon Mandaeism. We also find the statement in the Mandaean literature that the Naṣoraeans (or proto-Mandaeans) were once the worshippers of Adonai.[273] It is therefore clear that proto-Mandaeism reflects a kind of Jewish hereticism, and, consequently, there may be a connection between the Naṣoraeans (proto-Mandaeans) and pre-Christian Jewish dissident Nasaraeans of Epiphanius.

On the other hand this theory, which traces back the Mandaean origin to the pre-Christian Nasaraeans, is not free from difficulties, one of which is the fact that sources for the pre-Christian Nasaraeans are quite late (from the fourth century A.D.).

When we compare the modern Mandaeans to the Nasaraeans in Epiphanius' account we also find a number of important differences. On the other hand, as far as Mandaeism is concerned, we have a tradition which has a long history, and which contains a number of foreign influences. Therefore it seems to us that the theory which makes a connection between the Mandaean Naṣoraeans and the pre-Christian Nasaraeans is probably correct. In any case the term *naṣuraiia* in the Mandaean literature clearly reflects the western background of the Mandaeans.

b. Jordan

iardna, "Jordan", is one of the most central and ancient concepts of the Mandaean tradition. It occurs quite often in the Mandaean literature, both in the

---

270See Drower, E.S., op.cit., p.xiv; Macuch, R., "Anfänge der Mandäer", pp.93-100; Rudolph, K., "Problems of a History of the Development of the Mandaean Religion", p.220.
271See Macuch, R., "Anfänge der Mandäer".
272See above pp.68-69, 83f.
273See above p.94.

manuscripts and in the lead amulets and bowl texts.[274] Jordan is the name of all living (running) baptismal water for the Mandaeans.[275]

> "...these souls who are descending to the Jordan..."[276]

> "The jordan in which we have been immersed."[277]

Also it symbolizes the heavenly Jordan: "...the great Jordan of Life."[278]

iardna is derived from the well-known river with the same name in Palestine.[279] Pallis has claimed that *iardna* reached the Mandaeans through Christianity.[280] It is difficult to accept this suggestion because this term is one of the most ancient and central concepts of Mandaeism, which, as we emphasized, occurs also in the magical texts in which no Christian influence appears.[281]

The usage of this concept is connected with the western background of Mandaeism. The importance of the river Jordan as a name for all running water of baptism, the central ritual of the Mandaean religion, completely fits all the other western characteristics of Mandaeism. Therefore, as Segelberg stated,[282] there is no reason to doubt that the word, *iardna*, refers to the well-known river with the same name.

c. Hauran

hauran or *hauraran* [283] occurs both in the literary texts and in the earliest lead amulet. In the literature Hauran refers to a celestial land:

---

274 See *MD*, p.187; *MIT*, pp.189, 209, 237.

275 "Praised be all jordans of living water": *CP*, p.50.

276 Ibid, p.11.

277 Ibid, p.91.

278 Ibid, pp.8, 13.

279 Lidzbarski, who stated that this peculiar concept was one of the important terms which clearly pointed to the Palestinian origin of the Mandaeans, pointed out how among certain Gnostics it had a meaning similar to that found among the Mandaeans. See *Jb*, pp.xixff; *GR*, p.vi; Lidzbarski, M., *Mandäische Liturgien mitgeteilt, übersetzt und erklärt* (hereafter *ML*), Berlin (1920), p.xix. Also see Kraeling, C.H., "The Origin and Antiquity of the Mandaeans", p.212; Drower, E.S., *The Secret Adam*, p.xiv n.2; idem, "Mandaean Polemic", p.441; Macuch, R., "Anfänge der Mandäer", pp.100-4; Rudolph, K., "Problems of a History of the Development of the Mandaean Religion", pp.220-21; Segelberg, E., *Maṣbūtā*, p.38. Kraeling says: "...it is hard to believe that the Mandaean sect if it had been born on the banks of the Euphrates or the Zab would in its ubiquitous use of the name Jordan have so completely submerged the tradition concerning its own local rivers": See Kraeling, C.H., op.cit., p.212.

280 Pallis, S.A., op.cit., p.149. Also some New Testament scholars such as Burkitt and Peterson suggested that it was derived from Syriac *ywrdnn*. See Burkitt, F.C., "The Mandaeans", p.228; Peterson, E., "Bemerkungen zur mandäischen Literatur", *ZNW*, 25, 1926, p.237; idem, "Urchristentum und Mandäismus", p.89.

281 See above p.103.

282 See Segelberg, E., op.cit., p.38.

283 Hauran and Hauraran are sometimes used together. Drower and Macuch remark that the second name is formed by the enlarging of the first. See *MD*, p.117.

> "Speak of them of the pure Hauraran."[284]

> "He lifted him up and showed him Hauraran in which souls become perfect."[285]

Hauran is also closely connected with Jordan, the running water of Mandaean baptism:

> "Moreover, thou wilt be blessed with the blessing
> Pronounced in the Jordan and in the land of Hauraran,
> The great land of light..."[286]

> "This living water has come from the great Hauraran."[287]

It is also sometimes personified as a celestial being (*hauraran ukarkauan*).[288] Finally Hauran is sometimes mentioned as the name of a ritual garment, a usage which could be metaphorical.

> "...our jordan and our baptism; with Hauran our vestment; with Hauraran our covering."[289]

In the lead amulet published by Lidzbarski, Hauran occurs in the phrase Bar-Hauraran, the name of a protective spirit.[290]

The term Hauran in Mandaean literature refers to the Ḥaurān.[291] This can obviously be seen in the statement: "...in the Jordan and in the land of Hauraran" (*CP*, p.298). Therefore the term is closely connected with the original homeland of the Mandaeans and refers to their western background. The term Hauran suggests some of the Mandaeans (or proto-Mandaeans) might have lived in that area.[292]

---

284 *GR*, p.302 (see *HG*, p.v).
285 *GL*, p.593 (see *HG*, p.v).
286 *CP*, p.298.
287 *Jb*, p.232 (see *HG*, p.v).
288 See *CP*, p.43. Also see *HG*, p.v.
289 *CP*, p.23.
290 "...by the might of Bar-/ Hauraran," "And I went in the strength of/ Bar-Hauraran": *MIT*, p.239.
291 See *ML*, p.xix; *GR*, p.vi; Kraeling, C.H., "A Mandaic Bibliography", p.50; Drower, E.S., "Mandaean Polemic", p.441.
292 Also see *GR*, p.vi; Kraeling, C.H., op.cit., p.50.

d. Manda

manda, "knowledge, gnosis", is another quite ancient and central Mandaic term. It appears in all parts of the Mandaean literature from the earliest magical lead amulet to the latest literary texts.

manda (West-Aram.: *mndᶜ*, Jew.-Aram.: *mndᶜʾ*)[293] is especially personified as *manda d̠-hiia*, "knowledge of Life". Manda d̠-Hiia, one of the most important Light-beings, is the Mandaean Saviour-spirit.[294] Also *manda* (or *mandi*), *bit manda* or *bimanda*, the name of the Mandaean cult-hut,[295] and *mandaiia*, the word for the laity of the Mandaeans,[296] are derived from the term *manda*.

Manda is thus clearly an important term from the earliest phase of Mandaeism. Lidzbarski and other Mandaean scholars, such as Macuch and Rudolph, have regarded this term as favouring a western background of the Mandaeans.[297]

As we have seen, well-known Mandaean technical terms, such as *naṣuraiia*, *iardna* and *hauran*, which are the most ancient and central concepts of the Mandaean tradition, demonstrate that Mandaeism is connected to the West.

B. Baptism

Baptism is one of the most striking characteristics of the Mandaean religion. The problem of the origin of Mandaean baptism has often been discussed by scholars. Some, such as H. Zimmern, G. Widengren and E.M. Yamauchi, as we have mentioned earlier,[298] pointed out similarities between Mandaean baptism and Mesopotamian water-purification ceremonies, and argued for the Mesopotamian origin of the Mandaean baptismal ritual. Others, such as H. Lietzmann, compared the Mandaean baptism with the eastern Christian baptismal ritual and claimed that the Mandaean rite was actually derived from the Syrian Christian, particularly the Nestorian, ritual.[299]

Both these theories were criticized and rejected by scholars who emphasized the western baptismal parallels for the Mandaean cult. We have earlier discussed the criticism of the theory which claimed a Mesopotamian origin for the Mandaean

---

[293]See *MD*, p.247.
[294]See Rudolph, K., "Mandean Sources", p.136.
[295]See *MD*, p.61. The older name for the Mandaean cult-cut is *maškna*. See Rudolph, K., op.cit., p.131; *MD*, p.255.
[296]See *MD*, 247.
[297]See *Jb*, ii, p.xvii; Macuch, R., "Anfänge der Mandäer", pp.82ff; Rudolph, K., *Mandaeism*, p.5. Even Pallis accepts that *manda* shows a western influence in Mandaeism. See Pallis, S.A., *Mandaean Studies*, p.146.
[298]See above p.78.
[299]See Lietzmann, H., op.cit., pp.597ff. For a summary of Lietzmann's thesis see Segelberg, E., *Maṣbūtā*, p.15.

baptism.[300] The other theory, which argued for a Syrian-Christian origin for the Mandaean baptism, was criticized and rejected by scholars such as Schlier, Segelberg and Rudolph.[301]

All of the central characteristics of Mandaean baptism reflect the western connection of this ritual. The essential concepts of *maṣbuta* are of western origin. As we have discussed earlier,[302] *iardna*, Jordan, the running water of baptism, is an important western element in this ritual. The terms *šilmai* and *nidbai*, two important guardians of Mandaean baptism, reflect a western connection of Mandaean baptism, since these terms are derived from Phoenician deities *šlmn* and *ndbk*(*h*).[303]

The terms used in the act centred on Jordan, such as *ṭmš*, immerse, *nht*, descend, *rušma*, signation, *šqa*, drinking of the water, *miša*, oil, *klila*, myrtle wreath, and *kušṭa*, imposition of hand, are, as Segelberg remarked, all of Semitic and western origin.[304] Moreover the term *maṣbuta* itself is of western Semitic origin.[305] On the other hand we have generally Iranian, particularly Parthian, loanwords which are used for non-central details and ritual objects such as the words for ritual dress, like *himiana*, *šaruala*, *burzinga* and *taga*.[306]

Another important characteristic of Mandaean baptism is that it is a repeated ritual. Repeated baptisms also occur in Elchasaite doctrine, which allows for multiple baptism for the healing of the sick or after a major defilement.[307] Moreover multiple baptisms occur in the Nag-Hammadi text the *Zostrianos*.[308] Finally J.-M. Sevrin points out the repeated baptisms in the Jewish tradition, of which he states that these are the probable forebears of the *Zostrianos* multiple baptism.[309]

There are also many points of resemblance between the central acts of the Mandaean baptism and those of the various baptismal rituals of the West. Comparing the Mandaean baptism to the ancient western Christian rite from the late second century A.D., preserved by Hippolytus, Segelberg notes the similarities between the two traditions as well as differences. He remarks that both of the rituals have a "three action

---

300See above pp.78f.

301See Schlier, H., "Zur Mandäerfrage", *ThR*, NF, 5, 1933, pp.83-91; Segelberg, E., *Maṣbūtā*, pp.155ff, 160ff; Rudolph, K., *Mandaeism*, p.10. Of Lietzmann's difficulty in explaining the striking characteristics of the Mandaean baptism, Segelberg states: "The name Jordan for the baptismal water and the threefold immersion both seem to him [Lietzmann] difficult to explain": Segelberg, E., op.cit., p.15.

302See above pp.111f.

303"Praised be Šilmai and Nidbai the guardian 'uthras of the Jordan": *CP*, p.22. See *MD*, pp.297, 462.Also see *Jb*, p.xx.

304See Segelberg, E., op.cit., p.177. Also see *MD*, pp.181, 217, 250, 270, 292, 432, 473.

305See Segelberg, E., op.cit., p.177; *MD*, pp.250-51.

306See above p.80. Also see Segelberg, E., op.cit., pp.177ff.

307See Yamauchi, E.M., *Gnostic Ethics and Mandaean Origins*, p.62; Buckley, J.J., "Why once is not enough: Mandaean Baptism (Maṣbuta) as an Example of a Repeated Ritual", *HR*, 29, 1989, p.25.

308See Sieber, J.N., "Zostrianos", in *The Nag Hammadi Library in English*, General ed. J.M. Robinson, 3rd edition, Leiden (1988), p.405.

309See Sevrin, J.-M., *Le Dossier Baptismal Séthien. Études sur la Sacramentaire Gnostique*, (Bibliothèque capte de Nag Hammadi, Section "Etudes" 2) Laval (Québec) (1986), pp.290-91.

shape": baptism-unction-meal.[310] Segelberg also points out the similarities between the main acts of Mandaean baptism and the initiation baptism of the western Christian tradition, and remarks that the main acts, such as descending, triple immersion and unction or signation, appear in both.

On the other hand some differences between the two rituals are also notable. For example, the Mandaean rite has a double triplex immersion (the first one is a self-baptism), while the Christian rite has only one. Also in Mandaean baptism after immersion there is a threefold signing of the forehead of the neophyte with water, but in the Christian rite, after immersion the candidate goes out of the water (ascent), and then unction with oil, which is peculiar to the Christian tradition, follows.[311]

The resemblance between the main acts of the baptismal rite which appears in the *Odes of Solomon* and those of the Mandaean baptism is also notable. The *Odes of Solomon* is generally dated to the second century A.D. by scholars.[312] According to Rudolph its writer was a gnostic.[313] Although they do not give a clear picture of a baptismal rite the Odes reflect a rite which has (1) baptism in water, (2) signation, (3) drinking of water, (4) coronation, and (5) meal.[314] Segelberg also points out several texts of the Odes which indicate investing with the baptismal garment.[315] All of these acts, baptism in water, signation, drinking of water, investiture, coronation and meal, fit the main acts of Mandaean baptism.

On the other hand the difficulty with the Odes is their nature. Some scholars, such as Harris and Mingana, do not agree that these texts are baptismal hymns, although they accept that some passages reflect certain baptismal acts.[316]

We also find parallel points with the baptismal ritual of the quasi-Jewish sect of the Elchasaites. Besides the acceptance of repeated baptisms, on which we have earlier remarked, the similarities between the two traditions are: (1) baptism for the forgiveness of sins, (2) immersions after being bitten by a rabid dog or other vermin, (3) the veneration of water, and (4) the invocation of certain elements as witnesses at baptism.[317] Witnesses for Elchasaite baptism are "heaven, water, holy spirits, angel of prayer, oil, salt and earth". On the other hand the Mandaeans invoke the following

---

[310]See Segelberg, E., op.cit., pp.161f.

[311]See ibid, pp.163-64. Also see Rudolph, K., "Mandean Sources", p.131. Segelberg remarks: "There is no reason to think that the one rite is dependent on the other one, but there is strong reason to think that they have a common origin": Segelberg, E., op.cit., pp.164-65.

[312]See Yamauchi, E.M., *Pre-Christian Gnosticism*, p.92.

[313]See Rudolph, K., "War der Verfassen der Oden Salamos ein 'Qumran-Christ'?", pp.523ff.

[314]See Schlier, H., op.cit., p.89.

[315]See Segelberg, E., op.cit., p.166.

[316]See Harris R. and A. Mingana, *The Odes and Psalms of Solomon*, Manchester (1916-1920), v.II, p.197.

[317]See Drower, E.S., op.cit., pp.92-94; Yamauchi, E.M., *Gnostic Ethics and Mandaean Origins*, pp.62-63.

witnesses at baptism: *pitha* (bread), *mambuha* (sacramental water), the Jordan (running water of baptism), *habšaba* (personified Sunday) and *zidqa* (alms).[318]

Although there are some similarities between Mandaean and Elchasaite rituals it is difficult to accept the views of those scholars such as Chwolsohn, Lady Drower and Mead who inclined to identify the Elchasaites with the Mandaeans mainly because of these similarities.[319] As well as some similarities we find also some important differences between the two traditions. For example, contrary to the Mandaeans the Elchasaites required circumcision, observed the Sabbath, prescribed a life according to the law, and prayed facing Jerusalem.[320]

The similarities between Mandaean and Elchasaite baptism point to a common sphere of origin of both traditions, i.e. point to the valley of Jordan and its various baptist movements.[321]

Some scholars also pointed out similarities between the baptism of the Mandaeans and that of the Qumran community. Rudolph remarked that the baptist terminology and baptist figurative discourse of the Mandaeans, as well as ancient Mandaean concepts, like their self-designation *bhire zidqa*, "chosen righteous", recur in the Qumran literature.[322] F. Braun, who inclined to trace the Mandaeans to the Essenes, also pointed out the similarities between the two traditions, such as the substitution of immersions and lustrations for bloody sacrifices, and the confession of sins by the initiates who receive baptism.[323]

Some similarities between Mandaean baptism and the baptismal rituals which appear in the *Testament of Levi*, *Pistis Sophia* and the *Book of Jeu* have also been pointed out by Segelberg.[324]

As we have seen there are important similarities between the central characteristics and acts of Mandaean baptism and those of the various western

---

318Drower, E.S., op.cit., p.93.

319See Chwolsohn, D., op.cit., v.I, pp.116ff; Drower, E.S., op.cit., pp.92ff; idem, "Adam and the Elkasaites", pp.406ff; Mead, G.R.S., op.cit., pp.53-54 n.5. Drower associates Elchasai, the founder of that sect, with the Adam Kasia, the secret Adam, of the Mandaean literature and says: "There is a much deeper ground for thinking that there is a common background and for believing that the Elkasaites were once closely related to our Naṣoraeans. The central cult of both is the Heavenly Man, Adam. In the secret scrolls the 'false prophet' of the Elkasaites can be recognized as the Naṣoraean Adam Kasia- no 'man' but Man, Anthropos, the Son of Man, the Son of God; El Kasia": Drower, E.S., *The Secret Adam*, pp.97-98.

320See Rudolph, K., *Die Mandäer*, I, pp.233ff; Segelberg, E., op.cit., p.176; Yamauchi, E.M., *Gnostic Ethics and Mandaean Origins*, p.63. On the other hand G. Quispel accepts Elchasaitism as the origin of the western elements in Mandaeism. He says: "the present day Mandaeans are indebted to the Elkesaites for the rites and legends and views they have in common with these Jewish Christians. This explains the Western elements undoubtedly contained in their tradition. This, of course, is only one half of the story: Elkesaitism may explain the ritualism of the Mandaeans, not their Gnosticism. But if the story is only half true, this half is true": Quispel, G., "Jewish Gnosis and Mandaean Gnosticism. Some Reflections on the Writing *Brontè*", p.115.

321See Segelberg, E., op.cit., p.176.

322See Rudolph, K., "Problems of a History of the Development of the Mandaean Religion", p.231.

323See Braun, F.M., op.cit., pp.193-229. Also see Yamauchi, E.M., op.cit., p.57.

324See Segelberg, E., op.cit., pp.167-74.

baptismal rituals. All of the striking features of Mandaean baptism reflect the western background of this ritual and, consequently, of the Mandaeans.

C. Mandaic script

Mandaic is one of the eastern dialects of Aramaic.[325] We have earlier seen that the earliest Mandaic magical texts (lead amulets) are dated from the third or fourth centuries A.D.[326] We have also seen that at least some of the liturgical texts of the Mandaeans must have already been redacted in the third century A.D., since some Manichaean writers adapted (or translated) them.[327] We know moreover that there is a Mandaean tradition that some of their liturgical texts were redacted by a certain Zazai in the third century A.D. All of these points indicate that the Mandaeans had a script before the third century A.D.

The problem of how the Mandaeans adopted their script has been discussed by many scholars. Some, such as Lidzbarski, Kraeling and Macuch, have pointed out the resemblances between the Mandaean and Nabataean scripts and argued for a Nabataean origin of the Mandaic script,[328] while others, such as Naveh, paid attention to the relations of this script to other Aramaic scripts, Elymaean and Characenian, and argued for the primacy of the Elymaean script over against the Mandaean script.[329] On the other hand, comparing the Mandaic letter-forms to the other middle Aramaic scripts, Klugkist recently held the view that the Mandaic script did not originate from a particular script but from the encounter of several middle Aramaic script traditions.[330]

Almost all scholars agree that there are some resemblances between the letter-forms of Mandaic and those of Nabataean.[331] Some resemblances also exist between the letter-forms of Mandaic and those of the other Aramaic scripts, such as Palmyrene, Old Syriac, Elymaean and Characenian. Here we will not enter the palaeographical discussions of the letter-forms of Mandaic and other Aramaic scripts, since the detailed

[325]Beyer, K., *The Aramaic Language*, tr. J.F. Healey, Göttingen (1986), p.46.
[326]See above pp.60-61.
[327]See above p.61. Also see below pp.122f.
[328]See Lidzbarski, M., "Mandäische Fragen", *ZNW*, 26, 1927, pp.70ff; *GR*, pp.vi-vii; Brandt, W., "Mandaeans", pp.385-86; Kraeling, C.H., "The Origin and Antiquity of the Mandaeans", p.211; Macuch, R., "Anfänge der Mandäer", pp.141-46; idem, "The Origins of the Mandaeans and Their Script", pp.174-92; Rudolph, K., *Die Mandäer*, I, pp.29ff. Also see Rosenthal, F., *Die aramäistische Forschung seit Th. Nöldeke's Veröffentlichungen*, Leiden (1939), p.246.
[329]See Naveh, J., "The Origin of the Mandaic Script", pp.32-37; Coxon, P.W., "Script Analysis and Mandaean Origins", *JSS*, 15, 1970, pp.16-30.
[330]See Klugkist, A., "The Origin of the Mandaic Script", in *Scripta Signa Vocis*, eds. H.L.J. Vanstiphout et. al., Groningen (1986), pp.111-20.
[331]Naveh, however, states that "there is no connection at all between the Nabataean and the Mandaic scripts". See Naveh, J., op.cit., p.33.

study of letter-forms is beyond the scope of this study and in any case requires considerable expertise in Aramaic palaeography.[332]

We have enough reason, quite apart from the letter-forms themselves, to believe that the Mandaeans probably had some contact with the Nabataeans in the West before their migration. As we have seen earlier,[333] terms such as Hauran (or Hauraran) and Jordan refer to Palestine and Transjordan, where the Mandaeans lived before they migrated. Since it is well-known that Transjordan and the Ḥaurān are places where the Nabataeans lived,[334] the Mandaeans probably made contact with the Nabataeans before their migration to the East. Also, as we have mentioned earlier,[335] we find in the Mandaean tradition the term *nbaṭ*, eponym of the Nabataeans, which appears as a Light-spirit.

Since the Mandaeans (or proto-Mandaeans) probably had some kind of contact with the Nabataeans in Palestine, they might have taken their script from the Nabataeans before their migration to the East. On the other hand we have seen that Mandaean beliefs and rituals have been influenced by the neighbouring traditions, such as Iranian, Babylonian and Syrian-Christian, in their new homeland. It is therefore possible that after the Mandaean migration Mandaic script was also influenced by some eastern Aramaic scripts, like Elymaean, and this might explain the resemblances between the letter-forms of Mandaic and those of these other Aramaic scripts.

However, the argument about the origins of the Mandaic script cannot on present evidence be regarded as settled. More evidence is needed before it can be resolved.

In this section we have seen that the central characteristics of Mandaeism, such as the most essential and ancient concepts of Mandaean literature and baptism, reflect the western background of the Mandaeans, and therefore confirm the Mandaean tradition that the original homeland of the Mandaeans is Palestine from where their ancestors migrated to the East because of persecution by official Judaism.

---

[332]For the palaeographical comparison of the Mandaic letter-forms to other Aramaic scripts we refer the reader to the comparative studies made by Klugkist, Naveh, Coxon and Macuch, which we mentioned in the footnotes above. A detailed study is also found in Klugkist, A., *Midden-Aramese Schriften in Syrië, Mesopotamië, Perzië en aangrenzende gebieden*, (Ph.D. Thesis) Groningen University (1982), pp.218-49.

[333]See above pp.111ff.

[334]See Wenning, R., *Die Nabatäer-Denkmäler und Geschichte*, (Novum Testamentum et Orbis Antiquus, 3) Göttingen (1987), p.14; Healey, J.F., *The Nabataean Tomb Inscriptions of Mada'in Salih*, (Journal of Semitic Studies Supplement 1) Oxford University Press (1993), pp.13f.

[335]See above p.83.

CHAPTER V

EASTERN SOURCES FOR THE MANDAEANS AND THE PROBLEM OF THEIR EARLY APPEARANCE IN MESOPOTAMIA

Another problem we face is that of the date of the settlement of the Mandaeans in Mesopotamia, where they still live. We have already seen that the Mandaeans migrated from their original homeland, Palestine, to the East, first to the Median mountains and then to southern Babylonia. In this chapter we will examine whether there is any external evidence on t the Mandaeans in the East.

1. Iranian evidence

The *Kartīr* inscription at Naqsh-i Rustam, which is a Pahlavi inscription in Parsik characters and dated to about 275 A.D.,[1] mentions the religious groups who were persecuted during the early Sassanian period:

> "...and Jews (YḤWD-y) and Buddhist monks (ŠMN-y? ...) and Brahmins (BRMN-y ...) and Nazarenes (N'Č=ṢL=R'-y) and Christians (KL=RSTYDAN ...) and MKTK-y ... and Zandīk (ZNDYK-y ...) within the empire were driven out..."[2]

Two groups mentioned in this inscription are important in our discussion: Nazarenes or Naṣoraeans (*n'čr'y*) and *mktky*. Regarding the first, the text apparently distinguishes the Naṣoraeans from the Christians. M. Sprengling stated that the distinction between the Christians and Naṣoraeans was not made clear in the text and

[1] See Sprengling, M., "A New Pahlavi Inscription", *AJSL*, 53, 1937, p.126; Widengren, G., *Mani and Manichaeism*, p.16.
[2] Sprengling, M., "Kartīr, Founder of Sasanian Zoroastrianism", *AJSL*, 57, 1940, p.221. Also see Widengren, G., *Die Religonen Irans*, Stuttgart (1965), p.277.

thought that perhaps the Naṣoraeans were the Bardaisanites.[3] He did not consider the possibility that the Mandaeans one of whose earliest self-designations is the name Naṣoraeans might be meant.[4] Mandaean sources point to a persecution of the Mandaean community during the Sassanian period. According to *Haran Gawaita* during the Parthian period rulers showed great toleration to the Naṣoraeans (Mandaeans) so that they built 400 cult-huts in Babylonia. When the Parthian dynasty was overthrown by the Sassanids, toleration for the Mandaeans came to an end, and many Mandaean cult-huts were destroyed by the rulers. The text remarks:

> "(*Nevertheless*) there remained one hundred and seventy banners and *bimandia* in Baghdad."[5]

Obviously, if *n'čr'y* in the *Kartīr* inscription refers to Mandaeans, the Mandaean sources confirm the *Kartīr* inscription in that there was indeed a persecution against the Naṣoraeans during the Sassanian period.

On the second name, *mktky*, Sprengling notes that it is possible to read *yn* for *t*, and also *n* for the first *k*.[6] Hence it can be read *mkynky*, *mnynky*, or *mntky*. If we accept the last reading we find Mantakeans,[7] a possible version of "Mandaeans", but this is not free from difficulties. Firstly there is a difficulty about the spelling: here we have *t* instead of *d*, and an extra *k*. Secondly the term *mandaiia*, Mandaeans, is, as we have remarked earlier,[8] a quite late name for the Mandaeans. On the other hand the second reading, *mnynky* might give the name of the "Manichaeans", as Sprengling noted.[9] Consequently it is best to assume that the first name only, *n'čr'y*, Naṣoraeans, refers to the Mandaeans who, as well as the other non-Zoroastrian people of the Sassanian empire, were persecuted when the Zoroastrianism was accepted as the state religion of the Sassanians, probably during the time of Shapur I (241-272 A.D.).[10]

Before leaving the Iranian evidence for the early history of the Mandaeans in Mesopotamia we must also recall the Iranian background of a number of terms and proper nouns in the Mandaean literature. We have earlier remarked that the names of some Mandaean cult-objects and many proper nouns in Mandaean literature are of Iranian derivation.[11] Widengren states that linguistic analysis of the Iranian words in

---

[3] See Sprengling, M., op.cit., p.221.
[4] See Rudolph, K., "Der Mandäismus in der neueren Gnosisforschung", pp.272-73.
[5] *HG*, p.14.
[6] See Sprengling, M., op.cit., p.221.
[7] Rudolph actually translates the word as Mantaeans: Rudolph, K., "Der Mandäismus in der neueren Gnosisforschung", p.273.
[8] See above p.109.
[9] See Sprengling, M., op.cit., p.221.
[10] See Rudolph, K., *Gnosis*, p.364.
[11] See above p.80. G. Widengren, who examines the Iranian loanwords in Mandaean literature, remarks: "Systematic examination of the loan-words is however a comparatively new development.

Mandaean tradition supports the existence of the Mandaeans and their literature in the Parthian period.[12]

2. Manichaean evidence

Another external evidence on the early history of the Mandaeans is that of Manichaeism. Scholars have often discussed the relationship between Mandaeism and Manichaeism. Some, such as Widengren, suggested that Mani was brought up amongst the Mandaeans.[13] Also Macuch remarked that Manichaeism was a descendant of Mandaeism and not vice versa.[14] On the other hand the *Cologne Codex*, published in 1970, confirmed that Mani had been raised among the Jewish-Christian sect of the Elchasaites.[15] On the other hand some scholars, such as W.F. Albright, claimed that Mandaeism was later than the Manichaeism.[16]

We understand from the Mandaean and Manichaean sources that there were some relations between the two traditions. For example the *Ginza* contains a controversy with the followers of *mar mani*, "Lord Mani".[17] Also the Coptic Manichaean *Kephalaia* contains some arguments with the Naṣoraeans,[18] which probably refers to the Mandaeans since "Naṣoraeans" is the ancient self-appellation of the Mandaeans.

The most important source for the relations between the Mandaean and Manichaean traditions is the Coptic Manichaean *Psalms of Thomas*. Thomas was one of the first disciples of Mani who died about 276 A.D.[19] According to classical

The difference between Middle Parthian and Middle Persian forms is crucial. In many instances either the form of a word is Parthian or the word itself has been met only in Parthian... Moreover the frequency of Middle Persian loan-words in Mandaean records itself confirms the replacement of Parthian by Sassanian influence": Widengren, G., *Mani and Manichaeism*, pp.17-18.

[12]See ibid, pp.18-19. Widengren also states: "Eminently important to dating the beginning of the Mandaean scriptures is the fact that many loan-words and linguistic adaptations indicate a feudalistic Parthian world. The theological language of the Mandaean religion quite simply presupposes a feudal structure of society": ibid, p.19.

[13]See ibid, pp.25-26.

[14]See Macuch, R., "The Origins of the Mandaeans and Their Script", p.189.

[15]See Rudolph, K., *Gnosis*, p.329; Yamauchi, E.M., "Jewish Gnosticism? The Prologue of John, Mandaean Parallels, and the Trimorphic Protennoia", p.474.

[16]See Albright, W.F., *From the Stone Age to Christianity*, p.281. Cf. idem, "Recent Discoveries in Palestine and the Gospel of St. John", p.154 n.1.

[17]See *GR*, p.229; Rudolph, K., *Gnosis*, p.364. Pognon and Rudolph have pointed out the resemblance between the Manichaean ideas and theogonic and cosmogonic traditions of the Mandaean literature. Pognon, however, interpreted this as a Mandaean borrowing from Manichaeism. See Pognon, H., *Inscriptions mandäites des coupes de Khouabir*, Paris (1898-1899), pp.253f; Rudolph, K., *Die Mandäer*, I, pp.176ff; idem, "Mandean Sources", p.142. Also see Säve-Söderbergh, T., *Studies in the Coptic Manichaean Psalm-Book: Prosody and Mandaean Parallels*, p.157.

[18]See Rudolph, K., "Der Mandäismus in der neueren Gnosisforschung", p.272; idem, *Die Mandäer*, I, pp.43f. Segelberg suggested that there were some Mandaean influences in the *Kephalaia* such as "the five mysteries or signs of the Primal Man" in *Kephalaia* IX. See Segelberg, E., "Trāṣa ḏ-tāga ḏ-Šišlām rabbā", pp.238-43.

[19]Säve-Söderbergh, T., op.cit., p.156.

sources, such as the *Acta Archelai* and *Alexander Lycopolitanus*, Mani sent Thomas to Egypt in order to preach Manichaean doctrine. Epiphanius stated that Thomas was also sent to Judea for preaching.[20] The Coptic *Psalms of Thomas*, found in Egypt, was dated to the fourth century A.D. by scholars and Säve-Söderbergh stated that it was presumably translated into Coptic from a Syriac version already in the fourth century A.D. Therefore he remarked:

> "Hence I am convinced that the original version of the Psalms of Thomas was composed by Mani's disciple and should consequently be dated to the last quarter of the 3rd century."[21]

In his remarkable comparative study Säve-Söderbergh pointed out the close similarity between the Mandaean liturgical texts, particularly the *masiqta* texts in the *Ginza Left*, and the Coptic *Psalms of Thomas*, and demonstrated that the *Psalms of Thomas* were adaptations, almost translations of the Mandaean texts.[22]

Säve-Söderbergh held the idea that Thomas had adopted the Mandaean texts in the West before the migration of the Mandaeans.[23] In our opinion it is difficult to accept this view, because we know from the various sources such as the *Kartīr* inscription that the Mandaeans were already in Babylonia in the third century A.D. It is thus quite clear that they migrated into Babylonia much earlier than Thomas' mission in Judaea. and it is simpler to assume that Thomas was already under Mandaean influence in Babylonia where the Mandaeans lived during his time.

The Mandaean influence upon Manichaeism therefore clearly shows that (1) Mandaeism certainly antedates Manichaeism, (2) certain Mandaean liturgical texts were already redacted in the third century A.D., which confirms the Mandaean tradition about redaction of some of their liturgical texts,[24] and (3) the Manichaean writers such as Thomas, one of Mani's first disciples, were in contact with the Mandaeans in Babylonia during the third century A.D.

---

[20]See ibid, pp.163-64.
[21]Ibid, p.156.
[22]See ibid, pp.160ff. Säve-Söderbergh states: "It is interesting to note that this comparative analysis not only demonstrates the pre-Manichaean date of nearly all the motives connected with the *massiqtā*, especially in the form in which we find them in the Left Ginza II and III — books which have already been supposed to belong to the older strata of Mandaean literature — but also of many other passages, as e.g. the parables used in a parenese [paranesis] which would otherwise be very difficult to date from their contents only": ibid, p.163.
[23]Säve-Söderbergh says: "It is of course *a priori* not quite excluded that Thomas may have been under the influence of some Mandaean or pre-Mandaean sect of baptizers in Babylonia. But it seems to be much easier to explain the Mandaean character of his psalms (which were probably written after he had left Babylonia and had started his preaching in Syria and Palestine, towards the end of Mani's life...) if we return to the view of Lidzbarski and many other scholars that the Mandaeans lived in those western tracts before they migrated into Babylonia": ibid, p.166.
[24]See above pp.57f.

3. Medieval Syriac and Arabic sources

Finally we may note some Islamic and non-Islamic medieval sources which refer to the history of the Mandaeans in the medieval period. As we have discussed earlier,[25] from the 7th century onwards the Qur'ān and other Islamic sources mention the Mandaeans generally under the name "Sabians".

Also the Syriac writer Theodore bar Konai (8th/9th century A.D.) speaks of the Mandaeans in his *Scholion*.[26] He states that a certain Ado who came from Adiabene with his brethren was the founder of the Mandaean community in Mesene where the Mandaeans were called "the Mandaeans and Mashkanians (Mesenians)".[27]

Bar Konai's account supports Mandaean tradition on the history of the migration of their ancestors, that they migrated from Palestine first to the Median mountains, and, then, to Babylonia.[28] Adiabene is in Media, in the district to the north of Mosul. In the first century A.D. Adiabene, which was subject to the Parthians, had an important Jewish community. It is stated by sources like Josephus that even the royal family of Adiabene had adopted Judaism.[29]

If we reconstruct the history of migration of the Mandaeans and their settlement in the East, it is quite probable that the Mandaeans migrated under Parthian protection from Palestine to the district of Adiabene, which they called *ṭura ḏ-madai*, "the Median mountains" or *haran gauaita*, in the first century A.D. Presumably because of the strong Jewish influence at Adiabene they continued their migration until they reached southern Mesopotamia, where they established their community.

---

[25]See Chapter II.

[26]See Hespel, R. and R. Draguet, *Théodore bar Koni Livre des Scolies (recension de Séert) II. Mimré VI-XI*, (Corpus Scriptorum Christianorum Orientalium, vol. 432, Scriptores Syri Tomus 188) Louvain (1982), pp.257-59.

[27]See ibid, pp.257-58. Also another Syriac writer Īšoʿdad of Merw (9th century A.D.) mentions the script and dialect of Mesene as Mesenian. See Macuch, R., "The Origins of the Mandaeans and Their Script", pp.190f; Altheim, F. and R. Stiehl, *Die Araber in der alten Welt*, V/2, Berlin (1969), pp.31f. Also see Coxon, P.W., op.cit., pp.16ff; Kraeling, C.H., "The Origin and Antiquity of the Mandaeans", pp.203ff, 211.

[28]See above pp.62ff.

[29]See Murray, R., *Symbols of Church and Kingdom*, Cambridge (1975), p.8; McCullough, W.S., *A Short History of Syriac Christianity to the Rise of Islam*, Chico (1982), p.8; Segal, J.B., *Edessa 'The Blessed City'*, pp41, 67.

CHAPTER VI

CULTS AND BELIEFS OF THE HARRANIANS

As we have seen earlier[1] the medieval pagans of Harran were called "Sabians" by medieval scholars. The baptising sect of the lower Iraq, the ancestors of the modern Mandaeans, was also called by the same name. Modern Mandaeans are still called Sabians (*ṣubbā*) by their neighbours. Medieval scholars after the caliph al-Ma'mūn, further, used the term Sabian for all pagans, particularly for star-worshippers. Consequently they, and even some modern Muslim scholars, generally considered both the Sabians of Harran and the Ṣubba of Iraq (the Mandaeans) as members of the same community, though some of them pointed out the differences between the two traditions.

According to Lady Drower's information, in the first half of the century an Arab author,[2] wrote an article in an Egyptian periodical about the Ṣubba in which he described them as star-worshippers like the Sabians of Harran. Lady Drower says:

> "Indignation broke out amongst the Mandaean priesthood, for it was the old accusation of paganism, so imperilling to Muslim toleration. Legal proceedings were taken against the author, and a *ganzibra*, or head-priest, was dispatched to Baghdad armed with the Ginza Rba, the Great Treasure, to translate before witnesses passages in the holy writ denouncing the worship of planets."[3]

It is still a subject of argument among modern scholars whether there is a connection between the two communities. Chwolsohn, who suggested the identification of the Sabians of the Qur'ān with the Mandaeans, pointed out the pagan characteristics

---

[1]See chapter II.

[2]Lady Drower does not mention the name of this author, but it was presumably ʿAbd al-Razzāq al-Ḥasanī. See al-Ḥasanī, *al-ṣābi'ūn fī ḥāḍirihim wa māḍihim*, pp.7-8.

[3]See *MII*, pp.xvii-xviii.

of the Harranians and stated that there was no connection between the Harranians and the Mandaeans, because the former publicly worshipped the planets while the latter held planet-worship in abhorrence.[4] On the other hand, basing her theory on some minor similarities between the Mandaean and Harranian traditions Lady Drower suggested that there was a connection between them.[5] Concerning the medieval Harranian scholars such as Thābit ʾibn Qurrah she stated:

> "...they may have been no pseudo-Ṣābians but genuine members of that sect, Naṣoraeans, who practised baptism and were faithful to the religion into which they had been born. In this case they would probably have been of the priestly clan which today still provides the intelligentsia."[6]

What, therefore, are the striking features of the religion of the Harranians? Is there any similarity between the characteristics of the Harranian religion and those of the Mandaean religion? If there is, is there any real religious identity between the Harranians and the Mandaeans?

In this chapter we will first look at the history of Harran as a background to the Harranian religion. We will, then, examine the theology, prophets, rites and religious regulations of the Harranians.

1. The history of Harran from the second millennium B.C. to its destruction by the Mongols

The ancient city of Harran was a stage on the trade route between the Mediterranean and the plains of the Middle Tigris. The city is first named in the Old Babylonian period.[7] The name of the city is expressed in cuneiform by an ideograph as *ḫarrānu*.[8] Although this name is not often mentioned in Old Assyrian texts it frequently occurs in texts from the 10th century B.C.[9]

The Aramaic name for the city of Harran is *ḥrn*,[10] which is also used in the Bible.

---

[4]See Chwolsohn, D., op.cit., v.I, pp.21f, 139ff.
[5]See Drower, E.S., *The Secret Adam*, pp.111ff; *MII*, pp.xvif.
[6]Drower, E.S., op.cit., pp.111-12.
[7]Postgate, J.N., "Harran" in *RLA*, v.4, p.123.
[8]See Labat, R., *Manuel d'épigraphie akkadienne*, 5th edition, Paris (1976), p.166; *CAD*, v.6, p.106.
[9]The forms which were frequently used at that time are *uru ḫar-ra-nu, uru ḫar-ra-a(n), uru ḫar-ra-na* and *uru ḫar-ra-ni*. Cf. Parpola, S., *Neo-Assyrian Toponyms*, pp.152-53. Also see Postgate, J.N., op.cit., p.123.
[10]An Aramaic inscription from Zinjirli mentions *bʿl ḥrn*, "the Lord of Harran", which quite possibly refers to the Moon-god of the city, i.e. *sin*. See Gibson, J.C.L., *Textbook of Syrian Semitic Inscriptions: v.II, Aramaic Inscriptions*, Oxford (1975), p.93.

Although several theories (classical and modern) on the origin of the name Harran have been suggested by scholars[11] it is universally accepted that the name of Harran comes from Akkadian *ḫarrānu*, "road, journey, caravan, caravan-station, business capital", which was probably given it on account of its being a crossing point of the Syrian, Assyrian and Babylonian trade routes.[12]

Harran was called Καρραν by the Greeks, and Carrhae by the Romans.[13] It was also called Hellenopolis, "the heathen city", by the Fathers of the Church because of the pagan religion of its inhabitants.[14] As a matter of fact pagan religion among the Harranians survived in its Christian and Muslim environment until Harran and the last pagan sanctuary were destroyed by the Mongols.

A. Harran in the pre-Assyrian period

The origin of Harran is lost in antiquity. In the first centuries of the third millennium, and probably in even earlier times, each of the cities of Ur and Harran was a centre of moon-worship.[15]

Harran was the seat of the minor king Astidakim at the time of Zimrilim of Mari.[16] In a letter from that time (c. 1777-1746 B.C.)[17] mention is made of a treaty which the tribe of Benjamin (Banū iamīna), an invading Amorite tribe, concluded with the kinglets of some neighbouring states "in the temple of *sīn* of Harran".[18]

Sin and Shamash of Harran later appear among the gods whose names are invoked in the treaty between Shuppiluliuma, the king of the Hittites, and Shattiwaza of Mitanni.[19]

---

[11]See Yāqūt al-Hamawī al-Rūmī, *mu'jam al-buldān*, v.2, p.235; al-Dimashqī, op.cit., p.191 (al-Dimashqī spells the name as *'arrān*); 'Ibn Jubayr, *The Travels of 'Ibn Jubayr*, tr. R.J.C. Broadhurst, London (1952), p.254; Weidner, E.F., *Politische Dokumente aus Kleinasien*, Leipzig (1923), p.46 n.3; Olmstead, A.T., *History of Assyria*, New York, London (1923), p.38.

[12]See Postgate, J.N., op.cit., p.123; *EJ*, v.7, p.1328; *CAD*, v.6, p.106.

[13]See Fehervari, G., "Harran", in *EI**, v.3, p.227; Hill, G.F., *Catalogue of the Greek Coins of Arabia, Mesopotamia and Persia*, London (1922), pp.lxxxviiff.

[14]See Fehervari, G., op.cit., p.227.

[15]See Lewy J., "The Late Assyro-Babylonian Cult of the Moon and its Culmination at the Time of Nabonidus", *HUCA*, 19, 1945-46, p.482. Cf. Postgate, J.N., op.cit., p.123.

[16]Postgate, J.N., op.cit., p.123.

[17]S. Lloyd and W. Brice state that the date was about 2000 B.C. See Lloyd, S. and W. Brice, "Harran", *AS*, 1, 1951, p.87.

[18]See Lewy, H., "Points of Comparison Between Zoroastrianism and the Moon-Cult of Harran", in *A Locust's Leg; Studies in Honour of S.H. Taqizadeh*, ed. W.B. Henning, London (1962), pp.139-40.

[19]See Smith, S., *Babylonian Historical Texts*, London (1924), p.39. Cf Postgate, J.N., op.cit., p.123.

B. Under Assyrian dominion

In connection with the Assyrians Harran is first mentioned in the annals of Adad-Nirari I. About 1310-1280 B.C., he conquered the "fortress of Kharani", and annexed it as a province, which was ruled by the turtan.[20]

The city was frequently lost by the Assyrians, as during the collapse of Assyrian power which occured after the reign of Tiglath-Pileser I.[21] Harran was probably incorporated into the Assyrian empire under Shalmaneser III (859-824 B.C.) at the time of the capture of Tilbarsip, and it was never out of Assyrian hands for long thereafter.[22] At that time Harran was so important that Shalmaneser III restored the temple of the local moon-god, *é-ḫúl-ḫúl*, so that he recognized *sīn* of Harran as one of his gods.[23]

Harran continued to be an important city during the reigns of Tiglath-Pileser III (745-727 B.C.) and the Sargonid kings for both religious and strategic reasons.[24]

Under Esarhaddon (680-669 B.C.) Harran was the home of a rebellion in support of a pretender to the throne, Sasī(a), *ḫazannu* of the city.[25] Both Esarhaddon, who had been a devoted worshipper of Sin, and his successor, Ashur-bani-apal (668-626 B.C.), proceeded at the beginning of their rule to Harran in order to receive the royal tiara from "Sin who dwells in Harran".[26]

Ashur-bani-apal undertook extensive restorations of the temple *é-ḫúl-ḫúl* in Harran.[27] Moreover he installed his youngest brother, Ashur-etil-shame-irsitim-ballitsu, as high priest for the service of Sin.[28]

After the collapse of Assyrian power and the destruction of Nineveh, an Assyrian general, Ashur-uballit II (611-606 B.C.), fled to Harran, calling himself king of Assyria and trying to assert his right to the throne by the aid of Egypt.[29] The fall of Nineveh did not involve the end of the nominal Assyrian kingdom, which was simply transplanted to Harran.[30]

---

[20]See Smith, S., op.cit., p.39; idem, *Early History of Assyria*, London (1928), p.272. Cf. Luckenbill, D.D., *Ancient Records of Assyria and Babylonia*, Chicago (1926-1927), v.I, p.27. Also see Postgate, J.N., op.cit., p.123.

[21]Smith, S., *Babylonian Historical Texts*, p.39.

[22]Postgate, J.N., op.cit., p.123. Cf. Luckenbill, D.D., op.cit., v.I, p.210.

[23]See Smith, S., op.cit., p.40; Lloyd, S. and W. Brice, op.cit., p.88.

[24]See Smith, S., op.cit., p.40; Postgate, J.N., op.cit., p.124; Pallis, S.A., *The Antiquity of Iraq*, Copenhagen (1956), pp.606-7; Luckenbill, D.D., op.cit., v.II, pp.25, 40, 51, 54-55, 60.

[25]Postgate, J.N., op.cit., p.124.

[26]See Lewy, H., op.cit., p.140; Olmstead, A.T., op.cit., p.495.

[27]Cf. Luckenbill, D.D., op.cit., v.II, p.353.

[28]Ibid, v.II, p.377.

[29]See Pallis, S.A., op.cit., p.633. Cf. Luckenbill, D.D., op.cit., v.II, p.420; Gadd, C.J., *The Fall of Nineveh*, London (1923), p.40.

[30]Gadd, C.J., op.cit., p.17.

C. The Neo-Babylonian period

According to the "Nabopolassar Chronicle", in 610 B.C., in the sixteenth year of Nabopolassar, a united army of the Babylonians and the Scythians marched on Harran and occupied the city. After leaving behind a garrison, Nabopolassar returned to Babylonia; the Scythians remained in possession of the city.[31]

After the collapse of the Assyrians, the Empire was divided, the Medes keeping Assyria and Northern Mesopotamia (presumably with Harran), whereas Nebuchadnezzar II (604-562 B.C.) in addition to his hereditary kingdom, Babylonia, occupied all Syria and Palestine.[32]

The period from the death of Nebuchadnezzar II in 562 B.C. to 555 B.C. is marked by rapidly changing rulers, and intrigues and disagreement within the royal family. But in 555 B.C. Nabonidus, the Aramaean from Harran (555-538 B.C.), acceded to the throne of Babylonia. His peaceful reign saw an extensive restoring and rebuilding of old temples.[33] Nabonidus' mother was a votaress of the moon-god of Harran throughout her long life, from the time of Ashur-bani-apal to the ninth year of Nabonidus, her son, i.e. 104 years.[34]

In 553-552 B.C., therefore, Nabonidus was able to commence the work of which he had dreamed dreams; *é-ḫúl-ḫúl* was restored. Not only did Nabonidus restore the temples; his native city, Harran, was rebuilt, and his parent who had patiently served the god through years of desolation lived to see the restoration.[35] Nabonidus was closely attached to the deity Sin who had from the old days had a magnificent temple in his native town of Harran, so that Marduk in Babylonia was neglected for the benefit of Sin. The priesthood were therefore opposed to him, especially when he failed to celebrate the *akītu* festival, the Babylonian New-Year's feast, and this also turned the mind of the people against him. It may have been as a result of the animosity of the

---

[31]See ibid, p.41; Luckenbill, D.D., op.cit., v.II, p.421.
[32]Pallis, S.A., op.cit., p.633.
[33]Ibid, p.634.
[34]Cf. Gadd, C.J., "The Harran Inscriptions of Nabonidus", *AS*, 8, 1958, pp.38, 49, 54. H. Pognon, who discovered some cuneiform tablets around Eski Harran in 1906, stated that these tablets were made by a pious worshipper of Sin, the moon-god. Then he claimed that he was a high priest who called the king of Babylon his son. After that E. Dhorme pointed out that the writer was a woman whose name was Šumûa-damga and she was the mother of Nabonidus. See Lewy, J., op.cit., pp.405-6. This idea was generally accepted by the Assyriologists. See ibid, p.407; Gadd, C.J., op.cit., p.38. But J. Lewy disagrees with this theory and states that Dhorme's deductions cannot be correct. He remarks that it is a priori unlikely that Nabonidus' mother was a priestess; for it is almost certain that in Babylonia and Assyria priestesses, and particularly high-ranking priestesses of Sin, were not permitted to have children. Lewy, J., op.cit., p.407. He also claims that Šumûa-damga was not Nabonidus' mother, but a governor of the city of Harran. Ibid, pp.409-10. But, as C.J. Gadd stated, there need be no hesitation in naming the writer of the inscription as Nabonidus' mother because the inscription is mostly a declaration by his mother. For example she says: "I (am) the lady Adda-guppi', mother of Nabium-na'id, king of Babylon, votaress of the gods Sin, Nin-gal, Nusku, and Sadarnunna, my deities": Gadd, C.J., op.cit., p.47.
[35]See Smith, S., op.cit., pp.52-53. Cf. Gadd, C.J., op.cit., pp.49, 57, 65.

population that he retired to the oasis of Taima in the Arabian desert, while his son Bêl-shar-usur (Belshazzar) ruled Babylonia.[36]

In the fourth century B.C., when Alexander the Great (331-323 B.C.), king of Macedonia, conquered the Greek city-states and the Persian Empire from Asia Minor and Egypt to India, Harran passed to Greek possession. From that time, Harran was deeply under the influence of Greece. Though speaking at this time Syriac, the people were in many cases partly Greek by extraction.[37]

D. Roman Period

Of Harran at this period we know little. In 55 B.C. a Roman army under the command of Crassus, a Roman general, was defeated by the Parthians.[38] At this time we learn that Harran was a fortified garrison town, in which Crassus was able to take refuge after his first reverse, that his lieutenant Octavius escaped to a mountainous region called Sinnaca in an unstated direction from Harran, and that Crassus made his last stand on a hill under the mountains of Sinnaca and connected with them by a long ridge, which ran through the plain.[39]

From that time until the Islamic period Harran was at the centre of a power-struggle between the Romans and the Parthians — later the Sassanians — and often changed hands between them.

During this period the people of Harran continued to cling to their pagan planet-cult despite the popularity of Christianity among their neighbours, the Edessans. The Syriac inscriptions of Harran from that period[40] bear no Christian influence. Harran continuously lost power against her young and dynamic neighbour, Edessa, which became the new capital of the province which included Harran.[41]

The Roman coinage in the district of Harran extends from Marcus Aurelius (161-180 A.D.) to Gordion III (238-243 A.D.).[42] When Lucius Verus campaigned in 164 A.D. to recover this territory from the Parthians, Harran was not one of the cities against which he had to mount a siege. At this time Harran was rewarded by being formally declared a colonia and a "friend of Rome" in return for her service.[43]

---

[36]Pallis, S.A., op.cit., p.634.

[37]See Browne, E.G., op.cit., v.I, p.304.

[38]Cf. Segal, J.B., *Edessa and Harran*, p.10.

[39]Lloyd, S. and W. Brice, op.cit., p.89. Also see Segal, J.B., op.cit., p.10.

[40]See Segal, J.B., "Two Syriac Inscriptions from Harran", (with an Appendix by D. Strong) *BSOAS*, 20, 1957, pp.513-22. Also see Healey, J.F., "Syriac *ḥašqbōl*: A further Note", *Biblica*, 68, 1987, p.258.

[41]See Segal, J.B., *Edessa and Harran*, pp.8ff.

[42]See Hill, G.F., op.cit., pp.lxxxviii, xc. Cf. ibid, pp.82-90.

[43]Segal. J.B., op.cit., p.11.

In 217 A.D. the Emperor Caracalla (211-217 A.D.) was murdered during his return to the palace from the temple at Harran, which was a little distance away, and the deity he had been adoring was the moon deity of Harran.[44] In 241 A.D. Harran was captured by Shapur, but one year later the Sassanians were forced to retreat and Harran was recovered by the Romans.[45] At the time of Shapur II the Sassanians launched a formidable invasion of Mesopotamia (359 A.D.). Ammianus Marcellinus, on this occasion, refers to the poor condition of the walls of Harran.[46]

In 361 A.D. the first bishop of Harran, Barses, was appointed. A Frankish woman pilgrim, Egeria, wrote in the fourth or fifth century:

> "In the city itself, apart from a few clergy and holy monks (who, however, stay outside its walls), I found not a single Christian; all were pagans."[47]

In 363 A.D. the young Emperor Julian visited Harran on his way eastward to take his army to Persia and India.[48] Julian paid his respects like Caracalla a century and a half earlier to the moon-deity of Harran.[49]

A Sassanian army in 502-3 A.D. marched upon Harran to fight against it. The garrison of Harran came to terms, because, Joshua the Stylite maintains, it was "afraid to fight".[50] In the sixth century the fortifications of the walls of Harran were repaired by Justinian (527-565 A.D.).[51]

E. The Islamic period and destruction by the Mongols

At the time of the second caliph ʿUmar, ʿIyāḍ ʾibn Ghanam, a Muslim general, conquered all Mesopotamia without fighting, including Edessa, Nisibis and Harran (639 A.D.).[52] We learn from the medieval scholars that Harran, was at that time under the political influence of Edessa.[53] We also hear that when the Muslims conquered it the people of Harran were Nabataeans (presumably Syriac-speaking pagans) and

---

44 See Lloyd, S. and W. Brice, op.cit., p.89; Jones, H.S., *The Roman Empire*, London (1908), p.262.

45 See Jones, H.S., op.cit., pp.288-89.

46 Cf. Ammianus Marcellinus, *The Later Roman Empire (A.D. 354-378)*, tr. W. Hamilton, Harmondsworth (1986), p.156.

47 Segal, J.B., "Mesopotamian Communities from Julian to the Rise of Islam", *PBA*, 41, 1955, p.124.

48 Idem, *Edessa and Harran*, p.16.

49 See Lloyd, S. and W. Brice, op.cit., p.89; Segal, J.B., "Mesopotamian Communities from Julian to the Rise of Islam", p.124.

50 See Joshua the Stylite, *Chronicle of Joshua the Stylite*, ed. and tr. W. Wright, Cambridge (1882), p.50. Cf. Segal, J.B., op.cit., p.124.

51 Lloyd, S. and W. Brice, op.cit., p.90.

52 See al-Balādhurī, op.cit., p.179; al-Ṭabarī, *tārīkh al-rusūl wa al-mulūk*, v.2, p.197; al-Yaʿqūbī, op.cit., v.2, p.150.

53 See ʾAbū Yūsuf, op.cit., p.43.

immigrants from Greece.[54] ʿIyāḍ ʾibn Ghanam made a peace agreement with the Harranians and fixed a certain tax, *jizyah*, for them.[55]

The Harranians were a political and military force in the fortunes of the Umayyad dynasty.[56] The Umayyad caliph ʿUmar II (682-720 A.D.) transferred a school of medicine from Alexandria to Harran.[57] In the last period of the Umayyad dynasty the caliph Marwān II (744-750 A.D.) made Harran his residence and moved the capital of the Umayyad Empire from Damascus to Harran.[58]

In the Abbasid period the most important event is the Abbasid caliph al-Maʾmūn's visit to Harran. In 830 A.D. he passed through Harran, threatening the pagans of Harran with death, unless they accepted Islam or one of the other religions which Allah mentioned in the Qurʾān.[59]

We hear of many famous scholars, of Harranic origin, who played an important part in the cultural field during the Abbasid period. The first person from Harran, who became famous, was Thābit ʾibn Qurrah (835-900 A.D.). He was born in Harran and, then, because of some theological arguments with the other pagans of his city, he migrated to Baghdad. In Baghdad he became a well-known person in philosophy, medicine and translation from Greek and Syriac into Arabic. Consequently the Abbasid caliph al-Muʾtadi Billāh (857-902 A.D.) accepted him into the palace. He never changed his religion and died a heathen.[60] After Thābit ʾibn Qurrah many Harranian scholars were accepted into the palace of the caliphs. Among them were Thābit ʾibn Sinān ʾibn Thābit ʾibn Qurrah al-Ḥarrānī (d. 365/975), who was famous in medicine and history at the time of the Abbasid caliphs al-Rāḍī Billāh (909-940 A.D.), al-Mustakfī (d. 949 A.D.), al-Muttakī Lillāh (d.968 A.D.) and al-Muṭiʿ Lillāh (d. 974 A.D.),[61] and ʾIbrāhīm ʾibn Hilāl al-Ḥarrānī (925-995 A.D.), who was famous in literary circles at the time of the Abbasid caliph al-Muṭiʿ Lillāh and later, at the time of Muʿizzuddawla ʾibn Buwayh (915-967 A.D.), became a secretary of state.[62]

At this time there were two cultural centres of the Harranian scholars: their native city Harran and the capital Baghdad. During the reign of the caliph al-Mutawakkil (822-861 A.D.) the school of philosophy and medicine which had been

---

[54]Ibid, p.43.
[55]al-Balādhurī, op.cit., p.179; al-Ṭabarī, op.cit., v.2, p.197.
[56]Segal, J.B., *Edessa and Harran*, p.20.
[57]See Fehervari, G., op.cit., p.228.
[58]See ibid, p.228; *CHI*, v.II, p.707.
[59]See above pp.33ff.
[60]See Yāqūt al-Hamawī al-Rūmī, *muʿjam al-ʾudabā*, v.2, p.397; Bar Habraeus, ʾAbū al-Faraj ʾibn al-ʿIbrī, *The Chronography*, tr. E.A.W. Budge, London (1932), pp.152-53; idem, *tārīkh mukhtaṣar al-duwal*, ed. A. Salhani, Beirut (1890), p.265; al-Ziriklī, op.cit., v.2, pp.81-82.
[61]See Yāqūt al-Hamawī al-Rūmī, op.cit., v.2, p.397; al-Ziriklī, op.cit., v.2, p.81.
[62]See ʾIbn al-Nadīm, op.cit., pp.193-94; al-Ziriklī, op.cit., v.1, pp.73-74. Also Hilāl ibn ʾIbrāhīm, famous physician, al-Battānī, astronomer, and ʾAbū Jaʿfar al-Hazīn al-Riyāzī were among these important Harranian scholars at that time. See ʾAmīn, ʾAḥmad, *ḍuḥā al-ʾislām*, 6th edition, Cairo (1961-1962), v.I, pp.258-59.

previously transferred from Alexandria to Harran gained in importance.[63] Also at Baghdad the Harranians won the esteem of their Muslim contemporaries by their integrity and ability; and they earned the licence of the Commander of the Faithful himself to practise their ceremonies openly at their places of worship in the vicinity of Harran.[64]

Between 990-1081 A.D. the Numairid dynasty ruled over the territory between Saruj, Harran and Raqqa.[65]

The medieval geographer al-Dimashqī states that the Egyptians, viz. Fatimids, captured the temple of the moon in Harran in 424/1032,[66] but there is no other evidence of any Fatimid action in this area at that time. The Fatimid frontier ran slightly north of Damascus. For a short time Shabīb, the lord of Harran, was obliged to pay tribute to the Byzantines. It was not until 429/1037 that he obeyed the summons of the Fatimid governor Dizbirī, who had captured Aleppo, to recognize the suzerainty of the Fatimids.[67]

In the twelfth century this part of Mesopotamia, including Edessa and Harran, was the theatre of a power-struggle between the Crusaders and the Saljuqs — later the Ayyūbids. The people of Harran generally kept alliance with the Muslims, while the Edessans supported the Crusaders. At that time Christian rulers of Edessa continuously tried to rule over Harran. For example, in 1104 A.D., when the Crusader army, joined with the Edessans, reached the plains of Harran, Baldwin of Edessa prevented the Harranians from giving the keys of the city to the Crusader commanders because, he thought, it belonged to him, being of his territory.[68]

Rabbi Benjamin of Tudela visited and described the city in 1160 A.D.[69] Twenty-four years later also 'Ibn Jubayr visited and described the city.[70]

In 1237 A.D. the Khawarazmians, who had been driven from their native land by the Mongols, became masters of the city but not of the citadel.[71]

---

63 See Hitti, P.K., *History of the Arabs*, p.314.

64 Segal, J.B., "Pagan Syriac Monuments in the Vilayet of Urfa", p.111.

65 See Rice, D.S., "Medieval Harran. Studies on its Topography and Monuments, I", *AS*, 2, 1952, pp.74ff.

66 See al-Dimashqī, op.cit., p.191. Also al-Ḥamawī (wrote 1233 A.D.), who may have used the same source as al-Dimashqī, reports that in 424/1032 some ʿAlids (*ʿalawiyūn*) captured Harran and the moon temple there. He also remarks that the Sabians had no other temple after its capture. See Rice, D.S., op.cit., p.43.

67 Rice, D.S., op.cit., p.44.

68 Cf. Tritton, A.S. (tr.), "The First and Second Crusades from an Anonymous Syriac Chronicle", *JRAS*, 1933, p.79.

69 See Benjamin of Tudela, *The Itinerary of Benjamin of Tudela*, tr. M.N. Adler, New York (c. 1965, First edition: London, 1907), pp.32-33.

70 'Ibn Jubayr writes: "This is a town with no beauty about it. It has no shade to mitigate its feverish heat. Its water bears no acquaintance with freshness and its squares and outskirts never cease to burn from the heat of its midday sun": 'Ibn Jubayr, op.cit., p.254.

71 See Rice, D.S., op.cit., p.45.

In 1259-60 A.D. the Mongols encamped against Harran. Hulagu first obtained the peaceful surrender of the city whilst the citadel, under a different governor, held out until one of the towers was breached.[72] Then the Mongols destroyed the last of the pagan temples and left the principal buildings in ruins. Harran had perished as a city.[73] The Mongols decided shortly afterwards that Harran offered too little strategic value to justify its retention and defence. ʾIbn Shaddād, who composed his work before 1280 A.D., states:

> "they deported the population to Mardin and to other towns, destroyed the Friday-Mosque, walled up the gates of the city and left it an empty shell."[74]

After the Mamlūk victory over the Mongols in 1303 A.D. north Mesopotamia, including Harran, came under Mamlūk rule. The town, however, was never rebuilt.

2. The religion of the Harranians

The medieval pagans of the city of Harran were called *al-ḥarrāniyyah*,[75] *al-ḥarnāniyyah*[76] or *al-ḥarbāniyyah*[77] by the medieval scholars. Their names, as al-Bīrūnī stated in the 11th century,[78] are derived from their place, Harran, and the last two names, i.e. *al-ḥarnāniyyah* and *al-ḥarbāniyyah*, are clearly corruptions of *al-ḥarrāniyyah*.

They were also called "the Sabians of Harran",[79] *al-kaldāniyyūn* (the Chaldaeans)[80] and *al-nibṭiyyūn* (the Nabataeans).[81]

Concerning the genealogy of the Harranians, medieval Syriac sources generally claim that they are the descendants of Āram, son of Shem and grandson of Noah.[82]

---

[72]See Bar Habraeus, *The Chronography*, p.4356; Rice, D.S., op.cit., p.45.
[73]Segal, J.B., *Edessa and Harran*, p.25.
[74]Rice, D.S., op.cit., p.45.
[75]See al-Bīrūnī, op.cit., pp.186, 188; al-Maqdisī, op.cit., v.4, p.22.
[76]See ʾIbn al-Nadīm, op.cit., p.318.
[77]See al-Shahrastānī, op.cit., p.248.
[78]See al-Bīrūnī, op.cit., p.186. al-Bīrūnī also points out that some of the medieval scholars, however, derived it from Ḥarān ʾibn Tarah, the brother of Abraham, saying that he among their chiefs was the most deeply imbued with their religion and its most tanacious adherent. See ibid, p.186.
[79]See al-Masʿūdī, *murūj al-dhahab wa maʿādin al-jawhar*, pp.61, 62, 68; idem, *kitāb al-tanbīh wa al-ʾishrāf*, p.161; al-Baghdādī, *al-farq bayn al-firāq*, pp.263, 278. For the connection of the Harranians with the name Sabians see Chapter II.
[80]See Ḥamzah al-ʾIsfahānī, op.cit., p.7; al-Khawārizmī, op.cit., p.36; ʾIbn al-Nadīm, op.cit., p.318.
[81]See ʾAbū Yūsuf, op.cit., p.43.
[82]See Ephrem Syrus, *The Book of the Cave of Treasures*, tr. E.A.W. Budge, London (1927), p.134; Solomon or Shelemen, the Bishop, *The Book of the Bee*, tr. E.A.W. Budge, Oxford (1886), p.36.

Information on the religion of the Harranians comes to us from three kinds of sources, (1) the writings of the Harranians, (2) archaeological materials and (3) some medieval writers who were interested in these people.

(1) The books of the Harranians which have survived are very limited. The most important of them is "The Book of Bābā the Harranian", or "The Prophecy of Bābā of Harran".[83] We possess two rather large fragments of the reputed writings of Bābā.[84] One of them is in Syriac, which is found in Dionysius Bar Salibi's work "Against the Muslims". He wrote in the 12th century. This text was first published, together with a Latin translation, by Ignatius Ephraem III Rahmani in his *Studia Syriaca*.[85] Another one is in Arabic, found in the volume dealing with geography of the *bughyat al-talab fī tārīkh ḥalab* by ʾIbn al-ʿAdīm (1192/93-1262 A.D.), and longer than the Syriac one.[86] Both were translated into English by F. Rosenthal.

Bābā, in this book, gives information about the religion of the Harranians and tells of some future events.

Another source is the book of "Five Mysteries" of the Harranians,[87] which contains initiation rite and some Harranian magical information. ʾIbn al-Nadīm, who quotes this book from a mutilated copy, states:

> "There came into my possession a passage which one of the translators transcribed from their [the Ḥarranian Ṣābians] books and which includes five of their mysteries, except that a page fell out from the description of the first part of the fifth mystery."[88]

We are not given any information about the writer of this book and its date.

The final book, which may be connected with the Harranians, is *al-fillāḥatu al-nibṭiyyūn*, "The Nabatean Agriculture", which was translated into Arabic presumably from an Aramaic original copy by ʾIbn al-Wahshiyya.[89] A magical treatise called

---

[83]See Rosenthal, F., "The Prophecies of Bābā the Ḥarranian", in *A Locust's Leg; Studies in Honour of S.H. Taqizadeh*, ed. W.B. Henning, London (1962), pp.220-32.

[84]For the Bābā the Harranian see below pp.159f.

[85]See Rosenthal, F., op.cit., p.227. On the Syriac text Rosenthal states that there is a good possibility that the Syriac text has, in fact, preserved remnants of Harranian gnostic literature that were only slightly adapted to the purpose which the Christian author had in mind when using them. Ibid, p.232.

[86]See ibid, pp.221-25. In Rosenthal's opinion the Arabic text was translated from an Aramaic original presumably dating from the Umayyad period. Ibid, p.232.

[87]See ʾIbn al-Nadīm, op.cit., pp.326-27.

[88]Ibid, p.326 (Dodge, v.II, p.769). ʾIbn al-Nadīm also remarks: "The translator of these five mysteries was awkward, lacking good Arabic diction. Or, perhaps by translating in this corrupt and wretched style, he wished to show the truth about them [the Ṣābians] and aimed to give their own phrases, which he left unchanged in spite of lack of cohesion and omission of words": ibid, p.327 (Dodge, v.II, p.772).

[89]See al-Majrīṭī, ʾAbū al-Qāsim Maslamah ibn ʾAḥmad (Pseudo-Majrīṭī), *ghāyat al-ḥakīm wa ʾahaqq al-natījatayn bi al-taqdīm (Picatrix)*, ed. H. Ritter, Studien der Bibliothek Warburg, v.XII, Leipzig (1933), p.179; Maimonides, M., *The Guide of the Perplexed*, tr. S. Pines, Chicago (1963), p.518.

ghāyat al-ḥakīm, or "Picatrix",[90] of about 440 A.H. (1048 A.D.), which was assigned to ʾAbū al-Qāsim Maslamah ʾibn ʾAḥmad al-Majrīṭī (Pseudo-Majrīṭī), contains what is ostensibly a lengthy exract from this book. "The Nabatean Agriculture" contains information about the cult of seven planets and rites such as initiation, human sacrifice and some magical practises.

Our medieval sources mention some other books of the Harranians, which unfortunately have not come down to us. Among them ʾIbn al-Nadīm records a book, entitled *al-ḥātifī*, which was about the incantations, enchantments and amulets of the Harranians.[91] According to *al-fihrist* another Syriac book of the Harranians, which contained an account of their doctrines and prayers, was translated into Arabic by order of Hārūn ʾibn ʾIbrāhīm, the judge of Harran. ʾIbn al-Nadīm also points out that this book was to be found widespread in the hands of the people.[92]

(2) We have two kinds of archaeological materials from the district of Harran: cuneiform and Syriac inscriptions and the ruins of the temples and tombs.

In 1906 H. Pognon discovered some cuneiform inscriptions from the time of Nabonidus (555-538 B.C.), king of Babylonia, at Eski Harran.[93] Then three stelae bearing inscriptions were discovered at Harran by D.S. Rice in 1956, while he was engaged in examining the architecture of the ruined Great Mosque at that place.[94] They too are from the time of Nabonidus. All of these inscriptions contain information about the religion of the people of Harran at that time, especially the cult of Sin, the moon-god, and *é-ḫúl-ḫúl*, the temple of Sin.

D.S. Rice discovered two Syriac inscriptions in Harran in 1951. One was dated to the second or third centuries A.D. by J.B. Segal, while other was dated to the fourth or fifth centuries A.D. (with some hesitation).[95]

We also have some monuments and several Syriac inscriptions around them, some of which contain the date 476 (164-5 A.D.), at Sumatar Harabesi which is

---

[90]al-Majrīṭī, op.cit. For the Picatrix also see Yates, F.A., *Giordano Bruno and the Hermetic Tradition*, London (1964), pp.49-50.

[91]See ʾIbn al-Nadīm, op.cit., p.321. Also see Chwolsohn, D., op.cit., v.II, pp.137f.

[92]ʾIbn al-Nadīm, op.cit., p.327. Maimonides, who, like many medieval scholars, uses the term Sabians for all pagans, but in particular describes the pagans of Harran as Sabians, mentions some books of the Sabians, which are probably connected with the Harranians. He states that these books have been translated into Arabic. These are "The Book of *al-ʾustumākhus*" that is ascribed to Aristotle (but, Maimonides states that he cannot have written it) and the books concerning talismans such as "The Book of *tumtum*", "The Book of *al-sarb*" and "The Book of the Degrees of the Sphere and the Forms appearing in each of these Degrees". Maimonides also mentions a book concerning talismans that is likewise attributed to Aristotle, a book, ascribed to Hermes, the book written by ʾIsḥāq al-Ṣābī on the defence of the religious community of the Sabians and the big book of this same author concerning the laws of the Sabians and the details of their religion, festivals, sacrifices and prayers. See Maimonides, op.cit., p.520-21. Also ʾAbū al-Fidā ʾIsmāʿīl ʾibn ʿAlī states that they have a book, titled *ṣuḥufu shīth*, "The Pages of Seth", concerning their ethics and laws. See ʾAbū al-Fidā, op.cit., p.148.

[93]See Lewy, J., op.cit., p.405.

[94]Gadd, C.J., "The Harran Inscriptions of Nabonidus", p.35.

[95]See Segal, J.B., "Two Syriac Inscriptions from Harran", pp.517, 520.

situated in the Tektek mountains, to the north-east of Harran.[96] These inscriptions give information about the religion of that area in that time.

At Harran and in its vicinity there are several ruins of buildings, some of which are quite possibly related to the temples of the Harranians. At Harran we have a prayer-house or place of worship, set on a hill, the foundation of which is associated with Abraham by medieval Arab writers, and a castle. Also at Aşağı Yarımca there is a very large stone building, just beneath the surface, with a stele and cuneiform inscription. Moreover at Sultantepe, to the north of Harran, and at Sumatar Harabesi there are some ruins of buildings.[97]

(3) Finally we have the studies of the Arabic scholars such as al-Masʿūdī, ʾIbn al-Nadīm, al-Bīrūnī and al-Shahrastānī about the religion of the Harranians. Our main Syriac sources are Dionysius of Tell-Mahre, who composed his work about 840 A.D., and Bar Habraeus. Our only Hebrew source is Maimonides.

A. Harranian theology

We know very little about the religion of Harran in pre-medieval times. All we know from that time is some information on the pantheon of the gods, their temples and some rites. But from medieval times we have plenty of information through our Arabic sources. We will examine Harranian theology under three categories, (i) from Assyro-Babylonian times to the Christian era, (ii) from the beginning of the Christian era until the Islamic period and (iii) in the Islamic period.

(i) In Assyro-Babylonian times, among the deities of Harran Sin, the moon-god, was at the top of the pantheon.[98] He was the supreme deity of Harran since at least the first centuries of the third millennium B.C.

The children of Sin, Ishtar, his daughter, and Shamash, his son, are mentioned with him in one of the Nabonidus inscriptions from Harran.[99] It seems there was a trinity of gods, but this may be due to the custom of mentioning gods in threes.[100] Ishtar and Shamash were certainly worshipped at Harran in that period because they are among the divinities occurring in the composition of proper names in the district of Harran at that time.[101] Also the emblems of the sun (disc with internal pattern of four

---

[96]See Segal, J.B., "Pagan Syriac Monuments in the Vilayet of Urfa", p.97; Drijvers, H.J.W., *Old Syriac (Edessean) Inscriptions*, Semitic Stud. Ser., New Ser. 3, Leiden (1972), pp.4-19.

[97]See Gurney, O.R., "The Assyrian Tablets from Sultantepe", *PBA*, 41, 1955, pp.21-22; Segal, J.B., op.cit., pp.112-14; Lloyd, S. and W. Brice, op.cit.,, pp.80, 96.

[98]For this deity and its cult see below pp.192ff.

[99]See Gadd, C.J., op.cit., p.47; Smith, S., *Babylonian Historical Texts*, p.45.

[100]See King, L.W., *First Steps in Assyrian*, London (1898), pp.182, 250. Cf. Smith, S., op.cit., p.67.

[101]Cf. Johns, C.H.W., *An Assyrian Doomsday Book*, Leipzig (1901), p.12.

points and spreading rays between these) and Ishtar-Venus (seven-pointed star in a circle) occur on two sculptured steles from Harran.[102]

Under the moon-god Sin's supreme authority we hear from the inscriptions of three more deities, Ningal, Sin's consort, Nusku, the fire god, and Sadarnunna, Nusku's spouse. In the Harran inscriptions of Nabonidus these three deities are often mentioned with the moon-god Sin. Nabonidus speaks of bringing back these three deities into Harran to dwell in *é-ḫúl-ḫúl*, the temple of Sin.[103]

We also find a number of lesser deities who were worshipped at Harran. Their names often appear in proper names. These are Nabu, god of writing, wisdom and human fate, Adadi, god of rain, thunder and lightning, Ter, Šer and Allai.[104]

Finally S. Smith states that also the gods Ashur, Ea and Marduk were worshipped at Harran in the Assyrian period,[105] though some Assyriologists, such as J.N. Postgate, disagree with him.[106]

(ii) From the beginning of the Christian era to the Islamic period the Harranians clung obstinately to their local cults of Sin and the other planets despite their Christian environment. In the second and third century Bardaisan (154-222 A.D.), a Christian heretic from Edessa, speaks of the cult of seven planets of the Babylonian Chaldaeans and of their books in which, he states, it is described what influence the stars in their constellations exercise upon the horoscopes of men.[107] Also the *Doctrine of Addai*, which was composed in c. 400 A.D., tells of the planet cult of the Harranians. It mentions the Sun and the Moon which were venerated by the inhabitants of Harran and the cult of the stars and planets, especially the Bright Star, i.e. Venus, the morning and evening star.[108] The moon-god Sin occurs in the "Homily on the Fall of the Idols" of Jacob of Saruǧ (c. 451-521 A.D.), in which he mentions Sin as one of the deities of Harran.[109] Evidently Sin in the "Homily" and the moon-god in the *Doctrine of Addai* are, as H.J.W. Drijvers remarked, the same deity, worshipped at Harran, but Jacob knows the name of Harran's moon-god.[110]

---

[102]Gadd, C.J., op.cit., p.41.
[103]See ibid, pp.47, 49, 65. Also see Johns, C.H.W., op.cit., p.12.
[104]See Johns, C.H.W., op.cit., pp.14ff, 34; Gadd, C.J., op.cit., p.47.
[105]Smith, S., op.cit., p.53. Also see King, L.W., op.cit., p.98.
[106]See Postgate, J.N., op.cit., p.124.
[107]See Bardaisan, *The Book of the Laws of Countries*, tr. H.J.W. Drijvers, Assen (1964), pp.29, 40-41, 51. The term "the Babylonian Chaldaeans" in Bardaisan's book may refer to the pagans of Harran as well as the other pagans of Babylonia. The Biblical writers generally used the term "Chaldaeans" in the sense of astrologers, astronomers and magicians. See Dan. The same sense is also seen in classical writers such as Strabo and Diodorus. See *DB*, v.1, p.368. The reason for this usage was evidently that Babylonia-Chaldaea had been the home and the chief seat of astrological knowledge and magic from early times. The city of Harran was also an important centre of paganism, astrology and magic, near its Christian neighbour Edessa. Also, as we remarked earlier, the medieval scholars pointed out that the pagans of Harran were known as Chaldaeans before they were called Sabians (see above p.33). See Bar Habraeus, *tārīkh mukhtaṣar al-duwal*, p.266.
[108]Cf. *The Teaching of Addai*, p.49.
[109]See Drijvers, H.J.W., *Cults and Beliefs at Edessa*, Leiden (1980), p.43.
[110]Ibid, p.44.

Another cult of the Harranians at that time, which is mentioned in the *Doctrine of Addai*, is the cult of Bath-Nikkal, "daughter of Nikkal".[111] Nikkal is an Aramaic name for Ningal, consort of the moon-god Sin. Hence Bath-Nikkal is clearly a local designation of Ishtar-Venus because Ishtar is the daughter of the moon-god Sin and the goddess Ningal.[112] Also Jacob of Saruğ points out the Ishtar-Venus cult of Harran, but he gives the name of deity as *trʿtʾ*.[113] Bardaisan and the *Doctrine of Addai* too remark on the cult of Tarʿata, but they do not mention it in connection with the pagans of Harran; the former refers to the Tarʿata cult at Edessa while the latter mentions Tarʿata as the deity of Mabbug.[114] Tarʿata (or Tarʿatha) is a different spelling of the well-known Syrian goddess Atargatis, a local form of the Semitic goddess Ishtar. H.J.W. Drijvers states that her name actually is a composite of ʿAštart and ʿAnat.[115] Her name is spelled in different ways, *ʿtrʿth*, *ʿtrʿthʾ*, *ʾtrʿth*, *ʾtrʿtʾ*, and *trʾt*.[116] The main sanctuary of Atargatis was in Hierapolis-Mabbug as the *Doctrine of Addai* mentioned.[117]

At that time another deity of Harran, according to the "Homily" of Jacob of Saruğ, was Baʿal šamên.[118] The same deity is also mentioned by Ephrem Syrus (306-373 A.D.).[119] The epithet *baʿal šamūn*, "the Lord of Heaven", is used in ancient Near Eastern inscriptions as a divine name and usually denotes the supreme god of any local pantheon.[120]

Jacob of Saruğ, moreover, mentions three more cults at Harran in his time: Bar Nemrê, "My Lord with (or of) his Dogs" and Gadlat.[121]

Bar Nemrê might be a local appellation of a particular god. *nmr* in Akkadian means "shine, radiate". *br nmrʾ* could have the meaning "Son of the Shining one" or

[111]Cf. *The Teaching of Addai*, p.49.
[112]J.B. Segal, however, suggests that Bath-Nikal (Bath-Nikkal) is possibly to be identified with Ningal, consort of Sin, the Moon deity. See Segal, J.B., "Pagan Syriac Monuments in the Vilayet of Urfa", p.108 n.35.
[113]Drijvers, H.J.W., op.cit., p.43.
[114]See Bardaisan, op.cit., p.59; *The Teaching of Addai*, p.49.
[115]Drijvers, H.J.W., op.cit., p.84.
[116]Ibid, p.84. Also in the Akkadian pantheon list from Ugarit the name of the deity occurs as *ʿṯtrt* (= Ishtar). See Healey, J.F., "The Akkadian 'Pantheon' List from Ugarit", *SEL*, 2, 1985, p.118.
[117]Cf. *The Teaching of Addai*, p.49. Hierapolis and Harran are considered as the centres of paganism in his time by Jacob of Saruğ and therefore he gives so much attention to both of them and their connections. He says:
"Mabbug made he (i.e., Satan) a city of the priest of the goddess(es)
And called it with his name in order that it would err forever (going after its idols),
A sister of Harran, which is also devoted to the offerings;
And in their error both of them love the springs": Drijvers, H.J.W. op.cit., pp.97-98.
[118]Drijvers, H.J.W., op.cit., p.43.
[119]See Ephrem Syrus, op.cit., p.153.
[120]See Teixidor, J., *The Pagan God. Popular Religion in the Greco-Roman Near East*, Princeton (1977), pp.26-27. J.B. Segal is inclined to identify Māri/alāhē of Sumatar Harabesi, "the Lord of the gods", with Baʿal šamên, although with some hesitation, mainly because Baʿal šamên at Palmyra bears the title *mrʾ*, "lord", and at Hatra too was addressed as "king" and the "great god". See Segal, J.B., *Edessa 'The Blessed City'*, p.60; idem, "Pagan Syriac Monuments in the Vilayet of Urfa", pp.115f. For Māralāhē of Sumatar Harabesi see below p.199.
[121]See Drijvers, H.J.W., op.cit., p.43.

"Son of Shining". Thus *br nmr'* is, as Drijvers stated, probably a local appellation of the fire-god Nusku.[122]

On identification of the enigmatic deity "My Lord with (or of) his Dogs" J.B. Segal states that this god is perhaps the hunter Orion, at whose heels are the constellations Canis major and Canis minor.[123] As a second possibility, this deity may be identical with "the Lord of Good Luck" of the medieval Harranians, whose dogs are mentioned in one of the ritual prayers of the Harranians.[124] Here "the Lord of Good Luck" is evidently Gad, Semitic god of fortune or luck.[125] But in this identification there is a difficulty because Jacob of Sarug̃ also mentions Gadlat (Gad and Allat) as a deity of these people. A more probable explanation is that "My Lord with (or of) his Dogs" could be a local appellation of Nergal, who is represented with three dogs in the religious art of Hatra.[126]

Finally Gadlat is clearly a combination of Gad, the god of fortune, and Allat, the Arab goddess widely worshipped by the desert people in Syria and Mesopotamia.[127]

(iii) From the tenth century A.D. onward we have plenty of information about the religion of the pagans of Harran in the medieval period. At that time there were many arguments and divisions of opinion concerning theological subjects, especially about the Creator and Cosmos, among the Harranians.[128] Thābit 'ibn Qurrah, for instance, differed with the other pagans of Harran over some theological subjects and left the city.[129] However, we know little about the differences between these sects.

The medieval Muslim scholars speak of different sects of the Sabians/Harranians. ʿAbd al-Qāhir al-Baghdādī (d. 429/1037) tells of two different sects: one, he states, is a group of Greeks who believe that the Universe is not eternal (*ḥudūth*) and there is a Maker (*ṣāniʿ*) who does not resemble anything else; he is Ever-living (*ḥayy*), Speaking, Seeing and the Regulator of the Universe. According to al-Baghdādī another group basically accepts these points, but says we cannot say that the Maker is Ever-living, Knowing and able to do everything (*qādir*), but we say he is neither dead nor ignorant nor unable.[130] As is clear, the only difference between them is about the description of Creator. The second group describe the Creator (Maker) as

---

122 See ibid, pp.144-45.

123 Segal, J.B., "Pagan Syriac Monuments in the Vilayet of Urfa", p.109.

124 "Oh diviners of good luck, here is bread for your dogs, barley and straw for your beasts, oil for your lamps and myrtle for your crowns (wreaths)": 'Ibn al-Nadīm, op.cit., p.324 (Dodge, v.II, p.761).

125 See below p.153.

126 In Hatra inscriptions Nergal is mentioned as *nrgl klb'* (or *nrwgl klb'*), "Nergal the dog". See Vattioni, F., *Le Iscrizioni di Hatra*, Naples (1981), p.47. Also see Drijvers, H.J.W., op.cit., p.44.

127 For Gad see Dhorme, E., *Les religions de Babylonie et d'Assyrie*, Paris (1945), p.405. Also for Allat see al-Kalbī, 'Abū al-Mundhir Hishām 'ibn Muḥammad, *kitāb al-'aṣnām*, 2nd edition, Cairo (1343/1924), pp.16-17.

128 See al-Baghdādī, *'uṣūl al-dīn*, pp.324-25; al-Shahrastānī, op.cit., pp.244, 246.

129 See above p.132.

130 See al-Baghdādī, op.cit., pp.324-25.

exempt from anything that is bad, using in their description the way of negative expression.[131]

We are informed about another division by al-Shahrastānī and later al-Dimashqī, who separate them into two groups, star-worshippers and idol-worshippers.[132] al-Shahrastānī calls the star-worshippers *ʾaṣḥāb al-hayākil* and the idol-worshippers *ʾaṣḥāb al-ʾashkhāṣ*.[133] The former group believes that the saints and heavenly spirits are the intermediaries of the Holy Beings. They therefore should be venerated directly. On the other hand the latter group says that the idols should be worshipped, since they are the representatives of the planetary spirits and the Heavenly Beings.[134] What we understand from the difference between the two groups is that the star-worshippers preferred to worship the saints and planets directly and opposed the belief that the idols are the intermediaries of the Holy Beings.

ʾIbn al-Nadīm also tells of the heretical sects of the Harranians.[135] One of them is called *rūfusiyyūn* (or *rūfusiyyīn*).[136] According to *al-fihrist* the women members of this sect never wore gold or adorned themselves with it under any circumstances. They did not wear red boots either. On their annual festival day they used to sacrifice pigs to their gods and eat the meat. Also there was another heretical sect, the members of which, both men and women, used to shave their heads with razors.[137]

According to our medieval sources, besides their central planet cult, which we will later examine, the medieval Harranians generally believed that there was a Holy Creator of the world who was far from every creature.[138] In their belief he is the prime cause (the transcendent creator) of the world. He is eternal and a unity, rather than multiple.[139] With this belief of theirs we understand that they, as al-Bīrūnī stated,

---

[131] al-Bīrūnī gives almost the same information about the theology of the Harranians, but he does not mention the other group and their beliefs. See al-Bīrūnī, op.cit., p.187.

[132] See al-Shahrastānī, op.cit., p.244, 246; al-Dimashqī, op.cit., p.44.

[133] al-Shahrastānī, op.cit., p.244.

[134] Cf. ibid, p.246; al-Dimashqī, op.cit., p.44.

[135] ʾIbn al-Nadīm narrates this account from a person of whom he remarks "a reliable authority" who states: "In ancient times they used to have creeds and heresies, but I do not know whether or not they still exist": ʾIbn al-Nadīm, op.cit., p.326 (Dodge, v.II, p.768).

[136] See ibid, p.326. Also see Chwolsohn, D., op.cit., v.II, p.42.

[137] ʾIbn al-Nadīm, op.cit., p.326.

[138] See al-Dimashqī, op.cit., p.47. Maimonides, however, states that they believe in the eternity of the world, since in their opinion heaven is the deity. See Maimonides, op.cit., pp.515, 516. This must be the opinion of one of the philosophical sects, because we hear from many other sources, such al *al-fihrist* of ʾIbn al-Nadīm and *ʾuṣūl al-dīn* of al-Baghdādī, that they generally believed that the world has been created. See ʾIbn al-Nadīm, op.cit., p.318; al-Baghdādī, *ʾuṣūl al-dīn*, pp.324f.

[139] "No attribute of things created is connected with Him. He has charged discerning persons whom He has created to acknowledge His lordship. He has shown them the way, sending apostles for their guidance and for confirmation of proof, ordering them both to call [people] to be approved by Him and to warn them of His anger. They [the apostles] have promised enduring contentment for the obedient, but for the person who is disobedient they have promised torment and punishment to the extent which he deserves": ʾIbn al-Nadīm, op.cit., p.318 (Dodge, v.II, p.746). Also see al-Maqdisī, op.cit., v.4, p.22.

professed a kind of monotheism, which we cannot see among their beliefs before the medieval period.[140]

al-Bīrūnī states that the Harranians "call the Holy Creator by the Nomina Pulcherrima, but only metaphorically, since a real description of him is excluded according to them".[141] Therefore they believe that it is necessary for creatures to accept their inability to understand him.[142]

On the other hand they attribute the rule of the Universe to the celestial globe and its bodies, which they consider as living, speaking, hearing and seeing beings,[143] because according to their belief this Holy Creator undertakes only the major task, leaving inferior matters to the mediators appointed by him to administer the world.[144] The heavenly bodies or the seven planets and twelve zodiac signs act as intermediaries between men and the supreme deity. They have great influence on the human beings. They cause such effects as love and hatred, and knowledge and healing, since they have good and bad characteristics.[145]

Also the pagans of Harran believed in the existence of certain primal elements which emanated from the Primal Cause, the transcendent deity. These are *al-ʿaql*, "the Mind (or Intellect)", *al-nafs*, "the Soul", *al-siyāsah*, "Governing (or World Order)", *al-ṣūrah*, "the Form", and *al-ḍarūrah*, "Necessity".[146]

There is an obvious resemblence between this doctrine of the Harranians and ancient Greek philosophy. Medieval scholars therefore interpreted the metaphysical significance of these doctrines in terms of Aristotle's philosophical works.[147] al-Bīrūnī too pointed out the relationship between these pagans and the ancient Greeks and stated that they were the remains of the followers of the ancient religion of the West, separated from it, since the Greeks adopted Christianity.[148]

In the belief of the Harranians these divine elements are too transcendent for man to reach, so that some mediators are necessary. When the spirit of man comes to earth, it finds a human body in which to dwell. In the same way, when one of these divine spirits comes to earth it seeks a temple in which to find lodging. Accordingly, the Harranians built earthly abodes to accommodate each one of these divine spirits, during

---

[140] See al-Bīrūnī, op.cit., p.187.
[141] Ibid, p.187.
[142] See al-Dimashqī, op.cit., p.47.
[143] See al-Bīrūnī, op.cit., p.187. Also see ʾIbn al-Ḥazm, op.cit., v.I, p.34.
[144] ʾIbn al-Nadīm, op.cit., p.318. Also see Rosenthal, F., *Aḥmad B. aṭ-Ṭayyib as-Sarahsi*, p.45.
[145] See al-Dimashqī, op.cit., p.47; Maimonides, op.cit., p.576. Also see below p.146.
[146] See al-Shahrastānī, op.cit., pp.250-51; al-Masʿūdī, *murūj al-dhahab wa maʿādin al-jawhar*, v.4, pp.61-62; al-Dimashqī, op.cit., pp.39-40. al-Masʿūdī gives the name *al-silsilah*, "the Sequence", instead of "Governing". See al-Masʿūdī, op.cit., v.4, p.62.
[147] See ʾIbn al-Nadīm, op.cit., pp.319-20; al-Maqdīsī, op.cit., v.4, p.24. Also al-Masʿūdī (10th century A.D.) states that he has seen some words of Plato, written in Syriac, on the gate of Harran. al-Masʿūdī, op.cit., v.4, p.64. For the connection of the Harranian doctrine to the ancient Greek philosophy see Tardieu, M., "Ṣābiens Coraniques et 'Ṣābiens' de Ḥarrān".
[148] See al-Bīrūnī, op.cit., p.314.

its sojourn on earth and as it was considered to be presumptuous for a worshipper to pray to the transcendant god, prayer was addressed to these lesser deities.[149]

Our medieval sources describe the temples. Some, especially al-Dimashqī, give detail. The temple of the Primal Cause was in the shape of hemispere, with forty-eight windows near the roof and others lower down on the east and west sides, through which the heavenly bodies could cast their light. In this temple they used to pray on certain feast days. The temples of the other primal elements were in the form of circle. In the temple of the Soul there was an image of man with many hands and feet, perhaps representing the activities of creation.[150]

The pagans of Harran were also deeply rooted in their ancient planet cult. In fact they were most famous for this cult. They generally believed that the seven planets, the Moon, the Sun, Saturn, Mars, Jupiter, Mercury and Venus, were the creators, rulers and regulators of the world. They also believed that the seven planets gave good and bad fortune and blessing.[151] In their belief these seven heavenly bodies are male and female and have passions for one another and also have bad and good luck.[152]

Among the seven planets the highest deity or supreme being is the Moon (*al-qamar*), who seems to have been worshipped as a male deity. The name of this moon-god is *sīn*, as in the earlier moon-cult. We will later discuss the moon-cult of Harran.[153]

The second planetary deity of the Harranians is the sun (*al-shams*).[154] Maimonides states that the sun, who in their belief governs the upper and the lower world, was one of the two greatest deities, the other being the moon.[155] This deity is also called *al-rabb al-ʿaẓīm*, "the Great Lord", *rabb al-khayr*, "the Lord of Well-Being",[156] and *ʾayliyūs*, "Helios".[157] Although the term *al-shams*, indicating this deity, is feminine in Arabic, it is probable that in Harran the sun-deity was thought of as male, because his other names which we have mentioned, i.e. *al-rabb al-ʿaẓīm* and *rabb al-khayr*, clearly show that he was a male deity.[158] This deity is presumably identical with the Assyro-Babylonian sun-god *šamaš* who was also worshipped at Harran in the Assyro-Babylonian period.[159]

---

149 See Dodge, B., op.cit., p.65. Cf. al-Shahrastānī, op.cit., pp.204, 224.
150 See al-Dimashqī, op.cit., p.39; al-Masʿūdī, op.cit., v.4, pp.61-62; al-Shahrastānī, op.cit., p.250.
151 See al-Majrīṭī, op.cit., p.225; ʾIbn Ḥazm, op.cit., v.i, p.34; ʾIbn al-Nadīm, op.cit., p.325; Theodor Abu Ḳurra, *Traktat über den Schöpfer und die wahre Religion*, tr. G. Graf, Beiträge zur Geschichte der Philosophie des Mittelalters, ed. C. Baeumker, Band XIV. Heft 1, Münster i.W. (1913), p.24; Maimonides, op.cit., p.514; Bar Habraeus, *tārīkh mukhtaṣar al-duwal*, p.266.
152 ʾIbn al-Nadīm, op.cit., p.325.
153 See below pp.192ff.
154 See ʾIbn al-Nadīm, op.cit., pp.321, 324; al-Bīrūnī, op.cit., p.316.
155 Maimonides, op.cit., p.514.
156 ʾIbn al-Nadīm, op.cit., p.324.
157 Ibid, p.321.
158 In Arabic *al-rabb* is the masculine form.
159 See above p.137.

The third planet is Venus (*al-zuhrah*), who is named *balfī* [160] or *balthā* (or *balthī*).[161] This name is presumably a local version of Belit (or Beltu), "lady". The Babylonian mother-goddess Ninlil, wife of Enlil who is the second god of the highest triad of the Babylonian pantheon, is called *bēlit-mātātē*, "lady of lands", as well as *bēlit-ilē*, "lady of the gods". Later this mother-goddess has been assimilated to Ishtar.[162]

Venus is also called *al-shaḥmīyah*, "the glowing or flashing goddess", by the medieval Harranians.[163]

We have two other deity names of the Harranians, which quite possibly refer to the Venus-cult. One of them is *ʿuzūz*[164] which is obviously a local name for Venus, who was worshipped by the Arabs as *ʿuzzā*.[165] The second name is *tirrathā*[166] which is presumably a local form of Tatʿatha or Atargatis, Ishtar-Venus.

According to al-Dimashqī's account of the temples of the Harranians the Harranians describe Venus as *zawjah al-shams wa al-qamar*, "the wife of the Sun and the Moon".[167] Evidently she was worshipped as a fertility goddess by the pagans of Harran at that time. They had some offering rites for this deity in which they offered to her many kinds of fragrant fruits, dry or fresh, including water plants.[168]

Finally al-Bīrūnī mentions the names of the idols of the Venus-cult of the Harranians. One of them is *tarsā*.[169] Its similarity to Tatʿatha (Atargatis) is noticeable. The others are *blyān* and *daylafatān*.[170] The last is a dual of Dilbat, the Akkadian astronomical designation of the planet Venus, the dual apparently being due to the fact that Venus is both evening and morning star.[171]

The planet Mars (*al-mirrīkh*) was worshipped under the name of *laris* or *ʾarīs* (Ares).[172] This planetary deity is also called "the Blind Lord" by the medieval Harranians. al-Majrīṭī states that he was called *mārā samyā* (or *mārā smayyā*) which means, in Arabic, *al-ʾilāh al-ḍarīr*, "the Blind God".[173] Also in the account in *al-fihrist* he is described as *al-ʾilāh al-ʾaʿmā*, "the Blind God", and in another passage

---

160 al-Bīrūnī, op.cit., p.316.
161 ʾIbn al-Nadīm, op.cit., p.321. Also see Chwolsohn, D., op.cit., v.II, p.23.
162 See Zimmern, H., "Babylonians and Assyrians", in *ERE*, v.2, pp.310-11.
163 ʾIbn al-Nadīm, op.cit., p.324.
164 See ibid, p.324.
165 See *Qurʾān*, 53: 19. Also this deity was worshipped as the morning star under the name *ʿazizos*, one of her twin forms, at Edessa. See Drijvers, H.J.W., *Cults and Beliefs at Edessa*, pp.146ff. Also see al-Kalbī, op.cit., pp.18f.
166 See al-Bīrūnī, op.cit., p.316.
167 See al-Dimashqī, op.cit., p.42.
168 See ʾIbn al-Nadīm, op.cit., p.324.
169 See al-Bīrūnī, op.cit., p. 316.
170 Ibid, pp.317, 318.
171 See Lewy, H., op.cit., p.143.
172 ʾIbn al-Nadīm, op.cit., pp.321, 322, 325.
173 al-Majrīṭī, op.cit., p.226.

as *al-rabb al-ʾaʿmā*, "the Blind Lord".[174] On the other hand *rabb al-ʿumyān*, "the Lord of the Blind", is also mentioned.[175] Although in the text he is separated from the seven deities, i.e. the seven planets, *rabb al-ʿumyān* presumably refers to the planet Mars, the Blind Lord.

Bābā the Harranian, one of the prophets of the Harranians, also mentions the Blind Lord and points out that he is the one who commanded him to make the prophecies known to the people.[176]

The planet Mars, *ʾarīs* or the Blind Lord, is described as a malevolent spirit.[177] The reference to blindness is explained by the fact that when he fell into a rage Mars dealt blows without seeing what he was doing, causing wars and other calamities.[178]

Another planet Saturn (*zuḥāl*) was named *qirqis* (Chronos) by the medieval Harranians.[179] According to the records of al-Bīrūnī they also called him "the Venerable Old Man".[180] The human-shaped idols in his temple could be connected with this title. Saturn was a malevolent deity.[181]

The planet Jupiter (*al-mushtarī*) was worshipped under the name of *bāl* or *bayl* (Bel).[182] This deity was also called *shaykh al-waqār*, "the Shaykh of Majesty".[183] The name, *bāl* (or *bayl*), might be connected either the supreme god of Palmyra, Bēl, or with Baʿal Shamên who was worshipped by the people of Harran earlier.[184]

Finally Mercury (*ʿuṭārid*) was venerated under the name of *nābiq*.[185] al-Bīrūnī records the feast of Hermes-Mercury of the Harranians.[186] Here the planet Mercury is identified with Hermes who occurs both among the deities and the prophets of the Harranians.[187] *nābiq* is evidently a local name for the Babylonian deity Nabu, whose cult was widespread in the district of Harran during the Assyro-Babylonian period.[188]

---

174 ʾIbn al-Nadīm, op.cit., pp.322, 325.
175 "They burn seven lambs for the seven deities, a sheep for the Lord of the Blind, and a sheep for the deities [which are] the devils": ibid, p.322 (Dodge, v.II, p.756).
176 See Rosenthal, F., "The Prophecies of Bābā the Harranian", pp.224-25.
177 See ʾIbn al-Nadīm, op.cit., p.325. Also see al-Majrīṭī, op.cit., p.199. B. Dodge, however, suggests that "a malevolent spirit" in *al-fihrist* may indicate some other deity. See Dodge, B., *The Fihrist of al-Nadīm*, v.II, p.765 n.99.
178 See Dodge, B., "The Ṣābians of Harran", p.67. Also cf. al-Majrīṭī, op.cit., p.226. H. Ingholt refers to the Blind Lord in connection with Simios (or Sameos), who was also worshipped in Hierapolis-Mabbug (*symy* in Syriac spelling). See Ingholt, H., *Parthian Sculptures from Hatra*, (Memoirs of the Conn. Academy of Arts and Sciences XII) New Haven (1954), pp.26-27. F. Rosenthal also suggests that the Aramaic *mrʾ smyʾ* originally referred to the Lord *smyʾ* and was misinterpreted by Arabic translators, and perhaps already by the Aramaic Harranians themselves, as the Blind Lord. See Rosenthal, F., op.cit., pp.224-25 n.7.
179 ʾIbn al-Nadīm, op.cit., p.321, 322.
180 al-Bīrūnī, op.cit., p.316. Chronos is an old man also in Greek mythology.
181 See al-Majrīṭī, op.cit., p.198.
182 See al-Bīrūnī, op.cit., p.316; ʾIbn al-Nadīm, op.cit., pp.321, 325.
183 ʾIbn al-Nadīm, op.cit., p.325.
184 See above p.139. Also for Bēl of Palmyra see Teixidor, J., op.cit., pp.113ff.
185 See ʾIbn al-Nadīm, op.cit., p.321.
186 al-Bīrūnī, op.cit., p.316.
187 For the Hermetic tradition of the Harranians see below pp.208ff.
188 See above p.138.

Also the Nabu-Hermes cult was widespread in Syria and this god was described as the god of wisdom, the god of writers and the one who conducts the soul journeying through the spheres of the planets.[189]

The pagans of Harran divided the days of the week among these planetary deities; Sunday to the Sun, Monday to the Moon, Tuesday to Mars, Wednesday to Mercury, Thursday to Jupiter, Friday to Venus and Saturday to Saturn.[190]

In their belief each of the planets had influence over a special category of persons — Saturn over persons of authority, Jupiter over wise men and philosophers, Mars over men of violence, the Sun over persons of distinction, Venus over women, children and artists, Mercury over men of learning and science and the Moon over cultivators and vagrants.[191]

The pagans of Harran also distributed the minerals, the colours and the different climates between the planets.

Each of the planets had its own colour and metal. Black and lead was peculiar to Saturn, green and tin to Jupiter, red and iron to Mars, yellow and gold to the Sun, red and copper to Venus, probably dark-blue and baked pot to Mercury and silver to the Moon.[192]

This tradition is closely connected with Babylonian religion. It has been noticed in the ruins of Ezida, the temple of Nabu at Barsippa, in the middle of the nineteenth century that the seven stages still retained their colours, and from the ground upward had the following order, each representing a planet: (1) black (Saturn), (2) brown-red (Jupiter), (3) rose-red (Mars), (4) gold (Sun), (5) white-gold (Venus), (6) dark-blue (Mercury) and (7) silver (Moon).[193]

Also each planet had its own climate and temperament. Saturn is cold, dry and malevolent. He causes many calamities. Jupiter is cool and benevolent. Therefore he causes fertility and abundance. Mars is hot and dry, and causes war, bloodshed, killing and destruction. The Sun is also hot and dry, but unlike Mars he has a dual nature, both good and bad. He therefore is both malevolent and benevolent. Venus is cold and cool. She is the chief benevolent planet, causing fertility, happiness and victory. Mercury is also a benevolent planet which causes knowledge and science. Finally the Moon is cool and has a benevolent character. Therefore he causes abundance of intelligence, happiness and success.[194]

According to the Harranians' belief every planet has its earthly residence, i.e. the temple which the deity owns. The deity's relation to his temple resembles that of the

---

[189] See Drijvers, H.J.W., "Bardaiṣan of Edessa and the Hermetica", *JEOL*, 21, 1970, pp.195-96.
[190] See al-Maqdīsī, op.cit., v.4, p.23; ʾIbn al-Nadīm, op.cit., p.321.
[191] Segal, J.B., op.cit., p.216. Cf. al-Majrīṭī, op.cit., pp.195-97.
[192] See al-Dimashqī, op.cit., pp.40-43. Also see Maimonides, op.cit., p.516.
[193] See Langdon, S.H., *Semitic Mythology*, (Mythology of All Races, v.V) Boston (1931), p.159.
[194] See al-Majrīṭī, op.cit., pp.198ff.

spirit to the body and thus the planets are the masters of the temples.[195] Consequently the Harranians built temples for each of the planets. The temples were each of a special shape.[196] They also set up statues in the temples and thought that the forces of the planets overflowed to these statues and that consequently these statues talked, had understanding, gave prophetic revelation to people and made known to people what was useful to them.[197]

Our Arabic sources give us a full description of these temples and statues though there are some differences between them. All of these sources follow almost the same order with one exception, when they describe the temples of the planets: the temple of Saturn is the first; of Jupiter the second; of Mars the third; of the Sun the fourth. According to al-Masʿūdī and al-Shahrastānī the fifth is of Mercury and the sixth is of Venus, but in al-Dimashqī's record the temple of Venus is the fifth and of Mercury is the sixth. The last one is of the Moon.[198] The *Picatrix* of Pseudo-Majrīṭī follows the same order as in al-Dimashqī's book, when he describes the characteristics of the planets.[199] Here we will follow al-Dimashqī's order because of his lengthy information about the temples of the Harranians.

The temple of Saturn was a hexagon.[200] It was built of black stone. Inside this temple there were four black statues representing Saturn: a man holding an axe in his hand, another man holding a young gazelle (رشأ), another discussing the ancient secret sciences and finally the image of a king, seated on an elephant and surrounded by cattle. Also in the middle of the temple there was an idol made of black lead or black stone and seated on a throne at the top of nine steps. On Saturday the worshippers wearing black suits and carrying olive branches used to go to this temple and sacrifice an ox as a burnt offering.[201]

The temple of Jupiter was triangular and coloured green.[202] Within the temple there was an idol made of tin. The worshippers holding cypress branches used to gather on Thursday to venerate him. Probably on that day there was an offering ceremony in this temple. A woman with her suckling baby was brought to the idol. Then the baby was prodded with a needle until it died.[203]

195See al-Dimashqī, op.cit., p.204.
196J.B. Segal identified the remains of the buildings at Sumatar Harabesi, which, he states, are seven in number, standing in an arc on hillocks to the north and west of a central mount with the Harranian planet temples. See Segal, J.B., "Pagan Syriac Monuments in the Vilayet of Urfa", pp.112-14. B. Dodge too remarked on the possibility of this identification. See Dodge, B., "Ṣābians of Ḥarran", p.66. On the other hand some scholars such as Drijvers disagree with this, suggesting that all of these buildings are tombs. See below p.200.
197See Maimonides, op.cit., p.516.
198See al-Masʿūdī, op.cit., v.4, p.62; al-Shahrastānī, op.cit., p.251; al-Dimashqī, op.cit., pp.40-43.
199See al-Majrīṭī, op.cit., pp.195-225.
200al-Masʿūdī, op.cit., v.4, p.62; al-Shahrastānī, op.cit., p.251; al-Dimashqī, op.cit., p.40.
201al-Dimashqī, op.cit., p.40.
202Ibid, p.41; al-Masʿūdī, op.cit., v.4, p.62; al-Shahrastānī, op.cit., p.251.
203al-Dimashqī, op.cit., p.41. For human sacrifice of the Harranians see below pp.211ff.

The temple of Mars, in the opinion of al-Masʿūdī and al-Shahrastānī, was rectangular,[204] but al-Dimashqī says that it was square and coloured red.[205] In the middle of the temple there was an iron idol seated on a throne at the top of seven steps. In one hand there was a sword while in the other he held a head hung by its hair. Both sword and head were covered with blood. On Tuesday the worshippers wearing red suits and carrying swords and daggers used to come into this temple for a special ceremony. al-Dimashqī also states that they suppose that this shrine was built before the temple of Solomon and that it contained an idol named Tammūz.[206]

The temple of the Sun was square and coloured yellow.[207] Within the temple there was a throne at the top of six steps on which there was an idol made of gold, adorned with a crown and jewels.[208] On every step of the throne there were various statues of kings who were dead. On Sunday the people used to practise a ceremony to the Sun.[209]

al-Bīrūnī also states, "they had temples and images, called by the name of the Sun. For instance, the temple of Baʿal-bek was sacred to the idols of the Sun".[210]

Concerning the temple of Venus al-Masʿūdī and al-Shahrastānī state that it was a triangle within a rectangle,[211] but al-Dimashqī says that it was shaped like an elongated triangle and painted blue.[212] In the middle of the temple there was an idol made of copper, coloured red, on a throne at the top of five steps. Around it there were other images representing passion and pleasure. On Friday the worshippers wearing white clothes and holding various musical instruments used to come into this temple and venerate the idol of Venus in a ceremony.[213]

Concerning the shape of the temple of Mercury we have three different opinions: al-Masʿūdī states that it was a triangle within a rectangle,[214] al-Shahrastānī says that it was shaped as a triangle in a square[215] and al-Dimashqī states that it was square outside but hexagonal within.[216] Inside the temple there was a throne at the top of four steps and an idol, made of baked pot. On his sacred day, Wednesday, special

[204]al-Masʿūdī, op.cit., v.4, p.62; al-Shahrastānī, op.cit., p.251.
[205]al-Dimashqī, op.cit., p.41.
[206]Ibid, pp.41-42.
[207]Ibid, p.42; al-Masʿūdī, op.cit., v.4, p.62; al-Shahrastānī, op.cit., p.251. Also see al-Bīrūnī, op.cit., p.187.
[208]al-Dimashqī, op.cit., p. 42. Maimonides too states that they had the gold idols of the planet Sun. See Maimonides, op.cit., p.516.
[209]al-Dimashqī, op.cit., p.42.
[210]al-Bīrūnī, op.cit., p.187.
[211]al-Masʿūdī, op.cit., v.4 p.62; al-Shahrastānī, op.cit., p.251.
[212]al-Dimashqī, op.cit., p.42.
[213]Ibid, p.42.
[214]al-Masʿūdī, op.cit., v.4, p.62.
[215]al-Shahrastānī, op.cit., p.251.
[216]al-Dimashqī, op.cit., p.43.

honour was paid to the god and at least once a year a young man was sacrificed by dividing the body into two and burning the parts.[217]

Finally the temple of the Moon was an octagon in the opinion of al-Masʿūdī and al-Shahrastānī and a pentagon in the view of al-Dimashqī.[218] His shrine was adorned with gold and silver inscriptions. Within the temple there was an idol made of silver, seated upon a throne, up to which there led three steps.[219]

al-Dimashqī also speaks of a temple for the Moon, called *al-mudarraq* (or *al-madraq*), at Harran which remained until its destruction by the Mongols. He also points out that there were some inscriptions in Pahlavi on its door.[220] Moreover in another chapter of his book he states that among their temples a temple of the Moon, named *al-mudawwar*, remained until the Egyptians, i.e. the Fatimids, captured it and they had no other like this.[221] We will later discuss the identification of the moon-temples in Harran.[222]

Besides these temples our sources give us additional information about the holy buildings of the Harranians.

According to al-Masʿūdī one is a temple, called *maghlītiyā* (or *mughallītiyā*) in Bāb al-Rik'a at Harran. al-Masʿūdī remarks that this is the only temple of the Harranians which remained until his time (10th century A.D.), and that it is the temple of Āzar, Abraham's father.[223] Moreover he narrates from 'Ibn ʿĪshun al-Ḥarrānī al-Qāḍī that there were four underground corridors for various idols representing heavenly bodies, i.e. planets, and saints.[224]

Another is *bayt al-bughdāriyyīn*, "the house (or shrine) of *bughdāriyyīn*", which occurs several times in "the Book of Five Mysteries" of the Harranians.[225] Once the name occurs as *al-baghdādiyyīn*, but this must be an error because the Harranians had nothing to do with Baghdad at the time when their cult and rituals were being formed.[226]

J.B. Segal once pointed out the possible connection between *bayt al-bughdāriyyīn* and *bwdr* in one of the Syriac inscriptions from Sumatar Harabesi. The

---

[217] Ibid, p.43.
[218] Ibid, p.43; al-Masʿūdī, op.cit., v.4, p.62; al-Shahrastānī, op.cit., p.251.
[219] al-Dimashqī, op.cit., p.43. Also see Maimonides, op.cit., p.516.
[220] al-Dimashqī, op.cit., p.43.
[221] Ibid, p.191.
[222] See below pp.202ff.
[223] al-Masʿūdī, op.cit., v.4, pp.62-63. The other variations of the name are *maghlibīnā, maghlīnā* and *muṣlīnā*, See Chwolsohn, D., op.cit., v.II, p.369. On the interpretation of the word *maghlītiyā* Chwolsohn suggested that it might come from the Greek Μεγαλοθεῖον, alluding to the temple of the great moon god. See Chwolsohn, D., op.cit., v.I, p.409.
[224] al-Masʿūdī, op.cit., v.4, p.63.
[225] 'Ibn al-Nadīm, op.cit., pp.326-27. Another variation of the word is *bayt al-buʿdāriyyīn*. See ibid, p.326.
[226] al-Bīrūnī mentions a feast of a Baghdādian house, which presumably refers to the same temple. See al-Bīrūnī, op.cit., p.317.

inscription, which is dated 476 (=164-5 A.D.) says: "May he be BWDR after Tridates the ruler".[227] It has also been suggested that the word is perhaps meant to be *al-ʿadhāriyyīn*, "helpers", referring to some deities.[228]

Although the interpretation of *bughdāriyyīn* is difficult it is certain that this shrine which is also called "the house of the victor"[229] was evidently a hall of initiation, since according to "the Book of Five Mysteries" initiation rites were practiced in this shrine.[230]

maghlītiyā and *bayt al-bughdāriyyīn* are possibly the same temple because *maghlītiyā* too was a place in which initiation rites were practiced. al-Masʿūdī states that they used to bring their children into the underground corridors to see and hear the idols, where the priests would speak through tubes to make the idols talk.[231]

Another temple of the Harranians is *ʿazzūz*, which is mentioned by Bābā the Harranian.[232] Bābā mentions this temple as a place where the people slaughter sacrifices and bring offerings. This was quite possibly the temple of Venus because *ʿuzūz*, a local name referring to the planet Venus, occurs in *al-fihrist* as a deity of the Harranians.[233]

Our Arabic sources also claim that there is a connection between some ancient buildings outside Harran and the Harranians. al-Bīrūnī, for example, states that one of their monuments is the cupola over the *miḥrāb* beside the *maqṣūra* in the great Mosque of Damascus.[234]

Moreover al-Bīrūnī, ʾAbū al-Fidā and ʾIbn Ḥazm state that the Sabians/Harranians venerate the Kaʿbah, the holy building in Mecca.[235]

Finally ʾAbū al-Fidā claims that they venerate the pyramids in Egypt because they suppose that these pyramids are the burial chambers of Shīth, ʾIdrīs and his son Ṣābī.[236]

---

[227]See Segal, J.B., "Some Syriac Inscriptions of the 2nd-3rd Century A.D.", *BSOAS*, 16, 1954, pp.26-28.

[228]See Gaster, T.H., *Thespis: Ritual, Myth and Drama in the Ancient Near East*, New York (1950), p.229; Dodge, B., op.cit., v.II, pp.769-70 n.121.

[229]ʾIbn al-Nadīm, op.cit., p.326.

[230]For instance, at the beginning of the text the author states: "As the lambs in the flock and the calf in the herd, so are the young men endeavoring, racing ahead, drawing near, sent to the *bayt al-bughadhāriyīn* [*al-bughdāriyyīn*]": ibid, p.326 (Dodge, v.II, p.769).

[231]al-Masʿūdī, op.cit., v.4, p.63.

[232]Bābā says: "Thereafter, the kings of the west will be roused, and they will come up to our place. They will slaughter sacrifices and bring offerings in the midst of ʿAzzūz. They will seek to abolish the religion, while unable to say so because others after them will believe and rule": Rosenthal, F., op.cit., p.230.

[233]See above p.144.

[234]See al-Bīrūnī, op.cit., p.187.

[235]Ibid, p.187; ʾAbū al-Fidā, op.cit., p.148; ʾIbn Ḥazm, op.cit., v.I, p.35.

[236]ʾAbū al-Fidā, op.cit., p.148. Cf. al-Dimashqī, op.cit., pp.33-34; al-Masʿūdī, *kitāb al-tanbīh wa al-ʾishrāf*, p.19. For Shīth and ʾIdrīs see below p.163.

Besides the divine elements and seven planets our sources point out that the Harranians believe in and venerate the twelve zodiac signs as the Holy Beings who rule and regulate the world.[237]

Further the Harranians have a number of lesser deities belonging to their pantheon, some of which, as we will see, represent the seven planetary deities while the others are mainly the local designations of various Semitic deities.

Among them *shamāl*, whom *al-fihrist* mentions several times, seems to be the most important. *al-fihrist* gives us a full description of this deity who is frequently mentioned with the seven planetary deities.[238] He is the greatest god who controls and scatters the devils and the jinn, and gives good luck.[239] Thus he is the lord of the jinn and the devils.[240] He is also closely connected with magic and mystery.[241]

The interpretation of his name and to whom the name *shamāl* refers are still a subject of discussion, in spite of the clear description of his nature in *al-fihrist*. B. Dodge, who has always translated the name as "the North", states that this god was probably the same as the ancient Semitic deity Ṣaphōn or Zephon, who derives his name from the North.[242] He also remarks that the people of Harran possibly identified the North with the Primal Cause, from which the cosmic existences emanated.[243] On the other hand J. B. Segal once claimed that Shamāl of Harran may perhaps be identified with Māralāhē of Sumatar.[244] Finally Chwolsohn, who always keeps the original word *shamāl* in his translation of passages from *al-fihrist*, suggested that it might be an ancient deity belonging to the agricultural cult of ancient Mesopotamia.[245]

There might be a connection between Shamāl of the Harranians and Samael of Jewish tradition, since both have demonic characteristics. In Jewish sources from different periods Samael appears as (1) Satan, (2) the angel of death, (3) the angel in charge of Mars and (4) a name for demons.[246]

In *al-fihrist* Shamāl is also mentioned twice as if he is a local form of the Sun-god. One reference is to the effect that the feast of Shamāl is celebrated on the fifteenth of April with offerings, Sun worship, sacrificial slaughter, burnt offerings, eating and

---

237 See Theodore Abu Ḳurra, op.cit., p.24; 'Ibn Ḥazm, op.cit., v.I, p.34.
238 See 'Ibn al-Nadīm, op.cit., pp.322-23.
239 Ibid, p.323.
240 See ibid, p.322. Also see Segal, J.B., "The Sabian Mysteries: The Planet Cult of Ancient Harran", p.216.
241 'Ibn al-Nadīm, op.cit., pp.322f.
242 See Dodge, B., "The Ṣābians of Ḥarrān", p.69. Adon Ṣaphōn and Baal Zephon were worshipped at Memphis as "Lord of the North". See *ERE*, v.2, p.288; Olmstead, A.T., *History of Palestine and Syria to the Macedonian Conquest*, New York (1931), p.222. Also see Ex 14:2, 9; Num 33:7.
243 Dodge, B., "The Ṣābians of Ḥarrān", p.70.
244 See Segal, J.B., op.cit., p.217.
245 See Chwolsohn, D., op.cit., v.II, p.219.
246 See Scholem, G, "Samael", in *EJ*, v.14, pp.719-22. Also see Chapter Iv, n.122.

drinking;[247] the same celebration also appears on the first day of May.[248] The second suggests that during the month of February, of which seven days beginning with the ninth are the fast for the Sun, the great Lord, the Lord of well-Being, they pray only to Shamāl.[249] So can we think that Shamāl is a local name for the Sun-god? The identification of Shamāl with the Sun-god is, it seems to us, difficult, because Shamāl, as we have seen, is mentioned several times as a separate deity from the seven planetary deities, one of whom is certainly the Sun-god.[250]

Besides *al-fihrist* there are some other sources which tell of the cult of the jinn and devils of the Harranians, but they do not mention Shamāl. Shamāl only occurs in the account of ʾAbū Saʿīd Wahb ʾibn ʾIbrāhīm, which is narrated in *al-fihrist* by ʾIbn al-Nadīm. al-Bīrūnī, who reports what Muḥammad ʾibn ʿAbd al-ʿAzīz al-Ḥāshimī says, tells of the Harranian cult of the demons,[251] and mentions the name *salūghā* as the prince of the Satans.[252]

Salūghā is presumably identical with Shamāl because of two points: (i) both Salūghā and Shamāl are the chief of the demons; (ii) al-Bīrūnī records a feast for Salūghā on the second of May which is the first feast of the month.[253] ʾIbn al-Nadīm mentions an offering festival for Shamāl on the first of the same month.[254] Although there is a confusion about the date both of them refer to the same feast, celebrated for the chief of the demons.

Which one, Shamāl or Salūghā, is the original name of the chief of the jinn and the devils is still an enigma, but it is obvious that this cult was so important in Harranian religion that we find a number of sacrificial rituals and ceremonies for this deity.

According to the account in *al-fihrist* another deity of the Harranians is the god *tāuz* for whom the women of Harran weep during the feast in July.[255] The same deity is also mentioned as *tammūzā* by al-Bīrūnī,[256] and as Tammūz by Maimonides.[257]

---

[247] ʾIbn al-Nadīm, op.cit., p.322.
[248] Ibid, p.322.
[249] Ibid, pp.324.
[250] For instance, we read: "They also slay nine lambs: seven for the seven deities, one for the god of the jinn, and one for the Lord of the Hours": ibid, p.322 (Dodge, v.II, p.757).
[251] See al-Bīrūnī, op.cit., p.316. Maimonides too speaks of the Harranian jinn-cult. See Maimonides, op.cit., p.581.
[252] al-Bīrūnī, op.cit., p.317.
[253] Ibid, p.317.
[254] ʾIbn al-Nadīm, op.cit., p.322.
[255] Ibid, p.322. Also in the Yezidi religion the title of Azaziel, the greatest of the seven angels who assigned the god in creation and the establishment of the world, is *Melek Tāʾūs* (Peacock Angel) who is represented by a peacock. It is suggested that Tāʾūs is derived either from Greek *taôs* or from the name of the god Tammūz. See Guest, J.S., *The Yezidis. A Study in Survival*, London and New York (1987), p.30; Empson, R.H.W., *The Cult of the Peacock Angel*, London (1928), pp.134ff.
[256] al-Bīrūnī, op.cit., p.317.
[257] Maimonides, op.cit., pp.519f.

This deity evidently corresponds to the well-known Sumero-Akkadian god Tammūz or Dumuzi, the god of vegetation whose annual death and resurrection were celebrated throughout the ancient Near East.[258] One of the main features of this cult is the mourning for the premature death of the young Tammūz.[259]

al-fihrist also mentions a pair of twins, *fsfr* (Phosphor), who is described as "The Good, the Perfect", and *qūsṭīr* (Castor), the Chosen Shaykh.[260] These two deities, i.e. Phosphor, the light bearer, and Castor, one of the Dioscuri, are, as H. Lewy stated, known in Akkadian mythology as Bilgi, "the Flame", and Nusku. They represent the planet Mercury as evening and morning star, respectively.[261]

Another deity is *hāmān*, who is described as "the chief and father of the gods".[262] In the region of Tyre Baal Shamin was worshipped as "the God of Hammon",[263] but this is likely meant to be the god Hamon worshipped at Palmyra.[264]

The deity *nmryā*, which appears in *al-fihrist*,[265] is obviously identical with Bar Nemrê, mentioned by Jacob of Sarug̃.[266]

al-fihrist also mentions a number of times *rabb al-bakht*, "the Lord of Good Luck", who was venerated with a ritual meal made by the people of Harran with bread, straw, fresh myrtle and oil.[267] This deity is evidently the Semitic deity Gad, a god of fortune and fertility.[268]

There is also a god named *rabb al-sāʿāt*, "the Lord of the Hours".[269] He is always mentioned with the seven planetary deities. B. Dodge remarks that he may be similar to Chronos or the Persian Zervan.[270]

Another deity is *dhāt janāḥ al-rīḥ*, "Possessor of the Wing of the Wind".[271] This may be a local title of Enlil, the chief deity of the Sumerian pantheon whose name characterizes him as "Lord Wind".[272]

---

258 See Lewy, H., op.cit., p.143.
259 See below p.181.
260 Ibn al-Nadīm, op.cit., p.325.
261 See Lewy, H., op.cit., p.142.
262 Ibn al-Nadīm, op.cit., p.323.
263 See Teixidor, J., *The Pagan God*, pp.40-41.
264 See ibid, pp.127f. Also see Tubach, J., op.cit., pp.175ff.
265 Ibn al-Nadīm, op.cit., p.323. Also see Chwolsohn, D., op.cit., v.II, p.27. Another version of the name is *nmzyā*.
266 See below p.182. B. Dodge states that the deity perhaps is Nemesis. See Dodge, B., op.cit., v.II, p.759 n.65.
267 Ibn al-Nadīm, op.cit., pp.323-24.
268 See below p.140.
269 Ibn al-Nadīm, op.cit., p.322. Also al-Bīrūnī mentions the same deity. See al-Bīrūnī, op.cit., p.317.
270 Dodge, B., op.cit., v.II, p.757 n.56.
271 Ibn al-Nadīm, op.cit., p.325.
272 See Lewy, H., op.cit., p.145. On the other hand Dodge suggests another possibility, that it was the Sun. See Dodge, B., op.cit., v.II, pp.765-66 n.102.

Another is *ṣārah*, who is described as "the daughter of *al-faqr*, from whose womb these have come forth".[273] Here Ṣāraḥ, which means "being clear", is mentioned as the mother of the deities. This is presumably a local appellation of Ishtar who is called "the Brilliant Goddess" as well as "the Mother of the Gods".[274]

al-fihrist also mentions *rabbat al-thill*, "Mistress of the Herd". In one place she is described as the deity who "received Tammūz".[275] In another place she is the goddess who "arranged to guard the sacred goats which none of them are permitted to sell, but which (instead) they offer as sacrificial victims".[276] In the former description she is associated with Tammūz or Dumuzi. Therefore she is probably Ishtar, because according to Babylonian mythology Tammūz is the youthful consort of Ishtar.[277] In the latter description she is associated with the sacred goats. The goats have some connection with fertility. In Greek art there is known a type of image showing Aphrodite (Venus) riding on a goat.[278] Also a plaque from Ugarit shows that there the fertility goddess was also associated with goats.[279] Consequently *rabbat al-thill* was another local name referring to the fertility goddess Ishtar-Venus.

Another deity of the Harranians is *ʾibn al-salm* (or *ʾibn al-salām*) for whom they hold a feast.[280] *ʾibn al-salm*, "Son of Sunset", or *ʾibn al-salām*, "Son of Well-Being (or Salvation)", might be a title for some deity rather than the name of a specific deity.[281] There is a Ugaritic deity of Sunset, *šlm* (*sa-li-mu*), who appears in receipt of offerings in cultic texts.[282] Moreover there is a goddess *šlmʾ* who appears in Hatra inscriptions.[283]

ṣanam al-māʾ, "the Idol of the Water", is also mentioned among the deities of the people of Harran. Of this deity *al-fihrist* states:

> "Among their deities there is the Idol of the Water (*ṣanam al-māʾ*), which fell among the gods during the days of the Tyrannic Star, going forth as they suppose, fleeing and seeking the land of India. They set out

[273] ʾIbn al-Nadīm, op.cit., p.325.

[274] Dodge states that the name "daughter of *al-faqr* (Poverty)" may be a mistake for Daughter of the Moon (*ibnat al-qamar*), as Ishtar was called by the title. See Dodge, B., op.cit., v.II, p.766 n.103.

[275] ʾIbn al-Nadīm, op.cit., p.325.

[276] Ibid, p.325 (Dodge, v.II, p.767).

[277] See *ER*, v.4, pp.512-13.

[278] See *DB*, Extra vol., p.115.

[279] See Dodge, B., op.cit., v.II, p.766 n.107.

[280] See ʾIbn al-Nadīm, op.cit., p.322. Also see Chwolsohn, D., op.cit., v.II, p.25. al-Bīrūnī records a name, *mār shalāmā*, in his lists of the feast of the Harranians. See al-Bīrūnī, op.cit., p.315. There may be a connection between the deity *ibn al-salm* (or *ibn al-salām*) and this festival.

[281] See Chwolsohn, D., op.cit., v.II, p.193; Dodge, B., op.cit., v.II, p.757 n.59. According to ʾAbū Saʿīd Wahb the feast in honour of *ibn al-salm* is carried out on the 2nd May. On the other hand al-Hāshimī records "the Feast of Salūghā, the prince of Satans" on the same day. See below p.180. Therefore *ibn al-salm* may be a title for Salūghā.

[282] See Healey, J.F., op.cit., pp.119-20. Also see Gaster, T.H., op.cit., pp.228f.

[283] Concerning the term *bšlmʾ*, which occurs in Hatra text 202: 11, J.T. Milik says that this is abbreviation of *byt šlmʾ*, "the temple of *šlmʾ*". See Vattioni, F., op.cit., p.74.

in quest of it, asking and imploring it to return without delay. But it said to them, 'I shall not again enter the city of Ḥarran. I will, however, come to here (*hāhunā*),' ... Thus it refused them, and until our own time they go out every twentieth day of the month of Nīsān (April), men and women together, expecting the arrival of the Idol of the Water and its coming to them."[284]

There are two possibilities concerning the identification of *ṣanam al-māʾ*. One is that this deity, who left the city of Harran and fled to the land of India, may refer to Tammūz, who has been slain and has gone to the underworld. The other possibility, which seems more likely, is that it refers to the Moon-god of Harran en route to his temple (a cult similar to the Babylonian Akītu).[285]

According to *al-fihrist* another deity is *ʾabū rim* (or *ʾibn rim*).[286] Chwolsohn suggests several possibilities for the interpretation of this name. One of which is that it may be meant to be Ram (Baʿal Ram), a Near Eastern deity, and the other that it may be identical with the god Rimmon (or Rammon) of Syria.[287] On the other hand B. Dodge suggests that this word is perhaps meant to be Abram,[288] but this seems not to be possible because according to the pagans of Harran Abraham was a heretic who rejected some of the beliefs and rites of the community and therefore left the city.[289] Besides these possibilities *ʾabū rim* (or *ʾibn rim*) may be connected with the Moon-god Sin, because Rīm is an epithet of the moon.[290]

The enigmatic deity "*ʾarū* the Lord" also occurs in *al-fihrist* among the deities of the Harranians.[291] B. Dodge first inclined to identify him with Hera, the wife of Zeus, in Greek mythology, who was worshipped at Hierapolis and other places,[292] but later he suggested that he is perhaps meant to be Azar, Abraham's father, because al-Masʿūdī tells of a temple of Azar at Harran.[293]

---

[284]ʾIbn al-Nadīm, op.cit., p.325 (Dodge, v.II, p.767). B. Dodge remarks that the Tyrannic Star, *ʾasṭah waṭiranīqūs*, refers to the Pleiades, which disappear between the 15th and 20th of March, shortly after their conjunction with the moon, which also goes out of sight at that time. See Dodge, B., op.cit., v.II, p.767 n.111.

[285]See below p.180.

[286]ʾIbn al-Nadīm, op.cit., p.325. Also see Chwolsohn, D., op.cit., v.II, p.40.

[287]See Chwolsohn, D., op.cit., v.II, pp.287-88.

[288]Dodge, B., op.cit., v.II, p.766 n.106.

[289]See below pp.162f.

[290]See Tallqvist, K., *Akkadische Götterepitheta*, Studia Orientalia Edidit Societas Orientalis Fennica: VII, Helsinki (1938), p.445. There is also an Akkadian personal name Rim-sin, "Servant of Sin". See idem, *Assyrian Personal Names*, (Acta Societatis Scientiarum Fennicae, Tom. XLIII, No 1) Helsinki (1914), p.188.

[291]ʾIbn al-Nadīm, op.cit., p.325.

[292]Dodge, B., "The Ṣābians of Ḥarrān", p.70.

[293]Idem, *The Fihrist of al-Nadīm*, v.II, p.766 n.108.

On the other hand in Aramaic *ʾrwʾ* as well as *ʾryʾ* means "lion".[294] Also the plural of *ʾryʾ* refers to the Zodiacal sign Leo.[295] We know that the pagans of Harran worshipped the twelve Zodiacal signs as well as the seven planets.[296] Therefore *ʾarū* may refer to Leo.

According to *al-fihrist* another deity is "*ḥitān al-fārisiyah*, their mother, who had six evil spirits with which she went to the seacoast".[297] This mother goddess otherwise unidentified possibly refers to Ningal, Sin's consort, the great lady, since Ningal is the mother of Shamash and Ishtar.[298]

Finally *al-fihrist* mentions "the Deity who makes the arrow fly", for whom the Harranians practiced a ceremony which was connected with magic.[299] During the ceremony they also worship *shamāl*. This name may therefore be a title of Shamāl.

Characteristic features of the theology of the Harranian religion can be summarized as follows:

a. The planet cult has always been the most important feature of this religion from the earliest time to its disappearing. Although various foreign elements entered their system of belief from time to time, the pagans of Harran clung to this cult. Also, among the planetary deities, Sin, the moon-god, was always head of the pantheon.

b. The Harranians had a number of lesser deities, like Shamāl and Tammūz, who generally belonged to ancient Mesopotamian and Semitic cults.

c. According to our medieval sources they also had a belief in a Holy Creator, which did not appear among their beliefs earlier than medieval times.

d. Finally astrology, magic and mystery played an important role in every aspect of their beliefs.

The names of the deities belonging to the Harranian pantheon changed from time to time, depending upon the influence of various foreign cultures. Particularly three influences seem to have affected the theology of the Harranians. The most important is Assyro-Babylonian influence, which especially appears in their planet cult and beliefs associated with magic and mystery. Many of the deities, such as Sin, Ningal and Tammūz, are the same as in the Assyro-Babylonian pantheon. Moreover their cults, such as agricultural and vegetation cults, are closely connected with their Assyro-Babylonian counterparts.

The second influence which must have entered the area after Alexander the Great is that of Greek. This influence especially appears in the names referring the

---

[294]See Smith, J.P., *A Compendious Syriac Dictionary*, Oxford (1903), p.28.
[295]See *MD*, p.37.
[296]See above p.151.
[297]ʾIbn al-Nadīm, op.cit., p.325. Other versions of *ḥitān* are *ḥsāb* and *ḥsb*. See Chwolsohn, D., op.cit., v.II, p.39.
[298]See above p.138.
[299]ʾIbn al-Nadīm, op.cit., p.322.

planetary deities, such as *'aylīyūs*, *lārīs* and *qirqis*. Also their beliefs concerning cosmology and divine elements are closely connected with ancient Greek philosophy.

Finally we find the influence of monotheistic cults, which appear in their belief in the Holy Creator. This may be Jewish, Christian or Islamic influence, but Islamic influence, as D.S. Margoliouth stated,[300] seems to be more likely because this belief only appears in medieval times and the pagans of Harran lived under Muslim dominion from the seventh century A.D.

B. Prophets and mediators

The pagans of Harran in medieval times believed in certain prophets who were intermediaries between men and the Holy Beings, though we do not see such a belief earlier than this period. According to their doctrine of prophets:

> "a man who is an announcer of God (*al-nabī*) is he who is free from evil in his soul and from imperfections of the body, who is perfect in everything praiseworthy, who does not fall short in answering every question correctly, who tells what is in the imaginings, whose prayer for rain is answered, who wards off pests from plants and animals, and whose doctrine improves the world, increasing its population."[301]

Among their prophets one of the most important figures is Hermes who is called *harmīs* in *al-fihrist*, *harmas al-harāmasah* by al-Dimashqī, *harmas al-munajjim* by al-Baghdādī and "*harmas* the Egyptian" by al Bīrūnī.[302] Our medieval sources generally identify him with *'idrīs*, one of the prophets mentioned by the Qur'ān.[303] Some of them also point out that 'Idrīs is *'akhnūkh*[304] or *khunūkh*[305] of whom al-Bīrūnī remarks that he is mentioned as Henokh (Enoch) in the Jewish Bible.[306]

The Harranians claim that Hermes is one of their first two teachers — the other being Agathodaimon —, who taught them the true way, gave them their laws and judgements and praised them.[307] They also believe that Hermes and Agathodaimon are

---

300 See Margoliouth, D.S., "Harranians", p.519.

301 'Ibn al-Nadīm, op.cit., p.319 (Dodge, v.II, p.749). Cf. al-Maqdīsī, op.cit., v.4, p.24.

302 See 'Ibn al-Nadīm, op.cit., p.318; al-Dimashqī, op.cit., p.44; al-Baghdādī, *'uṣūl al-dīn*, p.324; al-Bīrūnī, op.cit., p.187.

303 See al-Bīrūnī, op.cit., p.188; 'Ibn Ḥazm, op.cit., v.1, p.35; al-Shahrastānī, op.cit., pp.202, 240; al-Dimashqī, op.cit., pp.34, 44. Also for prophet 'Idrīs see *Qur'ān*, 19:56, 57; 21:85.

304 al-Dimashqī, op.cit., p.44.

305 'Abū al-Fidā, op.cit., p.148.

306 al-Bīrūnī, op.cit., p.188.

307 See al-Shahrastānī, op.cit., pp.203, 228.

their masters, deities, intermediaries to the Holy Beings and interceders for them to God who is the master of masters and deity of the deities.[308] We will later discuss the identification of Hermes and the Hermetic tradition of the Harranians.[309]

Another important prophet is Agathodaimon whose name is spelled differently by the medieval scholars: *ʿadīmūn* by al-Dimashqī, *ʿaẓīmūn* by ʾIbn Ḥazm, *ʾaẓīmūn* by al-Shahrastānī, *ʾaghādhīmūn* by al-Bīrūnī, *ʾaghāthdīmūn* by al-Masʿūdī, *ʾaghāthādhīmūn* in *al-fihrist*, *ʾaghāthādīmūn* by Bar Habraeus and *ʾadīmūt* by ʾAbū al-Fidā.[310] The medieval scholars usually state that he is identical with the prophet *shīth* (Seth), the son of Adam.[311]

Like Hermes, Agathodaimon is connected with Egypt because the Harranians believed that one of the three big pyramids in Egypt is his tomb where, according to the account of al-Dimashqī, they perform pilgrimage and slaughter a cock.[312] Agathodaimon is evidently Agathos Daimon in Greek mythology. In the view of the Hermetic writers the Agathos Daimon is not a man, but a god, — an personification of the divine noûs —, who gives instruction to the man Hermes.[313]

In Harranian tradition Agathodaimon, like their other prophets, is a philosopher-prophet. Concerning his philosophy, al-Shahrastānī, who presumably quotes this from the books of the Harranians, states that according to Agathodaimon's philosophy the first beginning is five: God, wisdom, sense, place and emptiness (cavity).[314] It is to be noticed that there is a connection between the first three, i.e. God, wisdom and sense, and the first three divine elements in the Harranians' belief.[315]

Another prophet of the Harranians is *ʾarānī*. The name occurs as *ʾarānī* in *al-fihrist*,[316] while it occurs as *ʾarānī al-ʾawwal wa al-thānī*, "Arani the First and Second", in the account of al-Masʿūdī[317] and as *ʾarānī al-kabīr wa ʾarānī al-ṣaghīr*, "Arānī the Great and Arānī the Little", in the account of ʾIbn Ḥazm.[318]

There are various possibilities for the identification of Arānī. Chwolsohn thought that Arānī is a corruption of Orpheus.[319] W. Scott states that Arānī was a name

---

[308] See ibid, p.203.
[309] See below pp.208ff.
[310] See al-Dimashqī, op.cit., p.44; ʾIbn Ḥazm, op.cit., v.1, p.35; al-Shahrastānī, op.cit., pp.202, 240, 241; al-Bīrūnī, op.cit., p.315; al-Masʿūdī, *kitāb al-tanbīh wa al-ʾishrāf*, pp.19, 161; ʾIbn al-Nadīm, op.cit., p.318; Bar Habraeus, *tārīkh mukhtaṣar al-duwal*, p.12; ʾAbū al-Fidā, op.cit., p.14.
[311] See al-Shahrastānī, op.cit., pp.202, 241; al-Dimashqī, op.cit., pp.34, 44; ʾAbū al-Fidā, op.cit., pp.14, 148; Bar Habraeus, op.cit., p.12.
[312] See al-Dimashqī, op.cit., pp.33-34.
[313] See Scott, W. and A.S. Ferguson, op.cit., v.4, p.254.
[314] al-Shahrastānī, op.cit., p.241.
[315] See above p.142.
[316] ʾIbn al-Nadīm, op.cit., p.318.
[317] al-Masʿūdī, op.cit., p.161.
[318] See Chwolsohn, D., op.cit., v.II, p.527.
[319] See ibid, v.I, p.800. In Greek mythology Orpheus of Thrace is the founder of the Orphic cult. Characteristic features of this cult were the worship of Dionysus and Apollo, belief in punishments in

invented by the Harranians for the eponymous founder of their city, i.e. Harran. He also states that this may perhaps have resulted from identification of the imaginary city founder with Haran, the brother of Abraham. Therefore, he remarks, the Harranians who used the Greek language wrote Arranios, and this was transcribed as Arani in Arabic. On the other hand he points out the difficulty of this theory, i.e. the absence of the guttural with which the name of the city begins.[320]

On the other hand B. Dodge suggests that the name might be connected with Heron, the ancient wise man.[321] Finally M. Tardieu points out the possibility that Arānī may be connected with Horus.[322]

In our opinion Arānī could be an Arabic translation of Uranus in Greek mythology: (i) Uranus (or in the Greek form Ouranos) is more appropriate to Arānī in regard to spelling; (ii) the most important characteristic feature of the prophets of the Harranians is their connection with ancient Greek mythology and philosophy, and Uranus is an important figure in Greek mythology, the child and husband of Gaea, the earth.[323]

Another prophet is Bābā. al-Bīrūnī, who mentions him as one of the prophets of the Harranians, also spells the name as *mābā* in another chapter of his book,[324] which is evidently a misspelling. Also Dionysius Bar Salibi and ʾIbn al-ʿAdīm, who quote the book of Bābā, give information on this. The former mentions him as "the God of Harran" at the beginning of the quotation, but later states that he is called by the pagans of Harran a prophet, and that they esteem him more than all the philosophers, and take refuge in him.[325] On the other hand ʾIbn al-ʿAdīm mentions him as "the Sabian from Harran" and states that Bābā is said to have made his pronouncements 367 years before the Hijrah (3th century A.D.).[326]

According to ʾIbn al-ʿAdīm, Bābā must have lived in the third century A.D., but Dionysius Bar Salibi's account assumes a pre-Christian date for Baba.[327] "The Book of Bābā the Harranian" indicates Bābā as a genuine Harranian, but it is difficult to say whether he is a native Harranian prophet or a mythological person with Greek origin, like Hermes and Agathodaimon.

On the other hand the name of Bābā is a familiar one. For instance, it appears in Dura-Europos in a Semitic inscription as *bbʾ* and in Greek as *baba*, and it may or may

the underworld and also in the transmigration of souls. For this religious movement in the 6th century B.C., see *ER*, v.11, pp.111ff.

320 See Scott, W. and A.S. Ferguson, op.cit., v.4, p.249.

321 Dodge, B., *The Fihrist of al-Nadīm*, v.II, p.746 n.5.

322 See Tardieu, M., *Les Paysages Reliques*, Louvain-Paris (1990), p.160 n.101.

323 See *ER*, v.2, p.255; v.3, pp.109-10.

324 See al-Bīrūnī, op.cit., pp.187, 315.

325 Cf. Rosenthal, F., "The Prophecies of Bābā the Ḥarrānian", p.228.

326 Rosenthal, F., op.cit., p.221.

327 See ibid, pp.228-31.

not be related to quite a few Aramaic (Syriac and Jewish) names spelled *bby*.[328] Baba appears as an Egyptian god[329] and a Sumerian goddess,[330] and a Syrian goddess Babaia or the like is also known.[331]

ʾIbn al-Nadīm and al-Shahrastānī also mention Solon among the prophets of the Harranians. They state that he was the ancestor of the philosopher Plato on his mother's side.[332] al-Bīrūnī mentions *swʾr* twice as one of their prophets and once describes him as Plato's maternal grandfather.[333] ʾIbn Ḥazm, too, mentions *swʾr*, but he remarks that the Sabians (Harranians) differ about his prophecy.[334] al-Bīrūnī's description obviously shows that he is identical with Solon, but the word Sawar, used for Solon, is very strange and it is difficult to make a statement on its origin.[335]

Also Plato, *ʾaflātūn*, is mentioned among the prophets of the Harranians by al-Baghdādī who moreover states that they claim prophecy for a number of philosophers.[336] Besides this, a statement of al-Masʿūdī, who remarks that he has seen some words of Plato written in Syriac on the gate of Harran, supports the account of al-Baghdādī.[337]

Another prophet of the Harranians, *walīs* (or *wālīs*), is mentioned by al-Baghdādī and al-Bīrūnī.[338] His name also appears as *ʾalūs* in another version of al-Bīrūnī's Chronology.[339] Rosenthal suggests that he is identical with *ʾalyūs*, Zoroaster's Harranian teacher according to a passage in the Chronology of al-Bīrūnī published by H. Taqizadeh.[340]

In al-Bīrūnī's list Pythagoras, the Greek philosopher of Samos of the sixth century B.C., is also mentioned among the Harranian prophets.[341]

---

328 Ibid, p.220. Cf. Frye, R.N., J.F. Gilliam, H. Ingholt, C.B. Welles, *Inscriptions from Dura-Europos* (Yale Classical Studies, ed. H.M. Hubbell, v.XIV) New Haven (1955), pp.172, 178, 180, 183.

329 See Pritchard, J.B. (ed.), *Ancient Near Eastern Texts Relating to the Old Testament*, 2nd edition, Princeton (1955), p.15.

330 Baba (or Bau in older reading), the gracious lady, was the consort of Ningursu, the city-god of Lagash. See ibid, pp.217, 390.

331 See Jalabert, C., R. Mouterde and C. Mondésert, *Inscriptions grecs et latines de la Syrie*, Paris (1955), v.IV, p.119.

332 ʾIbn al-Nadīm, op.cit., p.318; al-Shahrastānī, op.cit., p.250.

333 Cf. al-Bīrūnī, op.cit., pp.187, 315.

334 See Chwolsohn, D., op.cit., v.II, p.527. Chwolsohn thought that *swʾr* should be read *swʾhā*, "the others of them". See ibid, v.II, p.527.

335 Rosenthal states that not even the assumption of a Pahlavi original would enable us to reconcile the forms Solon and Sawar. See Rosenthal, F., op.cit., p.220.

336 al-Baghdādī, *al-farq bayn al-firāq*, p.279.

337 al-Masʿūdī, *murūj al-dhahab wa maʿādin al-jawhar*, v.4, p.64.

338 al-Baghdādī, op.cit., p.279; al-Bīrūnī, op.cit., pp.187, 315.

339 See Rosenthal, F., op.cit., p.220.

340 Cf. ibid, p.220. Also see Taqizadeh, S.H., "A New Contribution to the Materials concerning the Life of Zoroaster", *BSOS*, 8, 1935-37, pp.952-53.

341 al-Bīrūnī, op.cit., p.187.

Another is *yūdāsaf* (or *nūdāshaf*), mentioned by ʾIbn Ḥazm.[342] Yudasaf is evidently a medieval Arabic name, referring to Buddha.[343]

ʾIbn Ḥazm also mentions "*ʾasqlānyūs*, the owner of the described temple" among the prophets of the Harranians.[344] Asqlānyus is obviously an Arabic spelling of Asclepius (Latin form Aesculapius), the Greek hero and god of healing.[345]

ʾaylūn occurs in the account of ʾIbn Ḥazm as a prophet and ʾIbn Ḥazm identifies him as the prophet Noah.[346] This cannot be correct since the Harranians are hostile to Noah.[347]

There are some other possibilities for the identification of Aylūn. There is a Greek term Elysium refers to the place where, according to Greek mythology, special heroes were taken by the gods without dying.[348] The name might also refer to Helen, daughter of Zeus and Leda in Greek mythology.[349]

According to al-Masʿūdī another prophet of the Harranians is *ʾamīrūs*.[350] This name, like the others, probably refers to someone in Greek mythology. Chwolsohn thought that it was Homer, the great Greek poet who was regarded as the author of the Iliad and Odyssey.[351] On the other hand there is another possibility, that this term may refer to the Greek writer of Messina, Euhemerus (4th century B.C.), who in a travel novel claimed to have visited an island in the Indian Ocean and seen a golden column on which were written the deeds of the gods.[352]

al-Masʿūdī also mentions *ʾarāṭas* as one of the Harranian prophets.[353] As suggested by Chwolsohn this name may refer to Aratus, the astronomer poet from Sicily.[354]

Another prophet of the Harranians in al-Masʿūdī's list is *ʾarībāsīs* (the other versions are *ʾarūbāsīs* and *ʾaryāsīs*).[355] This name probably refers to the Greek medical writer Oribasius.[356]

---

[342]ʾIbn Ḥazm, op.cit., v.1, p.35.
[343]Medieval Arabic sources also used the names *būdāsaf, būdāsat* and *byūrāsaf* for Buddha. See Chwolsohn, D., op.cit., v.I, pp.798f.
[344]ʾIbn Ḥazm, op.cit., v.1, p.35. Another version of the name is *ʾasqlābyus*. See Chwolsohn, D., op.cit., v.II, p.527.
[345]For Asclepius see Hammond, N.G.L. and H.H. Scullard, *The Oxford Classical Dictionary*, (hereafter *OCD*) 2nd edition, Oxford (1970), pp.129-30.
[346]See ʾIbn Ḥazm, op.cit., v.1, pp.35, 115.
[347]See below p.163.
[348]See *OCD*, p.23.
[349]See ibid, pp.492-93. Also see Chwolsohn, D., op.cit., v.I, p.800.
[350]al-Masʿūdī, *kitāb al-tanbīh wa al-ʾishrāf*, p.161.
[351]See Chwolsohn, D., op.cit., v.I, pp.782, 795.
[352]See *OCD*, pp.414-15.
[353]al-Masʿūdī, op.cit., p.161.
[354]See Chwolsohn, D., op.cit., v.I, pp.782, 796.
[355]al-Masʿūdī, op.cit., p.161. Also see Chwolsohn, D., op.cit., v.II, p.379.
[356]See *OCD*, p.756.

dūr and *tayūs* are mentioned among the prophets of the Harranians by al-Baghdādī.[357] There are two possibilities for identification of Tayūs: (i) the term may refer to Tatius, traditionally a Sabine king;[358] (ii) it may refer to the Syro-Egyptian god, Thot or Thoth, who is one of the oldest Egyptian gods. He is the god of wisdom and inventor of writing. He is also identified with the moon-god by the Egyptians and with Hermes by the Greeks.[359] On the other hand the identification of Dūr is difficult. We have some geographical names such as Dor, an Egyptian place name,[360] and Dur-ul or Durul, a Sumero-Akkadian canal name,[361] but they, presumably, are not connected with the Harranian prophet Dūr.

Finally al-Shahrastānī mentions *ʾaʿyānā* (or *ʾaʿyān*) and *ʾawādhī* (or *ʾarādī*) among their prophets and states that they believe that Awādhī forbade them to eat certain vegetables, such as onions and broad beans.[362] Awādhī or Arādī may be identical with Arānī. Aʿyānā or Aʿyān is possibly identical with Aylūn, mentioned by ʾIbn Ḥazm.

Besides these mythological figures and ancient philosophers, of the prophets mentioned by the Bible and the Qurʾān the Harranians accept only Adam. They deem Adam to have been an individual born of male and female like other human individuals, but they glorify him and say that he was a prophet, the envoy of the Moon, who called people to worship the Moon, and that there are works compiled by him on the cultivation of the soil.[363] Of Adam they also tell a mythological story about his journey from India to Babylon.[364]

On the other hand they are hostile to Abraham, Noah and Seth. According to the account of ʾIbn Sankilā, quoted by al-Bīrūnī, they claim:

> "Abraham left their community simply because leprosy appeared on his foreskin, and that everybody who suffered from this disease was considered impure, and excluded from all society. Therefore he cut off his foreskin, i.e. he circumcised himself. In this state he entered one of their idol-temples, when he heard a voice speaking to him: 'O Abraham, you went away from us with one sin, and you return to us with two sins. Go away, and do not again come to us.' Thereupon Abraham, seized by wrath, broke the idols in pieces, and left their community."[365]

---

[357] al-Baghdādī, op.cit., p.279.
[358] See *OCD*, p.1037.
[359] See *ER*, v.14, pp.493-94.
[360] See Pritchard, J.B., op.cit., p.26.
[361] See ibid, pp.217, 271.
[362] al-Shahrastānī, op.cit., p.250.
[363] Maimonides, op.cit., p.515.
[364] See ibid, p.516.
[365] al-Bīrūnī, op.cit., p.187.

After this Abraham repented and wished to sacrifice his son to the planet Saturn.[366]

They believed that Noah, who was a cultivator of the soil, never worshipped an idol, and that he was beaten and put into prison because of worshipping God.[367] They also believed that Seth disagreed with the opinion of his father Adam concerning the worship of the Moon.[368] Nor do they accept the prophecies of Jacob, Isaac, Ishmael, Ṣāliḥ, Hūd, Shuʿayb and Muḥammad.[369]

The Harranians, furthermore, believed that the idols and certain trees, which Maimonides calls Asheroth, were the intermediaries between the Holy Beings and the prophets. They thought that the idols and the trees gave prophetic revelation to the prophets, spoke to them in the course of such revelation and made known to them what is useful and what is harmful.[370] They also believed that in certain circumstances the jinn get in touch with people, come to them in dreams, inform them of secret things and are useful to them.[371]

As we saw, the most important characteristic feature of Harranian prophets is the connection with ancient Greek mythology and philosophy. It is difficult to know when the belief in such prophets entered their belief-system, but it must have been after Alexander the Great because Greek culture influenced the area only after his conquests.

Generally medieval scholars identified some of the Harranian prophets like Agathodaimon and Hermes with the prophets who are mentioned in the Qur'ān, such as Shīth (Seth) and 'Idrīs, though mostly these identifications are against the Harranians' own beliefs. The reason for these identifications is probably that these scholars thought of a monotheistic origin for these pagans.

C. Rites of the Harranians

Our medieval sources give plenty of information about the rites and ceremonies of the Harranians. Their main aim in practising these rites was to be close to the Holy Beings.[372] In this section we will discuss their prayers, fasts, sacrifices, initiation rites and feasts.

---

[366] See ibid, p.187.
[367] See Maimonides, op.cit., pp.515-16.
[368] Ibid, p.516.
[369] See 'Ibn Ḥazm, op.cit., v.1, p.35.
[370] See Maimonides, op.cit., p.576.
[371] See ibid, pp.585-86.
[372] al-Maqdīsī, op.cit., v.4, p.23.

a. Prayers

The medieval scholars generally remark that the Harranians have three compulsory times for prayers daily. Our main sources such as al-Bīrūnī, 'Aḥmad 'Ibn al-Ṭayyib al-Sarakhsī, al-Baghdādī and al-Shahrastānī have this idea.[373] According to the account of al-Sarakhsī:

> "The first one of these is half an hour or less before the rising of the sun, finishing at sunrise. It is composed of eight inclinations [of the body], with three prostrations during each inclination. They end the second prayer at the time of [the beginning of] the descent of the sun [noon]. It is composed of five inclinations, with three prostrations in the course of each inclination. The third is like the second, finishing at sunset. These three times [for prayer] are necessary because of the directions of the three fixed points, which are the fixed point of the east, the fixed point of the zenith, and the fixed point of the west. None of them mention that among the ordinances there is a prayer for the time of the fixed point of the earth."[374]

Besides this they have voluntary prayers which are not obligatory thrice daily, the first one of which is at the second hour of the day, the second at the ninth hour of the day, and the third during the third hour of the night.[375]

'Abū al-Fidā tells of their prayer for the dead and remarks that it has no prostration.[376]

According to our medieval sources all of the prayers are preceded by purification and washing.[377]

Concerning the direction for prayer, *qiblah*, there are two different opinions. In his quotation from 'Aḥmad 'ibn al-Ṭayyib al-Ṣarakhsī, 'Ibn al-Nadīm states that "they have adopted one direction for prayer, which they fixed towards the North Pole (*qutb al-shimāl*) in its course".[378] Bar Habraeus also remarks that their direction for prayer is to the North Pole.[379]

---

[373] See ibid, v.4, p.23; 'Ibn al-Nadīm, op.cit., p.318; al-Bīrūnī, op.cit., p.188; al-Baghdādī, *'uṣūl al-dīn*, p.324; al-Shahrastānī, op.cit., p.250; Bar Habraeus, *tārīkh mukhtaṣar al-duwal*, p.266.

[374] 'Ibn al-Nadīm, op.cit., pp.318-19 (Dodge, v.II, p.747). Cf. al-Maqdīsī, op.cit., v.4, p.23; al-Bīrūnī, op.cit., p.188; al-Baghdādī, op.cit., p.324.

[375] See 'Ibn al-Nadīm, op.cit., p.319; al-Bīrūnī, op.cit., p.188.

[376] 'Abū al-Fidā, op.cit., p.148.

[377] See al-Bīrūnī, op.cit., p.188; 'Ibn al-Nadīm, op.cit., p.319; al-Baghdādī, op.cit., p.325.

[378] 'Ibn al-Nadīm, op.cit., p.318 (Dodge, v.II, p.746). B. Dodge translates *qutb al-shimāl* as "the North Star".

[379] Bar Habraeus, op.cit., p.266.

On the other hand al-Masʿūdī, al-Bīrūnī and ʾIbn Ḥazm state that their direction in prayer is to the South. al-Masʿūdī, one of the earliest sources on the medieval Harranians, states:

> "the remnant of the Egyptian Sabians are, at this time [10th century A.D.], the Sabians from Harran; their direction in their prayer is towards *al-tayman* (or *al-tayammun*) which is the *qiblah*, and their back (*ʾistidbāruhum*) is the North."[380]

Apart from the statement "their back is the North" in the text, *al-tayman* may be interpreted to indicate a *qiblah* to the South, since it may be a common noun referring to the South direction.[381] As a matter of fact Chwolsohn gives the French translation of this sentence in al-Masʿūdī's account as follows:

> "qui se tournent, pour prier, vers le midi, ayant le dos au nord."[382]

al-Bīrūnī, who compares the Harranians with the Sabians of the Marshes (whom he calls the real Sabians), also states:

> "The Harranians turn in praying towards the South pole, the Sabians towards the North pole."[383]

ʾIbn Ḥazm says that they turn in praying to the Kaʿbah (in Mecca).[384]

Of these two views the one that mentions the South as their *qiblah* seems to be correct. First of all there is a difficulty in the *al-fihrist* version of the account of al-Sarakhsī where the North is mentioned as the *qiblah* of the Harranians. According to this quotation, also quoted by al-Maqdisī, al-Sarakhsī states that "they fix a direction in prayer (*qiblah*) by taking the North pole in *nuqrah al-qafāʾ*."[385] al-Sarakhsī does not say "they face to the North in prayer". *nuqrah al-qafāʾ* is an obscure phrase, which

---

380 al-Masʿūdī, op.cit., p.161. al-Masʿūdī also mentions *kaldāniyyūn* (Chaldaeans) who live in the marshes between Basra and Wasit and states that they are the remnants of the Babylonians and their direction in prayer is to the North Pole. See ibid, p.161.

381 We have many places known as *al-tayman* such as (1) a locality between *tabalah* and *jurash* in Yemen, (2) a hill in *diyār maḥārib* near *al-rabadhah* and (3) a place between *bilād banī tamīm* and *najrān*. It is noteworthy that all of these places are to the South of Harran. See Yāqūt al-Hamawī al-Rūmī, *muʿjam al-buldān*, v.2, p.68.

382 Chwolsohn, D., op.cit., v.II, p.378.

383 al-Bīrūnī, op.cit., p.329. He also states: "I believe that the Manichaeans, too, turn towards the North pole, because this is, according to them, the middle of the dome of heaven and its highest place": ibid, p.329.

384 See ʾIbn Ḥazm, op.cit., v.1, p.34.

385 al-Maqdisī, op.cit., v.4, p.23. Rosenthal translates this sentence as "they established a direction of prayer in such manner that the North pole was at one's neck": Rosenthal, F., *Aḥmad B. aṭ-Ṭayyib as-Saraḫsī*, p.44.

simply means "back of the head". There is also a phrase, *al-nuqrah fi al-qafā'*, which, according to *lisān al-ʿarab*, means "split of protuberance behind the ear".[386] The meaning is obscure, but a somewhat similar description, as we saw, occurs in the account of al-Masʿūdī, who states, "their direction in their prayer is towards *al-tayman* which is the *qiblah* and their back is the North".[387]

Also the Kaʿbah, the direction of the Muslims in praying, was, as we mentioned before, among the holy buildings, which the Harranians venerated.[388] According to 'Ibn Ḥazm they turned to it in prayer.[389]

Finally in the Arabic version of "the Book of Bābā the Harranian" the term *qiblah* is used in the meaning of "the South".[390] Although we do not know which word was used in the Aramaic original of this book, the term may be connected with their direction in prayer, i.e. the South.

Consequently all of these points suggest the South as the direction of the Harranians in praying.

b. Fasts

Our main sources about the fasts of the Harranians are al-Bīrūnī, who quotes the account of Muḥammad 'ibn ʿAbd al-ʿAzīz al-Hāshimī, and 'Ibn al-Nadīm, who quotes from al-Sarakhsī and 'Abū Saʿīd Wahb 'ibn 'Ibrāhim. al-Hāshimī's account is more detailed than the others. According to these writers the Harranians had a number of fasts scattered in the months of the year,[391] some of which were obligatory for priests only. Here we will follow the order in al-Hāshimī's account.

---

[386]See 'Ibn Manẓūr, op.cit., v.5, p.229. On the other hand as a geographical term *al-naqrah* (or *al-naqirah*) refers to a place between *ʿudākh* and *māwān*, which is one of the places of pilgrimage of Kūfah, and a mountain near Hama, both of which are to the South of Harran. Thus there are two possible meanings of the statement of al-Ṣarakhsī; either it means "by taking the North in the back of the head" or "by taking the North in *naqrah*". The latter possible meaning is quite difficult to accept, since all of the geographical places, which known as *naqrah* (or *naqirah*) are to the South of Harran. See Yāqūt al-Hamawī al-Rūmī, op.cit., v.5, pp.298-99.

[387]See above p.165.

[388]See above p.150.

[389]All of the information about their prayers and *qiblah* is connected with the medieval period of Harran. On the other hand we do not know whether they had prayers and *qiblah* like these before medieval times. The possibility exists that the medieval Harranians turned to the Kaʿbah in prayer because they lived under Muslim dominion from the 7th century. It is quite plausible that they adopted some Islamic rituals in order to get the sympathy and protection of the Muslims. For example, there is a similarity between features of their prayers and Islamic ones; both of them include prostrations in the course of each inclination. Also medieval sources, such as al-Bīrūnī and 'Ibn Ḥazm, point out the other points of similarity between the rituals and rules of the Harranians and those of the Muslims, like the regulations about women and penal laws. See al-Bīrūnī, op.cit., p.188; 'Ibn Ḥazm, op.cit., v.1, pp.34-35.

[390]For example Bābā states: "the Abyssinians, who are the most excellent of the people of the South (*al-qiblah*), will be roused": Rosenthal, F., "The Prophecies of Bābā the Harranian", p.222. Also he states: "*sumaysāṭ* will be destroyed and the water which belongs to *kwzn*, they will take South (*'ilā al-qiblah*)": ibid, p.224.

[391]al-Bīrūnī states that the Harranians derived their year from the revolution of the sun, and month from the revolution of the moon, and that their feast and fast days might be regulated by lunar computation, and at the same time keep their places within the year. See al-Bīrūnī, op.cit., p.13. He

According to the account of al-Hāshimī their first fast of the year begins on the 21st of Kānūn al-ʾAwwal (December). This is broken on the day after the day of conjunction (probably at the beginning of next month, January).[392] This nine-day fast is also among the three most important fasts of the Harranians in the list of al-Sarakhsī. On the other hand al-Sarakhsī states that it begins on the 9th of the month.[393] During this fast they do not eat meat. At the time when they break their fast they practise almsgiving and charitable work.[394] Moreover ʾAbū Saʿīd Wahb ʾibn ʾIbrāhim tells of a nine-day fast, beginning with the 21st of Tishrīn al-Thānī (November), and states that this is for the Lord of Good Luck (Gad).[395] This fast may be the same as the fast in December mentioned by al-Hāshimī and al-Sarakhsī. ʾAbū Saʿīd Wahb also remarks that during this fast every night they break soft bread with which they mix barley, straw, frankincence and fresh myrtle and over which they sprinkle oil. Then they mix it and distribute it among their houses.[396]

In Kānūn al-Thānī (January) they have a seven-day fast, which appears only in the list of al-Hāshimī. This fast begins on the 8th of this month and is broken on the 15th.[397]

In Shubāṭ (February) there is another seven-day fast. al-Sarakhsī mentions this fast among the most important Harranian fasts and states it begins on the 8th of this month.[398] On the other hand al-Hāshimī describes it as a minor fast, beginning with the 9th of the month, and states it is broken on the 16th.[399] ʾAbū Saʿīd Wahb also mentions this fast and states that the first day of the fast is 9th February. He also points out that this fast is for the Sun, the great Lord, the Lord of Well-Being.[400] During this time they do not eat meat, fat or anything from the feast-meals. ʾAbū Saʿīd Wahb also remarks that they do not drink wine.[401]

The Harranians have two fasts in ʾĀdhār (March). One of them, which is mentioned by al-Hāshimī only, is the fast of *ʾay* (اى) which begins on the first day of this month and is broken on the 4th, lasting three days.[402] The other is a thirty-day fast

---

also states that they call the months by the Syriac names and use them in a similar way to the Jews. Moreover he points out that they add the word *hilāl*, "new moon", to the names of the month. Ibid, p.315.

392 Ibid, p.316.

393 See ʾIbn al-Nadīm, op.cit., p.318.

394 al-Bīrūnī, op.cit., p.316.

395 ʾIbn al-Nadīm, op.cit., pp.323-24.

396 See ibid, p.324.

397 al-Bīrūnī, op.cit., p.316.

398 ʾIbn al-Nadīm, op.cit., p.318.

399 al-Bīrūnī, op.cit., p.316.

400 ʾIbn al-Nadīm, op.cit., p.324.

401 See al-Bīrūnī, op.cit., p.316; ʾIbn al-Nadīm, op.cit., p.324.

402 al-Bīrūnī, op.cit., p.316.

which many of our sources about the Harranians mention.[403] This is the first of the three most important fasts in the list of al-Sarakhsī and it is called "the Great Fast" by al-Hāshimī. According to the account of ʾAbū Saʿīd Wahb they hold this fast in honour of the Moon.[404] This begins on 8th March.[405] The breaking of this fast falls in most cases on 8th Nīsān (April).[406]

Moreover al-Sarakhsī mentions some extra fasts, prescribed for the Harranians, for sixteen and twenty-seven days, but they do not appear in the list of al-Hāshimī.[407]

Besides these fasts, in each of the months of the year there is a fast of certain days which is obligatory for only the priests. al-Hāshimī, who tells about this, is not sure about the extent of this fast and its beginning date. He states, "I think, either it lasts fourteen days of each month, or it falls on the fourteenth. I cannot make out the truth."[408]

c. Sacrifices and offerings

Perhaps the most important rites of the Harranians are the sacrifices and offerings to the Holy Beings and their representatives, i.e. idols. As an important characteristic these rites are practised in honour of the intermediaries and their images and temples, rather than the Holy Creator directly. The intermediaries are, as we mentioned before, the deities attached to the heavenly bodies, i.e. planets and zodiac signs.[409] al-Sarakhsī states:

> "Some of them say that it is a bad omen for the sacrifice to be offered in the name of the Creator, for, in their opinion, he undertook only the major

403See ibid, p.317; ʾIbn al-Nadīm, op.cit., pp.318, 324-25; al-Baghdādī, op.cit., p.325; ʾIbn Ḥazm, op.cit., v.1, p.34; ʾAbū al-Fidā, op.cit., p.148; Bar Habraeus, op.cit., p.266. ʾIbn Ḥazm claims that this fast is the fast of Ramaḍān (of the Muslims), but this is completely wrong.

404ʾIbn al-Nadīm, op.cit., p.324.

405See al-Bīrūnī, op.cit., p.317; al-Baghdādī, op.cit., p.325; ʾIbn al-Nadīm, op.cit., p.318. al-Hāshimī states: "...during which [this fast] only meat is forbidden. Its *Signum* is this, that they begin to lament on a day of this month, when the sun stands in the sign of Pisces (...). They continue their lamentations until the 31st day, when the sun stands in the sign of Aries, and the moon in the sign of Cancer, both standing in the same degree. The former day is the beginning of the fast, the latter is its breaking. Frequently this fast lasts only 29 days, when Ḥilāl Adhār has less than 30 days": al-Bīrūnī, op.cit., p.317.

Also ʾAbū al-Fidā states that they sometimes fast only twenty-nine days if the month is deficient. See ʾAbū al-Fidā, op.cit., p.148.

406al-Bīrūnī, op.cit., p.317. Concerning 8th April ʾAbū Saʿīd Wahb remarks that on this day they fast and then break the fast with lamb-meat. ʾIbn al-Nadīm, op.cit., p.322.

407See ʾIbn al-Nadīm, op.cit., p. 318.

408al-Bīrūnī, op.cit., p.318. al-Hāshimī also records the "Fasting of *dflnā* (دفلنا)" on the 14th of September. See ibid, p.318.

409See above p.142.

task, leaving inferior matters to the mediators appointed by him to administer the world."[410]

They also practised various offerings for their ancestors (the dead) whom they quite possibly believed in as the intermediaries of deities.[411]

Their main purpose in practising sacrificial offerings is to be close to the deities.[412] By this means they also think they elicit knowledge of the future of the man who offers the offering and the answer to his inquiries.[413] Moreover they believe that they are informed about secret and hidden knowledge which they want to know while the victim still moves.[414] They also examine the organs of the slaughtered animals and try to guess the events of the next year.[415]

According to the account of al-Sarakhsī there were four times of offering during the month: at the conjunction, the opposite position, on the seventeenth day, and the twenty-eighth day,[416] but this statement is not appropriate to the practices of the Harranians because they made offerings to their deities at any time of the month, as we hear from our other sources.[417]

The Harranians generally practised sacrificial offerings, especially human sacrifices and slaughtered and burnt animals, in the temples, which were mostly connected with the seven planets.[418] *ʿazzūz*, mentioned by Bābā the Harranian,[419] was an important sanctuary where they slaughtered sacrifices and brought offerings. The sacrifices were carried out by the priests.[420] After the sacrificial rites a local official or head-priest (*al-raʾīs*) used to collect money, usually two silver coins (*dirham*), from the people who joined the ceremony.[421]

Their sacrificial offerings can be categorized in three groups: (i) human sacrifices, (ii) sacrificial animals and (iii) other offerings.

(i) According to our medieval sources human sacrifices for planetary deities were common among the Harranians. ʾAbū Saʿīd Wahb, ʾIbn Sankilā, ʿAbd al-Masīh

---

410ʾIbn al-Nadīm, op.cit., p.318. For the translation of this sentence see Rosenthal, F., *Aḥmad B. aṭ-Ṭayyib as-Saraḫsī*, p.45.
411See ʾIbn al-Nadīm, op.cit., p.323.
412See al-Maqdisī, op.cit., v.4, p.23.
413al-Bīrūnī, op.cit., p.188.
414al-Dimashqī, op.cit., p.34.
415See al-Masʿūdī, *murūj al-dhahab wa maʿādin al-jawhar*, v.4, p.69.
416ʾIbn al-Nadīm, op.cit., p.319.
417See ibid, pp.322ff.
418See al-Dimashqī, op.cit., pp.40ff.
419See above p.150.
420See al-Bīrūnī, op.cit., p.188.
421See ʾIbn al-Nadīm, op.cit., pp.323, 324, 325.

ʾibn ʾIshāq al-Kindī, al-Majrīṭī, al-Dimashqī and Dionysius of Tell-Maḥre tell of various human sacrifices of the Harranians. We will later discuss this rite.[422]

(ii) It was very common among the Harranians to sacrifice various animals to their deities. This rite used to be practised in almost every month of the year. According to their regulations the priest who performed the sacrifice was forbidden to enter the sanctuaries during the day.[423] The Harranians generally sacrificed the following animals:

a. Lambs and sheep: lambs were the most common sacrificial animals. Generally seven, eight or nine were sacrificed together.[424] The deities to whom they were sacrificed were the seven planetary deities, Shamāl, Lord of the Hours and Hāmān.[425] They also sacrificed sheep to "the Lord of the Blind" (Mars) and to devils.[426]

b. Cattle: they sacrificed male cattle to their deities.[427] ʾAbū Saʿīd Wahb tells of their various rites in which they sacrifice bulls to the deities Sin, the moon-god, Saturn, Mars and Hermes.[428] Also al-Masʿūdī points out that they sacrifice a black ox by hitting its face with a block of salt and taking its eyes out by this means.[429] al-Majrīṭī gives an account of ox-sacrifice in honour of Saturn (*zuhāl*).[430]

c. Goats: goats were also among the sacrificial animals.[431] ʾIbn al-Nadīm refers to their sacred goats, none of which they are permitted to sell, but which instead they offer as sacrificial victims. No pregnant women can approach them or come near to them.[432]

---

422 See below pp.211ff.
423 See ʾIbn al-Nadīm, op.cit., p.318.
424 See ibid, pp.322-23. Also among the Jewish offerings there was the sacrifice of the Paschal lamb. See *ERE*, v.11, p.28. Further, lamb-sacrifice was common among the Babylonians. See Moore, G,F., *History of Religions*, Edinburgh (1931), v.1, p.220.
425 Cf. ʾIbn al-Nadīm, op.cit., pp.322-23.
426 See ibid, p.322. Sheep were among the most important sacrificial animals. Sheep or rams were sacrificed commonly by the Jews, the Babylonians and the Greeks. See Lev 1:10, 3:7; *ERE*, v.1, p.527; Moore, G., op.cit., v.1, p.220.
427 See ʾIbn al-Nadīm, op.cit., p.318. Cattle were important sacrificial animals for the Jews, the Babylonians and the Greeks. The bull was one of the chief sacrificial animals in the cult of Zeus. See Lev 1:5; Moore, G.F., op.cit., v.1, p.220; *ERE*, v.1, p.508. Also the central act of worship in Mithraism appears to have been the sacrifice of the bull, the prototype of which was the slaying of the bull by Mithra himself. See *ERE*, v.8, p.757.
428 See ʾIbn al-Nadīm, op.cit., p.322.
429 al-Masʿūdī, op.cit., v.4, pp.68-69.
430 See al-Majrīṭī, op.cit., p.227.
431 Goats were sacrificed by the Jews, the Babylonians and the Greeks. See Lev 1:10, 3:12; Moore, G.F., op.cit., v.1, p.220; *ERE*, v.1, p.517; v.11, p.33.
432 See ʾIbn al-Nadīm, op.cit., p.325. Also see ibid, p.318.

d. Other four-legged beasts: all kinds of four-footed beasts which do not have teeth in both of the jaws, with the exception of the camel, used to be sacrificed.[433] According to *al-fihrist* they offered these beasts to Venus and Shamāl.[434]

e. Cocks and chickens: they were among the most common sacrificial victims of the Harranians.[435] ʾAbū Saʿid Wahb especially mentions Mars and "the Lord of Good Luck" (Gad) as the deities to whom cocks and chickens were offered.[436] ʾIbn al-Nadīm states that they preserve the left wing of the chickens which are used for the mystery of the shrine of the gods. The men pare off the flesh with great care and hang the wing bone on the necks of boys and the collars of women, as well as the waists of pregnant women, believing this to be a great safeguard and protection.[437]

f. Other birds: the Harranians also sacrificed other birds which do not have talons, except the pigeon.[438] They sacrificed them to Shamāl and Venus.[439]

Besides these animals, according to *al-fihrist* one of the heretic sects of the Harranians, *rūfusiyyūn*, used to sacrifice pigs to their gods once a year.[440] Also Maimonides says that the Harranians sacrificed field-mice.[441]

According to *al-fihrist* the Harranians used to make amulets from the organs of animals, like donkey, pig, crow and other species, as well as from the charred remains of animals burned as offerings.[442]

According to our sources they also believed that some animals were sacred: dogs, ravens and ants.[443] As we understand from "the Book of Five Mysteries", during the initiation rites these animals are mentioned and described as "the brothers".[444]

---

433 See ibid, p.318. Also the Israelites neither ate nor sacrificed camels, but among the Arabs the camel was common food and a common offering. Smith, W.R., *The Religion of the Semites*, (Revised edition) London, (1894), p.218.

434 Cf. ʾIbn al-Nadīm, op.cit., p.324.

435 See ibid, p.318.

436 See ibid, pp.322-24. ʾAbū Saʿid Wahb tells of the chicken sacrifice of the Harranians on the twenty-sixth of ʾAylūl (September): "Whoever is bound by a vow to the Lord of Good Luck takes either a grown rooster or young chicken. On its wing he fixes a firebrand, the top of which has been kindled with a flame, and he sends forth the chick to the Lord of Good Luck. If the whole chicken burns up, the vow is accepted but, if the firebrand is extinguished before the chicken is burned, the Lord of Good Luck does not accept from him either the vow or the offering": ibid, p.323 (Dodge, v.II, p.760).

437 See ibid, p.325-26.

438 See ibid, p.318. As regards sacrificial birds, the Levitical law of the Jews admits pigeons and turtle-doves, but only as holocausts and in certain purificatory ceremonies. See Lev 1:15, 12:6, 8, 14:22. Also see Smith, W.R., op.cit., p.219 n.2.

439 See ʾIbn al-Nadīm, op.cit., p.324.

440 See ibid, p.326. For pig sacrifices in various traditions see Smith, W.R., op.cit., pp.290-91.

441 See Chwolsohn, D., op.cit., v.II, p.456.

442 See ʾIbn al-Nadīm, op.cit., p.321.

443 Dogs were, as we mentioned before, sacred to Nergal. See pp.241f. Also in ancient Egypt and ancient Persia dogs were commonly respected. See *ERE*, v.1, p.512. Ravens were sacred to Nebo. See Dodge, B., *The Fihrist of al-Nadīm*, v.II, p.770 n.122.

444 See ʾIbn al-Nadīm, op.cit., p.326.

They practised animal sacrifice to their deities in two ways: one was to slaughter the animal by cutting the jugular veins and the wind-pipe, reciting the name of the deity simultaneously with the slaughter with no interval intervening.[445] After slaughtering they carefully observed the movements of its eyes and mouth and its convulsions. Then they drew an augury from it, employed magic, and sought an omen about what would happen.[446] ʾAbū Saʿīd Wahb states:

> "If they wish to slay a large victim like a *zabrūkh*, which is a bull or a sheep, they pour wine over it while it is still alive. If it quivers they say, 'This offering is received', but if it does not quiver they say, 'The god is angry and will not receive this offering.'"[447]

Concerning the eating the sacrificial offerings ʾIbn al-Nadīm, who quotes from al-Sarakhsī, and Bar Habraeus remark that they do not eat the sacrificial offerings, but burn them.[448] On the other hand al-Maqdisī, who also quotes from al-Sarakhsī, states that they eat the flesh, but burn the bones and fats.[449] Also Maimonides points out that they eat the sacrificial flesh,[450] while ʾAbū Saʿīd Wahb states a number of times that they eat the slaughtered victims.[451] Therefore the statement that they never eat sacrificial flesh seems to be an exaggeration.

The other way of sacrifice is to burn animals alive.[452] ʾAbū Saʿīd Wahb states:

> "If they wish to burn a large animal, such as one of the cows, sheep, or cocks, while it is still alive, they hang it up with clamps and chains. Then a group of them exposes all sides of it to the fire until it burns. This is their great offering, which is for all of the gods and goddesses together."[453]

---

[445]See ibid, p.318.
[446]See ibid, p.325.
[447]Ibid, p.325 (Dodge, v.II, p.764).
[448]Cf. ibid, p.318; Bar Habraeus, op.cit., p.266.
[449]al-Maqdisī, op.cit., v.4, p.23.
[450]See Maimonides, op.cit., p.585. Also Maimonides states that they deemed that blood was the food of the devils and that consequently whoever ate it fraternized with the jinn so that they came to him and let him know future events. Accordingly they used to slaughter an animal, collect its blood in a vessel or in a ditch, and eat the flesh of this slaughtered animal close by its blood. In doing this they imagined that the jinn partook of this blood, this being the jinn's food, whereas they themselves ate the flesh. In this way fraternization was achieved, because all ate at the same table and in one and the same gathering. Consequently these jinn would come to them in dreams, inform them of secret things and be useful to them. See ibid, pp.585f. For the ritual of blood-eating among the northern Semites see Smith, W.R., op.cit., p.343.
[451]See ʾIbn al-Nadīm, op.cit., pp.322, 324.
[452]For example, according to the account of ʾAbū Saʿīd Wahb, on 24th January they used to burn eighty creatures, both four-footed beasts and birds, in honour of Shamāl. See ʾIbn al-Nadīm, op.cit., p.324. Also see ibid, pp.322ff. Burnt offerings also appear among the Babylonians and the Jews. See Lev 7:37; Moore, G.F., op.cit., v.1, p.220. Also see Smith, W.R., op.cit., p.371.
[453]ʾIbn al-Nadīm, op.cit., p.325 (Dodge, v.II, p.765).

(iii) Besides human and animal sacrifices the Harranians used to make bloodless offerings to their deities from time to time. For example, during the feast which is celebrated for Shamāl and "the deity who makes the arrow fly" on 27th June, they set up a table on which they placed seven portions for the seven planetary deities and Shamāl.[454] They also offered various fruits, roses and the other plants to their deities. According to the account of 'Abū Saʿīd Wahb, on 4th December they used to erect a dome named "Chamber of *balthā* (Venus)", on the marble of the inner shrine, hanging many kinds of fragrant fruits on it, with dried roses, citrons, small lemons, and other such fruits, whether dry or fresh.[455] Evidently these offerings would be practised in honour of Venus, the fertility goddess. Moreover they would offer various water plants to this goddess.[456]

The Harranians also made burnt offerings of various foods, sweetmeats and wine to their ancestors. In the middle of October they would cook varieties of cooked food and sweetmeats, all of which would be burned during the night in honour of their ancestors. They would also cook a camel-bone with this food and give it to the dogs so that they would not bark and terrify the spirits of the ancestors. In this offering they would also offer wine to them, pouring it over the fire.[457] Moreover they offered the new wine to the gods during the harvest in August.[458]

Another kind of food offering is bread and salt which they offered to the planetary deity Mars and possibly Venus.[459]

Finally they used to burn incense in honour of their deities.[460] 'Abū Saʿīd Wahb states that at the birthday of the moon-god on 24th January they would eat and drink and in honour of their gods and goddesses they would burn *al-dādhī*, which are rods of pine.[461]

d. Initiation rites

Our main source on these rites is "The Book of Five Mysteries" extracted by 'Ibn al-Nadīm.[462]

---

454 See ibid, p.322. The bloodless or grain offerings were also common among the Babylonians and the Jews. The Babylonians offered dates, figs, wine, oil, milk and honey to their deities. On the other hand the Hebrew offerings of grain, meal wine and oil were the most important. See Smith, W.R., op.cit., p.219, and cf. Lev 2:1. Also see Moore, G.F., op.cit., v.1, p.220.

455 See 'Ibn al-Nadīm, op.cit., p.324.

456 Cf. ibid, p.324.

457 See ibid, p.323.

458 See ibid, p.323.

459 See ibid, pp.324-25.

460 See al-Masʿūdī, op.cit., v.4, p.62; 'Ibn Ḥazm, op.cit., v.1, p.34. Also the Babylonians offered incense of sweet-smelling woods to their deities. See Moore, G.F., op.cit., v.1, p.220.

461 See 'Ibn al-Nadīm, op.cit., p.324.

462 For this book see above p.135.

For the temples in which they performed the initiation rites we have three names: The Book of Five Mysteries mentions *bayt al-bughdāriyyīn* several times, evidently a temple for these rites.[463] al-Masʿūdī mentions *maghlītiyā*, which is possibly identical with *bayt al-bughdāriyyīn* because it had underground corridors, used as initiation halls.[464] al-Majrīṭī mentions *bayt sirrihim*, "the House (or the Shrine) of their Mystery", and states that they take the children who were born outside Harran into this shrine.[465] This may be a temple in which the initiation rites take place.

Initiation rites were always performed in the temple under the supervision of the priests. As we understand from the sources, these rites were carried out only for the boys.[466] This was not an initiation into the priesthood, but the reception of a child into the faith. We do not know whether they had an initiation rite for priesthood.

According to The Book of Five Mysteries initiation rites last seven days. During this time the priests narrate to the candidates twenty-two allegories or tales, sung and chanted. The boys eat and drink in the temple, but during these seven days no woman sees them. From seven cups set in a row they take the draught which is called *yusūr*, "right, healthy or free-will offering". They anoint their eyes with this drink, and before they speak, the priests feed them bread and salt from these cups and also loaves and chickens. On the seventh day they eat the last of it. A sacrament of wine is also practised in the temple.[467]

According to The Book of Five Mysteries there were five stages of initiation,[468] each of which had a mystery. During the rite the candidates are called "the sons of *al-bughdāriyyīn*".[469] The characteristic features of the mysteries, which the priests teach the boys during the initiation, are that (1) the boys are always described as follows: "as the lambs among the sheep and the calves among the cows, so are the young men; frightened and fleeing", (2) their god is described as "the victor" and (3) dogs, ravens and ants are described as "the brothers".[470]

There is a resemblance between the initiation rites of the Harranians and those of the Mithra cult because Mithra is spoken of as "the victor" and "invincible". Also dogs and ravens are the names of two stages in the Mithra initiation cult.[471]

---

[463] See ʾIbn al-Nadīm, op.cit., pp.326-27.
[464] See al-Masʿūdī, op.cit., v.4, p.63. Also see above pp.149-50.
[465] See al-Majrīṭī, op.cit., p.226.
[466] See ʾIbn al-Nadīm, op.cit., pp.326-27.
[467] Cf. ibid, p.327.
[468] B. Dodge states that "as the initiation lasted for seven days and there were seven heavenly bodies, it is likely that there were actually seven stages of initiation, information concerning the last two being lost out of the old manuscript": Dodge, B., *The Fihrist of al-Nadīm*, v.II, p.771 n.124.
[469] See ʾIbn al-Nadīm, op.cit., p.327.
[470] Cf. ibid, pp.326-27.
[471] For the Mithra initiation cult see Moore, G.F., op.cit., v.1, p.595.

e. Feasts

A number of medieval sources tell of the feasts of the Harranians.[472] Among them the accounts of al-Hāshimī, extracted by al-Bīrūnī, al-Sarakhsī and ʾAbū Saʿīd Wahb, which ʾIbn al-Nadīm quotes, are the most important.

In addition to the festival days when the periods of fasting came to an end, there were a number of feasts occuring on fixed days of the year. They often used to celebrate the feasts outside Harran. The ceremonies would generally include sacrifices and offerings to the deities. Here we will follow the order of al-Hāshimī because he gives a full list of their feasts.

In *tishrīn al-ʾawwal* (October), al-Hāshimī states, they celebrated four feasts: on the sixth of this month there was a "Feast of *al-dhahbāna*", which possibly lasted a few days because al-Hāshimī remarks that the seventh is the beginning of the celebration of the feast.[473] They also had the "Feast of *fūdī ʾilāhī*" on the thirteenth, the "Feast of *ʾilāti fūdī*" on the fourteenth and the "Feast of the Lots (Festum sortium)" on the fifteenth.[474] These three were possibly the same feast which began on the thirteenth and ended on the fifteenth, lasting three days. Besides these feasts, according to the account of al-Sarakhsī, there was "the Feast of Pregnancy" on the twenty-fifth of this month, which was possibly celebrated in honour of Venus, the fertility goddess.[475] On the other hand ʾAbū Saʿīd Wahb tells of burnt offerings of food for their ancestors in the middle of this month.[476] These offerings might have been practised during the feast mentioned by al-Hāshimī, which occurred on the thirteenth, fourteenth and fifteenth of this month.

According to al-Hāshimī's account they hold the following feasts in *tishrīn al-thānī* (November): "The Great *bakht*" on the first, "*mār shalāmā*" on the second, the "Feast of *dāmū mlḥ* for the shaving of the head" on the fifth, the "Feast of *tarsā*, the idol of Venus", on the seventeenth, on which day they used to go out of Harran to Batnae, and the "Feast of Saruğ" on the eighteenth, which was, al-Hāshimī states, the day of the renewal of dresses.[477] On the other hand al-Bīrūnī states that according to ʾAbū al-Faraj al-Zanjānī they celebrate "the Feast of Tents" in this month, beginning with the fourth and ending on the eighteenth.[478] Consequently it is clear that the last

---

472 In this limited study we will not generally enter the problem of interpretation of Harranian feasts, since a detailed study based on comparison between the feasts of the Harranians and those of the other traditions needs further research and is beyond the limit of this study. A chart of calendar of the feasts of the Harranians will be given at the end of this chapter. See below pp.188ff.

473 al-Bīrūnī, op.cit., p.315.

474 Ibid, 315.

475 ʾIbn al-Nadīm, op.cit., p.319.

476 Ibid, p.323.

477 al-Bīrūnī, op.cit., p.316. al-Hāshimī also mentions "Tarsā the idol of Venus" on the ninth of this month, which is presumably a celebration for Venus. See ibid, p.316.

478 Ibid, p.316. Cf. ʾIbn al-Nadīm, op.cit., pp.323-24.

three feasts mentioned by al-Hāshimī, are various celebrations of the same feast. They also presumably had a festival at the end of the nine days fast which began with the twenty-first.[479]

According to al-Hāshimī the first feast of the month of *kānūn al-ʾawwal* (December) is "the Feast of addressing *tsān* (or *nsān*), the idol of Venus," on the seventh of this month.[480] ʾAbū Saʿīd Wahb, too, tells of an offering ceremony to Venus, beginning with the fourth of this month and lasting seven days.[481] Both of the sources must be referring to the same festival, celebrated in honour of Venus. ʾAbū Saʿīd Wahb's account of this festival is more detailed than the other. During this feast they used to carry out plenty of slaughtered and burnt sacrifices in front of a dome named "the Chamber of *balthā* (Venus)", on which they hung a number of fruits and plants.[482]

al-Hāshimī also mentions "the Feast of the idols of Mars", celebrated on the tenth of this month, "the Feast of the Demons" on the twentieth, "the Feast of the invocation of the Demons" on the twenty-eighth, "the Feast of the *fata* for the Demons" on the twenty-ninth,[483] none of which occur in the account of ʾAbū Saʿīd Wahb. al-Hāshimī also mentions "the Feast of consultation" on the thirtieth of this month,[484] which seems to occur in the account of ʾAbū Saʿīd Wahb, though he does not mention it as a feast. ʾAbū Saʿīd Wahb states that thirtieth of this month is the beginning of the month of the *raʾīs al-ḥamd* and says:

> "On this day the priest sits on [the top step of] an elevated pulpit with nine steps. He takes a tamarisk rod in his hand and then, as the procession passes by him, he strikes each one of them with the stick three, five, or seven times. Then he preaches a sermon to them."[485]

After the sermon the worshippers and priest eat the slaughtered victims and drink. Evidently this was a feast of encouragement of unity for the community because the priest, in his sermon, prays for the people to live, to increase the number of their offspring and to gain power and superiority over all nations so that their sovereignty and days of rule may return to them and that places like the Mosque of Harran and the Greek Orthodox Church may be destroyed.[486]

---

479 See above p.167.
480 al-Bīrūnī, op.cit., p.316.
481 See ʾIbn al-Nadīm, op.cit., p.324.
482 Cf. ibid, p.324.
483 al-Bīrūnī, op.cit., p.316.
484 Ibid, p.316.
485 ʾIbn al-Nadīm, op.cit., p.324 (Dodge, v.II, pp.762-63).
486 Cf. ibid, p.324.

According to al-Sarakhsī's account on the eighteenth of this month the Harranians must have been celebrating the breaking of a nine-day fast which began on the ninth.[487]

Moreover 'Abū al-Faraj al-Zanjānī states that they used to celebrate "the Feast of Nativity" on the twenty-fourth of this month.[488]

According to al-Hāshimī's account on the first of *kānūn al-thānī* (January) the Harranians used to celebrate "the Feast of New-Year's Day", according to the calendar of the Greeks.[489] He also mentions their two feasts, "the Feast of *dayr al-jabal*" and "the Feast of *balfī* (Venus)", on the fourth of this month.[490] These two must be the same feast, celebrated in honour of Venus in Dayr al-Jabal. al-Hāshimī also records "Invocation of *wḥswā*" on the twelfth of this month.[491]

As we mentioned before,[492] the Harranians had seven days fast in this month, beginning with the eighth. Consequently they must have been celebrating the breaking of this fast with a festival on the fifteenth.[493]

Both al-Sarakhsī and 'Abū Saʿīd Wahb also mention a "Birthday Feast", celebrated in this month. The former states that it was on the twenty-third, while the latter says that it was on the twenty-fourth.[494] 'Abū Saʿīd Wahb states that this is the birthday of the Lord who is the Moon and tells of their slaughtered and burnt sacrifices carried out on this day.

al-Hāshimī mentions their two feasts, "the Feast of the idol of *tirrathā* (Atargatis-Venus)", celebrated on the twenty-fifth, and "the Feast of the Nuptials (wedding) of the Year" on the twenty-sixth.[495]

al-Hāshimī also points out that according to their belief all the invocations, fast and feast days of this month are sacred to the Demons.[496] On the other hand concerning the sacred month of the demons 'Abū Saʿīd Wahb mentions February and states that during this month they pray only to Shamāl, the jinn and devils.[497]

There are four feasts celebrated in Shubāṭ (February) in the list of al-Hāshimī: "the Feast of the House of the Bridegroom for the Sun" on the tenth of this month, the "Feast of *mnṭs* for the Sun" on the twenty-second, "the Feast of the Venerable Old

---

[487]See above p.167.
[488]al-Bīrūnī, op.cit., p.316.
[489]Ibid, p.316.
[490]Ibid, p.316.
[491]Ibid, p.316.
[492]See above p.167.
[493]Cf. 'Ibn al-Nadīm, op.cit., p.319.
[494]See ibid, pp.319, 324.
[495]al-Bīrūnī, op.cit., p.316. According to al-Bīrūnī's record the Harranians pray to the Bel of Harran on the twentieth. See ibid, p.316.
[496]Ibid, p.316.
[497]See 'Ibn al-Nadīm, op.cit., p.324.

Man, i.e. Saturn" on the twenty-fourth and "the Feast of the nuptials of *ʿlmātā* (or *ʿlmānā*)" on the twenty-fifth.[498]

On the fifteenth and sixteenth of this month they probably celebrated the breaking of seven days fast which began with the eighth (or ninth according to al-Hāshimī and ʾAbū Saʿīd Wahb), because al-Sarakhsī, who also mentions this fast, points out that they have a feast called "the Feast of Breaking of the Fast of Seven" which lasts two days.[499]

According to al-Hāshimī's account they used to celebrate "the Feast of Hermes-Mercury" on the seventh of *ʾādhār* (March).[500] On the other hand ʾAbū Saʿīd Wahb tells of their celebration at *qubbah al-ʾujurr* (the Cupola of al-Ujurr) in honour of Mars on the twenty eighth.[501] This festival was celebrated with slaughtered and burnt sacrifices. He also states that at the end of this month there was a festival in honour of the marriage of the gods and goddesses, but he does not tell us whether this feast was especially related to Tammūz or Venus, or served in a more general way as an occasion when fertility rites could be observed.[502]

On 4th March the Harranians must also have been celebrating the breaking of the fast of *ʾāy*.[503]

Concerning their feasts in *nīsān* (April) there is a great resemblance between the accounts of al-Hāshimī and ʾAbū Saʿīd Wahb, though al-Hāshimī mentions some feasts which are not in ʾAbū Saʿīd Wahb's list. According to ʾAbū Saʿīd Wahb, during the first three days of this month they used to celebrate a special festival for their goddess *balthā* (Venus).[504] On the other hand al-Hāshimī does not mention any feast on the first day, but he records "the Feast of *damīs*" on the second and "the Feast of the Stibium" on the third,[505] which may be the same festival, celebrated in honour of Venus, in ʾAbū Saʿīd Wahb's account. ʾAbū Saʿīd Wahb also states that when entering the shrine of the goddess on these days, group by group in a scattered way, they slaughter sacrificial victims and burn animals alive.[506] Also al-Hāshimī mentions their "celebration of Ploutos" on the fourth and the "Feast of *blyān*, the idol of Venus" on the fifth.[507] The last one was obviously a feast for Venus. Hence it is possible that the feast celebrated for this goddess lasted five days.

---

[498] al-Bīrūnī, op.cit., p.316.
[499] See ʾIbn al-Nadīm, op.cit., p.319. Also cf. ibid, p.324.
[500] al-Bīrūnī, op.cit., p.316. al-Hāshimī also records "Weaning of the children" on the 10th March. See ibid, p.317.
[501] ʾIbn al-Nadīm, op.cit., p.325. Also see Chwolsohn, D., op.cit., v.II, p.37.
[502] See ʾIbn al-Nadīm, op.cit., pp.324-25.
[503] See above p.167.
[504] ʾIbn al-Nadīm, op.cit., p.322.
[505] al-Bīrūnī, op.cit., p.317.
[506] ʾIbn al-Nadīm, op.cit., p.322.
[507] al-Bīrūnī, op.cit., p.317.

This April feast may be an annual spring feast of Semitic origin, because the burning of living animals, performed during the festival period, answers to the ceremonies observed at Hierapolis in the great feast of the Syrian goddess at the incoming of spring, when goats, sheep and other living creatures were suspended on a pyre, and the whole was consumed.[508] Also at Babylon the New-Year's Festival (*akītu*) was celebrated each year at the beginning of this month, during the first twelve days of the first month, *nisan*, in honour of the highest deity. In the course of this celebration, the statue of the god proceeded, first by chariot and then by barge, on a river, from its metropolitan sanctuary to a suburban shrine, the Akītu-temple. This exodus symbolized the deity's descent to the Netherworld, the crossing of the "River of the Dead" being represented by a procession by barge on the nearest river or stream.[509]

It is obvious that this five days feast of the Harranians was not an Akītu festival, but it was a spring festival, celebrated for the fertility goddess Ishtar-Venus. Akītu was celebrated for the patron deity of a city and Venus never became the patron deity of Harran.

On the sixth of this month they had a celebration for the moon-god. al-Hāshimī mentions the name of this festival as "the Feast of *smār* and of the Living Being of the Moon".[510] On this day they used to go to *dayr kādī* where they would slaughter a bull in honour of this deity.[511]

The eighth of this month was generally the day of breaking their most important fast which began on 8th March. On this day they held a feast in honour of the seven deities, the devils, the jinn and spirits. al-Hāshimī calls this feast "the Feast of the birth of the spirits".[512] They used to celebrate it with burnt sacrifices to these deities. According to al-Sarakhsī this feast would last two days.[513]

al-Hāshimī also mentions "the Feast of the Lords of the Hours" on the ninth of this month.[514]

According to al-Hāshimī's account, on the fifteenth they used to celebrate "the Feast of the mysteries of *al-simāk*".[515] ʾAbū Saʿīd Wahb also tells of the same feast, but he mentions it as "the mystery of Shamāl".[516] They would celebrate this feast with sun-worship, sacrificial slaughter, burnt offerings, eating and drinking.

---

[508]See Smith, W.R., op.cit., pp.470-71.
[509]For Babylonian Akītu festival see Black, J.A., "The New Year Ceremonies in Ancient Babylon: 'Taking Bel by the Hand' and A Cultic Picnic", *Religion*, 11, 1981, pp.39-59; Pallis, S.A., *The Babylonian Akītu Festival*, Copenhagen (1926).
[510]al-Bīrūnī, op.cit., p.317.
[511]See ibid, p.317; ʾIbn al-Nadīm, op.cit., p.322.
[512]See al-Bīrūnī, op.cit., p.317; ʾIbn al-Nadīm, op.cit., p.322.
[513]See ʾIbn al-Nadīm, op.cit., p.319.
[514]al-Bīrūnī, op.cit., p.317.
[515]Ibid, p.317.
[516]ʾIbn al-Nadīm, op.cit., p.322.

Both of our sources also mention a festival celebrated on the twentieth of this month, at *dayr kādī*, a sanctuary near one of the gates of Harran known as *bāb funduq al-zayd*,[517] where they used to sacrifice bulls to Saturn, Mars and Sin, and other sacrifices in honour of Shamāl, the deity of devils, Lord of the Hours and the seven deities.[518]

According to another account in *al-fihrist* this feast was celebrated for the "Idol of the Water", who was awaited at the shrine at Dayr Kādī.[519] This festival was similar to the Babylonian Akītu feast, from which the name *kādī* was probably derived, although the local people thought that the name came from Syriac *kādhā*, meaning "to here".[520] The feast was based on an ancient myth to explain the disappearance of the Moon after its conjunction with the Pleiades during the third week of March. Although the people implored Sin, the moon-god, to return to Harran, he refused to do so, but said "I will come 'to here'", referring to Dayr Kādī. So a month after the moon's disappearance, the worshippers went to this shrine to welcome Sin back again. It seems certain that the return of the moon-god was dramatized by bringing an idol along the canal in a barge. Then the idol was very likely taken ashore to the shrine with chanting, dancing and impressive ritual, followed by feasting and revelry.[521]

The final feast in April was a feast at the Moon Shrine, *dayr sīnī*, on the twenty-eighth.[522] ʾAbū Saʿīd Wahb does not mention this name, but only states that it was a sanctuary in a village named *sabtā*. He also remarks that they used to celebrate it with various sacrificial offerings to Hermes, seven deities, Shamāl and the Lord of the Hours.[523]

According to al-Hāshimī's account, on the second of *ʾayyār* (May) they used to celebrate "the Feast of *salūghā*, the prince of Satans".[524] Salūghā is, as we mentioned earlier, presumably identical with Shamāl, the chief and the god of jinn and devils in the account of ʾAbū Saʿīd Wahb.[525] ʾAbū Saʿīd Wahb also mentions a feast for the deity ʾIbn al-Salm on the same day.[526]

Moreover al-Hāshimī mentions ten more feasts celebrated in this month. He states that on the third of this month the Harranians used to celebrate "the Feast of a Baghdādian house".[527] This evidently refers to the *bayt al-bughdāriyyīn* which occurs

---

517 See al-Bīrūnī, op.cit., p.317; ʾIbn al-Nadīm, op.cit., p.322.
518 ʾIbn al-Nadīm, op.cit., p.322.
519 Ibid, p.325.
520 See ibid, p.325.
521 See Dodge, B., "The Ṣābians of Ḥarrān", p.78; Lewy, H., op.cit., p.144.
522 al-Bīrūnī, op.cit., p.317. This shrine may be identical with Dayr Kādī, moon temple.
523 See ʾIbn al-Nadīm, op.cit., p.322.
524 al-Bīrūnī, op.cit., p.317.
525 See above p.152.
526 See ʾIbn al-Nadīm, op.cit., p.322. For this deity see above p.154.
527 al-Bīrūnī, op.cit., p.317.

several times in The Book of Five Mysteries. al-Hāshimī possibly misspelled the name as *baghdādiyyūn*.[528]

He also mentions "the Feast of the vows" on the 4th May, which according to the list in *al-fihrist* occurs on the second,[529] "the Feast of *'amīṣlḥ*, or Feast of Baptism" on the fifth or sixth, "the Feast of *ḍaḥḍāq*, the idol of the Moon" on the seventh, "the Feast of *ḍaḥḍāq* and *jurūshyā*" on the eleventh, "the Feast of *jurūshyā*" on the twelfth, "the Feast of *barkhūshyā*" on the thirteenth, "the Feast of *barkhurūshyā*" on the fifteenth, "the Feast of *bāb al-tibn* (the straw-gate)" on the seventeenth and "the Feast of perfection of *ḍaḥḍāk* (Ḍaḥḍāq)" on the twentieth. He also states that on the same day, i.e. on the twentieth, they celebrated "the Feast of *tara'ūz*".[530] Tara'ūz probably refers to the famous Babylonian god Tammūz. al-Hāshimī states that his commemoration with lamentation and weeping was on the seventh day of *ḥazīrān* (June),[531] but according to 'Abū Sa'īd Wahb's account this commemoration took place in the middle of *tammūz* (July) under the name of "the Feast of *al-būqat*.[532] Maimonides also tells of this commemoration for Tammūz and states that it took place on the first day of *tammūz*.[533]

'Abū Sa'īd Wahb states that on this day the women weep for this god because his master slew him by grinding his bones under a millstone and winnowing them in the wind. So the women eat nothing ground by a millstone, but rather moistened wheat, chick-peas, dates, raisins and similar things.[534] Maimonides also tells a similar story, saying that it is related that an individual from among the prophets of idolatry, named Tammūz, called upon a king to worship the seven planets and the twelve signs of zodiac. Thereupon that king killed him in an abominable manner.[535]

Concerning their feasts in *ḥazīran* (June) al-Hāshimī also records "the Feast of *al-kurmūs* or Feast of genuflection (bending the knee)" on the twenty-fourth and "the Feast of the butcher's house" on the twenty-seventh.[536] 'Abū Sa'īd Wahb too mentions a feast, celebrated with a magical ceremony for the seven deities and Shamāl, on the twenty-seventh. According to this account on this day they set up a table on which they place seven portions for these deities. Then the priest brings a bow which he strings,

---

[528]See above p.149.
[529]'Ibn al-Nadīm, op.cit., p.322.
[530]al-Bīrūnī, op.cit., p.317.
[531]See ibid, p.317.
[532]'Ibn al-Nadīm, op.cit., p.322. He also gives the name of deity as *tā-ūz*.
[533]Maimonides, op.cit., p.520.
[534]See 'Ibn al-Nadīm, op.cit., p.322. A parallelism to this story occurs in the Ugaritic texts, in the conflict between Ba'lu and Mōtu. According to the text the goddess 'Anatu attacks Mōtu, splits him with a sword, winnows with a sieve, burns with fire, and grinds with mill-stones. See Healey, J.F., "Burning the Corn: new light on the killing of Mōtu", *Or*, 52, 1983, pp.248ff. Also see Livingstone, A., *Mystical and Mythological Explanatory Works of Assyrian and Babylonian Scholars*, Oxford (1986), pp.161-64.
[535]Maimonides, op.cit., pp.519-20.
[536]al-Bīrūnī, op.cit., p.317.

and which he fixes an arrow to which there is attached a firebrand. It has a flame at its head and is made of a wood which grows in the region of Harran. On it there is a piece of cloth upon which the flame is ignited like a candle. The priest shoots twelve arrows. Then the priest walks as a dog does on his hands and feet, until he fetches the arrows. He does this fifteenth times and then makes an augury, i.e. if the firebrand is extinguished, the feast in his estimation is not acceptable, but if it is not put out, then the feast is accepted.[537]

al-Hāshimī records their four feasts in *tammūz* (July), "the Feast of the youths" on the fifteenth, "the Feast of the nuptials of the elements" on the seventeenth, "the Feast of the elements" on the eighteenth and "the Feast of the elements" on the nineteenth.[538] These last three are clearly the same festival, celebrated in honour of the elements, which may be the primal elements of the Harranians, i.e. the First Mind, the Soul, World Order, Form and Necessity.[539] ʾAbū Saʿīd Wahb too tells of a festival for the jinn, the devils and the deities on the seventeenth of this month, which they used to celebrate with various offerings to Hāmān, the chief and the father of the gods, and to Nmryā.[540]

Finally al-Sarakhsī states that they held a feast on the twenty-ninth of this month, but he does not give any information about it.[541]

According to the account of ʾAbū Saʿīd Wahb during eight days of *ʾāb* (August) they celebrated the fruit harvest by treading new wine for the gods, and also sacrificing a new-born infant.[542] al-Hāshimī also mentions "the Feast of *dailafatān* (Venus)" on the third and seventh of this month.[543]

It is clear that this was the Semitic agricultural feast of harvest. The Babylonians celebrated a great festival in honour of the fertility goddess Ishtar-Venus, which was repeated in the next month. The Israelites too celebrated "the Feast of Harvest" or "Feast of Weeks" in the third month. During this pilgrimage-feast the first fruits of the harvest were offered.[544]

al-Hāshimī also mentions "the Feast of bathing in the baths of Saruğ" which begins on the twenty-fourth and ends on the thirtieth. Moreover on the twenty-eighth they celebrated "the Feast of Kepharmīsā".[545]

---

[537]See ʾIbn al-Nadīm, op.cit., p.322.
[538]al-Bīrūnī, op.cit., pp.317-18.
[539]See above p.142.
[540]See ʾIbn al-Nadīm, op.cit., pp.322-23.
[541]Ibid, p.319.
[542]Ibid, p.323.
[543]al-Bīrūnī, op.cit., p.318.
[544]See Fohrer, G., op.cit., p.202; *ERE*, v.3, p.77.
[545]al-Bīrūnī, op.cit., p.318. al-Hāshimī also records a feast on the 26th of August which might be a part of the Feast of bathing. See ibid, p.318.

According to ʾAbū Saʿīd Wahb they held a feast, celebrated with a magical ceremony, during three days of *ʾaylūl* (September) which were possibly the first three days. During this time they used to heat water and throw into it some materials like tamarisk, wax, pine, olives and cane. Then they would cause it to boil and before sunrise pour it over their bodies as the magicians do. They would also sacrifice animals to their seven deities and Shamāl.[546]

al-Hāshimī mentions "the Feast of the Column of our Houses for the women" on the thirteenth of this month. He also mentions "the Feast of the Lords of the coming forth of the New Moons" on the twenty-fourth.[547] None of them is found in the account of ʾAbū Saʿīd Wahb.

According to al-Hāshimī's account on the twenty-fifth they used to celebrate "the Feast of the candle on the hill of Harran".[548] ʾAbū Saʿīd Wahb too mentions this festival, but he gives the date as the twenty-sixth and states that on that day they used to go forth to the mountain and observe the opposite position of the Sun, Saturn and Venus.[549] On this day they would also burn chickens for the Lord of Good Luck.

In ʾAbū Saʿīd Wahb's account, on the twenty-seventh and the twenty-eighth they used to celebrate a festival for Shamāl as well as for the devils and the jinn with various burnt and slaughtered sacrifices and offerings.[550]

Besides these feasts al-Bīrūnī states that on the seventeenth of each month they celebrate a feast, the reason for which is the beginning of the deluge on the seventeenth of the month; further the days of the equinoxes and solstices are festivals.[551] ʾAbū Saʿīd Wahb remarks that every twenty-seventh of the lunar month they go out to their sanctuary, which is known as Dayr Kādī, and slaughter and burn various offerings to the moon-god Sin.[552]

We can summarize the characteristic features of the rites of the Harranians under three points:

i. In their rites three kinds of influence are noticeable, the most important of which is Assyro-Babylonian influence which appears in a number of feasts and sacrifices. For example, magical ceremonies and the feasts such as the festival which is similar to Akītu and the commemoration of Tammūz clearly show this influence. Jewish influence is also important because there is a similarity between many sacrifices of the Harranians and those of the Jews. Moreover we find Iranian influence because

546 See ʾIbn al-Nadīm, op.cit., p.323.
547 al-Bīrūnī, op.cit., p.318.
548 Ibid, p.318.
549 ʾIbn al-Nadīm, op.cit., p.323.
550 See ibid, p.323.
551 al-Bīrūnī, op.cit., p.318.
552 See ʾIbn al-Nadīm, op.cit., p.325.

there is a resemblance between some of the rites, like initiation, and their counterparts in the Mithra cult.

ii. Magical ceremonies are one of the most important features of their rites. Magic seems to be connected especially with the devils, the jinn and their chief, Shamāl. During the feasts the priests used to try to make the feasts acceptable by performing magic, but it was not only practised in connection with their feasts: they also used it on every occasion. When they slaughtered or burnt an animal they paid attention to every movement and to the organs of the victim, and by this method guessed what would happen in the next year.

iii. Finally idolatry is the most important feature of their ceremonies, because all their rites were practised in honour of the idols symbolizing the deities — and most of them, like sacrifices and offerings, were carried out in front of the idols.

D. Harranian religious regulations

The medieval pagans of Harran had plenty of regulations about eating and drinking, pollution and impurity and marriage.

a. Eating and drinking

It was illegal to slaughter and eat some animals. Among them camel was the most important.[553] They also forbade the eating of all animals with teeth in both jaws, such as the pig, the dog and the donkey.[554]

There is an obvious similarity between these taboos and those mentioned in Leviticus for the Jews, because the Jews too were forbidden to eat camel and pig.[555] According to al-Bīrūnī's account, some of them did not eat fish and chicken.[556] Moreover among birds they forbade the eating of the pigeon and such birds as have talons.[557]

They did not eat whatever had not been positively slaughtered, i.e. any animal which had died of disease or by accident rather than being slaughtered.[558] Moreover they generally forbade consuming the blood (though some of them used to consume it),

---

[553]See al-Maqdīsī, op.cit., v.4, p.23; 'Ibn al-Nadīm, op.cit., p.319; al-Baghdādī, *'uṣūl al-dīn*, p.325; al-Shahrastānī, op.cit., p.250. al-Sarakhsī states: "They are so extreme in their abhorrence of the camel that they say that anyone who walks under the halter of a camel will not attain his desire": 'Ibn al-Nadīm, op.cit., p.319 (Dodge, v.II, p.749). Also see al-Maqdīsī, op.cit., v.4, p.23.

[554]See 'Ibn al-Nadīm, op.cit., p.319; al-Maqdīsī, op.cit., v.4, p.23; al-Baghdādī, op.cit., p.325; al-Shahrastānī, op.cit., p.250.

[555]Cf. Lev 11:1-20. The other animals which are illegal to eat for the Jews are the rock badger, the hare, sea creatures without fins and scales and the birds, like eagle, osprey and black vulture.

[556]al-Bīrūnī, op.cit., p. 188. Also see al-Maqdīsī, op.cit., v.4, p.23.

[557]See 'Ibn al-Nadīm, op.cit., p.319; al-Baghdādī, op.cit., p.325; al-Shahrastānī, op.cit., p.250.

[558]See 'Ibn al-Nadīm, op.cit., p.319; 'Ibn Ḥazm, op.cit., v.1, p.35.

deeming that it was the food of the devils and that, consequently, whoever consumed it fraternized with the jinn so that they came to him and let him know future events.[559]

Certain vegetables were also illegal to eat. They forbade the eating of garlic because in their opinion it produced headache and burnt the blood of the sperm on which the existence of the world depended. Also peas were forbidden because they thought that they stupified and impaired the intellect and originally grew in the skull of man.[560] Moreover some of them forbade the eating of some other vegetables, like broad beans, green beans, cauliflower, cabbage, onion and lentils.[561]

Some of our sources also tell us that they forbade alcoholic drinks,[562] but this information is possibly incorrect, because we hear from other sources that the Harranians used to make wine during the harvest and offer the new wine to their deities, and that they would eat and drink it in their festivals.[563]

b. Pollution and impurity

The Harranians considered some occasions as causing pollution or uncleanness. Among them touching a dead body, sexual intercourse and touching a woman in menstruation involved serious impurity.[564] Menstruation itself was also considered a cause of impurity for a woman.

It is clear that most of the regulations concerning pollution are closely connected with Hebrew tradition. Uncleanness caused by a dead body is familiar among the Hebrews. According to them contact with the carcases of animals causes impurity until evening. The human corpse was regarded by them as the most defiling. Also uncleanness caused by menstruation and by touching a woman in menstruation are familiar among the Hebrews.[565]

According to the regulations of the Harranians there are two ways of washing away impurities: one of them is to take a bath. They used to perform it after intercourse, contact with the dead and menstruation.[566] Anyone who touches a woman in menstruation must use natron (carbonate of soda) in washing.[567] It seems to imply washing the whole body, like *ghusl* of the Muslims, though we do not know exactly

559 See Maimonides, op.cit., p.585; ʾIbn Ḥazm, op.cit., v.1, p.35. Also according to Hebrew tradition the blood of animals slain for human food was forbidden. See Gen 9:4.

560 See al-Bīrūnī, op.cit., p.188.

561 See ʾIbn al-Nadīm, op.cit., p.319; al-Maqdisī, op.cit., v.4, p.23; Bar Habraeus, *tārīkh mukhtaṣar al-duwal*, p.266; al-Shahrastānī, op.cit., p.250. al-Shahrastānī states that ʾAwādhī, one of their prophets, forbade them to eat vegetables like onions and broad beans.

562 See al-Baghdādī, op.cit., p.325; al-Shahrastānī, op.cit., p.250.

563 See ʾIbn al-Nadīm, op.cit., pp.322-23. They also offered wine to their dead. See ibid, p.295.

564 See ibid, p.319; al-Maqdisī, op.cit., v.4, p.23; al-Baghdādī, op.cit., p.325; al-Shahrastānī, op.cit., p.250.

565 See Num 19:7, 11ff; Lev 15:19ff.

566 See al-Maqdisī, op.cit., v.4, p.23; al-Bīrūnī, op.cit., p.188; al-Baghdādī, op.cit., p.325.

567 See ʾIbn al-Nadīm, op.cit., p.319.

how they performed it. According to information in *al-fihrist*, impurity is also washed away by a change of garments. For anyone who touches a woman in menstruation a change of garments is required.[568] These two ways of removing impurity were possibly practised together, i.e. they would first wash themselves and then change garments.

In fact women were regarded as unclean by the Harranians. They were not eligible to take part in the most important mysteries of the cult. Also during the seven days initiation ceremony no woman should see the boys; if any woman saw them this would be regarded as impurity for the boys.[569]

They also regarded everything which might be separated from the body, such as hair, nail and blood, as unclean. In their opinion every barber is therefore unclean because he touches blood and hair.[570]

They avoid anybody with whiteness of skin and leprosy, and also with a contagious disease,[571] because these diseases are regarded as unclean. In their opinion particularly leprosy is the most defiling. For example Abraham left their community simply because leprosy appeared on his foreskin, and everyone who suffered from this disease was considered impure and excluded from all society.[572]

This regulation is also closely connected with the Hebrew tradition because according to this tradition leprosy involved exclusion from the community and the leper was looked upon, not only as defiled himself, but as a source of defilement to his neighbours.[573]

Finally they shun circumcision, not making any change in the work of nature.[574]

c. Marriage

The Harranians marry in front of witnesses. It is forbidden to marry with close relatives. A man cannot divorce his wife, unless there is clear proof of adultery; nor can he take back a divorced woman.[575] They do not tolerate polygamy.[576]

---

568 Ibid, p.319.
569 See ibid, pp.323, 327.
570 See Maimonides, op.cit., p.595.
571 See 'Ibn al-Nadīm, op.cit., p.319; al-Baghdādī, op.cit., p.325; al-Maqdisī, op.cit., v.4, p.23.
572 See above pp.162f.
573 Cf. Lev 13:2ff; Num 12:10ff.
574 See 'Ibn al-Nadīm, op.cit., p.319; al-Bīrūnī, op.cit., p.188; al-Baghdādī, op.cit., p.325; al-Shahrastānī, op.cit., p.250.
575 See 'Ibn al-Nadīm, op.cit., p.319; al-Maqdisī, op.cit., v.4, p.23; al-Baghdādī, op.cit., p.325; 'Ibn Ḥazm, op.cit., v.1, p.35; al-Shahrastānī, op.cit., p.250.
576 See al-Baghdādī, op.cit., p.325; al-Shahrastānī, op.cit., p.250.

According to them a man should only have sexual relations with his wife for the sake of producing a child.[577] Women are equal to men in following the rules of religion. They receive shares of inheritance equal to those of males.[578]

577 ʾIbn al-Nadīm, op.cit., p.319.
578 See al-Maqdīsī, op.cit., v.4, p.23; ʾIbn al-Nadīm, op.cit., p.319.

The Calendar of the Feasts of the Harranians*

	al-Hāshimī	'Abū Saʿīd Wahb	Others
Tishrīn al-'Awwal (October)			
6	*al-dhahbāna*		
13	*fūdī 'ilāhī*		
14	*'ilāfī fūdī*		
15	The Lots		
25			Pregnancy (al-Sarakhsī)
Tishrīn al-Thānī (November)			
1	The Great *bakht*		
2	*mār shalāmā*		
4-18			The Tents ('Abū al-Faraj al-Zanjānī)
5	*dāmū mlḥ* for the shaving of the head		
17	*tarsā*, the idol of Venus		
18	Saruğ		
30		Breaking of the nine-day fast	
Kānūn al-'Awwal (December)			
4-11		Offering ceremonies in honour of Venus	
7	The addressing *tsān* (or *nsān*), the idol of Venus		
10	The idols of Mars		
18			The breaking of nine-day fast (al-Sarakhsī)
20	The demons		
24			The Nativity ('Abū al-Faraj al-Zanjānī)
28	The invocation of the demons		
29	The *fata* for the demons		
30	The consultation	The celebrations for the beginning of the month of the *ra'īs al-ḥamd*	

*Besides these festivals recorded in this calendar according to our medieval sources the Harranians celebrated a feast on the 17th and 27th of each month.

Kānūn al-Thānī (January)

1	The New-Year's Day		
4	*dayr al-jabal* and *balfi*		
12	Invocation of *wḥswā*		
15	Breaking of the seven-day fast		
23			The Birthday (al-Sarakhsī)
24		The celebration of the birthday of the Lord (Moon)	
25	The idol of *tirrathā* (Atargatis-Venus)		
26	The nuptials (wedding) of the year		

Shubāṭ (February)

10	The house of the Bridegroom for the Sun		
15-16			The breaking of the fast of seven (al-Sarakhsī)
16	Breaking of the fast of seven	Breaking of the fast of seven	
22	*mnṭs* for the Sun		
24	The venerable old man, Saturn		
25	The nuptials of *ʿalmātā* or *ʿalmānā*		

ʾĀdhār (March)

4	Breaking of the three-day fast		
7	Hermes-Mercury		
28		A celebration at *qubbah al-ʾujurr* in honour of Mars	
30		A festival in honour of the marriage of the gods and goddesses	

Nīsān (April)

1-3		A special festival in honour of the goddess *balthā* (Venus)	
2	*damīs*		
3	The Stibium		
4	The celebration of Plautos		
5	*blyān*, the idol of Venus		
6	*smār* and the living being of the Moon	Bull-sacrifice in honour of the Moon	
8	The birth of the spirits. The break of the fast of thirty	Breaking of the thirty-day fast. Celebrations in honour of the seven deities, the devils, the jinn and spirits	
8-9			The breaking of the thirty-day fast (al-Sarakhsī)
9	The Lords of the Hours		
15	The mysteries of *al-simāk*	Celebration of the mystery of Shamāl	
20	A festival at Dayr Kādhī	Celebrations at Dayr Kāḍī	Celebrations of coming of the Idol of Water at Dayr Kādhī
28	A festival at the Moon shrine *dayr sīnī*	Celebrations in a sanctuary in a village named Sabtā	

'Ayyār (May)

2	Salūghā, the prince of Satans	Celebrations for the deity 'Ibn al-Salm and making vows	
3	Baghdādian house		
4	The vows		
5 or 6	*'amīṣlḥ* or feast of baptism		
7	*ḍaḥḍāq*, the idol of the Moon		
11	*ḍaḥḍāq* and *jurūshyā*		
12	*jurūshyā*		
13	*barkhūshyā*		
15	*barkhurūshyā*		
17	*bāb al-tibn*		
20	The perfection of *ḍaḥḍāk* (Ḍaḥḍāq) and the feast of *tarāʿuz*		

Ḥazīrān (June)

7	The commemoration of Tammūz with lamentation		
24	*al-kurmus* or feast of genuflection		
27	The butcher's house	A celebration with a magical ceremony	

Tammūz (July)**

1			Commemoration of Tammūz (Maimonides)
15	The youth		
17	The nuptials of the elements	A festival for the jinn, the devils and the deities	
18-19	The elements		
29			A festival (al-Sarakhsī)

ʾĀb (August)

1-8		Celebration of harvest	
3 and 7	*dailafatān* (Venus)		
24-30	Bathing in the baths of Sarug̃		
28	*kapharmīsā*		

ʾAylūl (September)

1-3		Celebrations with magical ceremonies	
13	The column of our houses for the women		
24	The Lords of the coming forth of the new Moon		
25	The candle on the hill of Harran		
26		Celebrations at the mountain	
27-28		A festival in honour of Shamāl, the devils and the jinn	

**According to ʾAbū Saʿīd Wahb's account the Harranians celebrated the commemoration of Tammūz (the feast of *al-būqāt*) in the middle of Tammūz (July).

CHAPTER VII

A COMPARISON OF MANDAEISM WITH HARRANIAN RELIGION

1. Some characteristic features of Harranian religion which do not appear in that of the Mandaeans

In this section we will examine some characteristics of the Harranians such as the Sin cult and the Hermetic tradition which do not appear in Mandaean religion.

A. The Sin cult of the Harranians

The cult of Sin, the moon god, was the central cult of Harranian religion from the earliest time to the destruction of the last pagan temple in Harran. In antiquity the city of Harran was perhaps important because of this cult rather than its strategic position or being a stage on the important trade route between east and west.

According to H. Lewy[1] the early worshippers of the moon were not farmers who tilled the soil, but Aramaean and proto-Aramaean nomads who roamed the Syro-Arabian desert. In ancient Mesopotamia the moon god was considered the oldest of the planets, preceding the sun as night precedes day. He was the father of the divine sun, as well as of Ishtar, and thus deserved precedence both by virtue of age and of family status.[2]

The name of the moon god, Sin, is presumably a borrowing from Sumerian. In Sumerian he was called *en-zu* (or *zu-en*), "the lord of knowledge", of which the name Sin may be a derivative.[3] The Semitic form of his name is Nannar (*na-an-na* or *na-an-*

---

[1]Lewy, H., p.151 n.2.

[2]Ingholt, H., op.cit., p.38.

[3]See Jastrow, Jr.M., *Aspects of Religious Belief and Practice in Babylonia and Assyria*, (American Lectures on the History of Religions, ninth series, 1910) New York and London (1911), pp.112, 211; Tallqvist, K., *Akkadische Götterepitheta*, p.442; Thierens, A.E., *Assyriology in Mesopotamian Culture*, Leiden (1935), p.32; Drijvers, H.J.W., *Cults and Beliefs at Edessa*, p.140. Jr. M. Jastrow also states that Sin may be a contraction of *si-in* and this in turn equivalent to En-zu inverted. See Jastrow, Jr.M., op.cit., p.112 n.2.

nar),[4] "illumination" or "luminary", and in Jastrow's opinion this appears to be a designation more particularly connected with the cult at Harran.[5] The moon god was also worshipped in the West, e.g. at Ugarit, under the name *yrḫ*.[6]

Before we examine the Sin cult of Harran we will briefly touch on the moon cult of ancient Mesopotamia. During the Sumerian period Sin was highly venerated together with his spouse Ningal, the great Lady, at Ur, the famous centre of a Sumerian dynasty. In the ancient hymns of Ur, where he is worshipped originally as the highest deity, the lunar god is called also "king" and "father" of the gods, like Anu. He is also called "the firstborn son of Enlil" who cosmically is the deity of the heavenly as well as of the earthly Earth. Moreover on the well-known stele of Ur-Nammu, founder of the third dynasty of Ur (2112-2095 B.C.), the god is represented enthroned with staff and sceptre in his right hand, Ningal is seated to his right and the king in front of them. The staff and the sceptre are the insignia with which the god invests the king.[7] Also in Sumerian mythology Sin, the moon god, is conceived as travelling across the heavens, thus bringing light to the sky.[8]

During the Assyro-Babylonian period two cities, Ur and Harran, were particularly important centres of the moon cult, of which Ur was more important than the other in early times, as is seen in the common designation of this centre as the "city of Nannar".[9] On the other hand the moon god was regarded as the supreme lord and owner not only of the countries of Harran and Ur, but also of the vast territories described by the geographic term Amurru.[10]

At the time of the First or Amorite dynasty of Babylon the god was universally popular. The Larsa dynasty was specially devoted to Sin of Ur, and Rim-Sin's sister served as a priestess of the goddess Ningal. Ashurbanipal's governor in the sea-lands rebuilt a shrine in É-giš-šir-gál, Sin's great temple at Ur.[11] Also at the time of Nabonidus (555-539 B.C.) the moon god was highly venerated in the whole of Babylonia, and, as we learn from the inscription of "the Cylinder of Nabonidus", he restored E-gi-par, an ancient seat of divination which was connected with E-giš-šir-gal.[12]

---

[4]Tallqvist, K., op.cit., p.442.
[5]Jastrow, Jr.M., op.cit., p.113.
[6]See Healey, J.F., "The Akkadian 'Pantheon' List from Ugarit", p.118.
[7]See Drijvers, H.J.W., op.cit., p.140; Thierens, A.E., op.cit., p.32.
[8]See Kramer, S.N., *Sumerian Mythology. A Study of Spiritual and Literary Achievement in the Third Millennium B.C.*, The American Philosophical Society, v.XXI, Philadelphia (1944), p.41. Also see Jastrow, Jr.M., op.cit., p.114.
[9]See Smith, S., *Babylonian Historical Texts*, p.53; Jastrow, Jr.M., op.cit., p.114.
[10]Lewy, J., op.cit., p.484.
[11]See Smith, S., op.cit., p.54. Also for É-giš-šir-gál see Langdon, S., "New Inscriptions on Nabuna'id", *AJSL*, 32, 1916, p.111.
[12]See Clay, A.T., *Miscellaneous Inscriptions in the Yale Babylonian Collections*, New Haven (1915), pp.66, 72-74.

There were close ties between the moon god Sin, who is described as "the majestic god whose word is constant" in one inscription of Nabonidus,[13] and kingship in ancient Mesopotamia. The physical appearance of the crescent looks like a royal crown, and Sin consequently is called "Lord of the Crown" (*bēl agī*) in the Babylonian creation epic *Enuma Elish*. The Code of Hammurabi states that Sin will deprive the transgressor of Hammurabi's laws of "the crown, of the throne of kingship", and Hammurabi himself is called "seed of the royalty, which the god Sin has created". In an ode to Hammurabi the first line reads : "Sin assigned the primacy to you".[14] Also a number of personal names from Assyria, such as *sīn-šar-ibni*, "Sin has created the king", *sīn-šar-iškun*, "Sin has established the king", and *sīn-šar-uṣur*, "Sin protect the king", prove that at that period the moon god Sin was regarded as a deity who had a great power over the kings of Assyria.[15]

In the Assyro-Babylonian pantheon Sin (or Nannar), the moon god, was at the top of the pantheon. He was regarded as the chief and the father of the gods. He is frequently called "father of the gods" in hymns.[16] His Akkadian titles were *ilu*^{MEŠ} *ša ilāni*^{MEŠ}, "god of the gods", and *bēl ilāni*^{MEŠ}, "lord of the gods".[17] Moreover Assyrian personal names, such as *sīn-ašarid*, "Sin is the first in place", *sīn-kabti-ilāni*, "Sin is the most mighty of the gods", and *sīn-šar-ilāni*, "Sin is king of the gods", clearly prove that he was the highest deity of the pantheon.[18]

Besides these characteristics, as we see from the personal names and the inscriptions, the moon god was considered as the physician, creator and guardian of mankind.[19]

In Ur, the moon god was represented in two forms: on seal cylinders he is depicted as an old man with a flowing beard, said in poetical compositions to be of a lapis-lazuli colour. His headgear consists of a cap on which the horns of the moon are generally indicated.[20] Secondly he is represented as a bull. At Ur this is attested, on the one hand, by a prayer which, invoking the moon god as the protector of the city and its principal temple, praises him as "the impetuous young bull with thick horns, perfect limbs and a lapis-lazuli beard" and, on the other hand, by an archaeological find obviously to be associated with this description of Sin's appearance: a figure of a young bull whose head is made of a thin sheet of gold hammered over a wooden core, while

---

[13]Ibid, p.74.

[14]Drijvers, H.J.W., op.cit., pp.140f.

[15]See Tallqvist, K., *Assyrian Personal Names*, p.201. Sin-šar-iškun was the last Assyrian king (614-606 B.C.). Cf. ibid, p.201.

[16]See Jastrow, Jr.M., op.cit., p.113.

[17]Lewy, H., op.cit., p.141.

[18]See Tallqvist, K., op.cit., pp.198, 199, 201.

[19]See ibid, pp.196-201; idem, *Akkadische Götterepitheta*, p.447.

[20]Jastrow, Jr.M., op.cit., pp.113-14. Jastrow also states that the horns became a general symbol of divinity which Naram-Sin attaches to his head on the famous monument on which he depicts himself as a ruler with the attribute of divinity. Ibid, p.114.

the heavy beard consists of tesserae of engraved lapis-lazuli.[21] This is from "the King's Grave", one of the oldest tombs of the so-called Royal Cemetery. Also in South Arabia the moon god was represented as a bull.[22]

Besides his cult at Ur the north-west centre of the moon god was at Harran. Concerning the origin of the moon cult at Harran Jastrow suggested that it may represent a transfer from Ur,[23] but, as S. Smith stated,[24] the cult at Harran was as old as or older than any in Babylonia and Assyria because from the first centuries of the third millennium B.C., and probably from even earlier times, the city of Harran was a centre of moon-worship.[25] At the time of Zimrilim of Mari (18th century B.C.) the city already had a temple of Sin.[26]

As in Ur Sin was the most popular deity in Harran during the Assyro-Babylonian period. As we see from the personal names from the district of Harran at that time many of the inhabitants of the area had Sin or *si'* incorporated into their names. We have such names as *si'-iababa, si'-aḫadi, si'-akaba(i), si'-dikir, si'-dilîni, si'-dada, si'-idri, si'-imku, si'-lukidi, si'-manâni, si'-nūri, si'-saka, si'-šimki* and *manki-si'*.[27] Here *si'* is certainly Sin, whose worship was so distinctive to Harran.

From the second millennium onward Sin of Harran was invoked in treaties over a wide area. In a letter from the time of king Zimrilim of Mari (1777-1746 B.C.) mention is made of a treaty which the tribe of *banū iamīna* concluded with the kinglets of some neighbouring states "in the temple of Sin of Harran".[28] There is later evidence also that Sin of Harran was considered a suitable guarantor for political treaties. In a compact between Shuppiluliuma, king of Hatti (c.1385-1345 B.C.), and Šattiwaza of Mitanni Sin and Shamash of Harran are invoked, and about the middle of the eighth century, Sin, "the god who dwells in Harran", is called upon to ratify the treaty of Ashur-nirari VI with Matiel of Arpad.[29]

Sin was widely worshipped as "lord of Harran" (*bēl-ḫarrān*) in the first millennium B.C.[30] An Aramaic inscription on a slab from Zinjirli in Northern Syria, which can be dated to about 730 B.C., mentions Baʿal Harran, referring to Sin of

---

21 Lewy, J., op.cit., pp.447-48.
22 See ibid, p.447.
23 Jastrow, Jr.M., op.cit., p.112.
24 Smith, S., *Babylonian Historical Texts*, p.64.
25 See Lewy, J., op.cit., p.482; Postgate, J.N., op.cit., p.123.
26 Postgate, J.N., op.cit., p.123.
27 See Johns, C.H.W., *An Assyrian Doomsday Book*, p.13. C.H.W. Johns remarks that there was in later Babylonian documents a tendency to replace the letter *n* by the breath ', as in writing *šaḫriʿ* for *šaḫrin*. See ibid, p.13. Also see ibid, pp.14, 17, 30.
28 See Lewy, H., op.cit., pp.139-40; Lloyd, S. & W. Brice, op.cit., p.87.
29 Luckenbill, D.D., op.cit., p.267; Smith, S., op.cit., p.39; Postgate, J.N., op.cit., p.124.
30 See Tallqvist, K., *Akkadische Götterepitheta*, p.443.

Harran: "My Lord is Baʿal Harran (*bʿl ḥrn*). I am Barrakkab, the son of Panammu".[31] Sin is also found in Assyrian personal names and later in the Sulaimanija district.[32] He is also mentioned in the first millennium hieroglyphic Hittite texts.[33]

The name of the famous Sin temple in Harran was *é-ḫúl-ḫúl* (Akkadian translation: *šubat ḫidāti*), "house of joy".[34] Although we do not have any information about when and by whom this temple was built, it may go back to the Old Babylonian period.

Of Assyrian kings we know that Shalmaneser III (859-824 B.C.) restored the temple of the local moon god, *é-ḫúl-ḫúl*, and recognized Sin of Harran as one of his gods.[35] Also Sargon II (721-705 B.C.) and Ashur-banipal (668-626 B.C.) did work on the *é-ḫúl-ḫúl*.[36] Ashurbanipal undertook extensive restorations of this temple. Moreover he installed his youngest brother, Ashur-etil-shame-ersiti-uballitsu, as high priest for the service of Sin in Harran.[37] After rebuilding *é-ḫúl-ḫúl* as early as the year of his accession to the throne he beautified the *bīt akīti*; he also reports the construction of another Sin sanctuary called *uzu-mu* and of a temple for Nusku named *e-melam-anna* both of which do not seem to have existed before.[38] *é-ḫúl-ḫúl*, which had been destroyed by the Babylonian-Scythian army when it occupied Harran,[39] was finally restored by Nabonidus, whose mother was a votaress of the Moon god through her long life.[40] This was in his third year (553-52 B.C.) following on his famous dream, as appears from one of his Harran inscriptions:

> "In the night season he [Sin] caused me to behold a dream (saying) thus '*é-ḫúl-ḫúl* the temple of Sin which (is) in Harran quickly build, (seeing that) the lands, all of them, to thy hands are verily committed'."[41]

---

[31]See Gibson, J.C.L., op.cit., v.II, p.93 (n.17, iii I); Ingholt, H., op.cit., p.22. H. Ingholt states that Baʿal Harran was the god through whom Bar-Rekub had been able to occupy the throne of his ancestors, albeit with Assyrian help. We learn from other Aramaic inscriptions found at Zinjirli that Baʿal Harran did not belong to the ancestral gods of Bar-Rekub and as a matter of fact the divine epithet *mr*, lord, is used at Zinjirli in connection with Ba al Harran only, hitherto a stranger to the pantheon of the Zinjirli kings. Ingholt, I., op.cit., p.27.

[32]Postgate, J.N., op.cit., pp.124-25. Also see Tallqvist, K., *Assyrian Personal Names*, pp.56-57.

[33]Postgate, J.N., op.cit., p.125.

[34]Ibid, p.124.

[35]See Smith, S., op.cit., p.40; Lloyd, S. & W. Brice, op.cit., p.88.

[36]Postgate, J.N., op.cit., p.124. Also see Smith, S., op.cit., p.44.

[37]See Olmstead, A.T., *History of Assyria*, pp.495-96; Smith, S., op.cit., p.40.

[38]Lewy, J., op.cit., p.455.

[39]See King, L.W., op.cit., p.97; Smith, S., op.cit., p.44.

[40]See above p.129.

[41]Gadd, C.J., "The Harran Inscriptions of Nabonidus", p.57. Also cf. King, L.W., op.cit., p.98; Smith, S. op.cit., pp.44, 49. According to Harran inscriptions Nabonidus also states: "*é-ḫúl-ḫúl* the temple of Sin anew I built, I finished its work. The hands of Sin, of Nin-gal, Nusku, and of Sadarnunna from Šuanna my royal city I clasped, and with joy and gladness I made them enter and dwell in their lasting sanctuary, generous libations before them I poured out and I multiplied gifts": Gadd, C.J., op.cit., p.65. Also cf. Smith, S., op.cit., p.44.

During the Assyro-Babylonian period the most important characteristic feature of Sin of Harran was his close ties with human rulers. Both Esarhaddon, who had been a devoted worshipper of Sin, and his successor Ashurbanipal proceeded at the beginning of their rule to Harran in order to receive the royal tiara from "Sin who dwells in Harran".[42] According to the Harran inscriptions, Sin also called Nabonidus to the kingship, as is often stated in these texts.[43]

Although Sin at Ur was depicted either as a man with lapis-lazuli beard and a crescent headgear or a young bull with horns, the emblem of Sin at Harran in Assyro-Babylonian times was a crescent. One of three divine emblems on the steles of Harran (H2,A and H2,B) from the time of Nabonidus is a whole circle with crescent below which obviously refers to the moon god; the others are a disc with an internal pattern of four points and spreading "rays" between these which refers to the sun and a seven-pointed star in a circle which refers to Ishtar-Venus.[44] Also a pole topped by a crescent and with a disc within the horns of the crescent representing either the moon with its earth-light or the moon in all its phases, was found at Aşağı Yarımca, about 4 miles from ancient Harran.[45] The same symbol has also been found in the house of a priestess of the god Sin at Sultantepe, a mound on the road between Harran and ancient Edessa, which dates from the latter half of the seventh century B.C.[46] Moreover a similar emblem is shown on the throne relief of king Bar-Rekub from Zinjirli, which obviously identifies the emblem, crescent and disc, as the Lord of Harran.[47]

During the Roman period Sin, the moon god, was still at the head of the Harranian pantheon, and its cult was the most important cult of the Harranians.

The Roman coins of Harran from the time of Marcus Aurelius (161-180 A.D.) to Gordion III (238-243 A.D.) are generally engraved with the emblem of the moon god, crescent with horns upwards, placed on a globe.[48] The crescent is usually represented with a single star, but occasionally there are two stars, which must be the sun and Venus, so that we have the trinity: Sin, Shamash and Ishtar.[49] On the other hand a few times the coins show the bust of the city goddess who is probably Ningal, the consort of the moon god Sin, because, on two coins, her bust (head wearing turreted crown) and a crescent with horns upwards are shown together.[50]

---

[42]See Olmstead, A.T., op.cit., p.495; Lewy, H., op.cit., p.140.

[43]The inscription of the King's mother, a votaress of Sin at Harran, phrases it as follows: "Sin, king of the gods, looked upon me and Nabu-na'id (my) only son, the issue of my womb, to the kingship he called, and the kingship of Sumer and Akkad from the border of Egypt (on) the upper sea even to the lower sea all the lands he entrusted hither to his hands": Gadd, C.J., op.cit., p.49.

[44]See Gadd, C.J., op.cit., p.41 and plate II.

[45]See Ingholt, H., op.cit., p.22.

[46]Ibid, p.22 n.6.

[47]See ibid, p.27.

[48]See Hill, G.F., op.cit., pp.82-90 (especially pl.XII. 3, 5, 9, 10, 12, 23; XIII. 4).

[49]Ibid, p.xcii.

[50]See ibid, pp.83, 88, 89 (pl. XII. 7, 24, 25; XIII. 1, 3).

The inscriptions and reliefs of Sumatar Harabesi from the second century A.D. also prove that at that period the Sin cult of Harran was widespread not only in the city of Harran but also in the whole district. Sumatar Harabesi is situated in the Tektek mountains, a rugged plateau to the east of the plain of Harran, 40-50 kilometres north-east of Harran. At Sumatar there are ruins standing in an arc on hillocks to the north and west of a central mount and caves around this central mount. As a result of studies on this site a number of Syriac inscriptions and some reliefs were found. First H. Pognon visited the place at the beginning of the century and recorded some inscriptions and reliefs in a cave.[51] Later J.B. Segal, in 1952, spent some time at Sumatar and discovered a whole series of Syriac inscriptions engraved on the bare rock of the central mount.[52] Finally H.J.W. Drijvers published some additional inscriptions and reliefs from Sumatar in 1973.[53] Drijvers has also republished most of the Sumatar inscriptions, which were published before by Pognon or Segal, without translation in his *Old Syriac (Edessean) Inscriptions*.[54]

The Sumatar inscriptions prove that this site was an important religious centre during the second century A.D. because a date by the Seleucid year of 476 (=164-5 A.D.) appears a number of times in the texts. Moreover an Aramaic inscription of three lines together with the remains of a Greek inscription, which may date from the second half of the fourth century B.C., was found by Drijvers. It is to be presumed that at that time Sumatar was inhabited and that for centuries it was an important pagan centre.[55]

Sumatar inscriptions generally have a religious content. The supreme deity of Sumatar, who occurs in the texts, is Sin, the moon god of Harran. An inscription on the left of a male bust on the northern slope of the central mount at Sumatar mentions "Sin the god" and states that the bust is the image of Sin.[56] Another inscription at the right of the figure of a full-length male person mentions "the god", referring to Sin, and gives the date 476 (164-5 A.D.).[57] Also "Sin the god" is mentioned by another Sumatar inscription, which occurs on the left of the bust in relief on the northern flank of the central mount.[58] Moreover the term "the god", which probably refers to Sin, occurs in another inscription of Sumatar Harabesi.[59]

---

[51]See Drijvers, H.J.W., *Cults and Beliefs at Edessa*, p.122.

[52]See Segal, J.B., "Pagan Syriac monuments in the Vilayet of Urfa", pp.97ff.

[53]See Drijvers, H.J.W., "Some New Syriac Inscriptions and Archaeological Finds from Edessa and Sumatar Harabesi", *BSOAS*, 36, 1973, pp.1ff.

[54]Idem, *Old Syriac (Edessean) Inscriptions*, pp.4-19 (no.3-25).

[55]See idem, "Some New Syriac Inscriptions and Archaeological Finds from Edessa and Sumatar Harabesi", pp.1-2.

[56]Cf. idem, *Cults and Beliefs at Edessa*, p.123; idem, *Old Syriac (Edessean) Inscriptions*, p.10 (no.14); Segal, J.B., op.cit., p.101; idem, "Some Syriac Inscriptions of the 2nd-3rd century A.D.", p.17.

[57]Cf. Drijvers, H.J.W., *Cults and Beliefs at Edessa*, p.124; idem, *Old Syriac (Edessean) Inscriptions*, pp.11-12 (no.16); Segal, J.B., "Pagan Syriac Monuments in the Vilayet of Urfa", p.101; idem, "Some Syriac Inscriptions of the 2nd-3rd century A.D.", pp.19ff.

[58]Cf. Drijvers, H.J.W., *Old Syriac (Edessean) Inscriptions*, pp.10-11 (no.15); Segal, J.B., "Some Syriac Inscriptions of the 2nd-3rd Century A.D.", pp.18-19. Segal reads the lines 11 and 12 of this

māralāhē is also mentioned a number of times in the Syriac inscriptions of Sumatar.[60] *mār ʾalāhē*, "Lord of the gods", is obviously a title of some deity. Segal, who prefers reading the title as *mārilāhā*, "Lord god",[61] is inclined to identify this with Baal Shamin at Palmyra, although with some hesitation.[62] He also suggests that the new moon of *šebaṭ*, the day on which the installation of the central mount was dedicated, must have been his festal day, and that his cult emblem was a pillar set upon a stool.[63]

On the other hand there is a close connection between the cult of the god *māralāhē* at Sumatar and the Sin cult of nearby Harran. Sin was, as we mentioned, the deity worshipped at Sumatar as well as at Harran. In the Nabonidus inscriptions of Eski Harran Sin is called *šar ilāni*, "king of the gods", and *bēl ilāni*, "lord of the gods".[64] Also during medieval times the pagans of Harran used the titles *ʾilāh al-ʾālihah*, "god of the gods", and *rabb al-ʾālihah*, "lord of the gods", for the moon god Sin.[65] Therefore it is, as Drijvers stated, obvious that this appellation is rendered in Syriac as *māralāhē*, "lord of the gods", a title which Sin also bears on the coins of Hatra, and it would seem reasonable to recognize Sin in *mār alāhē*, his position as head of the pantheon in Sumatar and in Harran being thus emphasized.[66]

Consequently we may assume that all the inscriptions at Sumatar Harabesi refer to the same deity, i.e. Sin, the moon god of Harran, who is called "Sin the god", "lord of the gods" or simply "the god".

Besides the inscriptions, in a cave (Pognon's cave) at Sumatar, there are horned pillars on both sides of a niche in the back wall of the cave which are clearly the symbol of Sin.[67]

Concerning the ruins of buildings at Sumatar, Segal once identified them with their grottos below them as the planet-temples around the central mount, based on the reports on the Sabians of Harran by medieval Muslim authors, especially al-Masʿūdī

---

inscription as "I am Sīn (?) the god (?)", but Drijvers thinks that here the identity of the god is very uncertain. See Drijvers, H.J.W., op.cit., p.11.

[59]See idem, *Cults and Beliefs at Edessa*, p.123; idem, *Old Syriac (Edessean) Inscriptions*, pp.9-10 (no.13); Segal, J.B., "Pagan Syriac Monuments in the Vilayet of Urfa", p.102; idem, "Some Syriac Inscriptions of the 2nd-3rd century A.D.", pp.16ff.

[60]See Drijvers, H.J.W., *Old Syriac (Edessean) Inscriptions*, pp.13-14, 16-18 (no.18, 23, 24).

[61]Segal, J.B., "Some Syriac Inscriptions of the 2nd-3rd century A.D.", p.22. Concerning Segal's reading Drijvers states that it is a reading not in accordance with the Harranian background of Sin's cult nor with the linguistic evidence. Drijvers, H.J.W., *Cults and Beliefs at Edessa*, p.128.

[62]See Segal, J.B., op.cit., p.15; idem, *Edessa and Harran*, p.13. Also Segal once suggested that Mārilāhā (*māralāhē*) of Sumatar might perhaps be identified with Shamāl of Harran. See idem, "The Sabian Mysteries: The Planet Cult of Ancient Harran", p.217.

[63]Idem, "Pagan Syriac Monuments in the Vilayet of Urfa", p.115.

[64]See Gadd, C.J., op.cit., pp.47, 49, 57, 59.

[65]See ʾIbn al-Nadīm, op.cit., p.325; al-Shahrastānī, op.cit., p.203; al-Dimashqī, op.cit., p.47.

[66]See Drijvers, H.J.W., "Some New Syriac Inscriptions and Archaeological Finds from Edessa and Sumatar Harabesi", pp.5-6.

[67]See idem, *Cults and Beliefs at Edessa*, p.137. Pognon thought that this cave was a temple, but Drijvers disagrees with him and remarks that it most likely was the place where various functionaries were invested with their offices, which were at the same time civil and religious ones. See ibid, p.139.

who gives a description of the various temples of the Harranians dedicated to the various planets and certain primal elements.[68] Hence Segal suggested that the cult at Sumatar was a planet cult, like the cult at Harran some seven or eight centuries later.[69] Segal's suggestion can be criticized from three points of view. First of all these buildings at Sumatar are, as Drijvers pointed out, clearly tombs.[70] Secondly the inscriptions at Sumatar only refer to the Sin cult, and a planet cult like that of the medieval Harranians does not occur in these inscriptions. Finally the accounts of al-Masʿūdī and other Muslim scholars are only concerned with the medieval Harranians, not with Sumatar. Therefore there is no connection between these accounts and the buildings of Sumatar belonging to the second century A.D. The cult at Sumatar consequently was not a planet cult, but in principle the local cult of Sin the moon god of nearby Harran connected with civil and military functionaries in that area.[71]

The Sumatar inscriptions and reliefs therefore prove that during the second century A.D. the cult of Sin was widespread in the district of Harran, and that Sin was the head of the pantheon not only in Harran, but in the whole area.

Also, during the time before the Muslim invasion into the area, Sin was still highly venerated. According to Roman historians, in 217 A.D. the Emperor Caracalla was murdered during his return to the palace from the temple in Harran, which was a little distance away, and the deity he had been adoring was a moon deity. Again it was the same moon deity to whom the Emperor Julian paid his respects at Harran during a halt on his expedition of 363 A.D.[72] The *Doctrine of Addai* (composed in c.400 A.D.) also mentions the moon among those deities which were adored by the Harranians,[73] while Jacob of Saruğ (451-521 A.D.) mentions Sin among the deities of Harran.[74] The moon god in the Doctrine of Addai and Sin in the account of Jacob of Saruğ are, as we mentioned before, the same deity, worshipped at Harran; the only difference between these sources is that Jacob of Saruğ knows the name of the Harranians' moon god.

During medieval times Sin was the principle deity of the Harranians. The city of Harran was still closely connected to the Sin cult, as earlier. According to the Syriac version of his book, Bābā the Harranian, one of the prophets of the Harranians, describes Harran as "the city of Sin".[75] al-Bīrūnī, one of our important sources on this subject, mentions Sin and states that the city of Harran was attributed to the moon, it

---

[68]See above pp.143, 147ff.
[69]See Segal, J.B., "Pagan Syriac Monuments in the Vilayet of Urfa", pp.112ff.
[70]Drijvers, H.J.W., op.cit., p.140. Segal himself, too, states this point, saying that at first sight they appear to be the familiar tomb-structures. Segal, J.B., op.cit., p.113.
[71]See Drijvers, H.J.W., op.cit., p.140.
[72]See Segal, J.B., "Mesopotamian Communities from Julian to the Rise of Islam", p.124; Lloyd, S. & W. Brice, op.cit., pp.89, 95-96.
[73]*The Teaching of Addai*, p.49.
[74]See Drijvers, H.J.W., op.cit. p.38.
[75]Cf. Rosenthal, F., "The Prophecies of Bābā the Ḥarrānian", p.228.

being built in the shape of the moon like a *ṭaylasān*.[76] He also remarks that close to Harran there is another place called *salamsīn*, its ancient name being *ṣanamsīn*, "the idol of Sin".[77] According to Yāqūt al-Hamawī al-Rūmī Salamsin is a village one parasang removed from Harran, and dedicated to the moon.[78] al-Bīrūnī also mentions *bel ḥarrānā* which probably refers to Sin, head of the Harranian pantheon.[79] Moreover he records the feasts of the Harranians in honour of the moon, one of which is the "Feast of *dayr sīnī* (shrine of Sin)" which was celebrateed on the twenty-eighth of April. Another festival is the "Feast of the Living Being of the Moon" on the sixth of April.[80] Finally al-Bīrūnī mentions *daḥḍāq*, the idol of the moon, and records three festival days for this idol, on the seventh, eleventh and twentieth of May.[81]

Another Muslim scholar ʾIbn al-Nadīm mentions the Sin cult of the Harranians and gives plenty of information about their sacrificial ceremonies, in which they generally slaughtered bulls, and burnt offerings to Sin.[82] ʾIbn al-Nadīm also mentions the title *rabb al-ʾālihah*, "Lord of the gods", for this deity.[83] Other medieval Muslim sources tell of the Harranian moon cult without giving the name of the moon god.[84]

Besides Muslim sources Maimonides too tells of the moon cult of the Sabians (Harranians), and states that the moon was one of their two greatest deities — the other being the sun.[85] He also remarks that they set up silver statues for the moon[86] and that according to their belief Adam was the envoy of the moon, who called people to worship the moon, but Seth disagreed with his father Adam concerning the worship of the moon.[87]

In medieval times the titles and the epithets of the moon god Sin were the same as in antiquity: *bel ḥarrānā*, as the deity is occasionally called, corresponds to the Assyrian epithet *bēl ḫarrāni*; the titles *ʾilah al-ʾālihah*, "God of the gods",[88] and *rabb al-ʾālihah*, "Lord of the gods", are translations of Sin's Akkadian epithets *ilu ša, ilāni* and *bēl ilāni*.[89]

[76]See al-Bīrūnī, op.cit., pp.187, 205. D.S. Rice, however, states that these comparisons are not of great value as the exact shape of the garment known as *ṭaylasān* is not easy to determine, and we are not told what kind of moon is meant. See Rice, D.S., op.cit., p.38.
[77]al-Bīrūnī, op.cit., p.187.
[78]See Yāqūt al-Hamawī al-Rūmī, *muʿjam al-buldān*, v.3, p.240; Chwolsohn, D., op.cit., v.II, p.551.
[79]al-Bīrūnī, op.cit., p.316.
[80]Ibid, p.317.
[81]Ibid, p.317.
[82]ʾIbn al-Nadīm, op.cit., pp.322, 324-25.
[83]Ibid, p.325.
[84]See al-Dimashqī, op.cit., pp.43, 47; al-Shahrastānī, op.cit., p.203.
[85]Maimonides, op.cit., p.514.
[86]Ibid, p.516.
[87]Ibid, pp.515-16.
[88]al-Shahrastānī, op.cit., p.203; al-Dimashqī, op.cit., p.47.
[89]See Lewy, H., op.cit., pp.140-41.

Our medieval sources also give some information about the moon temples of the pagans of Harran, which may throw some light on their localizations in Assyro-Babylonian times. First of all we must examine the inscriptions from Assyro-Babylonian times concerning the localization of the moon temples at Harran.

A letter from Marduk-šum-uṣur to king Ashurbanipal concerning Esarhaddon's campaign against Egypt records:

> "When the father of the king, my lord, went to the land of Egypt, he observed in the district of Harran a temple built of cedar. Therein Sin (was represented) supported by a staff, with two crowns upon his head. The god Nusku stood before him."[90]

According to this letter the moon temple which Esarhaddon saw was outside the city of Harran. On the identification of this temple we follow J. Lewy who states that this "temple of cedar wood" cannot be identical with *é-ḫúl-ḫúl*; in the first place because *é-ḫúl-ḫúl* was situated within the city of Harran, and secondly because Ashurbanipal's reports on his care for the Harranian sanctuaries emphasize that, in the years prior to his accession to the throne and, accordingly, at the time of Esarhaddon's visit to Harran, *é-ḫúl-ḫúl* was in a ruinous condition. On the other hand "long-lasting wood" was among the materials used for the embellishment of that Harranian temple which served as *bīt akīti*. Since, furthermore, temples designated as *bīt akīti* were always situated outside the gates of the large towns, there can hardly be any doubt that the sacred building referred to in the letter here under discussion was the Akītu temple known from two other Neo-Assyrian letters as a sanctuary of Sin of Harran.[91]

Also one of the Nabonidus inscriptions from Harran records:

> "...and in the midst of Harran in *é-ḫúl-ḫúl* the abode of their hearts' ease with gladness and rejoicing, he let them dwell."[92]

This inscription obviously claims that famous moon temple, *é-ḫúl-ḫúl*, was in the middle of Harran.

Moreover according to Assyrian inscriptions there was another Sin temple at Harran, named *uzu-mu*, which was provided with images of the moon god and the

---

[90]Waterman, L., *Royal Correspondence of the Assyrian Empire*, Ann Arbor, Part: II (1930), pp.140-41, Letter: 923, Part: III (1931), pp.261-62. Also see Parpola, S., *Letters from Assyrian Scholars to the Kings Esarhaddon and Assurbanipal*, Part: I (AOAT, Bd. 5/1), Kevelaer (1970), pp.82-83, No. 117, Part: II (AOAT, Bd. 5/2), Kevelaer (1983), p.100; Lewy, J., op.cit., pp.457-59; Pfeiffer, R.H., *State Letters of Assyria*, New Haven (1935), No. 248.

[91]See Lewy, J., op.cit., p.458 n.246.

[92]Gadd, C.J., op.cit., p.49 (H_1, B, Col. II: 19-21).

other gods of Harran.[93] On the other hand we do not know whether it was within the city centre or in the suburb of Harran.

Secondly our medieval sources describe the moon temples of the medieval Harranians. One of them is *dayr kādī*. ʾIbn al-Nadīm, who quotes from ʾAbū Saʿīd Wahb, states that on the twentieth day of April they go out to *dayr kādī*, which is a sanctuary near one of the gates of Harran known as *bāb funduq al-zayt*, "Inn of the Oil Gate", and slaughter bulls for Saturn, Mars and the Moon.[94] He also remarks that every twenty-seventh of lunar month they go out to this sanctuary, where they slaughter and burn various offerings to the moon god Sin.[95] Moreover ʾIbn al-Nadīm states that every twentieth of April they go out to the place called *kādhā* near Harran, to the east, expecting the arrival of the Idol of the Water (*ṣanam al-māʾ*).[96] Here *kādhā* and *dayr kādī* are presumably identical, and the celebration at this sanctuary, practised for the Idol of the Water, is similar to the Akītu festival, symbolizing the deity's descent to the Netherworld, which was celebrated in honour of the city's patron deity in the major cities of Assyria and Babylonia. The Idol of Water therefore probably refers to the Harran's patron deity, Sin the moon god.[97]

Besides this account of ʾIbn al-Nadīm, Yāqūt al-Hamawī al-Rūmī too tells of *dayr kādhī* (*kādī*) and states that it is a Sabian temple, and the only one left in Harran.[98] al-Majrīṭī mentions this sanctuary in connection with the Harranian human sacrifices, and tells of an idol within it.[99]

Concerning the site of Dayr Kādī (or Dayr Kādhī) S. Lloyd and W. Brice suggested that it can be identified on a hill close to Raʾs al-ʿAyn al-ʿArūs, about two kilometres west of Tel Abyad and about 30-40 kilometres south of Harran; first this place still retains the name Dayr Kādhī, and secondly ʿAyn al-ʿArūs is a copious spring, which forms the traditional source of the Balikh River.[100] This identification is not free from difficulties: first of all ʾIbn al-Nadīm places Dayr Kādī to the east of Harran, but ʿAyn al-ʿArūs lies to the south, and Lloyd and Brice are aware of this difficulty.[101] Secondly ʾIbn al-Nadīm remarks that it is near to Harran, but ʿAyn al-ʿArūs is very far from Harran. Consequently we must look for a place near to Harran. ʾIbn al-Nadīm recorded that it was near Bāb Funduq al-Zayt, one of the gates of Harran, and that it was to the east of Harran. Also ʾIbn Shaddād (1216-1285 A.D.), another medieval

---

[93] See Lewy, J., op.cit., p.455 n.227.
[94] ʾIbn al-Nadīm, op.cit., p.322.
[95] Ibid, p.325.
[96] Ibid, p.325.
[97] See above pp.154f., 180.
[98] Yāqūt al-Hamawī al-Rūmī, *marāṣid al-ʾiṭṭilāʿa ʿalā ʾasmāʾi al-ʾamkinah wa al-buqāʿa*, Cairo (1954), v.2, p.572; Chwolsohn, D., op.cit., v.II, p.630.
[99] al-Majrīṭī, op.cit., p.228.
[100] See Lloyd, S. & W. Brice, op.cit., p.94.
[101] See ibid, p.95.

Muslim scholar, mentions Bāb al-Mā', "the Water Gate", on the east side of Harran, which must have faced the river Jullab, a few miles from Harran.[102] Since both of these gates, i.e. Bāb Funduq al-Zayt and Bāb al-Mā', are on the east of Harran they are presumably identical. Consequently Dayr al-Kādī, where the Harranians celebrated festivals similar to Ạkītu, must have been near the river Jullab on the east of Harran. On the other hand the difficulty with this theory is that there is no archaeological evidence supporting it.

Another Muslim scholar, al-Dimashqī, writing in the early fourteenth century, states that there is a building of the moon in Harran, and it is said that it was its castle, named *al-mudarraq* (or *al-madraq*), and it continued until the Tatars (Mongols) destroyed it. He also remarks that there were some inscriptions in Pahlavi on its door.[103] al-Dimashqī also states in another chapter of his book that Harran was the city of the Sabians. He says that among the remains of the Sabians a castle, named *al-mudawwar* which was a temple for the moon, survived to his time (14th century A.D.). He also remarks that the Sabians (Harranians) continued to worship there until 424 A.H. (1032 A.D.) when the Egyptians (the Fātimids) conquered this temple. Moreover he points out that they had no other temple like this, and that after the Fatimid invasion most of them became Muslim.[104] According to this account the moon temple of Harran was the castle, *qalᶜah*, or the citadel which was at the south-east of the medieval Harran, near one of the gates of Harran (according to S. Lloyd and W. Brice Bab al-Baghdad). The names *al-mudarraq* and *al-mudawwar*, which al-Dimashqī uses, probably refer to the same castle. Besides al Dimashqī, some other medieval scholars, like Mustawfī, writing in the fourteenth century, mention the castle of Harran.[105] They speak of the walls of the castle, but none of them mention the castle as a moon temple. Basing their view on the account of al-Dimashqī, S. Lloyd and W. Brice suggest that during the medieval period there was a moon temple in the core of the castle in Harran.[106] However, al-Dimashqī wrote about one century after the last pagans of Harran disappeared after the Mongol invasion into the area. None of our medieval writers, who lived before the Mongol invasion, such as al-Maqdīsī, 'Ibn al-Nadīm and al-Bīrūnī, mentions the castle in Harran among the temples of the Harranians. Therefore there is no evidence which supports al-Dimashqī's suggestion.

---

[102] Cf. Rice, D.S., op.cit., p.40.
[103] al-Dimashqī, op.cit., p.43.
[104] Ibid, p.191. For discussion about the Egyptian invasion into the area see above p.133.
[105] See Lloyd, S. & W. Brice, op.cit., p.92.
[106] See ibid, p.96.

Yāqūt al-Hamawī al-Rūmī speaks of Salamsin, "the moon idol", a village one parasang removed from Harran, and dedicated to the moon god.[107] al-Bīrūnī too, as we noted, records Salamsin and points out that its ancient name was *ṣanam sīn*.[108]

Archaeological excavations in the district of Harran may throw light on the moon temples of Harran. Before discussing the excavations we must remark that in Assyrian times the city of Harran seems to have been situated slightly to the east of the Greek or Roman colony, Carrhae, probably at Eski Harran, where some inscriptions were found. The Roman colony was near the source of the river Balikh.[109] S. Smith thinks that the ancient town may have been at Sinnaka, where, he suggests, is the site of the temple of the moon god.[110]

As a result of excavations in 1949 at Aşağı Yarımca, about four miles north-west of Harran, a stele, bearing the emblem of the god Sin, a crescent, and a cuneiform inscription were found. This discovery also led to the recognition of a very large stone building, appearently of the Assyrian period, just beneath the surface.[111] S. Lloyd and W. Brice suggested that the building at Aşağı Yarımca was the temple of the moon goddess Selene (or local Nikkal, spouse of Sin) for the following reasons. First, from Herodian's account of the murder of Caracalla, we learn that the event occurred during the Emperor's return to the palace from the temple, which was a little distance away, and that the deity he had been adoring was a moon goddess, Selene. Secondly it was a female moon deity to whom Julian paid his respects at Harran. The site at Aşağı Yarımca fits the case well by being not only a little way outside the town, but also in the general direction of Edessa because according to Spartian's account the temple, which Caracalla visited, was in the direction of Edessa.[112]

We agree with Lloyd and Brice on the point that the temple at which Caracalla and Julian paid their respect may have been at Aşağı Yarımca, but we disagree with them on the identity of the deity who was the patron of that temple. First of all if we examine the accounts of the Roman writers concerning the murder of Emperor Caracalla we see that some of them such as Spartian remark that the deity whom the Emperor respected was masculine. Also Eutychius speaks of a male deity, Sin, at the city.[113] On the other hand some Roman writers such as Herodian thought that the moon deity of Harran was Selene.[114] Selene is, in fact, the moon deity of the Greeks, and the Romans always thought of the moon deity as feminine. It is therefore quite normal that

---

[107] See Chapter VII n.78.
[108] See above p.201.
[109] See Smith, S., *Babylonian Historical Texts*, p.38.
[110] See ibid, p.38.
[111] See Lloyd, S. & W. Brice, op.cit., p.80.
[112] See ibid, pp.89, 95-96.
[113] See Chwolsohn, D., op.cit., v.II, p.508.
[114] Ibid, v.I, p.400.

some Roman writers, who were informed about the moon cult of Harran, simply mentioned the moon deity of Harran as Selene just as in their own tradition. Also the emblem on the stele which was found at Aşağı Yarımca is clearly the emblem of the moon god Sin; the same emblem, a crescent with horns upwards, as we mentioned before, also frequently appears on the Roman coins during the second and third centuries A.D.[115] Consequently it is clear that the temple at Aşağı Yarımca was a temple of the moon god Sin.

O.R. Gurney, who joined the excavations at Sultantepe, a large mound about 20 miles north of modern Harran, in 1952, suggested that the main building occupying the site in Assyrian times was a large temple of the moon god Sin.[116] Moreover Ingholt remarks that an emblem of Sin, a crescent, was found at Sultantepe.[117] The difficulty with this identification is that Sultantepe is very far from Harran.

After considering these accounts of medieval sources and archaeological excavations we see that there is a close connection between the *bīt akīti* temple of Harran in Assyro-Babylonian times and Dayr Kādī in medieval period because both were situated outside the city of Harran, and they served as *akītu*-type temples. It is therefore possible that the *bīt akīti* temple of Sin at Harran in antiquity may be identical with medieval Dayr Kādī. Although we do not know the exact site of this temple it must have been situated in the east suburb of Harran near the Jullab.

On the other hand we cannot identify the exact sites of the famous *é-ḫúl-ḫúl* and Uzu-mu, another Sin temple in Harran according to Assyrian inscriptions. Any suggestion on this subject is only speculation.

Briefly we have seen that from the earliest time to the destruction of Harran, Sin, the moon god, was the patron deity of the Harranians. In other words they have always clung to their Sin cult.

On the other hand we do not see this cult among the Mandaeans. In Mandaean literature the moon has two characteristics: firstly it is one of the seven planetary purgatories (*maṭarta*, pl. *maṭarata*), which are the places of purification of the soul, or a kind of hell.[118] According to the belief of the Mandaeans these planetary spheres and their guardians are basically evil, demonic in nature, and persist in obstructing the way of the soul on its ascent. Their primary task is to seize sinful souls and subject them to

---

[115]See above p.197.

[116]See Gurney, O.R., "The Assyrian Tablets from Sultantepe", pp.21-22.

[117]See Ingholt, H., op.cit., p.22 n.6.

[118]For *maṭarta* see *MII*, pp.197-98; *MD*, pp.241-42; Rudolph, K., "Mandean Sources", p.133. "This, the purgatory of the moon, occupies up to two thousand parasangs... In this purgatory of the moon those who defraud (*rob*) their partners are put to the question, and those who remove boundary lines and take away boundary stones are questioned therein, and those who loosen their (*sacred*) girdles for their own ease. In this purgatory executioners stand and flog": *DA*, p.30. Also see ibid, pp.21-22.

abominable punishments in their purgatories.[119] Secondly the moon is associated with death, deformity, destruction and darkness. A waning moon is an unlucky time to wed, plant or sow seed.[120]

According to Mandaean writings Sin, (other name: Sira[121]) the moon god, who lives in the moon-ship, is a malevolent spirit. He appears to be regarded as a sinister influence, and he is described as "overthrower", "unclean", "striker" and "bringer about of deficiency".[122] The light-sprits in the moon prevent him from doing evil things against humans.[123]

In Mandaean literature Sin is also regarded as the son of Ruha (*ruha ḏ-qudša*), mother of the planets and devils.[124] He is therefore frequently associated with Ruha, Qin, the queen of darkness and grandmother of Ur,[125] Ur (*ʿur*), the king of darkness and son of Ruha,[126] and the demons.[127] Moreover a few times Sin is regarded as Ṣauriel, angel of death.[128]

Finally the moon and his worshippers are reviled in Mandaean writings:

"'Who will be your witness?'
'Lo, Moon who shineth above us,
He will be our witness!'
'It is not he whom I seek,
Not he whom my soul desireth.
The moon, of whom ye spake,
Riseth at dusk and setteth at dawn.
The moon of which ye spake,
The moon is vanity and cometh to an end
And his worshippers come to an end and are vanity'."[129]

119Rudolph, K., op.cit., p.137.

120*DA*, p.40 n.9. Also see *Jb*, pp.187-88. Moreover in modern Mandaean legends the moon, Sin, has a sinister character, and he is described with his seven heads branching out like a tree. Cf. *MII*, pp.389-93 (Legend XXVII : "The Man who sought to see Sin, the Moon"). Also see ibid, p.275.

121See *MII*, p.329 n.1.

122Cf. *DA*, p.40. Also see *MII*, p.329 n.1.

123"The light-*melki* in the moon prevent Sin and the King of Darkness from bemusing the children of men. Under the influence of those two, men do deeds of madness and shame that they would not wish to perform by day; and without the counteracting influence of the ten, men's moral sense would disappear... If a man says, 'There is no God, no spirits', he is entirely in the power of the King of Darkness and it is harmful even to sit with such a one": *MII*, p.79.

124See *DA*, p.40; *MD*, p.428.

125*MD*, p.410.

126*MD*, p.345.

127See *DA*, pp.28, 40; *GR*, p.132; *MD*, p.328.

128"Sin whose name is moon, his name is Ṣauriel": *GR*., pp.28, 46.

129*CP*, pp.16-17.

B. Hermetic tradition

According to our medieval sources Hermes was one of the most important figures in the religion of the Harranians.[130] In their belief Hermes was the founder of their cult, their prophet, and their fount of wisdom. Also in Arabic sources from the tenth century onwards the belief of the Harranians that two great pyramids in Egypt are the graves of Agathodaimon and Hermes occurs repeatedly, and some of our sources remark that the Harranians habitually went on pilgrimage to those pyramids because of this belief.[131]

Besides his human and prophetic character Hermes was also regarded as a deity by the Harranians. al-Shahrastānī, for example, states that Hermes and Agathodaimon are their deities as well as their masters and intermediaries to the Holy Beings.[132] ʾIbn al-Nadīm, who quotes from ʾAbū Saʿīd Wahb, mentions *hermes al-ʾilāh*, "Hermes the god", among the deities of the Harranians, and states that they slay a large bull to this god in their sanctuary in the village named Sabtā, near one of the gates of Harran called Bāb al-Sarāb.[133] It is therefore clear that Hermes was also one of the lesser deities of the Harranians.

Moreover al-Bīrūnī records the "Feast of Hermes-Mercury" of the Harranians.[134] Here the planet Mercury, who was venerated under the name of Nabiq by the medieval Harranians,[135] refers to the god Nabu. Not only in Harran but in Edessa and other Syrian towns the god Nabu (or local Nebo) was worshipped and identified with Hermes. Thus Pseudo-Lucianus can call Hermes the god of Hierapolis-Mabbug.[136] Nabu was the third person of the Babylonian triad, Bel-Nanai-Nabu. Nabu-Hermes had a very complex function in Syria: he is the god of wisdom, who

---

130 See Chapter VI n.302.

131 See al-Masʿūdī, *kitāb al-tanbīh wa al-ʾishrāf*, p.19; ʾAbū al-Fidā, op.cit., p.148; al-Dimashqī, op.cit., p.34. Concerning their belief about the two great pyramids in Egypt W. Scott states that it must have originated among people who knew the Hermetica and revered the supposed authors of the Hermetic teaching, as there could hardly be any other ground for coupling these two names together; and as there is no reason to think that the Hermetica were generally known in Egypt after the fifth century, it is most likely that the notion first arose among the Sabians of Harran or Baghdad (who must have known of the pyramids by report, and in whose eyes Agathodaimon and Hermes were the two greatest men of Egypt), and was conveyed thence to Egypt by Arabs. Scott also remarks that it can hardly be supposed that Sabians of Harran or Baghdad habitually went on pilgrimage to the Egyptian pyramids; it is more likely that the worshippers were Copts, among whom some remnants of the ancient pagan cults of Egypt still survived. But whether the worshippers themselves called the objects of their worship Agathodaimon and Hermes, is more doubtful. See Scott, W. & A.S. Ferguson, op.cit., v.4, pp.253-54.

132 al-Shahrastānī, op.cit., p.203.

133 ʾIbn al-Nadīm, op.cit., p.322.

134 al-Bīrūnī, op.cit., p.316.

135 See ʾIbn al-Nadīm, op.cit., p.321.

136 See Drijvers, H.J.W., "Bardaiṣan of Edessa and the Hermetica", p.195.

affords insight into the secrets of the cosmos; he is the god of writers, having invented writing, and he conducts the soul journeying through the spheres of the planets.[137]

Lady Drower, who suggested the Harranians had points of common belief with the orthodox Mandaeans, claimed that the Harranians camouflaged the Mazdean name Hormuz, Hirmiz, Hirmiş (Ahura-Mazda) in the name Hermes;[138] and she consequently suggested that there was a connection between the Harranians and Mandaeans because Hirmiz was a popular name with the Şubba (the Mandaeans). Drower's suggestion on the etymology of the name Hermes in Harranian religion is hardly acceptable. First of all although al-Bīrūnī suggested that there was a relationship between Zoroaster and the Harranians[139] there is no important similarity between the Harranians and the religious systems of Iran, but there are important differences between them. For example the most striking feature of Zoroastrianism is a certain dualism between Ahura-Mazda and Ahriman, but we cannot see such a dualism in Harranian beliefs. Also according to the Iranian tradition the planets are creatures of Ahriman, and consequently evil,[140] but in Harranian religion the cult of the seven planets has always been the most striking characteristic, and they worshipped the seven planets publicly.

On the other hand, as we have seen,[141] Mandaeism bears some elements from the religious systems of Iran. The name Hirmiz among the Mandaeans might therefore be taken from the Mazdean name Hormuz, but for the name Hermes of the Harranians we must look to other sources.

There is a close relationship between Harranian religion and ancient Greek mythology and philosophy. As we mentioned before, most of the Harranian prophets such as Agathodaimon, Solon, Pythagoras and Asclepius are originally persons of Greek mythology and philosophy.[142] Greek influence on Harranian religion is also seen in the deity names of the medieval Harranians, as they generally used Greek names for their planetary deities.[143] Therefore it seems probable that the Harranians adopted Hermes, like many of their other prophets, from Greek mythology.

In ancient Greek mythology there are two important figures connected with the name Hermes. One is one of the most ancient Greek gods. He is connected with fertility, and sometimes united with Aphrodite. He is also guide of souls. In mythology Hermes was son of Zeus and Maia, and the messenger of the gods. He was identified

---

137Ibid, p.196. Drijvers points out that Nabu-Hermes is also identified with Orpheus, the divine singer, and so represented with the lyre. See ibid, p.195.
138Cf. *MII*, p.96; Drower, E.S., *The Secret Adam*, p.113.
139See Taqizadeh, S.H., "A New Contribution to the Materials concerning the Life of Zoroaster", pp.952-53.
140See *MII*, p.96.
141See above pp.79ff.
142See above pp.157ff.
143See above pp.156f.

with the Roman Mercury and Egyptian Thoth.[144] The second figure is Hermes Trismegistus (Thrice-Great), under whose name a large literature in Greek developed, concerned with astrology and the occult sciences. It is not known when the Hermetic framework was first used for philosophy, but the Hermetic literature, such as the *Corpus Hermeticum*, is probably to be dated between 100 and 300 A.D.[145]

For a long time Hermes Trismegistus was considered as a real person and all-wise Egyptian priest who lived in times of remote antiquty and wrote many magical treatises and philosophical revelations known as Hermetic literature, but, today, it is accepted that Hermes Trismegistus is a mythological person, and that the Hermetic literature which contains popular Greek philosophy of the period, a mixture of Platonism and Stoicism combined with some Jewish and Persian influences, was not written by an Egyptian priest but by various unknown authors.[146]

According to Hermeticism Hermes has two striking characteristics: firstly he is the bearer of revelation, and consequently the messenger and revealer of the gods; and secondly he is the teacher of wisdom.[147] It is therefore clear that the Egyptian god Thoth, the scribe of the gods and the divinity of wisdom, was identified by the Greeks with their Hermes and sometimes given the epithet "Thrice-Great".[148]

There was a big influence of Hermeticism on the pagans of Harran. First of all they adopted Hermes with all his characteristics into their religious system. Consequently they venerated him both as a prophet and a teacher of wisdom, and as a lesser deity. Hermetic literature was also translated into Arabic via Syriac by the medieval Harranians.[149] Hermetic beliefs, ideas and actions were widespread among them.[150] Besides their belief in Hermes as a prophet, a teacher and the founder of their religion they quite often practised talismanic magic, one of the important features of Hermeticism, in its philosophical, religious, and magical aspects.[151]

---

[144]See Parrinder, G., *A Dictionary of Non-Christian Religions*, Buckinghamshire (1971), p.121.
[145]See Yates, F.A., op.cit., p.2.
[146]See ibid, pp.3, 6.
[147]See Drijvers, H.J.W., "Bardaisan of Edessa and the Hermetica", p.195; Dodd, C.H., op.cit., p.15.
[148]Yates, F.A., op.cit., p.2. Also see Dodd, C.H., op.cit., p.11.
[149]See Drijvers, H.J.W., op.cit., p.194; Yates, F.A., op.cit., p.49.
[150]Drijvers states: "Hermetism is, in fact, not a seperate religion with its own canon of sacred writings, but an attitude of mind characterised by intensive preoccupation with esoteric philosophy and astrology and by a hankering after the mysterious": Drijvers, H.J.W., op.cit., p.195. For further information about Hermetic influence upon the Harranians see Peters, F.E., "Hermes and Harran: The Roots of Arabic-Islamic Occultism", in *Intellectual Studies on Islam. Essays Written in Honor of M.B. Dickson*, ed. M.M. Mazzaoui et. al., University of Utah Press (1990), pp. 185-215.
[151]Magic and mystery were the most important parts of their sacrificial rites. See below pp.230f. They were also famous for practising magic in the area. For example, Bar Habraeus gives an account of the magic of the Harranians in 737 A.D.: "When this man (Bāshīr) entered Edessa he went inside the altar, and he took in his hands the offering from the Table of Life, according to the custom of the kings of the Rhomāye. And he called upon the Jews to bring up (his ancestors) for him by enchantments, and he also commanded the chief of the Ḥarrānites to examine for him a liver and to see whence his family sprung. Finally the miserable man was exposed, and he was killed": Bar Habraeus, *The Chronography*, p.110.

Therefore it is certain that Hermes of the Harranians is identical with Hermes Trismegistus of the Hermetica.

On the other hand in constrast to its importance in the religion of the Harranians, Hermeticism has no important place in Mandaeism.

C. Human sacrifice

According to our medieval sources one of the characteristic rites of the Harranians is human sacrifice, combined with magic and mysteries, on which they give plenty of information. Before discussing whether this rite really existed in this pagan community we will examine the accounts of medieval sources concerning this subject.

Dionysius of Tell-Maḥrē (9th century A.D.), who examines the Harranians under the name "the Manichaeans of Harran", tells of the Harranian human sacrifice. He states that the Harranians used to perform a ceremony of human sacrifice once a year in a temple situated outside Harran.[152]

ʾAbū Saʿīd Wahb ʾibn ʾIbrāhīm, whose account is related by ʾIbn al-Nadīm, tells about the Harranian human sacrifice in ʾĀb (August):

> "During eight days they tread new wine for the gods. They call it by many varied names. On this day they sacrifice an infant boy when he is born to the gods who possess the idols. They slaughter the boy and then boil him until he disintegrates. Then the flesh is taken and kneaded with fine flour, saffron, spikenard, cloves, and oil, and made into cakes as small as figs, which they bake in a new clay oven. This takes place every year for those who observe the mystery of the North [Shamāl].[153] No woman, slave, son of slave girl, or lunatic eats it [the cake] or watches the slaughter of this child. When carried out, the rite is performed by only three priests. The priests burn whatever remains of the bones, the organs, the cartilages, the veins, and the jugular veins as an offering to the gods."[154]

This infant sacrifice was evidently carried out during the Harvest festival,[155] in which they also tread new wine for the gods. On the other hand al-Hāshimī records a feast for Venus on the third and seventh days of this month,[156] which was possibly the same festival; the only difficulty with this is that ʾAbū Saʿīd remarks that this celebration was

---

[152]See Chabot, J.-M., *Chronique de Denys de Tell-Maḥré*, 4e Partie, Paris (1895), pp.68ff.
[153]B. Dodge, whose translation we generally use, translates *shamāl* as "the North". For Shamāl see above pp.1521f.
[154]ʾIbn al-Nadīm, op.cit., p.323 (Dodge, v.II, p.759).
[155]See above p.182.
[156]See above p.182.

performed for the gods, and especially for Shamāl, the god of the jinn and devils, but, on the other hand, Venus, for whom, according to al-Hāshimī's account, this festival was performed, is a goddess.

al-Majrīṭī also tells of the Harranian human sacrifices. He gives two accounts concerning this subject: first he remarks that when the sphere rises up eight degrees and falls they slaughter a child, and they say that Hermes commanded them to do this.[157] Secondly, he describes another human sacrifice. He states that when the sun enters the lion they bring a boy (or a slave) from Cyprus; first they clothe him and adorn him with jewels, then, on 28th ʾAyyār (May) they take him out of the city at night and cut off his head. After that, al-Majrīṭī states, they bury the body and take the head into Dayr Kādī; then they put the head in front of the idol within the sanctuary. As soon as they do this a horrible cry rises up, and from this they try to guess whether their number will increase or decrease. al-Majrīṭī remarks that Barthīm al-Barahmā, who died in India, introduced this practice.[158]

al-Bīrūnī quotes two accounts concerning Harranian human sacrifices: one is that ʿAbd al-Masīḥ ʾibn ʾIsḥāq al-Kindī states:

> "They are notorious for their sacrificing human beings, but at present [9th century A.D.] they are not allowed to do it in public."[159]

The other is that, when he tells of Abraham in the Harranians' belief, ʾIbn Sankīlā (Syncellus) relates that according to them after Abraham broke the idols into pieces and left their community, he repented and wished to sacrifice his son to the planet Saturn, it being their custom to sacrifice their children. Saturn, however, on seeing him truly repentant, let him go free with the sacrifice of a ram.[160] The former account shows that the Muslim governors forbade them to practise this rite, while the latter points out that it was their custom to sacrifice their children.

Finally al-Dimashqī records the Harranian human sacrifices carried out in various planet temples. First of all he speaks of an infant sacrifice for the planet Jupiter in his temple. A woman with her suckling baby is, al-Dimashqī narrates, brought in front of the idol of Jupiter within the temple probably on Thursday, the sacred-day of this planetary deity. Then the baby was prodded with a needle until it died.[161] al-Dimashqī also speaks of a child sacrifice to the planet Mercury. He states that at least

[157]Cf. al-Majrīṭī, op.cit., p.225.
[158]Cf. ibid, p.228.
[159]al-Bīrūnī, op.cit., p.187.
[160]Ibid, p.187.
[161]al-Dimashqī, op.cit., p.41.

once a year a child was sacrificed for this planet in his temple by dividing the body into two parts and burning them.[162]

Although the rite of human sacrifice of the Harranians was, as we said, well-known among the medieval scholars, some modern scholars, such as W.R. Smith[163] and J.B. Segal,[164] are suspicious about it because it is always unwise to trust a hostile narrator.

We agree with them that it is difficult to trust hostile narrators, but, on the other hand, we cannot completely neglect these accounts, because human sacrifice was common among the pagan communities of this area in antiquity.[165] According to al-Kindī's statement Muslim governors forbade the Harranians to practise it publicly; it is therefore possible that they practised this rite before the Muslim invasion.

On the other hand nobody accused the Mandaeans of practising this rite. On the contrary, in Mandaean religion killing any creature is generally regarded as a sin,[166] though they slaughter a dove or a sheep during their ritual meals.[167]

D. Idolatry

Idol-worship was the most important part of the Harranian rites. According to our medieval sources they had a number of idols and statues representing the planetary deities within various temples.[168] In their belief, the forces of the planets overflow towards these idols who, therefore, can talk, understand, give prophetic revelation to the people, and let them know what is useful and what is harmful. According to the statement of al-Masʿūdī, when they brought their children into the temple to see and hear the idols the priests would speak through tubes behind the idols in order to make them talk.[169] By this trick the priests obviously wanted the young followers to believe that those idols could talk and understand.

The Harranians generally practised their rites, especially sacrificial offerings, in front of the idols. During the rites they would adorn the idols with various things, depending on the deity the idol represented.[170] They also celebrated some festivals in

---

162Ibid, p.43.
163See Smith, W.R., op.cit., p.368 n.1.
164See Segal, J.B., "The Sabian Mysteries: The Planet Cult of Ancient Harran", p.217.
165For the human sacrifice of various traditions in antiquity see Smith, W.R., op.cit., pp.362ff; Fohrer, G., op.cit., p.59.
166"Fast with your hands from committing murder and do not commit robbery": *GR*, p.18 (Rudolph, K., "Man.Sour.", p.290). "The Mandai answered them, 'We may not fight, because it is forbidden to us to kill men'": *MII*, p.267.
167See *MII*, p.48.
168See above pp.147ff.
169Cf. al-Masʿūdī, *murūj al-dhahab wa maʿādin al-jawhar*, v.4, p.63.
170See above pp.147ff.

honour of the idols of planets, such as *blyān*, the idol of Venus, and *ḍaḥḍāq*, the idol of the moon.[171]

On the other hand in Mandaean religion idolatry is certainly rejected and idol-worshippers are abhorred. Through the Mandaean literature the people of Mandai and Naṣorai are commanded not to worship idols and images, and idolatry is regarded as a sin.[172] The Mandaeans are described as follows:

> "They have forsaken images, pictures and idols of clay, gods (made) of blocks of wood, and vain rites, and have testified to the name of the great, strange (sublime) Life. To them the gate of sin is closed and for them the gate of life is open."[173]

2. Some characteristics of Mandaeism which do not appear in Harranian religion

Many of the characteristic features of Mandaism do not have a part in the religion of the Harranians. Among them we will examine the most important ones.

A. Gnostic dualism

Throughout Mandaic literature there is a kind of dualism: on the one side a World of Light, *alma ḏ-nhura*, and the Light Beings, and on the other a World of Darkness, *alma ḏ-hšuka*, and the Evil Beings.[174] There is a mutual hostility between these two principles:

> "Behold and learn that betwixt Darkness and Light there can be no union or pact; on the contrary, (*between them exist*) hatred, enmity and dissension, although we are aware of all that takes place and which

---

171 See al-Bīrūnī, op.cit., p.317.

172 "Do not worship Satan, the idols, the images, the error, and the confusion of this world": *GR*, p.16 (Rudolph, "Man.Sour.", p.289).

"The whole world comes to an end, and idolatry comes to nothing": *GR*, p.23 (Rudolph, "Man.Sour.", p.289).

173 *CP*, p.34.

174 "Reveal to me about Radiance and Light, about (*Light and* ?) Darkness, Good and Evil, Death and Life, Truth and Error, and about blow and healing, about baptism and boundary-stone, about Bihram's jordan and about the oblation that is in our laps... Good and Evil of which thou didst speak I mingled together, for they are living waters and turbid water; they are life and death. Error and truth (*or* 'reliability') are wound and healing, they are Pthahil and Hibil-Ziwa, they are spirit and soul": *ATŠ*, pp.210-11.

seeketh to take place. For Darkness is the adversary of Light, for they are Right and Left; they are (*earthly*) spirit and (*immortal*) soul; they are sun and moon, day and night, earth and sky; (moreover) they may be called Adam and Eve."[175]

According to Mandaean theology these two principles are essential and need each other.[176] In other words they are the complements of one body.[177]

Good and Evil exist from the beginning. Worlds of Light and Light Beings emanate from the "Mighty Mana" or "Life" while Worlds of Darkness and Evil Beings emanate from the chaos or the "Black Waters". Concerning the origin of the Worlds of Light the *Ginza* states:

"When the fruit was in the fruit, when the ether was in the ether, and when the great and glorious Mana was (there), from whom the mighty and great manas came into being."[178]

On the other hand concerning the origin of the Worlds of Darkness:

"At that time there was no solid earth and no inhabitants in the black waters. From them, from those black waters, Evil was formed and emerged, One from whom a thousand thousand mysteries proceeded and a myriad myriad planets with their own mysteries."[179]

At the summit of the World of Light there is a sublime being, a kind of "unknown god" who bears different names, some of which are old and some new.

---

[175] *ATŠ*, p.146. On the other hand according to Lady Drower's statement modern Mandaeans do not accept the enmity between Darkness and Light. She says: "The old man [Hirmiz bar Anhar, one of the head-priests of the modern Mandaeans] replied, 'Lady, the enmity between Ruha and her children and the world of Light does not exist in reality. Between the Darkness and the Light there is no enmity, because both are the creations of One and the Same. The enmity that you read of is the creation of priests, and those who wrote the *ginzi* (treasures, holy books). Why should there be enmity between us and the powers of darkness, or between the powers of darkness and those of the Light? There is only love! Love holds all things together so that they form a whole'": *MII*, pp.398-99.

[176] "...Light and darkness are bound together: if there had been no darkness, then light would not have come into being": *ATŠ*, p.134.

[177] "The worlds of darkness and the worlds of light are Body and Counterpart, (*they are complements*) of one another, Neither can remove from or approach the other, nor can one distinguish either from its partner, moreover each deriveth strength from the other": ibid, p.213. Also see ibid, pp.264-65.

[178] *GR*, p.65 (Rudolph, K., "Man.Sour.", p.155). Also *CP* states: "...in the name of that Primal Being who was Eldest and preceded water, radiance, light and glory, the Being who cried with His voice and uttered words. By means of His voice and His words Vines grew and came into being, and the First Life was established in its Abode": *CP*, p.1.

Concerning the supreme being of Light, *mara ḏ-rabutha*, *ATŠ* states: "Thus did Mara-d-Rabutha create himself": *ATŠ*, p.116.

[179] *CP*, p.1. "Its own evil nature exists from the beginning and to all eternity. The worlds of darkness are numerous and without end": *GR*, p.277 (Rudolph, K., "Man.Sour.", p.159).

Among the oldest belong "Life" (*hiia*) or "Great Life", then "Lord of Greatness" (*mara d̠-rabuta*) and "mighty Mana" (i.e. container, spirit), and among the more recent is "King of Light (*malka d̠-nhura*).[180] From this supreme being a series of Lives, i.e. "Second Life", "Third Life" and "Fourth Life", and a countless number of beings of Light emanate. These light beings, *ʿutra* (pl. *ʿutria*) or more rarely *malaka*, surrounding the supreme being, live at Jordan in the Light worlds, perform cultic acts, and praise the "Life".[181]

The World of Darkness is a similar construction to the World of Light. Very varied explanations are given concerning its origin. On the one hand it began in the form of the King of Darkness, issuing forth from the "black waters"; on the other, the "Lord of Darkness" (Ur, giant, monster, dragon) is a product of Ruha, the fallen "spirit", who has become the adversary of the World of Light.[182] The King of Darkness then calls forth every kind of demonic beings, and spreads them abroad.[183]

There are two kinds of Darkness beings in Mandaean theology: on the one hand there are evil beings who originally belong to the Darkness such as the King of Darkness (*malka d̠-hšuka*) and his creatures; on the other some fallen light beings have a place among the beings of Darkness.[184] The most important of these fallen light beings is Ruha (*ruha d̠-qudša*, the Holy Ghost),[185] who is the mother of devils, the seven planets and twelve zodiac signs as well as Ur, giant or monster of the Worlds of Darkness. Joshamin (*iušamin*), Abatur (*abatur*) and Ptahil (*ptahil*), who are originally from the Worlds of Light, are, also, among the powers of Darkness.[186]

According to the *Ginza* on the Day of Judgement the powers of Darkness, such as the seven planets and twelve zodiac signs, will be destroyed, but the three fallen Light beings, Joshamin, Abathur and Ptahil, will be baptised in the Jordan by Hibil Ziwa, and then will ascend to the Worlds of Light.[187] It seems that Ruha too will finally

---

180Rudolph, K., "Mandean Sources", p.134. Also see *MII*, p.73.

181See *GR*, pp.66f, 70; *GL*, p.594; *CP*, pp.1ff.

182Rudolph, K., op.cit., p.135.

"From the black water the King of Darkness was fashioned through his own evil nature and came forth": *GR*, p.277 (Rudolph, "Man.Sour.", p.160).

183"He [*malka d̠-hšuka*] waxed strong, mighty, and powerful, he called forth and spread abroad a thousand thousand evil generations without number and ten thousand times ten thousand ugly creations beyond count. Darkness waxed strong and multiplied through demons, devs, genii, sprits, hmurthas, liliths, temple- and chapel-spirits, idols, archons, angels, vampires, goblins, noxious spirits, demons of apoplexy (?), monsters, spirits of nets and locks, and Satans, all the detestable forms of darkness of every kind and type, male and female of darkness": ibid, p.277-78 (Rudolph, "Man.Sour.", p.160).

184"Thou, Manda d'Haiye, does it please thee that the Uthras of Light have abandoned the Light and turned their faces to the Darkness, to the great Suf-Sea, to howling Darkness, to the consuming, corrupting water, to the Place which is full of Demons who talk in a loud voice, in which speaks the consuming Fire?" *GR*, p.67 (R. Haardt, *Gnosis Character and Testimony*, tr. J.F. Hendry, Leiden (1971), p.355).

185*MD*, pp.428-29.

186These three fallen uthras act as the demiurges and mediators between good and evil. They also personify the Second, Third and Fourth Life. See ibid, pp.2, 191, 384.

187"When the house is destroyed
and the spirit of the Seven ends,

be saved.[188] On the other hand we do not know what will happen to Darkness, i.e. the Black Waters and King of Darkness, but it seems that Darkness will exist to all eternity because the *Ginza* states:

> "Its own evil nature exists from the beginning and to all eternity."[189]

This gnostic dualism is one of the most important characteristics of Mandaean religion. On the other hand we cannot see such a dualistic system in the religion of the Harranians.[190]

B. Water cult

Immersion in flowing (living) water, which is regarded not only as a symbol of Life, but to a certain degree as Life itself, is the central rite of the Mandaeans.[191] Mandaean baptismal water bears the name "Jordan", *iardna.*[192] It is believed that these Jordans are fed from the celestial worlds of Light, in which there are also heavenly Jordans as on earth. The presence of the heavenly Jordan in the earthly Jordans establishes the connection between the world of Light and the earthly world and this means that there is a readily available source of life in the world. If the water from the

---

the form of the twelve stars shall fall to ruin
.....
On that great Day of Judgement
over Joshamin, Abathur and Ptahil shall sentence be pronounced.
Afterwards comes Hibil-Ziva
and raises them out of this World.
Joshamin and Abathur
shall be baptised in the Jordan of the powerful, first Life.
Thereupon they fetch Ptahil-Uthra
out of the clouds of fog with the putrefaction in which he sits.
He shall be baptised in the Jordan of the powerful, first Life;
in that Jordan the purtefaction shall be scraped from him.
He shall embrace the first Life
and tell of the ball and chain which he had to bear in the World.
He shall tell of the suffering
which befell him from his Father.
He shall be called King of the Uthras
and receive dominion over the entire Race of Souls": *GR*, pp.311-12 (Haardt, R., op.cit., pp.396-97). Also see *CP*, p.201.

188 See Buckley, J.J., *Female Fault and Fulfilment in Gnosticism*, Chapel Hill (1986), p.38. Cf. *CP*, p.74.

189 Ibid, p.277 (Rudolph, "Man.Sour.", p.159).

190 Like all Semitic communities in antiquity the Harranians, too, believed in the existence of the jinn, demons and satans. In their belief Shamāl, one of their lesser deities, for instance, was the god and chief of those beings (see above pp.151ff.). Also one of their deities, *ḥitān al-fārisiyah*, had an evil character, like some deities in Assyro-Babylonian pantheon (see above p.156). But this kind of belief did not play an important part in Harranian religion. Its most striking feature was the planet cult, especially the cult of Sin, the moon god.

191 See above pp.114ff.

192 See above pp.111f.

heavenly Jordan had not been poured out, the waters of the earth would have remained black and without life as they were after the creation.[193]

According to Mandaean literature the prototype of baptism was performed by spirits of Light in order to purify Hibil Ziwa on his return from the worlds of Darkness. One of the Diwans of the Mandaeans, "The Scroll of the Baptism of Hibil-Ziwa", is generally connected with this baptism, the Great Baptism.[194] The baptism of a human being was first carried out for Adam, the first man, by Hibil Ziwa, when Adam was created.[195]

There are three kinds of ceremonial ablutions: one of them is *maṣbuta* or "full baptism", which should take place every Sunday, after major defilements such as marriage, birth, touching the dead, illness, and after a journey, after such sins as uttering falsehoods, talking low talk, after violent quarrels, or, in fact, any deed of which a man is ashamed. Besides Sunday it also takes place at certain feasts, especially the five intercalary days of the Panja festival.[196] In the main the *maṣbuta* consists of the actual baptismal rite in the water, which involves a threefold self-immersion of the neophyte, who wears his white sacral dress throughout, a threefold immersion by the priest, a threefold signing of the forehead of the neophyte with water, a threefold draught of water, the crowning with a myrtle wreath (*klila*), and the laying on of hands; further there is the ceremony on the bank which consists of anointing with oil, the offering of the sacrament of bread (*pitha*) and water (*mambuha*), and the "sealing" of the neophyte. Both parts are always concluded by a hand shake (*kušṭa*) between the priest and the neophyte.[197] These rites are accompanied by recitations (prayers and hymns) from the canonical prayer-book.

In addition to *maṣbuta* there are two lesser ablutions which are performed without priestly assistance. The first is called *rišama* which should be performed daily before sunrise, and before every religious ceremony.[198] The second is called *ṭamaša*, which may be performed at any time and in any river after an uncleanness, such as menstruation, childbirth and touching a dead body, and after a sin. This ablution is a triple complete immersion in the river.[199] Rudolph remarks both these lustrations are to a large extent modelled on the *maṣbuta*, so that their origin is uncertain. At all events they take into account the purificatory character of the Mandaean water-cult.[200]

193Franzmann, M., op.cit., p.158.

194See *DMHZ*, pp.25ff. Also see *ATŠ*, p.143 n.6.

195"This is the baptism wherewith Adam the first man was baptised by Hibil-Ziwa when he breathed the pure *mana* into him and he got up, sneezed and lived": *CP*, pp.28-29.

196*MII*, p.102.

197For the description of *maṣbuta*, see *MII*, pp.100ff; Segelberg, E., *Maṣbūtā*; Buckley, J.J., "Why once is not enough: Mandaean Baptism (Maṣbuta) as an Example of a Repeated Ritual", pp.26ff.

198Lady Drower states that this rite corresponds in many ways to the Muslim *tawaḍḍuʿ*, especially the more rigorous ablutions of the Ḥanafi sect. See *MII*, p.101.

199Ibid, pp.101-2.

200Rudolph, K., "Mandean Sources", p.132.

Mandaean baptism contains three important purposes: firstly it signifies the intimate act of communion by means of which the beings of Light impart power to mankind through the "living water" that flows from heaven to earth; thus baptism, continually repeated, gives mankind strength to conquer all difficulties, before and after death. Secondly by immersion in *iardna* the neophyte receives a purification from sins and evil which was caused by his connection with this world and its wickedness, and therefore he, thirdly, passes through all purgatories (*maṭarata*) safely by the magical effect of baptism, and ascends to the world of Light.[201]

The Mandaeans believe that a man cannot pass through the purgatories, and ascend to the world of Light without performing rites, most important of which is baptism. They therefore always live in groups of varying size scattered along the rivers, especially the Euphrates, Tigris and Kārūn, in order to practice their baptismal rite in these running (living) waters.

On the other hand the water cult does not play an important part in Harranian religion, though our medieval sources tell of their ablution and purification before prayer and after some defilements such as menstruation and touching a dead body.[202] We also find no baptismal rite, parallel to *maṣbuta* of the Mandaeans, among the rites of the Harranians. In fact, it is difficult to think of such a rite, of which the most important part is to immerse in the river, at Harran where the people usually lived in arid conditions.

C. Masiqta

masiqta (pl. *masqata*), "ascent" or "raising up",[203] is the other important rite of the Mandaeans. It is a commemorative sacrament for the benefit of the dead performed by priests only. It is the mass for the dead. It is a characteristic feature of Mandaean religion to resolve the problem of death by a firm belief in the after-life of the soul. Accordingly, for the Mandaeans the fate of the soul is a chief concern, while the body is treated with disdain. An extensive number of ritual performances are developed with this aim in view, commencing with the ones which take place at death, and including the various funeral feasts and commemorations of the dead.[204]

According to Mandaean belief when a man dies the body (*pagra*) dies and is integrated back into mother earth, but the soul (*nišimta*) which is pre-existent and

---

201"Those souls who descend to the jordan and are baptised shall be without sins, trespasses, follies, mistakes and evil deeds: they will rise and behold the great Place of Light and the Eternal Abode. And praised be the Great Life in light": *CP*, p.6. Also see Pallis, S.A., *Mandaean Studies*, pp.43, 162; Rudolph, K., op.cit., pp.131-32; *MII*, p.100.

202See above pp.185-6.

203*MD*, p.249; *ATŠ*, p.13.

204Rudolph, K., op.cit., pp.132-33.

attached by destiny to its earthly partners, the *ruha* (spirit) and the *pagra*, with which it associates reluctantly while yearning for its home in the world of Light, does not die. The soul, contaminated by its association with the lower personality, the *ruha*, and by its sojourn in the flesh, is tied to corruption until it is released by funeral rites and sacraments celebrated in its name. It does not emerge from its prison alone, but with the purified *ruha*; both are raised up and eventually united in a celestial body.[205] Therefore the *masiqta* has three major goals: (i) to join the spirit with the soul, (ii) to incorporate them into a new celestial body and (iii) to help the newly deceased to join his ancestors in the world of Light.[206]

There are a number of death masses, *masqata*, such as the Masiqta of Shwalia, the Masiqta of the Mandi (cult-hut) and the Masiqta of Adam;[207] they differ somewhat with respect to prayers and the number of required participants, but all of them are performed within the cult-hut (*mandi*) by the priests. For a deceased Mandaean the *masiqta* ceremony begins on the third day after death because it is believed that on that day the *nišimta*, the soul, is finally released from the body and sets out on its forty-five days' journey.[208]

Besides the appropriate recitations, which are all connected in some way with the ascent of the soul, the focal point of the ceremony lies in the intricate preparation of sixty small flat loaves (*paṭira*, "unleavened bread") daubed with oil and administered with doves' flesh and spices. Only the priest is allowed to consume any food, together with a draught of wine (*hamra*). At the close of the ceremony the loaves are buried next to the cult-hut.[209]

Like the *maṣbuta* there is also a prototype for the *masiqta*. According to Mandaean writings the beings of Light recite a *masiqta* for Hibil Ziwa every day in order to secure for him a safe ascent from the numerous realms of Darkness.[210]

On the other hand nothing like the *masiqta* ceremony and the belief concerning the ascent of the soul after death appears in Harranian religion.[211]

---

205 See *ATŠ*, p.5; *WW*, pp.243-44; Drower, E.S., *The Coronation of the Great Šišlam*, p.xii.

206 See Buckley, J.J., "The Mandaean Tabahata Masiqta", *Numen*, 28, 1981, p.139.

207 See *MII*, pp.210-11; *WW*, p.242. Also cf. *ATŠ*, pp.130ff, 224f.

208 "When a soul is set free and leaves the body, (then) do not weep or lament for it, shed no tears for it... Offer alms (*zidqa*) on its behalf and distribute bread for it, and recite Masiqtas for it": *GR*, p.37 (Rudolph, "Man.Sour.", p.282).

209 Rudolph remarks that these loaves represent souls in whose names (besides the deceased, other "forefathers" are also invoked) the masiqta is recited. By this act they are supposed to gain strength for the ascent; it is a kind of food supply. Rudolph, K., op.cit., p.133. Also for various masiqta ceremonies see Buckley, J.J., op.cit., pp.139ff; *MII*, pp.132ff, 156ff; Pallis, S.A., *Mandaean Studies*, pp.76-77. Also cf. Drower, E.S., *The Coronation of Great Šišlam*, pp.26ff; *CP*, pp.32ff.

210 See Pallis, S.A., op.cit., p.76.

211 ʾAbū Saʿīd Wahb ibn ʾIbrāhīm, however, states that in the middle of October the Harranians would cook varieties of cooked foods and sweetmeats, all of which would be burned during the night for their ancestors (see above p.175), but obviously there is no similarity between this and *masiqta*.

3. Elements which are treated differently in Harranian and Mandaean religion

Here we will examine some characteristic beliefs and rituals which appear in both religions, and compare them with each other.

A. The seven planets and twelve zodiac signs

Planet worship was the most striking feature of Harranian religion. As we have seen,[212] the Harranians believed that the seven planets and twelve zodiac signs were the deities who created the world, regulate it and rule over it. The medieval pagans of Harran also believed that above all there was a holy being, but this belief did not play any part in their cultic rituals and ceremonies; on the other hand the planet cult was always the focal point of every ritual. Consequently they built temples for the planets, set up statues and idols symbolizing them, and practised various ritual ceremonies such as sacrifices, fasts, feasts and prayers in honour of their planetary deities. In other words they publicly worshipped the planets and zodiac signs which played a positive role.

The seven planets and twelve zodiac signs are also important in Mandaean religion, but, contrary to the Harranians' belief, they are regarded as the evil beings; therefore they play a negative role.

According to Mandaean writings the seven planets and twelve zodiac signs are the sons of Ruha, mother of all evil creatures in the macrocosmic domain, and Ur, who is regarded sometimes Ruha's son and sometimes her brother.[213] They live in the world

---

[212]See above pp.142ff.
[213]"She spoke to him:
'Arise, see how the radiance of the alien Man has diminished,
(how) his radiance has become deficient and imperfect.
Arise, sleep with your mother
.......'
When the evil one heard this
he trembled in his bones.
He slept with Ruha,
and she conceived seven forms by the *one* act.
After seven days she was in labour
and brought forth the despicable ones.
She gave birth to the Seven (Planets)
from which seven forms (or: counterparts) emanated.
....
She spoke to him:
....
'I am your sister!
If you sleep with me,
your strength shall be doubled'.
When he slept with her,
she conceived twelve monsters by the *one* act.
She conceived twelve monsters by him,
none of which was good for anything.
After twelve days
Ruha was in travail.

of Darkness, bring pain, blemishes and sufferings, and plot various kinds of evil.[214] Consequently they are regarded as the reason for all black magic and calamities, and the Mandaeans therefore try to prevent the effects of their black magic by practising the rituals, prayers and exorcism.[215]

They also believe that the seven planets and twelve zodiac signs have created the demonic beings and the other evil creatures.[216] Moreover according to Mandaean cosmology the seven planetary spheres are regarded as purgatorial houses or a kind of hell through which the soul must pass to the realm of Light.[217] At the end of time both the seven planets and the twelve zodiac signs will fall to ruin and will be destroyed.[218] It is also stated that the planet worshippers will come to an end as well as the planets themselves, and that they will be destroyed.[219]

Throughout Mandaean literature the Mandaeans are therefore commanded not to worship and praise the seven planets and twelve zodiac signs:

> "Do not praise the Seven and the Twelve, the ringleaders of the world, who travel day and night, those who seduce the family (*kanna*) of souls, who were transplanted here from the House of Life. Do not praise the sun and the moon."[220]

They are also warned that the seven planets and twelve zodiac signs are their enemies:

> "Every day the Seven were thine enemies,
> The Seven were thine enemies and the Twelve
> Beset thee with persecution."[221]

She was in labour and gave birth to twelve forms": *GR*, pp.99-101 (Rudolph, "Man.Sour.", pp.172-73). Also see *CP*, p.62.

214"the World of Darkness,
of Hatred, Envy and Discord,
the Habitation in which dwell the Planets,
which bring Sufferings and Maladies": *GL*, p.511 (Haardt, R., op.cit., p.385).
"The abode in which the planets go about,
Bringing pains and blemishes,
Pains they bring, and blemishes,
Everyday causing them tribulation": *CP*, p.97. Also see ibid, p.98.

215See Naveh, J., "Another Mandaic Lead Roll", pp.48-49.

216See *GR*, p.106; *CP*, pp.22, 110.

217"The purgatories which lie before you are the seven spheres (stages) that are above you: they are the waters (of death) which ye feared": *ATŠ*, p.253. Also cf. *CP*, p.62; *GL*, pp.498-500.

218See *GR*, p.311.

219See *CP*, pp.16-17.

220*GR*, pp.24-25 (Rudoph, "Man.Sour.", p.289). Cf. *CP*, p.110; *ATŠ*, pp.171, 251.

221*CP*, p.98.

B. Prophecy

As we have seen earlier the Harranians believed in some prophets such as Hermes, Agathodaimon, Bābā, Arānī and Plato, who were, in their belief, the mediators between the holy beings and humans.[222] Among them particularly Hermes and Agathodaimon, whom they believed to be the founder of their laws and judgements and their first two great teachers, were very important. They also believed that Adam was the envoy of the moon.

None of the prophets of the Harranians appears in Mandaean religion. Throughout Mandaic literature the term *nbiha* (pl. (ʿ)*nbihia*, or *nbiia*)[223] is usually used in speaking of John. In the *Ginza* John, Anuš and his two brothers, Hibil and Šitil, are spoken of as *nbihia ḏ-kušṭa*, "prophets of truth".[224]

Although the Mandaeans, when talking to people of another faith, say that John (*iaḥia iuhana*) is their prophet[225] it is questionable whether there is a real belief in prophets as part of their system, because they do not pretend that either their religion or baptismal cult originated with John.[226] Some of their ancestors, such as John the Baptist, are mentioned as great teachers and true believers. In addition some mythological figures such as Hibil Ziwa and Manda ḏ-Hiia,[227] who descend from the world of Light in order to teach the Mandaeans their rituals, are mentioned as the envoys of the world of Light.

Although he does not play a central role in Mandaeism, Yahia Yuhana, John the Baptist, is an important historical person in the Mandaean tradition. It is claimed for him that he was a great teacher, performing baptisms in the exercise of his function as a priest. They believe that he was a Naṣurai, and that he was skilled in the white magic of the priests and concerned largely with the healing of men's bodies as well as their souls.[228] John has no place in Harranian religion.

Another important person is Šitil, Seth.[229] According to the *Ginza*, as a human, Šitil bar Adam is the son of the first man Adam who has reached the respectable age of 1000 years and still refuses to die. When Ṣauriel, the angel of death, comes to him a second time, he suggests a substitute for himself, viz. his youngest son Šitil, who is only 80. Finally, as an obedient son, Šitil agrees to die and ascends to the world of

---

[222] See above pp.157ff.
[223] *MD*, p.288.
[224] *GR*, p.26.
[225] See *MII*, p.2.
[226] Ibid, p.3.
[227] See *MD*, pp.141, 247. Hibil Ziwa is sometimes identified with Manda ḏ-Hiia.
[228] See *MII*, p.3. Also see above pp.105-6.
[229] See above p.88.

Light.[230] According to the Mandaeans' belief, since Šitil has died for his father, his soul is the most pure among human beings. Every Mandaean soul is therefore weighed against Šitil's soul in the scales of Abatur at the entrance of the world of Light.[231] So Šitil is one of the most respected ancestors of the Mandaeans. On the other hand the Harranians disapprove of Seth because they believe that he disagreed with his father, Adam, concerning the worship of the moon.[232]

The Mandaeans respect Noah (*nu*),[233] while the Harranians reject him.[234] Adam, the first man, is also regarded as a true believer by the Mandaeans.[235] The Harranians, too, respect and glorify Adam and claim that he was a prophet, the envoy of the moon, who called people to worship the moon.[236] Obviously there is a big difference between the Harranians and the Mandaeans concerning Adam, as both of them describe him according to their own belief-system.

As a final point both the Harranians and Mandaeans speak ill of Abraham. In Mandaean literature he is called "the prophet of Ruha".[237] Of him a similar story to that of the Harranians[238] is told by the modern Mandaeans. According to oral Mandaean tradition Abraham was first a Mandaean, a Naṣurai. Then he was circumcised because of a sore, and he henceforth became unclean. Therefore he left the Mandaeans, and, together with other unclean and deficient persons, began to worship Yurba, one of the powers of Ruha. Abraham became strong by the power of Yurba, and tortured and killed the Mandaeans.[239]

230Cf. *GR*, pp.425ff. Consequently in Mandaean literature Šitil is more respectful than Adam: "When they beheld children, by testing the mysteries (?), Adam and Šitil came into being, and yonder the mysteries called Šitil 'the soul' and they called Adam 'the Body', because in that place Adam was blood and Šitil was the soul. And, in another sense, Adam was darkness of the eyes and Šitil was vision, and Adam was earth, whilst in all the mysteries Šitil is the jordan, for all of them are connected with the Jordan (flowing water)": *ATŠ*, p.173.

231See Buckley, J.J., "The Mandaean Šitil as an Example of 'The Image Above and Below'", p.188; *MII*, p.199; *CP*, p.106 n.4.

232See above p.163.

233See above p.88.

234See above p.163.

235"He praised his Father Adakas-Ziva,
the Mana, by whom he had been created.
....
He overturned the Planets,
overturned the Lords of the World.
He denied the Sons of the House
and all the works which they had created.
He bore witness for the Name of Life
and the Uthra, who had let him hear his voice.
He denied the works of the Tibil
and raised his eyes to the Place of Light": *GR*, p.113 (Haardt, R., op.cit., p.376).
"Adam heard and became a believer. — Hail to him who hears after thee and who believes. Adam accepted Kushta. Hail to him who after thee accepts Kushta. Adam gazed up full of hope and ascended. — Hail to him who after thee ascends": *Jb*, p.57 (Haardt, R., op.cit., p.381). Also see above pp.86-7.

236See above p.162.

237See above p.89.

238For Harranians' story of Abraham see above pp.162f.

239For this version see the legend "Of Abraham and Yurba", *MII*, pp.265-68. The Mandaeans might have taken the story of Abraham from the Harranian tradition, since from the 10th century A.D. many

There are important differences between these two stories, in spite of some similarities like being unclean because of circumcision, and leaving the community. First, according to the Harranians when Abraham became deficient he entered the temple and broke the idols within the temple, and then left the city, but this does not appear in the Mandaeans' version. Secondly, after doing this, in the Harranians' belief, he repented, but according to the Mandaeans after leaving the community Abraham took his place on the side of Darkness, and by the powers of Darkness tortured and killed the Mandaeans. Finally a story of human sacrifice appears in the Harranians' version: when Abraham repented he wished to sacrifice his son to the planet Saturn. On seeing him truly repentant, Saturn let him go free with the sacrifice of a ram. This human sacrifice version does not appear in the Mandaeans' story either. It is obvious that both communities shaped the story according to their own cult.

C. Some cultic rituals

Here we will examine the similarities and differences between the rituals of the Harranians and those of the Mandaeans.

a. Prayers

In prayers there are some important differences between the Harranians and the Mandaeans. First of all the Harranians evidently performed their prayers, like their other rituals, in honour of their planetary deities. They prayed every day to the planet who was, in their belief, the Lord of that day, but the Mandaeans do not pray to the planets. They perform their prayers to the King of Light and other Light beings such as Manda d̲-Hiia.[240]

There is also a difference between them concerning the time and number of the prayers. The Harranians, as we mentioned earlier,[241] had three prayer times in a day, the first of which was half an hour or less before the rising of the sun, finishing at sunrise; the second ended at the time of the beginning of the descent of the sun; and the third finished at sunset. Besides these obligatory prayers they had three voluntary prayers, two of which were during the day, and the other during the night. On the other hand according to the *Ginza* the Mandaeans have five prayer-times in a day:

Harranian pagan scholars, such as Thābit ibn Qurrah, settled in South Babylonia where the Mandaeans lived.

240 See *GR*, p.16.

241 See above p.164.

> "Teach them prayer and praise, in order that they may take their stand and praise <the exalted King of Light>, the Lord of all the worlds: three times daily and twice at night."[242]

Another important difference is concerning the direction of prayer. Although there is some confusion in the medieval sources concerning this subject, the Harranians, as we discussed earlier,[243] faced south when they were at prayer, but the Mandaeans definitely turn to the north in prayer as well as in death and on every occasion.[244] In their belief the north is the source of Light, instruction and healing.[245] The north is also the place where the King of Light and other Light beings live.[246]

b. Sacrifices

The sacrificial rituals of the Mandaeans differ from those of the Harranians in several points: first of all the Harranians offered their sacrificial victims to the planetary and some lesser deities such as Shamāl. On the other hand the Mandaeans believe that slaughter of a sacrificial animal is the order of Hibil Ziwa, one of the important Light beings, and they therefore slaughter it in the name of the Light beings, particularly Life and Manda ḏ-Hiia.[247] Secondly by practising this rite the Harranians want to be close to their planetary deities, and to elicit the knowledge of the future by observing the organs of the victims during and just after the slaughter,[248] but the Mandaeans practise sacrificial ceremonies just before the ritual meals for the dead. Consequently these ceremonies are part of the ritual meals such as *masiqta* and *zidqa brika*. They use some of the meat and fat of sacrificial victims in preparing the ritual food. The death of the sacrificial animal symbolizes the death of man, and, hence, its flesh represents the deceased for whom the ritual meal is prepared.[249]

---

[242] *GR*, p.16 (Rudolph, "Man.Sour.", p.288). On the other hand *CP* mentions ten times prayers: "Like a servant lying prostrate before Thee, our eyes are lifted to Thee, our lips give Thee praise and blessing seven hours of the day and the three watches of the night": *CP*, p.35. *CP* also mentions 7 times prayer in another passage. See *CP*, p.39.

[243] See above pp.164ff.

[244] See *MII*, pp.18-19; Pallis, S.A., op.cit., pp.37ff.

[245] "Whosoever is in the northern region is light, but whosoever is in the lower one is black, and their bodies are as ugly as those of the demons": *GR*, p.281 (Pallis, S.A., op.cit., p.39).

[246] "He sits in the lofty north, he is mighty, glorious and exalted, the source of all beings of Light and the father of all Uthras": *GR*, p.7. Also see ibid, p.280; *MD*, p.92.

[247] According to Lady Drower's information, during the slaughter the priest murmurs into the right ear of animal: "In the Name of the Life! The name of Manda ḏ Hiia is pronounced upon thee. Pṯahil calls thee; Hibil Ziwa ordered thy slaughter. Thy flesh is pure; everyone who eats of it shall live, shall be made healthful, shall be established. The name of the Life and the name of Manda ḏ Hiia are mentioned upon thee": *MII*, p.137.

[248] See above p.169.

[249] See *CP*, p.49; Buckley, J.J., "The Mandaean Tabahata Masiqta", p.153.

Another difference between these two rituals is concerning the animals which are sacrificed. The Mandaeans slaughter doves and sheep as sacrificial animals. Sheep must be a male, for no female must be slaughtered, but a dove's sex is not important; it may be of either sex.[250] Dove sacrifice is practised quite often, and they name this ceremony *qnasa d-iauna*, "the sin-offering of the dove".[251] After using some of its meat in preparing the ritual food they bury the remains of the dove with the sacred bread in a space to the north-west of the cult-hut (*mandi*).[252] On the other hand according to the information of our medieval sources the Harranians never slaughtered doves.[253] The Harranians offered oxen and bulls to their deities as sacrificial animals,[254] but the Mandaeans consider it a crime to kill either buffalo or ox.[255] Moreover the Harranians quite often slaughtered or burnt chickens as a sacrifice, but the Mandaeans never sacrifice chickens, though they eat them as daily food.[256]

There is also a difference between them concerning the method of sacrifice. To burn alive the sacrificial animals as well as to slaughter was very common among the Harranians,[257] but burning alive does not appear in Mandaean sacrificial ceremonies. On the other hand the Mandaeans consider important four points during the slaughter of the victim, which do not appear in Harranian sacrificial rite: (1) threefold immersion of the priest with the knife and stick used in slaughter in the river before and after the slaughter, (2) use of an iron knife, (3) holding of a small stick, about 6 inches in length, when the throat was cut; after slaughter this stick is allowed to float away in the river, and (4) facing to the north during the slaughter.[258] Also the Mandaeans do not allow anybody, who has not been baptised, to touch the sacrificed animals.[259]

Finally, besides animal sacrifices the Harranians also offered wine, various foods and incense to their deities, which do not happen in Mandaean religion.

c. Eating and drinking

Concerning regulations for eating and drinking there are important differences between them, despite some similarities. We will first note the similarities: both

[250]See *MII*, pp.49, 136.
[251]*MD*, p.414. For the description of dove sacrifice of modern Mandaeans, see *MII*, pp.134-35; *WW*, pp.247ff.
[252]*MII*, p.135.
[253]See above pp.171, 184.
[254]See above p.170.
[255]Lady Drower remarks that the Mandaeans believe that these animals were created for ploughing, for draught, and for the production of milk, and not for food. *MII*, p.48.
[256]Ibid, p.48. For chicken sacrifice of the Harranians see above p.171.
[257]See above p.172.
[258]See *MII*, pp.137f.
[259]Ibid, p.139.

communities forbid eating of the flesh of camel, pig and dog.[260] Also both forbid blood and the animals which have not been slaughtered positively or which have been found dead.[261] Finally both the Harranians and the Mandaeans use wine in their ritual meals. According to medieval sources the Harranians made wine and offered it to their deities during the harvest. They also often drank it in ritual meals, and offered wine to their ancestor spirits.[262] The Mandaeans too drink a kind of wine, *hamra*, which is specially prepared by the priests, in ritual meals and at certain festivals such as wedding ceremonies.[263]

On the other hand we can examine the differences between them under two headings: first of all the Mandaeans immerse everything with the exception of salt and oil in the river before eating,[264] which does not appear among the regulations of the Harranians. Secondly, concerning instructions for eating food, the Mandaeans believe that Hibil Ziwa instructed Adam as to what was lawful for food, when Pthahil created the living creatures of the earth. They believe that among the vegetables and fruits everything that has seed is lawful; hence the mushroom is forbidden. On the other hand according to the Harranians garlic, peas, broad-beans, cauliflower, cabbage, lentils and green-beans are forbidden, which is a clear difference between them. Among the animals the Mandaeans forbid the eating of ox or buffalo and cow, which they believe were created for ploughing, and for the production of milk, not for meat, but the Harranians slaughtered or burnt these animals during sacrificial ceremonies. The Mandaeans also forbid the eating of rabbit and hare, but this does not appear in Harranian religion. On the other hand according to the Harranians it is forbidden to eat pigeon which is one of the important sacrificial animals of the Mandaeans. Moreover according to the information of al-Bīrūnī, some of the Harranians forbid the eating of fish and chicken, but the Mandaeans use fish in preparing ritual food and also eat chicken as a daily food, though it is forbidden as a ritual food. Among the birds the Harranians forbid the eating of whatever has talons, but according to the Mandaeans the raven, which has talons, is lawful.[265]

---

[260] See above p.184. Also see *MII*, p.47.

[261] "Do not eat the blood of animals, not one dead, not one pregnant, not one casting its young (?), not one standing (?) [or what has fallen], and not one which a wild animal attacked. But slaughter with iron": *GR*, p.20 (Rudolph, "Man.Sour.", p.292).

"And eat not of that which was killed by lion or wolf, or of anything disgorged or (*found*) dead": *CP*, p.27. For the regulations of the Harranians see above pp.184-185.

[262] See above pp.173, 185.

[263] Hamra is not fermented juice but water reddened by the maceration of grapes or raisins, on the other hand according to the *Ginza* fermented drinks are forbidden to the Mandaeans:
"Drink not and do not become intoxicated,
and do not forget your lord in your thoughts": *GR*, p.387 (Rudolph, "Man.Sour.", p.293). Also see *MII*, pp.68, 160ff; *WW*, pp.239ff; Drower, E.S, *The Secret Adam*, p.86.

[264] Also pots and pans which are used in preparing the food must at certain times be baptised, especially at Panja festival, when every house-wife brings her kitchen utensils of all kinds to receive ritual ablution. See *MII*, p.50.

[265] See above p.184. Also see *MII*, pp.47ff; *WW*, p.9; Drower, E.S., *The Secret Adam*, p.70.

d. Fasts

Fasts played an important part in Harranian religion. As we mentioned earlier,[266] they had a number of fasts scattered in various months of the year. Some of their fasts were abstention from eating meat. On the other hand fasting does not play an important part in Mandaean religion. In the *Ginza* the Mandaeans are commanded to fast not from eating or drinking, but from sin and evil.[267]

e. Feasts

The Harranians, as we showed earlier,[268] had a number of festivals celebrated in honour of planetary deities, demons, jinns and satans. The most important part of the ceremonies was to slaughter or to burn the sacrificial victims and the worship of the deities in whose honour the festival was celebrated.

On the other hand the Mandaeans have only a few feasts, the most important of which is Panja which is celebrated during the five intercalary days between the end of the month Šumbulta and the beginning of Qam Qaina.[269] Five days before Panja, or the last five days of Šumbulta, are considered as *mbaṭṭal*, "useless" or "inauspicious", for they are dedicated to the five lords of Darkness, but the period of Panja is the happiest time of the whole year.[270] Another festival is Dihba Rba (or Dehwa Rabba) which is the New Year's Feast, celebrated at the beginning of Qam Daula, the first month of the year. They also use the Persian Nauruz Rba for this festival. Thirty-six hours before the second day of Qam Daula, i.e. the night before the New Year and the first day of the

[266]See above pp.166-168.

[267]"I say to you, my chosen, I instruct you, my faithful: Fast the great fast (*ṣauma*), which is not a fasting from the eating and drinking of the world. Fast with your eyes from (immodest) winking, and do not see or practise evil. Fast with your ears from eavesdropping at doors which do not belong to you. Fast with your mouths from wanton lies and do not love falsehood and deceit. Fast with your hearts from wicked thoughts, and do not harbour malice, jealousy, and dissension in your hearts... Fast with your hands from committing murder and do not commit robbery. Fast with your body from the married woman who does not belong to you. Fast with your knees from prostrations before Satan and do not kneel before images of deception. Fast with your feet from going craftily after something that does not belong to you. Fast this great fast and do not break it until you depart from your body": *GR*, p.18 (Rudolph, "Man.Sour.", p.290).

Lady Drower, however, remarks that modern Mandaeans observe the Muslim ʿArafāt as a fast, which is not prescribed by their holy books, and states abstention from animal food is the only form of Mandaean fasting. See *MII*, p.92.

[268]See above pp.175ff.

[269]The Mandaeans have a lunar year, which is divided into twelve months of thirty days each, with five intercalary days named Parwanaiia, which fall between Šumbulta, the 8th month, and Qam Qaina, the 9th month. The beginning of Panja festival changes depending upon the movements of lunar months in the year. Lady Drower, however, remarked that in 1932, 1933, 1934 and 1935 the feast began on April 5th, in 1936 on April 4th, and in 1954 and 1955 on March 31th. See Drower, E.S., "Colour Film Taken in a Mandaean Sanctuary in Lower Iraq", in *Proceeding of the Twenty-third International Congress of Orientalists*, Cambridge (1954), p.107; idem, "Scenes and Sacraments in a Mandaean sanctuary", *Numen*, 3, 1956, p.73; *MII*, pp.83-84, 90.

[270]*MII*, p.89.

New Year, is called the Day-of-Lacking, during which period nobody goes out of the house and no religious ceremony can take place.[271] They also celebrate Dehwa Hnina, or Little Feast, which lasts three days beginning with 18th Taura, and Dehwa Daimana (Dihba Daima), which falls ninety days after Panja.

The Mandaean festivals are the commemorations of mythological events. Therefore the rituals practised during the festivals symbolize these events. They believe that in the five days of Panja five celestial beings of Light were created, and that consequently the doors of the world of Light are open during these five days.[272]

Dehwa Hnina celebrates the return of Hibil Ziwa from the underworlds to the worlds of Light, and the New Year's Feast commemorates the Creation, for Mana Rba Kabira, the Great Mana, the Lord of Greatness, completed his work of creation on this day.[273] Finally Dehwa Daimana celebrates the baptism of Adam; therefore all Mandaeans should be baptised like their ancestors.[274]

During these festivals, especially in Panja, every Mandaean should be baptised as many times as he can; this symbolizes creation and new life. There are also various sacramental rites, such as lofanis, zidqa brikas and dukranas (the first two are ritual meals for the deads, and the last one is the rite of commemoration of the dead by name) and consecration of the cult-hut, which are carried out during the festival days.

There are important similarities between the feasts of the Mandaeans and that of Iranian tradition, while the Harranian feasts generally correspond to the Assyro-Babylonian or Semitic festivals.[275]

D. Astrology, magic and mystery

Magic and mystery were part of almost every Harranian rituals. Their sacrificial rituals especially were mixed with various magical ceremonies. For example, they examined every organ of sacrificial victims during as well as just after the slaughter, and foretold future events and divined whether the ceremony was accepted by the deities. The priests also performed various magical rites during the ceremonies in order to cause them to be accepted. In Harranian religion magic and mystery seem to be connected especially with the jinn, the devils and their chief, Shamāl.

---

[271] See ibid, pp.85-86.

[272] "During those Five Days the three hundred and sixty-five days of the year were created, so that in each one, one day (*Being*?) was created, and then the five days of *Parwanaiia* which are called (days of) Commemorations... For they are five Kings, in them they created themselves, and they are the five mysteries of the Beginning in which spirit and soul rejoice (at?) the seven crowns that are placed upon them": *ATŠ*, pp.116-17.

[273] See *ATŠ*, pp.200, 238; *MII*, pp.86, 88.

[274] See *ATŠ*, p.238; *MII*, p.91.

[275] See above pp.80, 183.

According to our medieval sources the Harranians carried amulets and charms made of bones or various organs, like wings of birds or bones of other animals, and of stones in order to prevent disease and to get good luck. Finally they were also famous sorcerers and magicians.[276]

The Mandaeans are prohibited to practice black magic, sorcery, soothsaying and exorcism in some of the holy books such as the *Ginza*:

> "Do not go to the soothsayers and lying Chaldeans, who are housed in darkness."[277]

Of the powers of Darkness the *Ginza* says:

> "Some among them are sorcerers, swindlers, liars, forgers, robbers, deceivers, exorcists, Chaldaeans, soothsayers."[278]

On the other hand in magical and astrological writings such as *Sfar Malwašia* and the rolls, called *qmahia* or *zraztia*, the main subjects are astrology, omens, exorcism of disease spirits, spirits of darkness, liliths, curses on those who wish ill and bring misfortune, and invocations of spirits of Light and Life.[279] According to Lady Drower many modern Mandaean priests, in spite of the *Ginza*'s prohibition of such practices, derive part of their income from the writing of amulets, and from sorcery, when legitimate fees are insufficient for their needs.[280] Consequently on this subject there is a contradiction in Mandaean literature, presumably between early and later writings; but as a matter of fact throughout the holy books black magicians, Chaldaeans and soothsayers are rejected, while the Mandaeans are called to practice white magic such as exorcism against the powers of Darkness.

Although magic has a part in both communities there is a clear difference between them: Harranian magical ceremonies, such as the examination of the organs of sacrificial victims, shooting arrows and walking like a dog on hands and feet, do not appear among the Mandaeans. The Mandaean priests read holy books, especially *Sfar Malwašia*, to forecast the events of the next year, and use the holy writings and prayers as exorcism against evil spirits. The Harranians usually practised magic in order to cause the rituals such as sacrifices and feasts to be accepted by the deities, but the

---

[276]See above p.171. Also see Chapter VII n.151.
[277]*GR*, p.22 (Rudolph, "Man.Sour.", p.292).
"Warn them, deliver them, save them and protect these souls which went down to the jordan, were baptised and received the pure sign from adultery, theft, black magic, from going to temples and worship in temples..": *CP*, p.27.
[278]*GR*, p.278 (Rudolph, "Man.Sour.", p.160).
[279]See *MII*, p.25; *AM*, p.1.
[280]*MII*, p.xviii.

Mandaeans practise it only against the effects of evil spirits, diseases, and for the invocation of spirits of Light.

CHAPTER VIII

CONCLUSION

All of the evidence we have discussed, such as the central characteristics of Mandaeism (various technical terms and baptism and extensive western elements in Mandaean tradition), support the theory that Mandaeism is derived essentially from western tradition and that the Mandaeans once lived in the West before they settled in Babylonia. Mandaean history in the West goes back to the pre-Christian period. Extensive Jewish elements in Mandaean tradition indicate that Mandaeism or proto-Mandaeism originated in heretical Jewish circles. The proto-Mandaeans who lived in Palestine had heretical Jewish characteristics, but they were also in close contact with the other traditions of the area, such as that of the Nabataeans from whom they may have adopted their script. Although this western period of Mandaeism explains the western characteristics of the Mandaean tradition, such as the central Jewish elements found throughout the Mandaean literature, it was also probably in this period that they adopted some eastern elements, such as the dualism of Light and Darkness, since some eastern cults were influential in the West even before the Christian period.

In the first century A.D. (presumably before the destruction of Jerusalem by Titus in 70 A.D.) a persecution of the Mandaeans in Palestine by official Judaism took place and this left great sorrow in the consciousness of the Mandaeans. Many of them were killed and others were forced to migrate. Eventually the migration of the Mandaeans to the East under the protection of the Parthians began. Mandaean writers showed gratitude to the Parthian kings under the name "King Ardban" because of this protection.

The Mandaeans presumably migrated to the East group by group. They first migrated to the mountainous lands of Media, probably to the district of Adiabene, known as *ṭura ḏ-madai* or *haran gauaita* in the Mandaean literature. The Mandaeans did not stay in Adiabene for a long time. Possibly because of the strong and influential Jewish community in Adiabene, they moved southward to the marshy regions of

Babylonia where they still live. By the second century A.D. they were in this new homeland where they settled under Parthian protection.

The second period of the history of the Mandaeans begins with settlement in their new homeland, southern Mesopotamia, where they were surrounded by various local traditions, mainly Babylonian, Iranian and eastern Christian (particularly Nestorian). Contact between the Mandaeans and these neighbouring traditions was unavoidable. They consequently in time adopted some elements from these traditions. This explains much of the eastern element and influence in the Mandaean tradition.

Because of the deep effects of persecution by official Judaism in Palestine the Mandaeans produced strong anti-Jewish polemics and hated the Jews. Also, as a result of their contact with the Christian tradition in their new homeland the Mandaeans adopted some Christian elements such as acceptance of Sunday as a holy day instead of Saturday. On the other hand, when the Christian mission became more active and more concerned with orthodoxy, Mandaean feeling towards Christianity changed and the Mandaeans produced strong anti-Christian polemics.

During the Parthian period the Mandaeans lived in great freedom, so that according to their own tradition they built up to 400 cult huts in this new homeland. But, when the Sassanians took over from the Parthians, Mandaean freedom and expansion came to an end. Especially in the third century A.D., when Zoroastrianism became the official religion of the kingdom, the Mandaeans, as well as the other non-Zoroastrian religious groups, were persecuted.

Some of the liturgical texts of the Mandaeans must have already been redacted in the third century A.D., because some of them were adopted by the Manichaean writer Thomas in that century. Also Zazai ḏ-Gawazta, the greatest Mandaean copyist, lived in this century.

There was confusion and schism among the Mandaeans from time to time. Notably a schism among the Mandaean priesthood happened about a century before the Islamic period.

After the conquest of Iraq by the Muslims, the Mandaeans were treated according to the status of *ʾahl al-kitāb* in Islamic law, since they were mentioned (under the name "Sabians") with the other "Peoples of the Book", i.e. with the Jews and Christians, in the Qurʾān. There was, however, some persecution against the Mandaeans, so that some of them migrated northwards towards Iran and northern Mesopotamia.

The early Muslim scholars who lived before 832-33 A.D., the date of death of the Abbasid caliph al-Maʾmūn, stated that the Sabians of the Qurʾān had a kind of monotheistic belief system bearing some features of Judaism, Christianity and the Iranian religion and they located them in the region of Iraq, particularly around Mosul and Kūtha. Their descriptions of the Sabians correspond with the statements of the Qur'ān.

832-33 A.D. was a turning point. Just before that date the Harranian pagans, who were never called "Sabians" but simply "Harranians" or "Nabataeans" (non-Arab Syriac-speaking people) in earlier sources, and whose essential characteristic was the planet cult of ancient Mesopotamia, adopted the name "Sabians" in order to ensure their status as a subject people. It was the appropriation of the term Sabian by the Harranians, who played such a prominent role in intellectual and court circles in the Islamic empire, which led to the dramatic change in the use of the term. Instead of referring to an obscure religious group in the south of Iraq, it referred to the self-assertive pagans of Harran. At the same time there began the speculations about the Sabians which appeared in medieval Muslim, as well as some non-Muslim, sources. Scholars from that date onwards described the Harranians as "Sabians", though the term "Sabian" could also be used for any pagan from China to Egypt.

Some of the later scholars mentioned a second specific group of Sabians whom they called by different names, such as al-Mughtasilah, al-Wāsitiyyah and al-Kūthā'iyyūn. They stated that this other Sabian sect, which lived in the marshy regions of southern Mesopotamia between Basra and Wasit, and which had such characteristics as the practice of baptising themselves and washing everything before eating, was different from the Harranians. This baptising group of Sabians, mentioned by the later Muslim scholars, and the Sabians of early Muslim scholars are presumably identical, since both lived in the same location and had similar characteristics.

There is a notable similarity between the characteristics of the Sabians of southern Iraq mentioned in early *and* later Muslim sources and those of the Mandaeans of today, who are still called Sabians by their Arab neighbours. It is therefore quite clear that the Sabians of the Muslim sources were the progenitors of the modern Mandaeans.

There is no religious identification or connection at all between the Harranian pagans and the Mandaeans (or the Sabians of the Qur'ān). The pagans of Harran had always clung to the planet cult of ancient Mesopotamia. Especially the cult of Sin, the moon god, was the most striking feature of Harranian religion from the earliest time to the destruction of Harran. During medieval times the Harranians continued to practise the pagan cults and rituals of ancient Mesopotamia, blended with Neo-Platonism and Hermeticism. They worshipped publicly idols which represented the planetary deities and offered sacrificial victims, celebrated feasts and held fasts for them.

We disagree with the scholars who suggested that there was a religious identity or connection between the Harranians and the Mandaeans, because there are vitally important differences between them: first of all the Mandaeans represent a kind of gnostic dualism between Light and Life and Darkness, or between Good and Evil, which does not appear in Harranian religion. Also the rituals, such as baptism in running water and various ceremonies of mass for the dead, are very important for the Mandaeans. They consider them at least as important as, or more important than, belief in Light and Life, because they believe that nobody can reach final salvation and the Worlds of Light without practising these rituals regularly. They therefore always live alongside rivers in order to practise regular baptism in running water. On the other hand these cultic rituals do not appear among the rituals of the Harranians. As a matter of fact it is impossible to think of the existence of regular baptism in running water at Harran because of the lack of water.

On the other hand many important characteristics of the Harranian religion, such as the Sin cult, the role of the Hermetic tradition, idolatry and human sacrifice, do not appear among the Mandaeans. The Mandaeans abhor planet-worship and believe the planets and the zodiac signs are the powers of Darkness, and therefore evil, while the Harranians worshipped them publicly.

Besides these vitally important points there are also many other differences between the religion of the Harranians and that of the Mandaeans, such as in prayers, fasts, feasts and sacrifices. It should therefore be accepted without any hesitation that Mandaeism and Harranian religion are two completely different traditions.

SELECTED BIBLIOGRAPHY

ʾAbū al-Faraj, ʿAbd al-Raḥmān ʾibn al-Jawzī al-Qurashī al-Baghdādī, *zād al-masīr fī ʿilm al-tafsīr*, Beirut (1384/1964).

ʾAbū al-Fidā, ʾIsmāʿīl ʾibn ʿAlī, *al-mukhtaṣar fī ʾakhbār al-bashar*, ed. H. Fleischer, Vogel (1831).

ʾAbū al-Suʿūd, Muḥammad ʾibn Muḥammad al-ʾAʿmādī, *ʾirshād ʿakl al-salīm ʾilā mahāyā al-qurʾān al-karīm*, Cairo (n.d.).

ʾAbū Yūsuf, Yaʿqub ʾibn ʾIbrāhīm, *kitāb al-kharāj*, 5th edition, Cairo (1396 A.H.).

Adam, A., *Die Psalmen des Thomas und das Perlenlied als Zeugnisse vorchristlicher Gnosis*, (*BZNW*, 24) Berlin (1959).

Addai, the Apostle, *The Teaching of Addai*, tr. G. Howard, Chico (1981).

Albright, W.F., "Recent Discoveries in Palestine and the Gospel of St. John", in *The Background of the New Testament and its Eschatology*, eds. W.D. Davies and D. Daube, Cambridge (1956), pp.153-72.

------- , *From the Stone Age to Christianity*, Baltimore (1946).

Altheim, F. and R. Stiehl, *Die Araber in der alten Welt*, V/2, Berlin (1969).

ʿAlyān, Rushdī, *al-ṣābiʾūn ḥarrāniyyīn wa mandāʾiyyīn*, Baghdad (1976).

al-Baghdādī, ʾAbū Manṣūr ʿAbd al-Qāhir ʾibn Ṭāhir, *al-farq bayn al-firāq*, Cairo (1328/1910) [tr. A.S. Halkin, *Muslim Schisms and Sects*, Tel-Aviv (1935)].

------- , *ʾuṣūl al-dīn*, Istanbul (1346/1928).

al-Balādhurī, ʾImām ʾAbū al-Ḥasan, *futūḥ al-buldān*, Beirut (1398/1978).

Bammel, E., "Zur Frühgeschichte der Mandäer", *Or*, 32, 1963, pp.220-25.

Bar Habraeus, ʾAbū al-Faraj ʾibn al-ʿIbrī, *The Chronography*, tr. E.A.W. Budge, London (1932).

------- , *tarīkh mukhtaṣar al-duwal*, ed. A. Salhani, Beirut (1890).

Bardaisan, *The Book of the Laws of Countries*, tr. H.J.W. Drijvers, Assen (1964).

Baumgartner, W., "Zur Mandäerfrage", *HUCA*, 23, 1950-51, pp.41-71.

Baumstark, A., "Der Mandäerpsalm Ginza R V 2 — Qolasta 75", *Br.Christ.*, 35, 1938, pp.157-74.

Bell, R., "Who were the Ḥanīfs?", *MW*, 20, 1930, pp.120-24.

------- , *The Origin of Islam in its Christian Environment*, London (1926, new edition 1968).

------- , *Introduction to the Qur'an*, Edinburgh (1958).

Benjamin of Tudela, *The Itinerary of Benjamin of Tudela*, tr. M.N. Adler, New York (c. 1965, First edition: London, 1907).

Benoit, P., J.T. Milik and R. de Vaux, *Les Grottes de Murabbaʿât*, Oxford (1961).

Beyer, K., *The Aramaic Language*, tr. J.F. Healey, Göttingen (1986).

al-Bīrūnī, 'Abū al-Rayhān Muḥammad 'ibn 'Aḥmad, *The Chronology of Ancient Nations*, ed. and tr. C.E. Sachau, London (1879).

Black, J.A., "The New Year Ceremonies in Ancient Babylon: 'Taking Bel by the Hand' and A Cultic Picnic", *Religion*, 11, 1981, pp.39-59.

Black, M., *The Scrolls and Christian Origins: Studies in the Jewish Background of the New Testament*, London (1961).

Böhlig, A., *Mysterion und Wahrheit*, Leiden (1968).

Bousset, W., "Die Religion der Mandäer", *ThR*, 20, 1917, pp.185-205.

Brandt, W., *Die mandäische Religion*, Leipzig (1889).

------- , "Mandaeans" in *ERE*, v.8, pp.380-93.

Braun, F., "Lé Mandéisme et la secte essénienne de Qumrân", *L'Ancien Testament et l'Orient: études présentées aux VI journées bibliques de Louvain 1954*, Louvain (1957), pp.193-230.

Buck, C., "The Identity of the Ṣābi'ūn: An Historical Quest", *MW*, 74, 1984, pp.172-86.

Buckley, J.J., "The Mandaean Šitil as an Example of 'The Image Above and Below'", *Numen*, 26, 1979, pp.185-91.

------- , "The Mandaean Tabahata Masiqta", *Numen*, 28, 1981, pp.138-63.

------- , "A Rehabilitation of Spirit Ruha in Mandaean Religion", *HR*, 22, 1982, pp.60-84.

------- , "The Making of a Mandaean Priest: The Tarmida Initiation", *Numen*, 32, 1985, pp.194-217.

------- , *Female Fault and Fulfilment in Gnosticism*, Chapel Hill (1986).

------- , "Why once is not enough: Mandaean Baptism (Maṣbuta) as an Example of a Repeated Ritual", *HR*, 29, 1989, pp.23-34.

------- ,"The Mandaean Appropriation of Jesus' Mother Miriai", *Novum Testamentum*, 35, 1993, pp.181-196.

Bultmann, R., *The Gospel of John: A Commentary*, tr. G.R. Beasley-Murray, General eds. R.W.N. Hoare and J.K. Riches, Oxford (1971).

Burkitt, F.C., *Church and Gnosis. A Study of Christian Thought and Speculation in the Second Century*, Cambridge (1932).

------- , "The Mandaeans", *JThS*, 29, 1928, pp.225-35.

------- , "Note on Ginza Rabba 174", *JThS*, 29, 1928, pp.235-37.

Caquot, A., "Un phylactère mandéen en plomb", *Semitica*, 22, 1972, pp.67-87.

Casey, R.P., "Gnosis, Gnosticism and the New Testament", in *The Background of the New Testament and its Eschatology*, eds. W.D. Davies and D. Daube, Cambridge (1956), pp.52-80.

Chabot, J.-M., *Chronique de Denys de Tell-Maḥré*, 4e Partie, Paris (1895).

Chwolsohn, D., *Die Ssabier und der Ssabismus*, St. Petersburg (1856).

Clay, A.T., *Miscellaneous Inscriptions in the Yale Babylonian Collection*, New Haven (1915).

Cohn-Sherbok, D., "The Alphabet in Mandaean and Jewish Gnosticism", *Religion*, 11, 1981, pp.227-34.

------- , "The Mandaeans and Heterodox Judaism", *HUCA*, 54, 1983, pp.147-51.

Coxon, P.W., "Script Analysis and Mandaean Origins", *JSS*, 15, 1970, pp.16-30.

Crehan, J.H., "The Mandaeans and Christian Infiltration", *JThS*, 19, 1968, pp.623-26.

Daniélou, J., *The Theology of Jewish Christianity*, tr. and ed. J.A. Baker, (The Development of Christian Doctrine before the Council of Nicaea, v.1) London (1964).

al-Dimashqī, Shams al-Dīn ʾAbī ʿAbd ʾAllāh Muḥammad, *nukhbat al-dahr fī ʿajāʾib al-barr wa al-bahr*, ed. M.A.F. Mehren, St. Petersburg (1866) [French tr. M.A.F. Mehren, *Manuel de la cosmographie du Moyen Age*, Copenhague (1874)].

Dodd, C.H., *The Interpretation of the Fourth Gospel*, Cambridge (1953, reprinted 1954).

Dodge, B., "The Ṣābians of Ḥarrān" in *American University of Beirut Festival Book (Festschrift)*, eds. F. Sarruf and S. Tamim, Beirut (1967), pp.59-85.

Drijvers, H.J.W., "Bardaiṣan of Edessa and the Hermetica", *JEOL*, 21, 1970, pp.190-210.

------- , *Old Syriac (Edessean) Inscriptions*, Semitic Stud. Ser., New Ser. 3, Leiden (1972).

------- , "Some New Syriac Inscriptions and Archaeological Finds from Edessa and Sumatar Harabesi", *BSOAS*, 36, 1973, pp.1-14.

------- , *Cults and Beliefs at Edessa*, Leiden (1980).

Drower, E.S., *The Mandaeans of Iraq and Iran. Their Cults, Customs, Magic, Legends, and Folklore*, Oxford (1937).

------- , "A Mandaean Phylactery", *Iraq*, 5, 1938, pp.31-54.

------- , "The Mandaeans To-day", *The Hibbert Journal*, 37, 1938-39, pp.435-47.

------- , "A Phylactery for Rue. An Invocation of the Personified Herb", *Or*, 15, 1946, pp.324-46.

------- , *The Book of the Zodiac*, Oriental Translation Fund, vol.36, London (1949).

------- , *Diwan Abatur or Progress Through the Purgatories*, Studi e Testi 151, Vatican City (1950).

------- , *The Haran Gawaita and the Baptism of Hibil-Ziwa*, Studi e Testi 176, Vatican City (1953).

------- , "A Mandaean Bibliography", *JRAS*, 1953, pp.34-39.

------- , "Colour Film Taken in a Mandaean Sanctuary in Lower Iraq", in *Proceeding of the Twenty-third International Congress of Orientalists*, Cambridge (1954), pp.107-8.

------- , *Water into Wine. A Study of Ritual Idiom in the Middle East*, London (1956).

------- , "Scenes and Sacraments in a Mandaean Sanctuary", *Numen*, 3, 1956, pp.72-76.

------- , *The Canonical Prayerbook of the Mandaeans*, Leiden (1959).

------- , *The Secret Adam. A Study of Naṣoraean Gnosis*, Oxford (1960).

------- , *The Thousand and Twelve Questions*, Deutsche Akademie der Wissenschaften zu Berlin Institut für Orientforschung, Veröffentlichung Nr.32, Berlin (1960).

------- , "Adam and the Elkasaites", *TU*, 79, (Studia Patristica, v.IV) 1961, pp.406-10.

------- , *The Coronation of the Great Šišlam. Being a Description of the Rite of the Coronation of a Mandaean Priest According to the Ancient Canon*, Leiden (1962).

------- , "Mandaean Polemic", *BSOAS*, 25, 1962, pp.438-48.

------- , *A Pair of Naṣoraean Commentaries (Two Priestly Documents). The Great 'First World' and the Lesser 'First World'*, Leiden (1963).

------- and R. Macuch, *A Mandaic Dictionary*, Oxford (1963).

Empson, R.H.W., *The Cult of the Peacock Angel*, London (1928).

Ephrem Syrus, *The Book of the Cave of Treasures. A History of the Patriarchs and the Kings Their Successors from the Creation to the Crucifixion of Christ*, tr. E.A.W. Budge, London (1927).

Fakhruddīn al-Rāḍī, Muḥammad ʾibn ʿUmar al-Khaṭṭāb, *mafātīḥ al-ghayb*, Istanbul (1307 AH).

------- , *ʾiʿtiqād firaq al-muslimīn wa al-mushrikīn* (with Tāhā ʿAbd al-Raʾūf Ṣaʿd and Muṣtafā Hawārī, *al-murshīd al-ʾamīn*) Cairo (1978).

Fohrer, G., *History of Israelite Religion*, tr. D.A. Green, London (1972).

Fossum, J.E., *The Name of God and the Angel of the Lord*, (Wissenschaftliche Untersuchungen zum Neuen Testament 36) Tübingen (1985).

Franzmann, M., "Living Water Mediating Element in Mandaean Myth and Ritual", *Numen*, 36, 1989, pp.156-72.

Frye, R.N., J.F. Gilliam, H. Ingholt and C.B. Welles, *Inscriptions from Dura-Europos*, (Yale Classical Studies, ed. H.M. Hubbell, v. XIV) New Haven (1955).

Gadd, C.J., "The Harran Inscriptions of Nabonidus", *AS*, 8, 1958, pp.35-92.

------- , *The Fall of Nineveh*, London (1923).

Gaster, T.H., *Thespis: Ritual, Myth and Drama in the Ancient Near East*, New York (1950).

Gibson, J.C.L., *Textbook of Syrian Semitic Inscription: v.II, Aramaic Inscriptions*, Oxford (1975).

Giversen, S., *Apocryphon of Johannis*, (Acta Theologica Danica, v.V) Copenhagen (1963).

Greenfield, J.C., "A Mandaic 'Targum' of Psalm 114", in *Studies in Aggadah, Targum and Jewish Liturgy in Memory of Joseph Heinemann*, eds. J.J. Petuchowski and E. Fleischer, Jerusalem (1981), pp.23-31.

------- , "A Mandaic Miscellany", *JAOS*, 104, 1984, pp.81-85.

------- and J. Naveh, "A Mandaic Lead Amulet with Four Incantations", *Eretz-Israel*, 18, 1985, pp.97-107.

Guest, J.S., *The Yezidis. A Study in Survival*, London and New York (1987).

Gurney, O.R., "The Assyrian Tablets from Sultantepe", *PBA*, 41, 1955, pp.21-41.

Haardt, R., *Gnosis: Character and Testimony*, tr. J.F. Hendry, Leiden (1971).

Ḥamzah al-ʾIṣfahānī, *tārīkh sīnī mulūk al ʿarḍ wa al-ʾanbiyā*, ed. Jawad al-Irani al-Tabrizi, Berlin (1340 AH) [V.M, Daudpota, *The Annals of Ḥamzah al Iṣfahānī*, Bombay (1932)].

Harris, R. and A. Mingana, *The Odes and Psalms of Solomon*, Manchester (1916-1920).

al-Ḥasanī, ʿAbd al-Razzāq, *al-ṣābiʾah qādiman wa ḥādīthan*, Cairo (1350/1931).

------- , *al-ṣābiʾūn fī ḥāḍirihim wa māḍihim*, Saida (1374/1955).

------- , *ṣābiʾah al-batāʾikh wa ṣābiʾah ḥarrān*, n.p. (1968).

Healey, J.F., "Burning the Corn: new light on the killing of Mōtu", *Or*, 52, 1983, pp.248-51.

------- , "The Akkadian 'Pantheon' List from Ugarit", *SEL*, 2, 1985, pp.115-25.

------- , "Syriac *ḥašqbōl*: A Further Note", *Biblica*, 68, 1987, p.258.

Hespel, R. and R. Draguet, *Théodore bar Koni Livre des Scolies (recension de Séert) II. Mimré VI-XI*, (Corpus Scriptorum Christianorum Orientalium, vol. 432, Scriptores Syri Tomus 188) Louvain (1982).

Hill, G.F., *Catologue of the Greek Coins of Arabia, Mesopotamia and Persia*, London (1922).

Hjärpe, J., *Analyse critique des traditions Arabes sur les Sabéens Harraniens*, Uppsala (1972).

Houtum-Schindler, A., "Notes on the Sabaeans", *PRGS*, 13, 1891, pp.663-69.

Howard, W.F., "The Fourth Gospel and Mandaean Gnosticism", *LQR*, 1927, pp.72-85.

ʾIbn ʾAthīr, ʾAbū al-Saʿādat Mubārak ʾibn Muḥammad, *al-nihāyah fī gharīb al-ḥadīth wa al-ʾāthār*, Beirut (n.d.).

ʾIbn Ḥayyān, ʾAthīr al-Dīn ʾAbī ʿAbd ʾAllāh al-ʾAndalusī, *al-tafsīr al-kabīr al-muthammā bi al-bahr al-muḥīt*, Riyād (n.d.).

ʾIbn Ḥazm, ʾAbū Muḥammad ʿAlī ʾibn ʾAḥmad al-ʾAndalusī, *kitāb al-faṣl fī al-milal wa al-ʾahwāʾi wa al-nihāl*, Cairo (1317 A.H.).

ʾIbn al-Jawzī, Jamāl al-Dīn ʾAbī al-Faraj ʿAbd al-Raḥmān, *talbīs ʾiblīs*, Beirut (1368 A.H.).

ʾIbn Kathīr, ʾAbū al-Fidā ʾIsmaʿīl al-Qurashī, *tafsīr al-qurʾān al-ʿaẓīm*, 3rd edition, Cairo (1376/1956).

------- , *al-bidāyah wa al-nihāyah*, Cairo (1932).

ʾIbn Khaldūn, *The Muqaddimah: An Introduction to History*, tr. F. Rosenthal, New York (1958).

ʾIbn Manẓūr, ʾAbū Faḍl Jamāl al-Dīn Muḥammad, *lisān al-ʿarab*, Beirut (c. 1975).

ʾIbn al-Nadīm, Muḥammad ʾibn ʾIsḥāq, *kitāb al-fihrist*, ed. G. Flügel, Leipzig (1872) [English translation by B. Dodge, *The Fihrist of al-Nadim*, New York-London (1970)].

ʾIbn Qudāmah, Muwaffaq al-Dīn ʾAbī Muḥammad ʿAbd ʾAllāh ʾibn ʾAḥmad, *al-mughnī*, Beirut (1392/1972).

ʾIbn Qutaybah, ʾAbū Muḥammad ʿAbd ʾAllāh ʾibn Muslim, *taʾwīl mushkil al-qurʾān*, 2nd edition, Cairo (1393/1973).

------- , *al-maʿārif*, Cairo (1934).

ʾIbn Saʿīd al-ʾAndalusī, ʾAbū al-Qāsim Saʿīd ʾibn ʾAḥmad, *kitāb al-taʿrīf bi ṭabaqāt al-ʾumam*, Cairo (n.d.).

Ingholt, H., *Parthian Sculptures from Hatra*, (Memoirs of the Conn. Academy of Arts and Sciences XII) New Haven (1954).

al-ʾIṣṭakhrī, ʾAbū ʾIsḥāq al-Farasī, *kitāb al-ʾaqālīm*, ed. J.H. Moeller, Gotha (1839).

Jalabert, C., R. Mouterde and C. Mondésert, *Inscriptions grecs et latines de la Syrie*, Paris (1955).

Jaṣṣāṣ, ʾAḥmad ʾibn ʿAlī, *ʾaḥkām al-qurʾān*, Cairo (1347 AH).

Jastrow, Jr.M., *Aspects of Religious Belief and Practice in Babylonia and Assyria*, (American Lectures on the History of Religions, ninth series, 1910) New York and London (1911).

Johns, C.H.W., *An Assyrian Doomsday Book or Liber Censualis of the District Round Ḥarran; in the Seventh Century B.C.*, Leipzig (1901).

Jonas, H., *The Gnostic Religion*, Beacon Hill (1958).

Joshua the Stylite, *Chronicle of Joshua the Stylite*, ed. and tr. W. Wright, Cambridge (1882).

Kaḥḥālah, ʿUmar Riḍā, *muʿjam al-muʾallifīn tarājīm muṣannifiyyi al-kutub al-ʿarabiyyah*, Damascus (1379/1960).

al-Kalbī, ʾAbū al-Mundhīr Hishām'ibn Muḥammad, *kitāb al-ʾaṣnām*, 2nd edition, Cairo (1343/1924) [N.A. Faris, *The Book of the Idols*, New Jersey (1952)].

al-Khawārizmī, ʾAbū ʿAbd ʾAllāh Muḥammad, *mafātīḥ al- ulūm*, ed. V. Vloten, Leiden (1968).

Klugkist, A., *Midden-Aramese Schriften in Syrië, Mesopotamië, Perzië en aangrenzende gebieden*, (Ph.D. Thesis) Groningen University (1982).

------- , "The Origin of the Mandaic Script", in *Scripta Signa Vocis*, eds. H.L.J. Vanstiphout et. al., Groningen (1986), pp.111-20.

Kraeling, C.H., "The Mandaic God Ptahil", *JAOS*, 53, 1933, pp.152-65.

------- , "The Origin and Antiquity of the Mandaeans", *JAOS*, 49, 1929, pp.195-218.

------- , "A Mandaic Bibliography", *JAOS*, 46, 1926, pp.49-55.

Labat, R., *Manuel d'épigraphie akkadienne*, 5th edition, Paris (1976).

Langdon, S., "New Inscriptions of Nabuna'id", *AJSL*, 32, 1916, pp.102-17.

Lewy, H., "Points of Comparison Between Zoroastrianism and the Moon-Cult of Harran", in *A Locust's Leg; Studies in Honour of S.H. Taqizadeh*, ed. W.B. Henning, London (1962), pp.139-61.

Lewy, J., "The Late Assyro-Babylonian Cult of the Moon and its Culmination at the time of Nabonidus", *HUCA*, 19, 1945-46, pp.405-91.

Lidzbarski, M., "Ein mandäische Amulett", in *Florilegium dédié à M. Vogué*, Paris (1909), pp.349-73.

------- , *Das Johannesbuch der Mandäer*, Giessen (1915).

------- , *Mandäische Liturgien mitgeteilt, übersetzt und erklärt*, Berlin (1920).

------- , *Ginzā. Der Schatz oder das grosse Buch der Mandäer übersetzt und erklärt*, Göttingen (1925).

------- , "Mandäische Fragen", *ZNW*, 26, 1927, pp.70-75, 245.

------- , "Alter und Heimat der mandäischen Religion", *ZNW*, 27, 1928, pp.321-27.

Lietzmann, H., "Ein Beitrag zur Mandäerfrage", *SPAW*, Phil.-Hist.Kl., 1930, pp.596-608.

Livingstone, A., *Mystical and Mythological Explanatory Works of Assyrian and Babylonian Scholars*, Oxford (1986).

Lloyd, S. and W. Brice, "Harran", *AS*, 1, 1951, pp.77-111.

Luckenbill, D.D., *Ancient Records of Assyria and Babylonia*, Chicago (1926-1927).

Lyall, C.S., "The Words 'Ḥanif' and 'Muslim'", *JRAS*, 1903, pp.771-84.

MacRae, G.W., "The Apocalypse of Adam", in *Nag Hammadi Codices, V, 2-5 and VI with Papyrus Berolinensis 8502, 1 and 4*, ed. D.M. Parrott (Nag Hammadi

Studies, eds. M. Krause, J.M. Robinson and W. Wisse, XI) Leiden (1979), pp.151-95.

Macuch, R., "Alter und Heimat des Mandäismus nach neuerschlossenen Quellen", *ThLZ*, 82, 1957, pp.402-7.

------- , "Anfänge der Mandäer", in *Die Araber in der Alten Welt*, eds. F. Altheim and R. Stiehl, v.II, Berlin (1965), pp.76-191.

------- , *Handbook of Classical and Modern Mandaic*, Berlin (1965).

------- , "Zur Frühgeschichte der Mandäer", *ThLZ*, 90, 1965, pp.649-60.

------- , "Altmandäische Bleirollen", in *Die Araber in der Alten Welt*, eds. F. Altheim and R. Stiehl, Berlin, v.IV (1967), pp.91-203, 626-31; v.V/1 (1968), pp.34-72, 454-69.

------- , "The Origins of the Mandaeans and Their Script", *JSS*, 16, 1971, pp.174-92.

------- , "Gnostische Ethik und die Anfänge der Mandäer", in *Christentum am Roten Meer*, v.II, eds. F. Altheim und R. Stiehl, Berlin, New York (1973), pp.254-73.

Maimonides, M., *The Guide of the Perplexed*, tr. S. Pines, Chicago (1963).

al-Majrīṭī, ʾAbū al-Qāsim Maslamah ʾibn ʾAḥmad (Pseudo-Majrīṭī), *ghāyat al-ḥakīm wa ʾaḥaqq al-natījatayn bi al-taqdīm (Picatrix)*, ed. H. Ritter, Studien der Bibliothek Warburg, v.XII, Leipzig (1933).

al-Maqdisī, al-Muṭahhar ibn Ṭāhir, *kitāb al-badʾi wa al-tārikh*, Paris (1899-1919).

al-Maqrīzī, Taqiaddin ʾAḥmad ʾibn ʿAlī ʿAbd al-Qādir ʾibn Muḥammad, *al-mawāʿiz wa al-ʾiʿtibār fī dhikr al-khitāt wa al-ʾāthār*, ed. G. Wiet, Cairo (1911-1924).

Margoliouth, D.S., "On the Origin and Import of the Names Muslim and Hanif", *JRAS*, 1903, pp.467-93.

------- , "Ḥarranians", in *ERE*, 6, pp.519-20.

Marquet, Y., "Sabéens et iḫwān al-ṣafāʾ", *SI*, 24, 1966, pp.35-80; 25, 1966, pp.77-109.

Marrānī, N.G., *mafāhīm ṣābiʾiyyah mandāʾiyyah tārīkh.dīn.lughah*, 2nd edition, Baghdad (1981).

al-Masʿūdī, ʾAbū al-Ḥasan ʿAlī ʾibn Ḥusayn, *murūj al-dhahab wa maʿādin al-jawhar*, text and translation into French by C.B. de Meynard, Paris (1861-1877).

------- , *kitāb al-tanbīh wa al-ʾishrāf*, ed. M.J. de Goeje, Leiden (1967).

McCullough, W.S., *Jewish and Mandaean Incantation Bowls in the Royal Ontario Museum*, (Near and Middle East Series 5) Toronto (1967).

------- , *A Short History of Syriac Christianity to the Rise of Islam*, Chico (1982).

Mead, G.R.S., *The Gnostic John the Baptizer. Selections from the Mandaean John-Book*, London (1924).

Meeks, W.A., *The Prophet-King. Moses Traditions and the Johannine Christology*, Leiden (1967).

Montgomery, J.A., *Aramaic Incantation Texts from Nippur*, (University of Pennsylvania the Museum Publications of the Babylonian Section vol.III) Philadelphia (1913).

de Morgan, J., *Études Linguistiques. Deuxième Partie. Textes Mandaïtes* (with notice of C. Huart), Paris (1904).

Morony, M.G., *Iraq After the Muslim Conquest*, Princeton, New Jersey (1984).

Naveh, J., "The Origin of the Mandaic Script", *BASOR*, 198, 1970, pp.32-37.

------- , "Another Mandaic Lead Roll", *Israel Oriental Studies*, 5, 1975, pp.47-53.

al-Naysābūrī, Niẓām al-Dīn al-Ḥasan ʾibn Muḥammad ʾibn Ḥusayn al-Qummī, *gharāʾib al-qurʾān wa raghāʾib al-furqān*, Cairo (1381/1962).

Nöldeke, Th., *Mandäische Grammatik*, Halle (1875).

Olmstead, A.T., *History of Assyria*, New York, London (1923).

------- , *History of Palestine and Syria to the Macedonian Conquest*, New York (1931).

Pallis, S.A., *Mandaean Studies*, tr. E.H. Pallis, London and Copenhagen (1926).

------- , *The Babylonian Akîtu Festival*, Copenhagen (1926).

------- , *Essay on Mandaean Bibliography 1560-1930*, Amsterdam (1933).

------- , *The Antiquity of Iraq*, Copenhagen (1956).

Parpola, S., *Letters from Assyrian Scholars to the Kings Esarhaddon and Assurbanipal*, Part I: Texts (AOAT, Bd. 5/1), Kevelaer (1970); Part II: Commentary and Appendices (AOAT, Bd. 5/2), Kevelaer (1983).

------- , *Neo-Assyrian Toponyms*, Kevelaer (1970).

Pedersen, J., "The Ṣābians", in *A Volume of Oriental Studies; Presented to Edward G. Browne*, eds. T.W. Arnold and R.A. Nicholson, Cambridge (1922), pp.383-91.

Peterson, E., "Bemerkungen zur mandäischen Literatur", *ZNW*, 25, 1926, pp.236-48.

------- , "Urchristentum und Mandäismus", *ZNW*, 27, 1928, pp.55-91.

Pognon, H., *Inscriptions mandaïtes des coupes de Khouabir*, Paris (1898-1899).

Postgate, J.N., "Harran", in *RLA*, v.4, pp.122-25.

al-Qifṭī, Jamāl al-Dīn ʾAbī Ḥasan ʿAlī ʾibn Yūsuf, *tārīkh al-ḥukamā*, ed. J. Lippert, Leipzig (1903).

Quispel, G., "Jewish Gnosis and Mandaean Gnosticism. Some Reflections on the Writing *Bronté", in Les Textes de Nag Hammadi*, ed. J.-É. Ménard, (Nag Hammadi studies, eds. M. Krause, J.M. Robinson, F. Wisse, VII) Leiden (1975), pp.82-122.

------- , "Gnosticism and the New Testament", in *The Bible in Modern Scholarship*, ed. J.P. Hyatt, Nashville (1965), pp.252-71.

al-Qurṭubī, ʾAbū ʿAbd ʾAllāh Muḥammad ʾibn ʾAḥmad, *al-jāmiʿ al-ʾaḥkām al-qurʾān*, Cairo (1387/1967).

Rice, D.S., "Medieval Harran. Studies on its Topography and Monuments, I", *AS*, 2, 1952, pp.36-84.

Robinson, J.M. and H. Koester, *Trajectories Through Early Christianity*, Philadelphia (1971).

Rosenthal, F., *Die aramäistische Forschung seit Th. Nöldeke's Veröffentlichungen*, Leiden (1939).

------- , *Ahmad B. aṭ-Ṭayyib as-Sarahsī*, New Haven (1943).

------- , "The Prophecies of Bābā the Ḥarrānian", in *A Locust's Leg; Studies in Honour of S.H. Taqizadeh*, ed. W.B. Henning, London (1962), pp.220-32.

Rudolph, K., "Ein Grundtyp gnostische Urmensch-Adam-Spekulation", *ZRGG*, 9, 1957, pp.1-20.

------- , *Die Mandäer I. Prolegomena: Das Mandäerproblem; II. Der Kult*, (Forschungen zur Religion und Literatur des Alten und Neuen Testaments, n.F. 56) Göttingen (1960-61).

------- , "Stand und Aufgaben in der Erforschung des Gnostizismus", in *Tagung für allgemeine Religionsgeschichte*, ed. Th. Lohmann, 1963 (Sonderheft der Wissenschaftlichen Zeitschrift der Friedrich-Schiller-Universität Jena. 13, 1964), pp.89-102. Reprinted in *Gnosis und Gnostizismus*, ed. K. Rudolph, Darmstadt (1975), pp.510-53.

------- , "War der Verfasser der Oden Salomos ein 'Qumran-Christ'? Ein Beitrag zur Diskussion um die Anfänge der Gnosis", *RQ*, 16, 1964, pp.523-55.

------ , *Theogonie, Kosmogonie und Anthropogonie in den mandäischen Schriften*, (Forschungen zur Religion und Literatur des Alten und Neuen Testaments, 88) Göttingen (1965).

------- , "Renderschinungen des Judentums und das Problem der Entstehung des Gnostizismus", *KAIROS*, 9, 1967, pp.105-22. Reprinted in *Gnosis und Gnostizismus*, ed. K. Rudolph, Darmstadt (1975), pp.768-97.

------- , "Problems of a History of the Development of the Mandaean Religion" (English translation by D.C. Duling, in consultation with J. Modschiedler), *HR*, 8, 1969, pp.210-35.

------- , Review of E.M. Yamauchi: *Gnostic Ethics and Mandaean Origins* (Cambridge, 1970), *ThLZ*, 97, 1972, pp.733-37.

------ , "Mandean Sources", in *Gnosis. A Selection of Gnostic Texts*, ed. W. Foerster, English translation edited by R.McL. Wilson (trs. R.McL. Wilson, P.W. Coxon and K.H. Kuhn), v.II, Part 2, Oxford (1974), pp.121-319.

------ , "Quellenprobleme zum ursprung und alter der Mandäer", in *Christianity, Judaism and Other Greco-Roman Cults. Studies for Morton Smith at Sixty*, ed. J. Neusner, Part 4, Leiden (1975) pp.112-42.

------- , "Die mandäische Literatur", in *Studia Mandaica*, ed. R. Macuch, Band I, Berlin, New York (1976), pp.147-70.

------- , "Der Mandäismus in der neueren Gnosisforschung", in *Gnosis. Festschrift für Hans Jonas*, ed. B. Aland, Göttingen (1978), pp.244-77.

------- , *Mandaeism*, (Iconography of Religions, Section 21) Leiden (1978).

------- , *Gnosis: The Nature and History of an Ancient Religion*, translation edited by R.McL. Wilson (trs. R.McL. Wilson, P.W. Coxon and K.H. Kuhn), Edinburgh (1983).

Säve-Söderbergh, T., *Studies in the Coptic Manichaean Psalm-Book: Prosody and Mandaean Parallels*, Uppsala (1949).

------- , "Gnostic and Canonical Gospel Traditions (with special reference to the Gospel of Thomas)", in *Le Origini dello Gnosticismo Colloquio di Messina 13-18 Aprile 1966*, ed. U. Bianchi, Leiden (1967), pp.552-62.

Schlier, H., "Zur Mandäerfrage", *ThR*, NF, 5, 1933, pp.1-34, 69-92.

Scholem, G., *Kabbalah*, New York (1974).

------- , *Major Trends in Jewish Mysticism*, London (1955).

Schonfield, H.J., *The Authentic New Testament*, London (1956).

Schweizer, E., *Ego Eimi*, Göttingen (1965).

Scott, W. and A.S. Ferguson, *Hermetica*, Oxford (1936).

Segal, J.B., "Pagan Syriac Monuments in the Vilayet of Urfa", *AS*, 3, 1953, pp.97-119.

------- , "Some Syriac Inscriptions of the 2nd-3rd Century A.D.", *BSOAS*, 16, 1954, pp.13-36.

------- , "Mesopotamian Communities from Julian to the Rise of Islam", *PBA*, 41, 1955, pp.109-39.

------- , "Two Syriac Inscriptions from Harran", (with an Appendix by D. Strong) *BSOAS*, 20, 1957, pp.513-22.

------- , "The Sabian Mysteries: The Planet Cult of Ancient Harran", in *Vanished Civilizations: Forgotten Peoples of the Ancient World*, ed. E. Bacon, London (1963), pp.201-20.

------- , *Edessa and Harran. An inaugural lecture delivered on 9 May 1962*, London (1963).

------- , *Edessa 'The Blessed City'*, Oxford (1970).

------- , Review of E.M. Yamauchi: *Gnostic Ethics and Mandaean Origins*, (Cambridge, 1970), *BSOAS*, 36, 1973, pp.134-35.

Segelberg, E., *Maṣbūtā. Studies in the Ritual of the Mandaean Baptism*, Uppsala (1958).

------- , "Old and New Testament Figures in Mandaean Version", in *Syncretism*, ed. S.S. Hartman, (Scripta Instituti Donneriani Aboensis III) Stockholm and Uppsala (1969), pp.228-39.

------- , "The Ordination of the Mandaean *tarmida* and its Relation to Jewish and Early Christian Ordination Rites", in *Studia Patristica*, ed. F.L. Cross, v.x, Part 1, Berlin (1970), pp.419-25.

------- , "The Mandaean Week and the Problem of Jewish Christianity and Mandaean Relationship", in *Judéo-christianisme: recherches historiques et théologiques offerts en hommage au Cardinal Jean Daniélou*, eds. B. Gerhardsson et. al., Paris (1972), pp.273-86.

------- , "*Trāṣa d̲-tāga d̲-Šišlām rabbā*. Studies in the rite called the Coronation of Šišlām Rabbā", in *Studia Mandaica*, ed. R. Macuch, Band I, Berlin, New York (1976), pp.171-244.

------- , "The Pitha and Mambuha Prayers to the Question of the Liturgical Development among the Mandaeans", in *Gnosis Festschrift für Hans Jonas*, ed. B. Aland, Göttingen (1978), pp.464-72.

Sevrin, J.-M., *Le Dossier Baptismal Séthien. Études sur la Sacramentaire Gnostique*, (Bibliothéque Copte de Nag Hammadi, Section "Études" 2) Laval (Québec) (1986).

al-Shahrastānī, ᵓAbū al-Fatḥ Muḥammad ᵓibn ᶜAbd al-Karīm, *kitāb al milal wa al-nihāl*, ed. W. Cureton, London (1842).

Sieber, J.N., "Zostrianos", in *The Nag Hammadi Library in English*, General ed. J.M. Robinson, 3rd edition, Leiden (1988), pp.402-30.

Smith, S., *Babylonian Historical Texts*, London (1924).

------- , *Early History of Assyria*, London (1928).

Smith, W.R., *The Religion of the Semites*, (Revised edition) London (1894).

Sokoloff, M., "Notes on Some Mandaic Magical Texts", *Or*, 40, 1971, pp.448-58.

Sox, H.D., "The Last of the Gnostics", *King's Theological Review*, 6, 2, 1983, pp.43-44.

Sprengling, M., "A New Pahlavi Inscription", *AJSL*, 53, 1937, pp.126-44.

------- , "Karīr, Founder of Sasanian Zoroastrianism", *AJSL*, 57, 1940, pp.197-228.

Stroumsa, G.A.G., *Another Seed: Studies in Gnostic Mythology*, Leiden (1984).

Sundberg, W., *Kushṭa. A Monograph on a Principal Word in Mandaean Texts, I. The Descending Knowledge*, Lund (1953).

al-Ṭabarī, ᵓAbū Jaᶜfar Muḥammad ᵓibn Jarīr, *jāmiᶜ al-bayān ᶜan taᵓwīl ᵓāy al-qurᵓān*, 3rd edition, Cairo (1388/1968) [*The Commentary on the Qurᵓan*, tr. J. Cooper, Oxford (1987)].

------- , *tārīkh al-rusūl wa al-mulūk*, ed. M.J. de Goeje, Leiden (1964) [*The History of al-Tabari*, tr. M. Perlmann, New York (1987)].

Tallqvist, K., *Assyrian Personal Names*, (Acta Societatis Scientiarum Fennicae, Tom. XLIII, No 1) Helsinki (1914).

------- , *Akkadische Götterepitheta*, Studia Orientalia Edidit Societas Orientalis Fennica: VII, Helsinki (1938).

Taqizadeh, S.H., "A New Contribution to the Materials concerning the Life of Zoroaster", *BSOS*, 8, 1935-37, pp.947-54.

------- , "An Ancient Persian Practice Preserved by a Non-Iranian People: The Mandaean Calendar", *BSOS*, 9, 1938, pp.603-19.

Tardieu, M., "Ṣābiens Coraniques et 'Ṣābiens de Ḥarrān"', *JA*, 274, 1986, pp.1-44.

------- , *Les Paysages Reliques*, Louvain-Paris (1990).

Teixidor, J., *The Pagan God. Popular Religion in the Greco-Roman Near East*, Princeton (1977).

Theodor Abū Ḳurra, *Traktat über den Schöpfer und die wahre Religion*, tr. G. Graf, Beiträge zur Geschichte der Philosophie des Mittelalters, ed. C. Baeumker, Band XIV, Heft 1, Münster i.W. (1913).

Tubach, J., *Im Schatten des Sonnengottes*, Wiesbaden (1986).

Vattioni, F., *Le Iscrizioni di Hatra*, Naples (1981).

Weidner, E.F., *Politische Dokumente aus Kleinasien*, Leipzig (1923).

Wenning, R., *Die Nabatäer -Denkmäler und Geschichte*, (Novum Testamentum et Orbis Antiquus, 3) Göttingen (1987).

Widengren, G., *The Ascension of the Apostle and the Heavenly Book (King and Saviour III)*, (UUA 7) Uppsala-Leipzig (1950).

------- , "Die Mandäer", in *Handbuch der Orientalistik*, ed. B. Spuler, VIII, Pt.2, Leiden (1961), pp.83-101.

------- , *Mani and Manichaeism*, tr. C. Kessler, London (1965).

------- , *Die Religonen Irans*, Stuttgart (1965).

------- ,"Heavenly Enthronement and Baptism. Studies in Mandaean Baptism", in *Religions in Antiquity*, ed. J. Neusner, Leiden (1968), pp.551-82.

------- (ed.), *Der Mandäismus*, Darmstadt (1982).

Williams, F., *The Panarion of Epiphanius of Salamis. Book I (Sects 1-46)*, (Nag Hammadi Studies, XXXV, vol. ed. J.M. Robinson) Leiden (1987).

Wilson, R. McL., *The Gnostic Problem. A Study of the Relations Between Hellenistic Judaism and the Gnostic Heresy*, London (1958).

------- , *Gnosis and the New Testament*, Oxford (1968).

Wisse, F., "The Apocryphon of John", in *The Nag Hammadi Library in English*, General ed. J.M. Robinson, 3rd edition, Leiden (1988), pp.104-23.

Yamauchi, E.M., "The Present Status of Mandaean Studies", *JNES*, 25, 1966, pp.88-96.

------- , *Mandaic Incantation Texts*, American Oriental Series, vol. 49, New Haven (1967).

------- , "A Mandaic Magic Bowl from the Yale Babylonian Collection", *Berytus*, 17, 1967-68, pp.49-63.

------- , *Gnostic Ethics and Mandaean Origins*, (Harvard Theological Studies XXIV) Cambridge (1970).

------- , *Pre-Christian Gnosticism. A Survey of the Proposed Evidences*, London (1973).

------- , "Jewish Gnosticism? The Prologue of John, Mandaean Parallels, and the Trimorphic Protennoia", in *Studies in Gnosticism and Hellenistic Religions Presented to Gilles Quispel on the Occasion of his 65th Birthday*, eds. R. Van den Broek and M.J. Vermaseren, Leiden (1981), pp.467-97.

Zimmern, H., "Das vermutliche babylonische Vorbild des Pethā und Mambūhā der Mandäer", in *Orientalische Studien Theodor Nöldeke zum siebzigsten Geburtstag gewidmet*, ed. C. Bezold, Gießen (1906), Bd.2, pp.959-67.

------- , "Nazoräer", *ZDMG*, 74, 1920, pp.429-38.

INDEX

A

B

Printed in the USA/Agawam, MA
February 14, 2023

805804.056